WORKING LIFE OF WOMEN
IN THE
SEVENTEENTH CENTURY

Working Life of Women in the Seventeenth Century, originally published in 1919, was the first comprehensive analysis of the daily lives of ordinary women in early modern England. It remains the most wide ranging introduction to the subject.

Clark uses a wide variety of documentary sources to illuminate the experience of women in the past. Gentlewomen left memoirs, letters, and household accounts detailing the administration of their family estates; craftsmen's wives and widows figure in the apprenticeship and licensing records of guilds and towns; the wives of yeomen, husbandmen and labourers are glimpsed in court evidence, petitions and the registers of parish poor relief. Alice Clark's evidence dates from the later sixteenth to the early eighteenth century, and her analysis addresses a broad transition, from a medieval subsistence economy to the industrial capitalism of the nineteenth and early twentieth centuries.

Clark's conclusions about the effects of industrial capitalism on women's working conditions and contribution to the economy were controversial in her own time and remain so today. Her vivid portrayal of the everyday lives of working women – and all women worked – in seventeenth-century England remains unsurpassed.

Alice Clark (1874–1934) was born into a Liberal Quaker family which believed in careers for women. Alice joined the family shoe firm in Street, Somerset and worked her way up, eventually becoming one of the directors. She worked at the firm throughout her life, but in 1912 she moved to London to take part in the leadership of the women's suffrage movement. The following year, at the age of 38, she enrolled at the London School of Economics and began to study the seventeenth century. When war broke out she took a course in midwifery and devoted much of her time to relief work. *Working Life of Women* was finished in 1918. and

turning her tremendous energy once again to the management of the firm and its employees' welfare.

Amy Louise Erickson is Research Fellow at Girton College, Cambridge. Her forthcoming book on *Women and Property in Early Modern England* will be published by Routledge in 1992.

Working Life of Women
in the
Seventeenth Century

ALICE CLARK

New edition
With a new introduction by Amy Louise Erickson

ROUTLEDGE

London and New York

First published in 1919 by George Routledge & Sons, Ltd

Second edition published in 1982 by Routledge & Kegan Paul Ltd

Third edition published by Routledge
11 New Fetter Lane, London EC4P 4EE

Simultaneously published in the USA and Canada
by Routledge
a division of Routledge, Chapman and Hall Inc.
29 West 35th Street, New York, NY 10001

Original text © the estate of the late Alice Clark
Introduction and Bibliography in third edition © 1992
Amy Louise Erickson

Printed in Great Britain by
T J Press (Padstow) Ltd,
Padstow, Cornwall

British Library Cataloguing in Publication Data
Clark, Alice.
Working life of women in the seventeenth century / Alice
Clark. – New ed. / with a new introduction by Amy Erickson.
    p.   cm.
Includes bibliographical references.
    1. Women–Employment–Great Britain–History–17th century.
    2. Women–Great Britain–History–17th century.   I. Title.
HD6135.C5   1992
331.4′0941′09032–dc20   92–5974

Library of Congress Cataloging in Publication Data

Also available

ISBN 0–415–06668–9

CONTENTS

INTRODUCTION[1]

'Those who don't make mistakes don't make anything.'

The anonymous author of the *Essay in Defence of the Female Sex* (1696) was under few illusions about women's subordinate position in her own day and the means used to perpetuate it:

> if any histories were anciently written by women, time, and the malice of men, have effectually conspired to suppress 'em; and it is not reasonable to think that men should transmit, or suffer to be transmitted to posterity, any thing that might shew the weakness and illegality of their title to a power they still exercise so arbitrarily, and are so fond of. [p. 23]

It is not surprising that the greater part of the history of women has had to be written by women. Nor is it surprising that they have been frequently preoccupied with the comparison between the past and the present. Was women's status in the past 'better' or 'worse' than it is now?

The two historical developments which are considered to have had the greatest impact on the life of everyone in the capitalist industrial world today are capitalism and industrialization. Historians since the later nineteenth century in England have been divided over whether capitalism and industrialization were good things or bad things for women, taking either an 'optimistic' or a 'pessimistic' view of the early modern period. Although it was first published more than seventy years ago, Alice Clark's *Working Life of Women in the Seventeenth Century* remains the leading exposition of the pessimistic view that capitalist industry seriously eroded

[1] I am grateful to Maxine Berg, Carole Erickson, Mary Fissell, Ann Hughes, Alasdair Palmer and Helen Weinstein for discussing Alice Clark, *Working Life*, and seventeenth-century historiography with me.

women's status, which had been higher in the pre-capitalist and pre-industrial past. Why, given the efflorescence of women's history, and social history generally, in the last twenty years, is Clark's book still so important?

In its late twentieth-century abundance, women's history has fragmented, splintered into myriad essays, each of which provides a mass of detail in individual case studies – on one type of work, one phase of the life-cycle, one parish or city, and so forth. These studies clarify the importance of regional variations and age differences in women's experience, but they make rather abstruse reading for the newcomer to early modern England. Clark's sweeping survey was reprinted in 1968, just in time for the revival of feminist history in the 1970s and 1980s, and it remains the starting point for many books and articles today. She is often set up as a straw woman in this later research, to be knocked down by a barrage of statistical data analysis. Such treatment is unlikely to have perturbed Clark, who was fond of saying that those who don't make mistakes don't make anything (Gillett n.d.: 18). Even today, her findings are as regularly confirmed as they are disputed, and *Working Life* remains the most comprehensive introduction to women's everyday lives in the late sixteenth, seventeenth and early eighteenth centuries.

Working Life traces the changes in women's work over a very gradual but very important transition in the economy of England. In the middle ages and even through the seventeenth century at some social levels, members of a household worked in what Clark calls 'domestic industry'. Domestic industry was what we would today call a subsistence economy, in which all production took place within the household and the family consumed everything it produced, without having to purchase additional supplies. Wives and husbands contributed jointly to the household economy in a system of domestic industry. The skills of housewifery then were more numerous and more various than those required in the twentieth century, and women's work was essential to the household and respected accordingly, whether it was in the manor house or in a small cottage.

In Clark's second stage of 'family industry' some members of the family worked for wages but that work, like domestic production, was still carried out mainly within the household, so work was still visibly shared by both spouses. Commercial textile production, for example, operated on a 'putting-out' basis whereby either the dealer gave raw materials to the workers and then paid them by the piece for finished work, or workers bought their own raw materials and sold their finished products to a dealer. This type of waged work became increasingly common in the course of the seventeenth century, as the seeds of 'capitalistic industry' began to sprout.

'Capitalistic industry' was Clark's final stage of economic development, beginning in the late seventeenth century and extending into her own lifetime. In this regime virtually all production is commercial and it takes place outside the home in factories. The wives of the 'capitalist' class, who before had shared in their husbands' businesses, were now confined to domesticity. The wives of yeoman farmers and wealthier husbandmen still had their land on which they could manage a dairy and produce food for the household as before, but many husbandmen and craftsmen were pushed down into the condition of labourers, reliant on wages alone. Labourers' wives, having no land on which to produce for their families' subsistence, had to work for wages themselves. But a man's wages were barely enough to feed himself, and a woman's wages were wholly inadequate to support herself and her children. At the middle and upper levels of society the household was no longer a producing unit, but rather a consuming one, and as such it was unhealthy, since women were deprived of productive work. At lower social levels inadequate wages threw labourers upon the poor law, and when these men and women went out to factories to work – or for that matter, when men of the capitalist class left home to go to their place of work – they were severed from what Clark sees as the beneficent moral influence of the home.

Clark's description of the development from 'domestic' to 'family' to 'capitalistic' industry is still largely accepted today, although the terminology has changed. Louise Tilly and Joan Scott (1978) call the three stages 'family economy', 'family wage economy', and 'family consumer economy'. Another recent set of terms is 'family economy', 'proto-industry', and 'industrial economy' or 'mechanized industry'. While there is an extensive literature on proto-industrialization as an explanatory theory in the development of factory industry (Clarkson 1985), in its descriptive, as opposed to theoretical usage 'proto-industry' means the same thing as Clark's 'family industry' – household or workshop production in rural areas as a commercial enterprise, managed on a putting-out basis rather than centralized in a factory.

The principal difficulty with this tripartite model is placing it chronologically. Clark saw the seventeenth century as one of great importance in a longer-term process (pp. 8, 11), but her chronology has been greatly extended. Industrialization, which is more precisely described as mechanization, Clark thought began late in the seventeenth century, whereas it is now agreed that mechanization only began in the late eighteenth century. Even then, the process of mechanization was slow and most people still worked in agriculture or in putting-out industries or in service – that is, not in factories – even in the second half of the nineteenth century. Many of the issues that Clark allocated to the seventeenth century, such as the removal of production from the home and the masculinization of previously female trades, are related today to the eighteenth and early nineteenth centuries (Rose 1988; B. Hill 1989; Valenze 1991).

While Clark specifically associates industrialization with capitalism, her intermediate economic stage of 'family industry', involving wages for piecework in the household, was clearly part of a capitalist, commercial enterprise. Such 'proto-industry', sometimes organized in a workshop which was a sort of non-mechanized factory, was prominent in textile production from the later middle ages. And the cash-less self-sufficiency of Clark's 'domestic industry' was probably rare even by the late middle ages, when people relied upon local or national markets to supply goods they did not produce themselves (Dyer 1989). So capitalism, strictly speaking, is much older than industrialization, although trade certainly grew increasingly commercial from the seventeenth century.

The personal history of Alice Clark

Clark was interested in the effect of economic changes upon women's work for two reasons: first, because as a middle-class woman she was personally involved in the women's movement to gain access to education, professions, politics and the vote; and second, because she observed around her the degrading and debilitating conditions in which working-class women lived and worked. Sociological inquiries into working-class life abounded in the late nineteenth and early twentieth centuries. The working lives of women were of particular concern not only because the investigators deplored the corrupting moral influence of factory and slum conditions, but also because they recognized women's double burden of having to raise children and simultaneously work for wages. Clark would have been familiar with studies such as Barbara Hutchins's *Working Life of Women* (1911) and *Women in Modern Industry* (1915), Maud Pember Reeves's *Round About a Pound a Week* (1913), Clementina Black's *Married Women's Work* (1915) and Margaret Llewellyn Davies's *Maternity: Letters from Working Women* (1915), to name only some of the better known of such inquiries.

But Clark's interest was personal as well as sociological. She was born in 1874 in Street, Somerset, into a Quaker manufacturing family. Growing up, she knew many prominent reformers as family friends, and her maternal grandfather was the Liberal MP John Bright. The Clark family, as Quakers and as Liberals, believed in women's professional achievement; Alice's elder sister became a teacher, her younger sister a doctor. After leaving school Alice took a housewifery course in Bristol, then entered the family shoe factory at the bottom to learn the business. In 1897, at the age of 23, she suffered the first of a series of illnesses and required a long convalescence, but returned to the firm and began taking part in the management. In 1904 when the business was made a private limited company she became one of five life directors, in charge of the Home Order Office, correspondence with customers, and all of the processes done by women in the factory. Her experience of working-class life was immediate, if not personal.

Again in 1909 Clark became ill with tuberculosis and required a lengthy recuperation, including a trip to the Middle East. Returning to England in 1912, she settled in London to work on the executive committee of the Union of Suffrage

Societies, where her colleagues included Millicent Garrett Fawcett, by then one of the leaders of the suffrage campaign for more than fifty years, and Mrs H. M. Swanwick, author of *The Future of the Women's Movement* (1913) among many other books. In 1913, at the age of 38, Clark was awarded Mrs Bernard Shaw's Research Studentship at the London School of Economics (LSE), and began to study the seventeenth century. She did her research in the British Museum, looking at works printed in London in the early modern period, and at a variety of primary sources published in the nineteenth century. They included guild and company records, mainly from London, but also collections of county and municipal records from all over England.

When war broke out in 1914, Clark took a course in mid-wifery, hoping to join her sister in Châlons at the Quaker maternity hospital for refugees, but ill health prevented her going. Instead, after completing her two-year studentship she returned to the family factory part-time in 1917, while continuing to work on the Friends' Committee for the Relief of War Victims in London.

Clark went to the LSE at a time when more women were active in the field of economic history than at any period since. In the years 1895–1932, 22 per cent of the LSE's regular teaching staff were female, a figure larger than the proportion of women among all full-time university teachers today. In the early days of professional journals such as *Economica* and *The Economic History Review* women contributed more articles than they do to the same journals today. (On women in early twentieth-century economics and economic history, see Berg 1992.) Many of these women chose to write at least one study specifically on the history of women, including Annie Abram, Ellen McArthur, Marian Dale, Eileen Power and Ivy Pinchbeck. Others, such as Clark's research supervisor Lilian Knowles, and Jocelyn Dunlop, Dorothy George, Ada Elizabeth Levett, Dorothy Marshall and M. G. Jones did not address women's history specifically, but they invariably displayed more awareness of women when writing histories of guilds, laws, schools, merchants and the poor than did their male contemporaries (see also B. G. Smith 1984: 709–10). These women were the first generation of professional academics, connected principally with the LSE, which had been coeducational since its foundation in 1895, and with Girton College, Cambridge, the first residential institution offering education to degree level for women in Britain.

The intellectual climate at the LSE emphasized the connection between economic history and social policy, between the past and the present. This cross-fertilization of history with economic and social policy meant that, for example, Dunlop could take her history of apprenticeship and child labour all the way from the middle ages to her own day, concluding with a report from the then (1912) chair of the parliamentary committee on juvenile labour. Barbara Hutchins, Annie Abram, Mabel Buer and Maud Davies investigated both contemporary and historical working conditions. And other women besides Clark wrote history without being professional historians: Lina Eckenstein, Rose Bradley and Ada Wallas also spent most of their lives doing other things. Like her contemporaries, Clark had no qualms about specifically comparing the past with the present. She found in medieval and early modern 'domestic industry' a model of women's self-sufficiency, productive labour and self-respect, to be applied to her own day.

Pessimistic and optimistic views of capitalist industry

Clark's admiration for pre-industrial and pre-capitalist systems of work was shared by Mabel Atkinson, in her *Economic Foundations of the Women's Movement* (1914), a tract published by the Fabian Society. Clark was not personally involved with the Women's Group of the Fabian Society, dedicated to the establishment of a socialist society by peaceful means; in fact she was active for most of her life in the Liberal Party, but the pessimistic view of the effects of capitalism and industrialization on women was widespread. Clark's preface to *Working Life* declares her intellectual debt to Olive Schreiner's *Woman and Labour* (1911). Like the earlier *Women and Economics* (1899) by Charlotte Perkins Stetson and *The Awakening of Women* (1899) by Frances Swiney, Schreiner's *Woman and Labour* stresses the biological and moral superiority of the female as the key to 'racial health'. These three books, which all went through multiple editions, deplored middle-class women's economic dependence on men at the dawn of the twentienth century and the evil effects upon women of consumption without production; Schreiner described their condition as 'parasitism'. Stetson, Swiney and Schreiner agreed that the removal of production from the home affected women of different classes differently, but in all cases adversely for the purpose of morals and motherhood. They looked for historical models of a pure, healthy and productive motherhood before the advent of capitalist industry (on early twentieth-century motherhood campaigns, see Lewis 1980). Clark shared their concern with women's 'maternal and spiritual functions', studying economic conditions because she believed they were a principal determinant of women's ability to be good mothers and to exert moral influence upon society as a whole.

Medieval historians also shared Clark's pessimistic view. Like her, they emphasized the pre-industrial self-sufficiency of the household, achieved by the joint labours of the husband and the housewife, the marital partnership in trade, and women's participation in the craft guilds. Clark does not refer to the work specifically on medieval and early modern women available to her at the time, but she was clearly familiar with the studies of law (Buckstaff 1893; Stopes 1894; Bateson 1904 and 1906), the trades (Dixon 1895; Abram 1916), the convents (Eckenstein 1896), mid-seventeenth-century politics (McArthur 1909) and women in general (G. Hill 1896). In addition, numerous works were available which, while not specifically about women, touched on their economic position: on guilds (L. T. Smith 1870), on social life or 'manners and morals' (Green 1894; Abram 1909 and 1913; Bradley 1912; Powell 1917), on poverty (Leonard 1900) and on landholding and agrarian change (Tawney 1912).

Clark was the only one among her contemporaries to concentrate on the seventeenth century rather than on the middle ages or on aspects of industrial labour. Unlike medievalists, those who studied the eighteenth century and later, including Hutchins, Knowles, George, Pinchbeck and Marshall, held the generally optimistic view that industrialization served as the catalyst of women's emancipation, at least in the long run. Pinchbeck, for example, in *Women Workers and the Industrial*

Revolution, concluded that while in the short term women lost economic opportunities, the mechanization of industry did relieve them of at least some heavy and arduous labour; women who worked in factories eventually became much better off than those in domestic service, needlework, agriculture or domestic industries, as gradually through the nineteenth century the experience of working together led women to organize for better wages and protective legislation, and ultimately for access to education and the vote (1930: 306–16).

The same pessimist–optimist dichotomy that divides early twentieth-century historiography also permeates women's history today, and the rift often appears between those who study the years before and those who study the years after 1750 (see further Hufton 1983). Of course, some of this difference of opinion is simply the result of each historian positing her 'own' period as the pivotal one. But the dominant historical tradition of modernization takes an optimistic view of both capitalism and industrialization, and assumes that women's status continually improved with the progress of time. The pessimistic vision therefore stands accused of romanticizing the past, of creating a pre-industrial 'golden age' of 'rough and ready equality' between the sexes.[2]

The pre-capitalist, pre-industrial golden age

Friedrich Engels, building on mid-nineteenth-century ideas of a pre-historic matriarchy, proposed that women's subordination arose out of the historical development of private

[2] The phrase 'rough and ready equality' appeared in Eileen Power's article 'The position of women' (1926), a piece which is not representative of her best work, and about which she was clearly angry from its inception. She wrote to G. G. Coulton that the editors rejected her first submission on medieval ideas about women as insufficiently

> respectful to (a) man (b) the church and (c) the proprieties!! . . . I had to . . . set to work to try and produce something which can safely be read aloud to the second form by the kindergarten mistress during needlework! – one of those 'gossips' about social life which ought to be bought by the yard at a department store. From this you may gather that I am in rage.

(Power Papers, dated only 5 Sept., Girton College Archives. I am grateful to Maxine Berg for drawing this letter to my attention.) It is unfortunate that this essay was reprinted by M. M. Postan in Power's posthumous collection *Medieval Women*.

property. Today, accounts of a medieval or early modern golden age appear most frequently in works with a marxist cast (for example, Figes 1970; Hamilton 1978; Oakley 1981). The influence of these books, which usually refer to Alice Clark, is considerable; they reach a wide general audience and they regularly go through multiple editions, unlike historical monographs. But their approach to history is sweeping, covering vast chronological expanses. Only two recent studies which focus on the early modern period romanticize about a golden age (Cahn 1987; M. George 1988), and they are able to do so only because of a failure to analyse historical evidence properly. These studies are based only on selectively chosen anecdotal material and didactic literature – that is, sermons, advice and conduct books, and other sources which prescribe how women ought to behave, but do not describe how they actually lived.

The problems of evidence are highlighted by the modern-day example of the eastern European socialist economies (before their recent upheaval). If the historian read only official – that is, didactic – sources in order to understand the position of women in mid-twentieth-century eastern Europe, she would have to reach the conclusion that socialism had created an egalitarian paradise. But in reality, the pressures on women in socialist states to work in the public sector while they remain solely responsible for the domestic sector, and the segregation of labour by sex, result in the same double burden that women in capitalist states suffer (Moore 1988: 136–49). Western marxist feminists make the important point that the relations between different classes of women are as important as the relations between women and men (Barrett 1980), as Clark emphasized that capitalism affected women of different classes differently. But the difference between capitalist class relations and pre- or post-capitalist class relations requires much more exploration. The possibility of a golden age in pre-capitalist England, then, is dimmed by observation of post-capitalist societies in the twentieth century, which do not encourage the hope that the patriarchal exploitation of female labour is unique to capitalism.

The credibility of a golden age in England before industrialization is likewise not bolstered by anthropological research, which has analysed many subsistence agricultural societies, virtually none of which can be described as gender-equal. Technological developments do affect the sexual division of agricultural labour, in so far as they tend to reduce women's agricultural labour. For example, the shift from the hoe to the plough, and from the sickle to the scythe, had this effect in the long run, since both women and men use the hoe and the sickle, while only men use the more 'advanced' tools, the plough and the scythe (see short-term qualifications in Roberts 1979). But this limitation of women's agricultural work, with the consequent decrease in their contribution to the household economy in an agricultural society, does not necessarily undermine their social status. Nor, on the other hand, does the lightening of women's heavy agricultural labour necessarily improve the regard in which they are held. Unjust as it may seem, the extent of women's contribution to the household economy bears no predictable relation to their ideological status in any given society.

Medievalists today, in the 'second wave' of feminist history, are less sanguine about medieval and early modern partnership and egalitarianism than those in the first wave at the beginning of the century. Examining the same records – court cases, probate documents, apprenticeship indentures and guild records – medievalists now emphasize patriarchal restrictions upon women in the family, in work, in religion, in law and so forth, demonstrating that the lives of medieval women were far from idyllic (Bennett 1988). Women's guild membership, lauded by earlier historians, was in fact extremely limited and always dependent upon their husbands; the few skilled women's trades which existed, all in textiles, failed to organize into guilds at all in England. Women had very little access to training, skilled work and adequate wages; their legal rights were severely curtailed when they married, which of course they were expected to do; and they had no political voice at any level (Middleton 1979; Charles and Duffin 1985; Hanawalt 1986; Bennett 1987; Kowaleski and Bennett 1989).

However, to present medieval and early modern conditions in a positive light is not necessarily the same as positing a golden age. In defence against the self-congratulatory optimism of modernization theory, some historians find the conditions of medieval and early modern women not wholly unrecognizable today.

Continuity in women's work

Despite the endurance of the argument between pessimists and optimists, both sides have been loath to establish the precise criteria by which they think women's status ought to be measured (Thomas 1988). But it is possible to go back one step further and question the assumption of the argument that the early modern period necessarily constituted a watershed in all aspects of English life. In fact, a comparison of medieval circumstances with those that prevail today reveals more continuity than change in the important features of women's working lives. Most startling, the ratio of women's wages relative to those of men has stuck at between one half and two thirds for the past seven centuries. In addition, access to training and skilled jobs in nineteenth-century mechanized industry was male-controlled in much the same way it had been in craft industries in the middle ages, and to some extent the way it is in skilled trades and professions today. Women were concentrated in low-paying jobs like charring, laundering, domestic work and nursing in the late seventeenth and early eighteenth centuries, as they are concentrated today in the service sectors – cleaning, secretarial work, nursing. The sexual division of capitalist industrial labour looks remarkably like the sexual division of feudal agrarian labour. And the domestic division of labour, or rather the fact that there is no division since housework is exclusively women's responsibility, remains virtually unchanged. In short, the essential features of women's economic position relative to men – the sex ratio of wages, access to training, concentration in the lowest-paid sectors of the labour market, and the sexual division of labour – appear to have been unaffected by either capitalism or industrialization. (For discussion of points in this paragraph, see Davidson 1982; Middleton 1985; Berg 1987; Bennett 1988; Earle 1989.)

Domestic work deserves specific attention, since one of Clark's most important contributions to subsequent feminist history is that she gave equal weight to women's paid and unpaid work. She could not say much about unpaid work because very little was ever written down, but whether labour was used to produce for domestic use or for wages, to Clark it was all production. In this she distinguished herself from economists who counted only paid employment as work, and hence ignored an enormous amount of female labour. When the washerwoman Mary Collier wrote her poem, 'The woman's labour' (1739), she too meant all kinds of labour – haymaking, laundering, cooking, gleaning, raising children, sewing, cleaning, brewing – whether it was for wages or for the family:

> No Learning ever was bestow'd on me;
> My Life was always spent in Drudgery:
> And not alone; alas! with Grief I find,
> It is the portion of poor Woman-kind.

Clark's pessimistic view relies heavily on the intuitive sense that if production is removed from the home and women's domestic work is no longer seen as productive, then necessarily their status will decline. But to what extent was women's work ever really seen as productive? Yes, the efficiency of Lady Brilliana Harley and Anne, Lady Fanshawe and that of the Fell sisters and other gentlewomen in managing their husbands' or fathers' estates (pp. 15–22) provides an impressive display of female competence; and their menfolk's trust in their capabilities suggests respect. Yes, women's labour was essential to the household economy. This is evident in manuals like Fitzherbert's *Book of Husbandrye* (1555), which Clark quotes at length (pp. 46–9), and in others too which Clark doesn't mention, like Gervase Markham's *English Housewife* (1631).

In terms of its importance to the family, women's work was not only essential but appears to have constituted at least half of the total household economy. When middle- and upper-class men began to investigate the condition of agrarian labouring families in the eighteenth and early nineteenth centuries, they observed that women's cash earnings alone produced nearly as much income as their husbands' wages (Snell 1985: 212; Humphries 1990). And this calculation did not begin to consider that most of women's labour took the invisible form of subsistence rather than the visible form of cash.

It is common for historians today to speak of women's work
'supplementing' the family income, or of women being
engaged in 'by-employments' or 'side-industries' (Hutton 1985:
90, 95, 97; Wright 1985: 104; Bennett 1987: 117). Women's
work was certainly 'supplementary' in the sense that their
wages were lower than those of men, that they worked overwhelmingly in the service trades, and that as wives they
adapted their labour to assist in their husbands' trades. But
the terminology of 'by-employments' reflects a later historical
development – the assumption that a man 'supported' his wife
and children and that any contribution they made to the family
economy was incidental. Clark rightly points out that this idea
simply did not exist in early modern England.

On the other hand, if the writers of sixteenth- and
seventeenth-century household manuals represent the roles
of husband and wife as complementary, that representation
is meretricious. Both the division of labour and the division
of power within the household was clearly hierarchical. There
is no evidence to support Clark's suggestion (p. 5) that early
modern men took any more responsibility for cooking, cleaning and childcare than they do today. All household manuals
made this women's work, and popular ballads mocked the
role-reversed household in which the husband washed the
baby's 'shitten clouts' (Pepys Ballad IV: 132, in Weinstein
1992). A practical, day-to-day complementarity of work
coexisted with a powerful theory of female subordination.
Ultimately, the husband and father ruled the early modern
household and his power could be legally or morally invoked,
should he choose, at any time that, according to him, his wife
failed to perform her housewifely duties in a sufficiently
prompt and obedient manner. The myriad household tasks
which we now identify as women's work were considered by
early modern men and women more as wifely duty than as
work, a social obligation rather than an occupation (Roberts
1985).

Clark was over-enthusiastic in supposing an egalitarian and
mutually supportive working relationship in the pre-industrial
family. But a pre-existing hierarchical conception of women's
and men's work was undoubtedly exacerbated when men's
work was separated from the home by the long-term develop-

ment of a cash economy. In the context of a wage economy, the early modern conception of male headship of the family easily slips into the idea that a man supports his wife and children economically. In addition, the centrality of cash in the economy encourages the devaluation of work which is not paid, like domestic work. Of course it is possible to pay someone (almost invariably female) to perform domestic work, but her wage is artificially low because such work is ordinarily performed free of charge by a female member of the family. There is no free market in domestic labour which may arrive at a just price through the mechanism of competition, since most of the competition is unpaid. In many ways housework is still defined today in the early modern sense, as women's obligation rather than as work.

Due to the constraints of the archive, Clark pays more attention to paid than to unpaid work, because that is what appears in the historical record, albeit irregularly. Women's paid work in the early modern period has been aptly described as 'improvising, casual, and impermanent' (Thirsk 1985: 15), and as 'unorganised, piecemeal, untrained and auxiliary' (Brodsky 1986: 142). Historically, women appear most prominently in crafts, trades and manufacturing when there were not enough men to do the jobs, as in time of war, or when the local economy was in difficulties. Economic crises had the simultaneous effects of removing institutional obstacles to women, and of requiring them to earn money in the absence of an adequate male income in the household (Prior 1985; M. Howell 1986). But should women's participation in the public economy be seen as evidence of their freedom to take advantage of new opportunities, or as a sign of household impoverishment which forced women to take paid work? The answer must be that women's public work was a mixture of choice and necessity. In certain circumstances financial dependence on a husband was perfectly satisfactory. On the other hand, work which offered some freedom from an onerous dependence – where a husband abused his power or where a widow preferred not to remarry – was welcomed. Most families could not survive on the husband's income alone. Clark is aware that most women worked of necessity, but she also regards paid work as an opportunity – not in its current sense of career advancement, but in so far as it offered the possibility of economic security or comfort.

Having examined Clark's perspectives on long-term change, and discussed the more recent evidence of consistent relative sexual inequality at this macroeconomic level, I now turn to the microeconomic: the descriptive aspects of Clark's research on early modern women's daily lives and the evidence for a short-term deterioration in relative status in the seventeenth century. It should be noted that, while her arguments pertain broadly to the whole of England, more recent studies distinguish fastidiously between different agricultural and economic regions of the country. In reviewing the history of women's work since Clark, I focus on publications of the last decade, and have regretfully excluded the large amount of unpublished research, since some of the published material will be difficult enough for the reader to track down. I follow the chapters in *Working Life*, dividing women into economic groups – 'capitalists', 'agriculture', 'textiles', 'crafts and trades' and 'professions'.

'Capitalists'

By 'capitalists' Clark means people with capital, in the form of land or equipment or cash, engaged in commercial enterprise for profit. This category ranges from aristocrats seeking concessionary benefits such as wardships or monopolies from the crown, to gentry women involved in estate management, to women who ran an ironmongery or a paper mill or an insurance office, to married couples engaged in a multitude of trades. Clark presents an impressive array of wives taking an active part in all kinds of home-centred businesses with their husbands, and carrying on those businesses as widows. She suggests that over the seventeenth century these women gradually lost contact with commercial affairs, as the place of work was more frequently removed from the home. These capitalist wives, who could afford to pay other women to perform their domestic work, gradually became merely ornamental in their husbands' homes, deprived of productive work and of self-respect. To support this hypothesis, Clark looks at three main sources: the Calendar of State Papers Domestic for wardship, monopoly and patent applications; contemporary upper-class comments on women's business activity; and the wills of men of the capitalist class.

No further research has been done since *Working Life* on women's applications to the crown for wardships, monopolies and patents (p. 25). Only two subsequent studies of individual women's financial enterprise have appeared, both of them in obscure periodicals: Joyce Jeffries of Hereford, in the decade between 1638 and 1648, derived her income partly from farming, but principally from financial dealing in loans and mortgages (Griffiths 1933); Elizabeth Parkin, in mid-eighteenth-century Sheffield, invested widely in the steel industry (Holderness 1973). Neither Jeffries nor Parkin ever married.

The second of Clark's sources is contemporary comments by people like Sir Josiah Child, Samuel Pepys and Mary Astell, who make unfavourable comparisons between English and Dutch women's commercial involvement (pp. 35–9). However, such individual pronouncements on the business inferiority of the English woman range across the whole century, and there is no evidence that they increase in number towards the end of the period, so they cannot demonstrate a change in women's actual working lives. In general, contemporary comments on the relative status of women in different countries – a subject regularly remarked upon by European travellers since the late sixteenth century – tell us more about what the commentator thought women ought to be like than they do about the actual condition of women in the countries being contrasted.

The use of business records as a historical source presents a different picture. The two available studies of eighteenth-century businesswomen (Berg 1987; Hunt forthcoming) suggest that, at the very least, female commercial enterprise was not limited to the pre-industrial period. The proliferation of varieties of trades and of commercial records renders businesswomen in the eighteenth century more visible to historians than those in earlier centuries, but the range of business undertaken by women in all periods deserves much more research. In medieval and early modern centuries, the principal sources for discovering businesswomen and tradeswomen

must be court records and tax returns (see for example Goldberg 1990 on the late fifteenth century).

The final source which Clark cites as evidence of women's
increasing alienation from their husbands' business activities
is men's wills. She states that fewer and fewer wives were
appointed executrix in their husbands' wills in the seventeenth
century (p. 39), but offers no precise figures to support this
claim. Wills are one type of record which has been examined
in detail in recent years. Their quantitative analysis has been
facilitated by the collection of probate documents into county
record offices and by the advent of computers. Subsequent
studies of sixteenth-, seventeenth- and eighteenth-century wills
confirm Clark's observation that a wife was usually named
executrix in her husband's will (Evans 1985: 66; Brodsky 1986:
145; Erickson forthcoming 1993a). But of the two studies
which specifically compare change over time in one place, one
finds no change over the period 1500–1700 in the proportion
of wives named executrix (Wrightson 1984: 330), and the other
finds a late seventeenth-century increase and concludes that
women's status improved (Vann 1979: 366), exactly opposite
to Clark's idea.

Will patterns vary in different regions of the country,
according to inheritance customs, and they also vary with the
wealth of the testator. A poor man was more likely to name
his wife executrix than a wealthy man (Wrightson 1982: 94;
Lebsock 1984: 36–7). This evidence confirms Clark's propo-
sition that poorer women exercised greater control in family
economic affairs than wealthy women, if they were more often
trusted to administer those affairs after their husbands' death.
But there is no indication that wealthy women were progress-
ively relieved of responsibility in their husbands' wills in the
early modern period. The executrix question has been extensively elaborated in the past ten years. Was she appointed
alone or jointly with someone else, and if so, with whom?
What restrictions might be placed upon her, particularly those
limiting her remarriage? Women's own wills, those made by
widows and those very few made by married women, are also
now being investigated (Prior 1990) to learn whether women
had attitudes to their property similar to or different from
those of men, and who they themselves appointed as execu-

tors. The answers so far remain inconclusive, but if clear patterns are not immediately forthcoming, wills are one source suggested by Clark whose possibilities subsequent historians have explored in both quantitative and qualitative detail.

'Agriculture'

Clark's description of the three-tiered agricultural structure, comprising farmers or yeomen, husbandmen, and labourers, is the same one historians use today. Her interest in the household economy at each of these three levels is also shared by historians today. Unfortunately neither of the two recent estimates of yeomen's household budgets has taken to heart Clark's lesson on the mutual participation of husband and wife in the domestic economy. Both consider exclusively the male contribution to that economy, since they are based principally on crop yields (Macfarlane 1970: 44, 49; Bowden 1985). This type of estimate fails to take into account that half of household production provided by women in landholding families, including vegetable, dairy and poultry production both for family use and for market, the making of cloth, clothing, bed and table linen, and so forth (Erickson forthcoming 1993b). The same is true of the one attempt to reconstruct the economy of a small landholder, or husbandman (C. Howell 1983: ch. 8).

Certainly there are difficulties in reconstructing women's half of the household economy; yeomen's account books survive much more frequently than those of their wives. Another problem is the transitory nature of most of women's production: produce for market was obviously for immediate consumption, and seventeenth-century textiles rarely survive to the present day. A craftsman or an owner might imprint his mark onto a wooden linen chest, or a pewter bowl, or a metal tool; but his wife carved her mark on her cheeses, or cut a certain design in the crust of a pie to identify its contents (Ulrich 1982: 47, 108ff), and it was eaten.

Evidence for the domestic economy of families below the level of yeomen and substantial husbandmen – families which combined waged work with subsistence agriculture or survived on wages alone – is hardest to obtain. Neither husbandmen's nor labourers' account books survive, if they were ever written

at all. Clark's estimate of the subsistence budget required by
a seventeenth-century wage-earning family was the first of its
kind and remains the most thoroughly documented investigation of the subject. Using poor relief rates, the diets of
workhouses and schools, and the levels of agricultural wages
which included food, she calculated the absolute minimum
costs of living which must have been met by these families.
(For recent discussions see Wrightson and Levine 1979: 40;
Wrightson 1982: 34.) But even this minimum expenditure,
Clark observed, amounted to more than the maximum wages
that a family could expect to bring in, even assuming that
both parents and two out of three children would work for
wages. This shortfall continues to baffle historians today, and
deserves more attention; it is still not really understood how
the majority of the population in early modern England survived from day to day.

The study of wage levels is complicated by a lack of source
material. A 'wage series' must cover some length of time and
relate to the same or a similar employer in order that the
levels of pay being charted are comparable. Those series so
far compiled have therefore studied construction workers on
cathedrals, universities or large civic projects (Phelps Brown
and Hopkins 1981). Construction workers were usually,
although not invariably, men. Women were most frequently
found in the heavy carrying trades, hauling stone, slate and
so on, which were paid by the piece or the barrow, rather
than at a daily rate. It is next to impossible to construct wage
series for work which was more 'traditionally' female, such as
midwifery or wetnursing. The only data available for payments
consists of occasional, scattered account entries such as
'expended in and about her deliverye of the childe . . . and
spent in baptizinge of it and at her Churchinge, £1'.[3] At least
an account entry like 'Emme epps came into my house to
sukle my child Lydia for 7s. 6d. per week'[4] lists payment for
one thing only and for a specified period of time, but a great
many such entries are needed to construct a series.

The only quantitative source which covers both men's and

---

[3] Lincolnshire Archives Office: Ad Ac 19/58.

[4] British Library: Egerton MS 2667, this entry dated 1717.

women's pay is the legally required wage assessments for domestic and agricultural servants set locally by justices of the peace at quarter sessions. Wage assessments were first collected by Thorold Rogers (1866), and Clark uses those from several counties. The condition of early modern servants in husbandry, agricultural workers who lived in their employers' homes, has recently been examined by Ann Kussmaul (1981). Almost one third of these servants in husbandry were female. However, as early as the end of the sixteenth century, it appears that agricultural servants did not usually live in their employers' homes; rather, both men and women hired out as day labourers, living independently (A. H. Smith 1989). In order to evaluate women's and men's day labour, it is necessary to establish not only daily rates of pay, but also how many days in the year any individual worked, figures which require a detailed series of surviving estate papers. More qualitative information about women's agricultural day labour can be gleaned from court indictments of those who took wages in excess of the assessments and otherwise transgressed against labour laws (Penn 1987). Domestic servants living either in or out of their employers' homes were overwhelmingly female, and they still await research, as they did when Dorothy Marshall wrote a brief pamphlet on the subject in 1949. The minimal work so far done on servants pertains to the eighteenth century, and principally to menservants (Marshall 1929; Hecht 1956). If middle- and upper-class women gradually retired from productive activity starting in the seventeenth century, then they must have been hiring increasing numbers of maidservants to facilitate that retirement.

The one fact that emerges clearly from all the scattered bits of evidence on women's agricultural and domestic wages, whether on an annual living-in basis or for day labour, is that they almost invariably ranged from only one half to two thirds of the wages of men (Gilboy 1931–2: 390; Campbell 1942: app. 3; Kussmaul 1981: 37; C. Howell 1983: 173–4; Snell 1985: 326, 346). Even that differential which is identifiable does not take into consideration the sexual differentiation in agricultural day labour which meant that women worked many fewer days than men.

Clark describes the grinding poverty endured by labouring

families, but many cottagers and even landless labourers had access to common land on which to graze a cow, gather fuel, pick berries or herbs and catch fish or birds. The value of this common land, along with the right to glean, probably meant at least as much to poor families as a daily wage. Rights to common land were exploited principally by women, since men could earn higher and more regular wages; but over the sixteenth, seventeenth and eighteenth centuries the process of enclosure, by destroying the commons, deprived more and more women of their means of livelihood. This trend, which has enormous importance for the household economy, was broached by Pinchbeck in 1930, but has received little attention since, largely because there is no obvious historical source which records the use of common land. Most evidence comes from the late eighteenth and early nineteenth centuries, with the advent of public inquiries (Snell 1985: ch. 4; Humphries 1990; King 1991), but the process had been ongoing for some three hundred years previously.

'Textiles'

Outside agriculture the textile industry employed the largest number of women in the population, and women heavily outnumbered men within the industry, but they were concentrated in the lower-paid jobs. Building on the costs of living calculated in her previous chapter, Clark found that women's wages in the wool industry were barely sufficient to keep body and soul together; those in linen and luxury cloths were wholly inadequate. She traces the decline of the silk trade from a virtual monopoly of gentlewomen in the fifteenth century to a seventeenth-century industry exploiting women's sweated labour (pp. 138–43). No further work has been produced on women's role in the luxury textile trades in England, even for the eighteenth century, when the demand for luxury fabrics increased the employment of women in their production, when the processes were mechanized, and from when ample records survive for study. (For silk production in sixteenth-century Tuscany, see J. Brown 1986; in eighteenth-century southern France, Hufton 1981.)

Even before it became mechanized and factory-centred, the textile industry was a hotbed of worker unrest. Clark reviews women's participation in petitioning and protest during the economic distress of the 1620s and 1630s in clothworking areas (pp. 119–23); recently Buchanan Sharp also found women in the textile areas of Gloucestershire involved in riots protesting against low wages and lack of work (1980: ch. 2). However, research specifically on women in riots has looked at the eighteenth century rather than earlier, and particularly at grain and food riots (Bohstedt 1988). Work on women's crime in the sixteenth and seventeenth centuries has touched only briefly on riot (Beattie 1975; Wiener 1975). Women's participation in 'subsistence' riots over grain or food prices has been explained by the facts that it was they who fed their families and they who were familiar with the marketplace.

But many questions remain. Since women made up the vast majority of textile workers, were they in fact the principal actors in wage riots too? If, instead, they constituted only a minority of the rioters, then why were male textile workers more likely to riot? Women were apparently also involved, at least prior to the civil war, in riots protesting at the hedging of common land and the drainage of fens (Houlbrooke 1986). Did they continue to protest against these and other types of enclosure later in the seventeenth century and into the eighteenth? Did, as seems likely, the loss of common rights affect women more immediately than men? Specific studies are needed of women in early modern popular protest, since gender is not adequately analysed in research which ostensibly addresses popular protest 'as a whole'. Women in the textile trades will probably be found to have been prominent in that unrest.

The association of women with textiles, especially spinning, is of at least biblical origin. Clark shows that early modern overseers of the poor, workhouse administrators and reformers had a penchant for setting poor and idle women on spinning work (pp. 129–37), a practice which merits further investigation into the mentality of these men, since it was clear that such work paid insufficient wages which were bound to keep the women poor and likely to lead them into desperate work like prostitution in order to survive. The rapid expansion of cities in the seventeenth and eighteenth centuries suggests that prostitution provided employment for an ever-growing number of women. Victorian prostitution – and its connection with low wages, usually for spinning or needlework – has received some attention of late, but only occasional, tantalizing glimpses are afforded of an earlier period. Even these illuminate only London, only prostitution which was organized into brothels, and only the perspective of the men trying to control the trade: for example, the rules by which the Bishop of Winchester managed the Southwark stews in the fifteenth century (Karras 1989); the records of the later sixteenth-century crackdown on bawdy houses by the Bridewell authorities and the courts (Archer 1991: 211–15); and the Shrove Tuesday 'tradition' for apprentices to attack and burn down bawdy houses in the first half of the seventeenth century (T. Harris 1986: 537–8). In other words, we know virtually nothing about medieval and early modern prostitution.

'Crafts and trades'

In her chapter on crafts and trades Clark discusses women's activities in guilds and companies, and in the retail and food provision trades. Little of her work has been followed up. In the records of the Stationers' Company Clark found that women had been excluded from the printing trades in the early seventeenth century, but that widows constituted nearly 10 per cent of all publishers in the period 1553–1640 (pp. 161–7). The only recent work on women publishers focuses on the Puritan Hannah Allen and the Quaker Mary Westwood in the mid-seventeenth century (Bell 1988 and 1989). It would be interesting to know some statistics for the period after 1640: for example, did the proportion of women publishers increase along with the number of women writers from the late seventeenth century? Clark's evidence on women in most of the crafts and trades is not extensive enough to identify a specific decline in their position, but more work may identify changes over time. Research today is commonly circumscribed by location rather than by occupation, such that a study of women's work in Salisbury or Shrewsbury or London or York will turn up many interesting occupations, but only a few examples of each. Comparison with other cities and towns is necessary to amass any considerable number of butchers or victuallers, watchmakers or mantua-makers.

Brewing is Clark's best example of a trade in which capitalization specifically displaced women. Brewing was originally an exclusively female domestic trade; in the 1620s and 1630s it was monopolized in large-scale production by men, with the specific encouragement of a government which wanted to control the taxation of ale and beer (pp. 221–32). However, this monopolization did not come out of the blue: antagonism towards brewsters, or female brewers, is evident from at least the late middle ages (Bennett 1991). And capitalist industry did not invariably exclude women. In late sixteenth-century Tuscany, for example, women's employment in the wool and silk industries increased (Brown and Goodman 1980; J. Brown 1986). But this occurred as men left wool and silk and moved into new luxury trades. Women's paid employment is largely a matter of filling the interstices of a male craft and trade structure, and the institutional attitude towards women will fluctuate with economic conditions. When labour was needed, there was no objection to female craft and trade workers, but when competition was stiff or demand slack, then women were complained about and restricted.

Most of the women listed as practising crafts and trades in tax returns and guild records had acquired their skills unofficially. Clark found very few girls among apprenticeship indentures for the skilled trades. The evidence for girls' apprenticeship to skilled trades in London is conflicting. A recent study found not one female apprentice in 8,000 indentures from the late sixteenth and early seventeenth centuries (Brodsky 1986: 141). An older study identified occasional girls bound apprentice in the Carpenters', Wheelwrights', and Clockmakers' Companies in the early eighteenth century (Dunlop 1912: 151). However, Clark points out (pp. 175–7) that in such cases it is not clear whether the girls were meant to learn the trade of the master or that of his wife, which could have been different from her husband's, or could have been housewifery.

The most recent study, of southeast England, traces a marked decline in girls' apprenticeship to trades and to agriculture in the late seventeenth and early eighteenth centuries (Snell 1985: ch. 6). Work on continental Europe confirms that girls were no longer apprenticed in the same numbers or to the same variety of trades as they had been previously, and whatever rights in trade guilds and companies the wives of members had ever enjoyed were whittled away, but that this was a gradual process over the fifteenth, sixteenth, seventeenth and eighteenth centuries (M. Howell 1986, Wiesner 1986).

Clark states in her preface that she hoped to write a second volume on girls' education and apprenticeship, but she never did. There is now a substantial body of work on the 'learned ladies' of the early modern period (for example, Warnicke 1983; Hannay 1985). But the best surveys of schools for more ordinary girls remain those of Dorothy Gardiner (1929), who covers twelve centuries but concentrates on the seventeenth and eighteenth, and M. G. Jones (1938) on the eighteenth century (see also Kamm 1965; Schnorrenberg 1980). Probably the extent of girls' and boys' education in the countryside consisted in learning to read at a village 'petty' or 'dame' school at the age of four or five. Some children, principally boys, subsequently learned to write. For cities, it is possible to unearth the records of individual schools, such as those of the charitable Red Maids School in Bristol, established in the early seventeenth century for 'poore women children' (Vanes 1986: chs 1–2).

'Professions'

Clark investigates the female 'professions' of teaching, nursing, medicine and midwifery. Women were not in any of these fields 'professional' in the sense of being institutionally trained and licensed to practise until the late nineteenth century. But through the seventeenth century, and perhaps later, women did predominate in the professional practice, in the sense of being paid for work in nursing, medicine and midwifery. While women were paid to teach young children, they probably did not predominate in the field, but surviving parish records occasionally document the licensing of schooldames, some of whom were the wives of labourers (Spufford 1981: 24, 35–6). Teaching and nursing have received very little historical attention in the past seventy years. Nursing was, as Clark observed, the occupation of the poor. The records of parish overseers of the poor regularly record payments to women, themselves in receipt of weekly relief, to care for other poor people – to nurse the sick, watch with the dying, wash and wind the dead, and cleanse the house after a visitation of plague. Probably these, and other women not on relief, were similarly employed on a private basis. From the prevalence of women in the chambers of the dying, it appears that death may have been as specifically female an event as birth. Even wives paid other women to look after their dying husbands, perhaps because the wives were obliged to work outside the home for wages, or perhaps because the hired women had special expertise in nursing. One Dorothy Chapman, for example, wife of a Lincolnshire labourer, paid Margaret Storr 3s. 3d. in 1633 for 'keeping' Dorothy's husband Tobias in his last sickness, as well as for 'certain honey'.[5] Regrettably, neither of the two studies of death and burial in England in this period does more than mention the work of women in passing (Gittings 1984: 112; Houlbrooke 1989b: 44).

The source material for teaching, nursing and medicine is scarce; as Clark makes clear, training for women in these areas was not an issue because the skills were assumed to be innately female, an extension of their housewifely duties. Most women were not institutionally educated or licensed for such work, and it is the processes of formal education and licensing which leave records. Prosecution of course also leaves records, and women accused of practising surgery illegally, as well as those few who were duly licensed as surgeonesses, have recently received consideration (Wyman 1984). Evidence from the patients' rather than the regulators' perspective is available in household and probate accounts and in corporate or borough records like those in which Clark found women being paid to look after plague victims (pp. 249–51). Likewise, the London hospital records from which Clark obtained her wage rates for nurses (pp. 243–9) could be further explored, and they may be available for other cities as well.

Clark's picture of the formerly entirely female occupations of medicine and midwifery gradually becoming 'professionalized' and therefore male is widely accepted, but the timing of the transition is now placed largely in the eighteenth, rather

---

[5] Lincolnshire Archives Office: Ad Ac 23/170.

than the seventeenth century (Donnison 1977; Versluysen 1981). But little is known about the actual practice of these women, since recent debate is preoccupied with the question of midwives' personal characters – were they slovenly and ignorant, or were they trained, albeit informally, and careful practitioners (Harley 1981; Wilson 1983; Boss and Boss 1983)? Studies of midwifery have been few compared with investigations of motherhood itself. Although childbirth was quintessentially women's 'labour', Clark does not go into any detail on what work was involved in bearing and raising children in the past, assuming that this process was equivalent in the seventeenth century to that in the early twentieth century. The recent popularity of the history of family relations has given rise to research on parental attitudes towards children, and to a limited extent on women's labour in childrearing, although most work focuses on personal relations (Pollock 1983; McLaren 1985; Crawford 1986; Fildes 1990). Of course, some aspects of childrearing left more records than others; wetnursing, for example (Fildes 1988), not only provides records of payment from the parents to another woman, but it was also continually going in and out of fashion, providing another topic for moralists to fulminate about in print.

Women alone

Throughout *Working Life* Clark holds up as a model for her own society the pre-industrial marital partnership in the household economy. She does not address the inadequacies of the way in which the marital relation itself has been historically constructed. Perhaps had she been married we would have heard more. Today the pre-industrial household still represents an ideal for some 'progressive' thinkers (for example, Illich 1982), but feminists question the value of both the household economy and the marriage on which it is based, since both are predicated upon female subordination and economic dependence (see the bracing critiques of Illich by Bowles *et al.* 1983).

Clark assumes that virtually all women in the seventeenth century married. Her emphasis on the importance of both marriage and maternity is intriguing, in view of her own life-long single state. (Whether her singleness was by choice or accident, and what she felt about it, are unknown. Alice Clark did not commit personal reflections to paper.) Research in the past decade in the new field of historical demography has deployed computer modelling to establish English rates of marriage in the past. It is now estimated that throughout the early modern period the proportion of English people who never married was in fact substantially higher than at any time since, fluctuating between about 10 per cent and 20 per cent of the population (Wrigley and Schofield 1981: 260; Schofield 1985: 9–10). This estimate makes no distinction by sex, but it is likely that more women than men never married. At the same time the rate of remarriage was declining, and as women remarried much less frequently than men, there were far more widows than widowers in the population (Dupaquier *et al.* 1981; Wrigley and Schofield 1981: 258–9). Then too, while divorce was infrequent and difficult to obtain, marital separation was probably not uncommon (P. Sharpe 1990). So, contrary to Clark's assumption, the proportion of single women in the population was in fact extraordinarily high.

How did these lone women live in a society which theoretically had no place in its social hierarchy, its 'great chain of being', for an unattached female? Surprisingly, they did not necessarily live as dependants in other men's households, as might be assumed. Single and widowed women were nearly three times as likely as single and widowed men to head their own household, or to live alone (Laslett 1972: 147; Wall 1981). Of course, statistics are static and cannot reflect the continual changes in family circumstances which characterized the early modern household (Chaytor 1980), or the way in which people regarded marriage, singleness and widowhood. To put flesh on the demographic bones of single women there is only a handful of studies of their lives. Some of the female-headed households identified by demographers were what Olwen Hufton calls 'spinster clusters' – that is, unmarried women and widows living together wherever work was available, particularly in textile-producing towns (1984). Hufton has also examined the gruelling lives of poor French girls in the eighteenth century, working to save a pathetically small dowry towards their marriages (1981). While most young women throughout early modern Europe planned to marry, many did not ultimately do so. Both variations in the age at which women married and the changing incidence of widows' remarriage deserve close attention.

Age at marriage has been correlated with men's real wages: when these wages improve, both men's and women's age at first marriage drops, presumably as the couple is able to set up a household earlier (Wrigley and Schofield 1981: table 10.2). But the same correlation appears unreliable for female wages in the seventeenth and eighteenth centuries (P. Sharpe 1991). In the nineteenth-century textile industry, where women's wages were good and work was readily available, women married later and more women never married. Conversely, where female wages were low, women's age at first marriage dropped. In other words, women married earlier when their opportunities for supporting themselves were limited, while a good wage and economic independence gave women the option to postpone marriage. For some women this may have been a decision not to marry, but for most it represented the freedom to exercise a choice of spouse.

On the issue of the declining incidence of widows' remarriage, the debate continues over the relationship between personal choice and economic necessity in a woman's decision to remarry (Rosenthal 1984; B. Todd 1985; Brodsky 1986; Boulton 1990). What part did social expectation play? Throughout the late sixteenth and the seventeenth century the possibility that a widow might remarry was something of a 'hysterical obsession among the middle and upper-class males' (Hufton 1984: 373). But it was precisely the widows of these men – those left relatively well off – who could afford not to remarry. One side of the debate has it that wealthy widows were snatched up by fortune-hunting men, the other side that these women opted to remain independent. The evidence so far is equivocal, but since it is so important to the explanation of gender differences in remarriage rates and changes in those rates over time, the question merits further research.

So do many other questions about how widows supported themselves and their children. For even modestly prosperous widows, moneylending was an important alternative or addition to physical labour as a means of securing an income (Holderness 1984), but for a substantial number of women, widowhood meant poverty. While Clark is attentive to the hardships of poverty for wage-earning labourers' wives, and the problems caused by women's low pay, she does not confront the systemic economic vulnerability imposed to varying degrees on all women. A woman's loss of her spouse was potentially severely impoverishing in a way in which a man's loss of his spouse was not, not only because of men's higher wages, but also because the common law gave all of her property legally to him. Women's legal rights to control of property within marriage have left considerable records, in the form of court cases, probate documents and legal treatises, and this aspect of women's economic situation has been extensively analysed in recent years (Cioni 1982; Spring 1983 and 1984; Okin 1983–4; Erickson 1990; Staves 1990; B. Todd 1990).

The inevitable result of legal disadvantages and low wages was that lone women – whether never-married, widowed or separated from their husbands – were the social group most vulnerable to poverty. That vulnerability has been measured in slightly different ways: in seventeenth-century Norfolk more than 60 per cent of all those in receipt of poor relief were female, and most of those were widows with young children (Wales 1984: 378); in one Hertfordshire parish in the course of the seventeenth century, more than one-third of all widows were on poor relief (W. Brown 1984: 412); and of all single parents dependent on relief in the eighteenth and early nineteenth centuries 86 per cent were female (Snell and Millar 1987: 397). But these rates should not be surprising since they are virtually identical to those that prevail in Britain and America today: women comprise about two-thirds of the adult poor, and more than one-third of all single mothers of minor children live in poverty (Scott 1984: ch. 2; Oppenheim 1990: ch. 6). While this kind of statistical comparison – in wages, in the division of public and private labour, and in levels of poverty – will never take the place of lived experience, only figures can reveal how impervious is the relative disadvantage of women to economic and technological change.

In so far as poverty was relieved by individual charity, rather than by poor relief, it is interesting that female benefactors were 'much more substantially committed to the care of the poor than were their husbands or fathers'; unlike male benefactors, women had 'but scant interest in financing municipal improvements of any kind' (Jordan 1959: 353–5). Women's philanthropic gifts comprised only a small percentage of the total number of donations, and an even smaller proportion of total philanthropic wealth – as is to be expected given women's economic disadvantages – but these donations were directed specifically to help other women. One new article looks at women's charitable bequests in medieval Yorkshire (Cullum forthcoming), but otherwise Jordan's work on early modern philanthropy has lain unelaborated for the past thirty years.

Current approaches to early modern women

'A book might be wholly filled with a story of the part taken by women in the political and religious struggles of the period,' Clark observed (p. 25). This book has not been written in the seventy years since *Working Life*, and only one article addresses politics specifically, in the form of the women petitioners to parliament in the 1640s (Higgins 1973). Two studies address different aspects of the role of gender in the maintenance of the seventeenth-century social order (Amussen 1988; Pollock 1989), but this is a separate issue from women's political activities as such.

A plethora of articles is, however, available on religion. While it is impossible to separate politics and religion in this period, most research focuses on less overtly political aspects of religion: the activities of individual protestant women in the religious upheavals of the sixteenth century (most recently, Shakespeare and Dowling 1982; Greaves 1985; Lake 1987; Newman 1990; Wabuda 1990); Catholic women in the same period (Rowlands 1985; Cross 1990); the ritual of churching (Coster 1990); the prophetesses of the mid-seventeeth century (Mack 1982 and 1988; Cohen 1984) and women in the civil war sects (Crawford 1988); the effect of protestant, and particularly puritan, ideology about women and the family (K. Davies 1981; Leites 1982; Ludlow 1985; Eales 1990; Laurence 1990); and one more general overview (Willen 1989). Noticeably lacking are studies of women and religion in the late seventeenth and first half of the eighteenth centuries, but this should be remedied, and the existing disparate material drawn together, in a new book-length analysis covering the entire period, 1500–1720 (Crawford forthcoming).

Another current approach to the study of early modern women is through the vast number of surviving legal records from many different courts. In addition to property law, mentioned above, there are articles on women's prominence in church court offences such as character defamation (J. Sharpe 1980; Gowing forthcoming), and one on women as victims of violent crime (Bashar 1983). Some interesting avenues for which there is a lack of direct source material, such as women's mental health (Laurence 1989), may also be approached obliquely through court records.

While Clark viewed the economic function of consumption as an almost parasitic act – the moral converse of healthy, uplifting production – today consumption is coming into its own as a subject of research. One approach is the study of 'material culture': probate inventories have been used by Lorna Weatherill to assess the acquisition of luxury goods (1986 and 1988), and by Carole Shammas for the consumption of more everyday commodities (1980 and 1983); Amanda Vickery has looked at gentlewomen's personal attitudes to consumer goods in the eighteenth century (1991). Clark focuses instead on supply (production) rather than on demand (consumption), when she looks at shopkeeping, trading and markets (pp. 32–3, 197–209). It was the wives of farmers, husbandmen and tradesmen who attended markets, to buy as well as to sell, and it was they who bought from itinerant pedlars. Recent work has found more women selling, as shopkeepers, market-stall holders, itinerant chapwomen and regrators (Spufford 1984; Thwaites 1984; Wright 1985), but it is more difficult to trace consumption activities.

Consumption is an essential part of any economy, and while the excesses of twentieth-century consumer societies are rightly coming under criticism, in its basic form consumption is a component of domestic management, which has for all of recorded history been undertaken by women (see further O. Harris 1982). Of course, housewives historically have not referred to what they do as consumption. In early modern England the process of deciding when and what to consume, when and what to save, was called thrift or 'oeconomy', and it represented the principal virtue a woman could display in the running of her household. In the middle of the nineteenth century George Eliot's farm wife Mrs Poyser still thought highly of her 'economy', saying hotly to the local squire in an argument over her husband's land, 'for all I'm a woman, . . . I've a right to speak, for I make one quarter o' the rent [from her dairy], and save another quarter' (*Adam Bede*, p. 335). The word 'economy' still carries its connotation of thrift today in a certain context: the largest but relatively least expensive box of washing powder in the supermarket is called the economy size. If domestic management always required the skills of thrift and consumption, the way in which those skills were exercised changed over the seventeenth and eighteenth centuries, as the number and choice of products available to consume multiplied exponentially.

The most popular approach in the second wave of feminist history is the literary one. Those very few women who wrote are the most frequently studied today. Margaret Cavendish, the Duchess of Newcastle (1623–73), Aphra Behn (1640–89) and Mary Astell (1661–1731) were all familiar to the early twentieth century. But in the last fifteen years, in addition to new biographies and editions of Cavendish, Behn and Astell, a wealth of witty, angry and eloquent women writers from the fifteenth to the eighteenth centuries has been rediscovered, reassessed and reprinted. Besides many anthologies, recent historical treatments which analyse books' readership and the circumstances of their publication, as well as their content, cover the sixteenth and early seventeenth centuries (Hull 1982; Henderson and McManus 1985; Shepherd 1985), the seventeenth century (Crawford 1985; Ezell 1987: chs 3–4; Hobby 1988) and the eighteenth century (Perry 1980; Rogers 1982; J. Todd 1989). Autobiographical writing, not meant for publication, offers another literary angle on early modern women (Mendelson 1985 and 1987; Graham *et al.* 1989).

Conclusion

Alice Clark worked hard all her life. After eleven years in London during which she campaigned for the vote, organized for war relief and wrote *Working Life*, she returned to her parents' house in 1922, now aged 48, as one of four in charge of the family business. Over the next twelve years she directed the Machine Room with 300 women, and introduced and took charge of personnel management, ensuring the suitability of work, earnings levels and pension arrangements, for each of some 1,400 employees. She died in 1934.

Although *Working Life* has become a required text for anyone studying women in early modern England, neither Clark nor more recent feminist historians of the period have succeeded in making any impact on the so-called 'standard' early modern economic history texts (for example, Clarkson 1971; Holderness 1976; Coleman 1977; Clay 1984). Likewise, while women's work has been centred on the family, has maintained the family and has helped determine its historical structure, general histories of family life take absolutely no notice of women's work (for example, Shorter 1975; Stone 1977; Mitterauer and Sieder 1982; Houlbrooke 1984 and 1989a; Macfarlane 1986; Casey 1989). The history of the domestic economy appears firmly separated in male historians' minds from the history of familial affection, and the latter seems to them a far more interesting topic. Female historians, more likely to experience personally the demands of the household economy and its effects upon familial relations, have yet to write an integrated history of these two artificially isolated spheres.

To some extent, Alice Clark's influence today is the result of *Working Life* having been reprinted in 1968, just before the second wave of feminist history, and again in 1982. Ivy Pinchbeck's *Women Workers and the Industrial Revolution 1750–1850* was likewise reprinted in 1969 and 1981. Eileen Power is best known today through her posthumous collection of essays, *Medieval Women* (1975). Other early twentieth-century historians of women whose works survive only in their original editions have largely fallen into oblivion, even among feminist historians. As a result, women's history – and it will be apparent from the bibliography to this introduction that a very large amount of work has been published on women in early modern England since 1919 – is liable to a certain amount of wheel reinvention. On the positive side, the historical sources available for study have mushroomed since Clark's time and more women, in absolute numbers, are studying women's history. *Working Life* is reprinted today because it still offers the most comprehensive introduction to women's everyday lives in the early modern period. We now know more, but our knowledge is of necessity scattered more widely, in local or regional studies and specialist journals.

Some of the work undertaken in the past seventy years confirms Clark's hypotheses, some of it directly challenges them, and some of it extends or qualifies her conclusions and suggests alternative means of enquiry. All of it owes its approach to the historical record to her use of a multiplicity of different sources to find out about ordinary early modern women – the supposedly silent majority. And all of it is indebted to Alice Clark for her willingness to make mistakes in order to make something.

BIBLIOGRAPHY

Abram, Annie (1909) *Social England in the Fifteenth Century: A Study of the Effect of Economic Conditions*, London: Routledge.
——(1913) *English Life and Manners in the Later Middle Ages*, London: Routledge.
——(1916) 'Women traders in medieval London', *Economic Journal* 26, 2: 276–85.
Amussen, Susan (1988) *An Ordered Society: Gender and Class in Early Modern England*, Oxford: Basil Blackwell.
Archer, Ian W. (1991) *The Pursuit of Stability: Social Relations in Elizabethan London*, Cambridge: Cambridge University Press.
Atkinson, Mabel (1914) *The Economic Foundations of the Women's Movement*, Fabian Tract no. 175.
Barrett, Michèle (1980) *Women's Oppression Today: Problems in Marxist Feminist Analysis*, 2nd edn, London: Verso.
Bashar, Nazife (1983) 'Rape in England between 1550 and 1700', in London Feminist History Group (ed.) *The Sexual Dynamics of History*, London: Pluto Press.
Bateson, Mary (1904 and 1906) *Borough Customs*, Selden Society Series 18 and 21.
Beattie, J. M. (1975) 'The criminality of women in eighteenth-century England', *Journal of Social History* 8: 80–116.
Bell, Maureen (1988) 'Mary Westwood, Quaker publisher', *Publishing History* 23: 5–66.
——(1989) 'Hannah Allen and the development of the puritan publishing business 1646–1651', *Publishing History* 26: 5–56.
Bennett, Judith M. (1987) *Women in the Medieval Countryside*, New York: Oxford University Press.
——(1988) ' "History that stands still": women's work in the European past', *Feminist Studies* 14, 2: 269–83.
——(1991) 'Misogyny, popular culture and women's work', *History Workshop Journal* 31: 166–88.
Berg, Maxine (1987) 'Women's work, mechanization and the early phases of industrialization in England', in Patrick Joyce (ed.) *The Historical Meanings of Work*, Cambridge: Cambridge University Press.
——(1992) 'The first women economic historians', *Economic History Review* 2nd ser. 45.
Black, Clementina (ed.) (1915) *Married Women's Work: Being a*

Report of . . . the Women's Industrial Council, London: G. Bell & Sons.

Bohstedt, John (1988) 'Gender, household and community politics: women in English riots 1790–1810', *Past & Present* 120: 88–122.

Boss, Bernice and Boss, Jeffrey (1983) 'Ignorant midwives: a further rejoinder', *Society for the Social History of Medicine Bulletin* 33: 71.

Boulton, Jeremy (1990) 'London widowhood revisited: the decline of female remarriage in the seventeenth and early eighteenth centuries', *Continuity & Change* 5, 3: 323–55.

Bowden, Peter J. (1985) 'Agricultural prices, wages, farm profits, and rents', in Joan Thirsk (ed.) *The Agrarian History of England and Wales* vol. v, pt 2, Cambridge: Cambridge University Press.

Bowles, Gloria et al. (1983) 'Beyond the backlash', *Feminist Issues* 3, 1: 3–43.

Bradley, Rose (1912) *The English Housewife in the Seventeenth and Eighteenth Centuries*, London: Edward Arnold.

Brodsky, Vivien (1986) 'Widows in late Elizabethan London', in Lloyd Bonfield, Richard M. Smith and Keith Wrightson (eds) *The World We Have Gained*, Oxford: Oxford University Press.

Brown, Judith C. (1986) 'A woman's place was in the home: women's work in renaissance Tuscany', in Margaret W. Ferguson, Maureen Quilligan and Nancy J. Vickers (eds) *Rewriting the Renaissance: The Discourses of Sexual Difference in Early Modern Europe*, Chicago: University of Chicago Press.

Brown, J. C. and Goodman, J. (1980) 'Women and industry in Florence', *Journal of Economic History* 40: 73–80.

Brown, W. Newman (1984) 'The receipt of poor relief and family situation: Aldenham, Hertfordshire 1630–90', in R. M. Smith (ed.) *Land, Kinship and Life-Cycle*, Cambridge: Cambridge University Press.

Buckstaff, Florence Griswold (1893) 'Married women's property in Anglo-Saxon and Anglo-Norman law', *Annals of the American Academy of Political and Social Sciences* 4: 233–64.

Buer, Mabel (1926) *Health, Wealth and Population in the Early Days of the Industrial Revolution*, London: Routledge.

Cahn, Susan (1987) *Industry of Devotion: The Transformation of Women's Work in England 1500–1660*, New York: Columbia University Press.

Campbell, Mildred (1942) *The English Yeoman Under Elizabeth and the Early Stuarts*, New Haven, N.J.: Yale University Press.

Casey, James (1989) *The History of the Family*, Oxford: Basil Blackwell.

Charles, Lindsey and Duffin, Lorna (eds) (1985) *Women and Work in Pre-Industrial England*, London: Croom Helm.

Chaytor, Miranda (1980) 'Household and kinship: Ryton in the late sixteenth and early seventeenth centuries', *History Workshop Journal* 10: 25–60.

Cioni, Maria L. (1982) 'The Elizabethan chancery and women's rights', in D. Guth and J. W. McKenna (eds) *Tudor Rule and Revolution*, Cambridge: Cambridge University Press.

Clarkson, L. A. (1971) *The Pre-Industrial Economy in England 1500–1750*, London: Batsford.

——(1985) *Proto-Industrialization: The First Phase of Industrialization?*, Basingstoke: Macmillan.

Clay, C. G. A. (1984) *Economic Expansion and Social Change: England 1500–1700*, Cambridge: Cambridge University Press.

Cohen, Alfred (1984) 'Prophecy and madness: women visionaries during the puritan revolution', *Journal of Psychohistory*: 11: 411–30.

Coleman, D. C. (1977) *The Economy of England 1450–1750*, Oxford: Oxford University Press.

Collier, Mary (1762) *Poems on Several Occasions*, Winchester: Mary Ayres.

Coster, William (1990) 'Purity, profanity, and puritanism: the churching of women, 1500–1700', in W. J. Sheils and Diana Wood (eds) *Women in the Church*, Studies in Church History 27, Oxford: Basil Blackwell.

Crawford, Patricia (1985) 'Women's published writings 1600–1700', in Mary Prior (ed.) *Women in English Society 1500–1800*, London: Methuen.

——(1986) ' "The sucking child": adult attitudes to child care in the first year of life in seventeenth-century England', *Continuity & Change* 1, 1: 23–51.

——(1988) 'Historians, women and the civil war sects', *Parergon* new ser. 6: 5–32.

——(forthcoming) *Women and Religion in England 1500–1720*, London: Routledge.

Cross, Claire (1990) 'The religious life of women in sixteenth-century Yorkshire', in W. J. Sheils and Diana Wood (eds) *Women in the Church*, Studies in Church History 27, Oxford: Basil Blackwell.

Cullum, Patricia (forthcoming) ' "And hir name was charite": women and charity in medieval Yorkshire', in P. J. P Goldberg (ed.) *Woman is a Worthy Wight: Women in Medieval English Society 1200–1500*, Gloucester: Alan Sutton.

Dale, Marian K. (1933) 'The London silkwomen of the fifteenth century', *Economic History Review* 1st ser. 4: 324–35.

Davidson, Caroline (1982) *A Woman's Work is Never Done: A History of Housework in the British Isles 1650–1950*, London: Chatto & Windus.

Davies, Kathleen M. (1981) 'Continuity and change in literary advice on marriage', in R. B. Outhwaite (ed.) *Marriage and Society*, London: Europa.

Davies, Margaret Llewellyn (ed.) (1915) *Maternity: Letters from Working Women*, London: G. Bell & Sons.

Davies, Maud F. (1909) *Life in an English Village: An Economic and Historic Survey of the Parish of Corsley in Wiltshire*, London: T. Fisher Unwin.

Dixon, E. (1895) 'Craftswomen in the *"Livre des métiers"* ', *Economic Journal* 5, 2: 209–28.

Donnison, Jean (1977) *Midwives and Medical Men*, London: Heinemann.

Dunlop, O. Jocelyn: (1912) *English Apprenticeship and Child Labour: A History . . . with a Supplementary Section on the Modern Problem of Juvenile Labour by O. J. Dunlop and R. D. Denman*, London: Unwin.

Dupâquier, Jacques, et al. (eds) (1981) *Marriage and Remarriage in Populations of the Past*, London: Academic Press.

Dyer, Christopher (1989) 'The consumer and the market in the later middle ages', *Economic History Review* 2nd ser. 42, 3: 305–27.

Eales, Jacqueline (1990) 'Samuel Clarke and the "lives" of godly women in seventeenth-century England', in W. J. Sheils and Diana Wood (eds) *Women in the Church*, Studies in Church History 27, Oxford: Basil Blackwell.

Earle, Peter (1989) 'The female labour market in London in the late seventeenth and early eighteenth centuries', *Economic History Review* 2nd ser. 42, 3: 328–53.

Eckenstein, Lina (1896) *Woman Under Monasticism*, Cambridge: Cambridge University Press.

Eliot, George (1906) *Adam Bede*, London: J. M. Dent (1st edn 1859).

Erickson, Amy Louise (1990) 'Common law *versus* common practice: the use of marriage settlements in early modern England', *Economic History Review* 2nd ser. 43, 1: 21–39.

——(forthcoming 1993a) *Women and Property in Early Modern England*, London: Routledge.

——(forthcoming 1993b) 'Maternal management and the cost of raising children in early modern England', in Richard Wall and Osamu Saito (eds) *Social and Economic Aspects of the Family Life Cycle*, Cambridge: Cambridge University Press.

An Essay in Defence of the Female Sex (1697) 3rd edn, London: A. Roper and R. Clavel (1st edn 1696).

Evans, Nesta (1985) 'Inheritance, women, religion and education in early modern society as revealed by wills', in Philip Riden (ed.) *Probate Records and the Local Community*, Gloucester: Alan Sutton.

Ezell, Margaret J. M. (1987) *The Patriarch's Wife: Literary Evidence and the History of the Family*, Chapel Hill: University of North Carolina Press.

Figes, Eva (1970) *Patriarchal Attitudes*, London: Faber & Faber (3rd edn 1986, Basingstoke: Macmillan).

Fildes, Valerie (1988) *Wetnursing: A History from Antiquity to the Present*, Oxford: Basil Blackwell.

——(ed.) (1990) *Women as Mothers in Pre-Industrial England*, London: Routledge.

Gardiner, Dorothy (1929) *English Girlhood at School: A Study of Women's Education through Twelve Centuries*, London: Oxford University Press.

George, M. Dorothy (1923) *English Social Life in the Eighteenth Century*, London: Sheldon Press.

——(1925) *London Life in the Eighteenth Century*, London: Kegan Paul, Trench & Trübner.

——(1931) *England in Transition: Life and Work in the Eighteenth Century*, London: George Routledge & Sons.

George, Margaret (1988) *Women in the First Capitalist Society: Experiences in Seventeenth-Century England*, Brighton: Harvester.

Gilboy, E. W. (1931–2) 'Labour at Thornborough: an eighteenth-century estate', *Economic History Review* 1st ser. 3: 388–98.

[Gillett, Margaret Clark] (n.d., but before February 1935) 'Alice Clark of C. & J. Clark Ltd., Street, Somerset', Oxford: privately printed by Oxford University Press.

Gittings, Clare (1984) *Death, Burial and the Individual in Early Modern England*, London: Croom Helm.

Goldberg, P. J. P. (1990) 'Women's work, women's role in the late medieval North', in Michael A. Hicks (ed.) *Profit, Piety and the Professions in Later Medieval England*, Gloucester: Alan Sutton.

Gowing, Laura (forthcoming) 'Gender and the language of insult in early modern England', *History Workshop Journal*.

Graham, Elspeth *et al.* (eds) (1989) *Her Own Life: Autobiographical Writings by Seventeenth-Century Englishwomen*, London: Routledge.

Greaves, Richard Lee (1985) 'Foundation builders: the role of women in early English nonconformity', in R. L. Greaves (ed.) *Triumph Over Silence: Women in Protestant History*, Westport, Conn.: Greenwood Press.

Green, Alice Stopford (1894) *Town Life in the Fifteenth Century*, London: Macmillan.

Griffiths, R. G. (1933) 'Joyce Jeffreys [*sic*] of Ham Castle: a 17th century business gentlewoman', *Transactions of the Archaeological Society of Worcestershire* 10: 1–32.

Hamilton, Roberta (1978) *The Liberation of Women: A Study of Patriarchy and Capitalism*, London: Allen & Unwin.

Hanawalt, Barbara A. (ed.) (1986) *Women and Work in Preindustrial Europe*, Bloomington: Indiana University Press.

Hannay, Margaret P. (1985) *Silent But for the Word: Tudor Women as Patrons, Translators, and Writers of Religious Works*, Kent, Ohio: Kent State University Press.

Harley, David (1981) 'Ignorant midwives: a persistent stereotype', *Society for the Social History of Medicine Bulletin* 28: 6–9.

Harris, Olivia (1982) 'Households and their boundaries', *Past & Present* 13: 143–52.

Harris, Tim (1986) 'The bawdy house riots of 1668', *Historical Journal* 29, 3: 537–56.

Hecht, J. Jean (1956) *The Domestic Servant Class in Eighteenth-Century England*, London: Routledge & Kegan Paul.

Henderson, Katherine Usher and McManus, Barbara F. (1985) *Half Humankind: Contexts and Texts of the Controversy About Women in England, 1540–1640*, Urbana: University of Illinois Press.

Higgins, Patricia (1973) 'The reaction of women, with special reference to women petitioners', in Brian Manning (ed.) *Politics, Religion and the English Civil War*, London: Edward Arnold.

Hill, Bridget (1989) *Women, Work and Sexual Politics in Eighteenth-Century England*, Oxford: Basil Blackwell.

Hill, Georgiana (1896) *Women in English Life, from Medieval to Modern Times*, London: Richard Bentley & Son.

Hobby, Elaine (1988) *Virtue of Necessity: English Women's Writing 1649–88*, London: Virago.

Holderness, B. A. (1973) 'Elizabeth Parkin and her investments, 1733–66: aspects of the Sheffield money market in the eighteenth century', *Transactions of the Hunter Archaeological Society* 10, 2: 81–7.

——(1976) *Pre-Industrial England: Economy and Society from 1500 to 1750*, London: J. M. Dent.

——(1984) 'Widows in pre-industrial society: an essay upon their economic functions', in R. M. Smith (ed.) *Land, Kinship and Life-Cycle*, Cambridge: Cambridge University Press.

Houlbrooke, Ralph (1984) *The English Family 1450–1700*, London: Longmans.

——(1986) 'Women's social life and common action in England from the fifteenth century to the eve of the civil war', *Continuity & Change* 1, 2: 177–81.

——(1989a) *English Family Life, 1576–1676*, Oxford: Basil Blackwell.

——(ed.) (1989b) *Death, Ritual and Bereavement*, London: Routledge.

Howell, Cicely (1983) *Land, Family and Inheritance in Transition: Kibworth Harcourt 1280–1700*, Cambridge: Cambridge University Press.

Howell, Martha C. (1986) *Women, Production, and Patriarchy in Late Medieval Cities*, Chicago: University of Chicago Press.

Hufton, Olwen (1981) 'Women, work and marriage in eighteenth-century France', in R. B. Outhwaite (ed.) *Marriage and Society*, London: Europa.

——(1983) 'Women in history: early modern Europe', *Past & Present* 101: 125–41.

——(1984) 'Women without men: widows and spinsters in Britain and France in the eighteenth century', *Journal of Family History* 9, 4: 355–76.

Hull, Suzanne W. (1982) *Chaste, Silent and Obedient: English Books for Women 1475–1640*, San Marino, Calif.: Huntington Library.

Humphries, Jane (1990) 'Enclosures, common rights, and women: the proletarianization of families in the late eighteenth and early nineteenth centuries', *Journal of Economic History* 50, 1: 17–42.

Hunt, Margaret (forthcoming) *The Culture of the Middling Classes: English Families in Trade, 1660–1800*, Berkeley: University of California Press.

Hutchins, Barbara (1911) *The Working Life of Women*, Fabian Tract no. 157.

——(1915) *Women in Modern Industry*, London: G. Bell & Sons.

Hutton, Diane (1985) 'Women in fourteenth-century Shrewsbury', in Lindsey Charles and Lorna Duffin (eds) *Women and Work in Pre-Industrial England*, London: Croom Helm.

Illich, Ivan (1982) *Gender*, New York: Pantheon.

Jones, M. G. (1938) *The Charity School Movement: A Study of Eighteenth-Century Puritanism in Action*, Cambridge: Cambridge University Press.

Jordan, W. K. (1959) *Philanthropy in England 1480–1660*, London: Russell Sage Foundation.

Kamm, Josephine (1965) *Hope Deferred: Girls' Education in English History*, London: Methuen.

Karras, Ruth Mazo (1989) 'The regulation of brothels in later medieval England', in Judith M. Bennett et al. (eds) *Sisters and Workers in the Middle Ages*, Chicago: University of Chicago Press (originally printed in *Signs* 14, 2).

King, Peter (1991) 'Customary rights and women's earnings: the importance of gleaning to the rural labouring poor, 1750–1850', *Economic History Review* 2nd ser. 44, 3: 461–76.

Knowles, Lilian (1921) *Industrial and Commercial Revolutions in Great Britain in the Nineteenth Century*, London: Routledge.

Kowaleski, Maryanne and Bennett, Judith M. (1989) 'Crafts, gilds, and women in the middle ages: fifty years after Marian K. Dale', *Signs* 14, 2: 474–88.

Kramer, Stella (1927) *The English Craft Gilds*, New York: Columbia University Press.

Kussmaul, Ann (1981) *Servants in Husbandry in Early Modern England*, Cambridge: Cambridge University Press.

Lake, Peter (1987) 'Feminine piety and personal potency: the "emancipation" of Mrs Jane Ratcliffe', *The Seventeenth Century* 1: 143–65.

Laslett, Peter (1972) 'Mean household size in England since the sixteenth century', in P. Laslett and Richard Wall (eds) *Household and Family in Past Time*, Cambridge: Cambridge University Press.

Laurence, Anne (1989) 'Women's psychological disorders in seventeenth-century Britain', in Arina Angerman et al. (eds) *Current Issues in Women's History*, London: Routledge.

——(1990) 'A priesthood of she-believers: women and congregations in mid-seventeenth-century England', in W. J. Sheils and Diana Wood (eds) *Women in the Church*, Studies in Church History 27, Oxford: Basil Blackwell.

Lebsock, Suzanne (1984) *The Free Women of Petersburg: Status and Culture in a Southern Town, 1784–1860*, New York: Norton.

Leites, Edmund (1982) ' "The duty to desire": love, friendship and sexuality in some puritan theories of marriage', *Journal of Social History* 15: 383–408.

Leonard, E. M. (1900) *The Early History of English Poor Relief*, Cambridge: Cambridge University Press.

Lewis, Jane (1980) *The Politics of Motherhood*, London: Croom Helm.

Ludlow, Dorothy (1985) 'Shaking patriarchy's foundations: sectarian women in England, 1641–1700', in R. L. Greaves (ed.) *Triumph Over Silence: Women in Protestant History*, Westport, Conn.: Greenwood Press.

McArthur, Ellen (1909) 'Women petitioners and the long parliament', *English Historical Review* 24: 698–709.

McArthur, Ellen and Cunningham, William (1895) *Outlines of English Industrial History*, Cambridge: Cambridge University Press.

Macfarlane, Alan (1970) *The Family Life of Ralph Josselin*, Cambridge: Cambridge University Press.

——(1986) *Marriage and Love in England 1300–1840*, Oxford: Basil Blackwell.

Mack, Phyllis (1982) 'Women as prophets during the English civil war', *Feminist Studies* 8, 1: 19–45.

——(1988) 'The prophet and her audience: gender and knowledge in the world turned upside down', in Geoffrey Eley and William Hunt (eds) *Reviving the English Revolution: Reflections and Elaborations on the Work of Christopher Hill*, London: Verso.

McLaren, Dorothy (1985) 'Marital fertility and lactation 1570–1720' in Mary Prior (ed.) *Women in English Society 1500–1800*, London: Methuen.

Markham, Gervase (1683) *The English Housewife*, 9th edn, London: Hannah Sawbridge (1st edn 1631).

Marshall, Dorothy (1926) *The English Poor in the Eighteenth Century*, London: George Routledge & Sons.

——(1929) 'The domestic servants of the eighteenth century', *Economica* 9, 25: 15–40.

——(1949) *The English Domestic Servant in History*, Historical Association Pamphlet, General Series 13.

Mendelson, Sara (1985) 'Stuart women's diaries and occasional memoirs', in Mary Prior (ed.) *Women in English Society 1500–1800*, London: Methuen.

——(1987) *The Mental World of Stuart Women*, Brighton: Harvester.

Middleton, Chris (1979) 'The sexual division of labour in feudal England', *New Left Review* 113/114: 147–68.

——(1985) 'Women's labour and the transition to pre-industrial capitalism', in Lindsey Charles and Lorna Duffin (eds) *Women and Work in Pre-Industrial England*, London: Croom Helm.

Mitterauer, Michael and Sieder, Reinhard (1982) *The European Family: Patriarchy to Partnership from the Middle Ages to the Present*, Oxford: Basil Blackwell.

Moore, Henrietta L. (1988) *Feminism and Anthropology*, Cambridge: Polity Press.

Newman, Christine M. (1990) 'The reformation and Elizabeth Bowes: a study of a sixteenth-century northern gentlewoman', in W. J. Sheils and Diana Wood (eds) *Women in the Church*, Studies in Church History 27, Oxford: Basil Blackwell.

Oakley, Ann (1981) *Subject Women*, Oxford: Martin Robertson.

Okin, Susan Moller (1983–4) 'Patriarchy and married women's property in England', *Eighteenth-Century Studies* 17, 2: 121–38.

Oppenheim, Cary (1990) *Poverty: The Facts*, London: Child Poverty Action Group.

Pember Reeves, Maud (1913) *Round About a Pound a Week*, London: G. Bell & Sons.

Penn, Simon A. C. (1987) 'Female wage-earners in late fourteenth-century England', *Agricultural History Review* 35: 1–14.

Perry, Ruth (1980) *Women, Letters and the Novel*, New York: AMS Press.

Phelps Brown, Henry and Hopkins, Sheila V. (1981) *A Perspective of Wages and Prices* (collected essays), London: Methuen.

Pinchbeck, Ivy (1930) *Women Workers and the Industrial Revolution 1750–1850*, London: Routledge (3rd edn 1981, London: Virago).

Pollock, Linda (1983) *Forgotten Children: Parent–Child Relations from 1500 to 1900*, Cambridge: Cambridge University Press.

——(1989) ' "Teach her to live under obedience": the making of women in the upper ranks of early modern England', *Continuity & Change* 4, 2: 231–58.

Powell, Chilton Latham (1917) *English Domestic Relations 1487–1653*, New York: Columbia University Press.

Power, Eileen (1922) *Medieval English Nunneries, c.1275 to 1535*, Cambridge: Cambridge University Press.

——(1926) 'The position of women', in C. G. Crump and E. F. Jacobs (eds) *The Legacy of the Middle Ages*, Oxford: Oxford University Press.

——(1975) *Medieval Women*, Cambridge: Cambridge University Press.

Prior, Mary (1985) 'Women and the urban economy: Oxford 1500–1800', in Mary Prior (ed.) *Women in English Society 1500–1800*, London: Methuen.

——(1990) 'Wives and wills 1558–1700', in John Chartres and David Hey (eds) *English Rural Society, 1500–1800: Essays in Honour of Joan Thirsk*, Cambridge: Cambridge University Press.

Putnam, Emily James (1910) *The Lady: Studies of Certain Significant Phases in her History*, New York: Sturgis & Walton.

Roberts, Michael (1979) 'Sickles and scythes: women's work and men's work at harvest time', *History Workshop Journal* 7: 3–28.

——(1985) ' "Words they are women, and deeds they are men": images of work and gender in early modern England', in Lindsey Charles and Lorna Duffin (eds) *Women and Work in Pre-Industrial England*, London: Croom Helm.

Rogers, Katharine (1982) *Feminism in Eighteenth-Century England*, Brighton: Harvester.

Rose, Sonya O. (1988) 'Proto-industry, women's work and the household economy in the transition to industrial capitalism', *Journal of Family History* 13, 2: 181–93.

Rosenthal, Joel T. (1984) 'Aristocratic widows in fifteenth-century England', in Barbara J. Harris and JoAnn K. McNamara (eds) *Women and the Structure of Society*, Durham, N.C.: Duke University Press.

Rowlands, Marie B. (1985) 'Recusant women 1540–1640', in Mary Prior (ed.) *Women in English Society 1500–1800*, London: Methuen.

Schnorrenberg, Barbara B. with Hunter, Jean E. (1980) 'The eighteenth-century English woman', in Barbara Kanner (ed.) *The Women of England from Anglo-Saxon Times to the Present*, London: Mansell.

Schofield, Roger (1985) 'English marriage patterns revisited', *Journal of Family History* 10, 1: 2–20.

Schreiner, Olive (1911) *Woman and Labour*, London: Unwin.

Scott, Hilda (1984) *Working Your Way to the Bottom: The Feminization of Poverty*, London: Pandora.

Shakespeare, Joy and Dowling, Maria (1982) 'Religion and politics in mid-Tudor England through the eyes of an English protestant woman: the recollections of Rose Hickman', *Bulletin of the Institute of Historical Research* 55: 94–102.

Shammas, Carole (1980) 'The domestic environment in early modern England and America', *Journal of Social History* 14, 1: 3–24.

——(1983) 'Food expenditures and economic well-being in early modern England', *Journal of Economic History* 43, 1: 89–100.

Sharp, Buchanan (1980) *In Contempt of All Authority: Rural Artisans and Riot in the West of England, 1586–1660*, Berkeley: University of California Press.

Sharpe, J. A. (1980) 'Defamation and sexual slander in early modern England: the church courts at York', University of York Borthwick Papers no. 58.

Sharpe, Pamela (1990) 'Marital separation in the eighteenth and early nineteenth centuries', *Local Population Studies* 45: 66–70.

——(1991) 'Literally spinsters: a new interpretation of local economy and demography in Colyton in the seventeenth and eighteenth centuries', *Economic History Review* 2nd ser. 44, 1: 46–65.

Shepherd, Simon (ed.) (1985) *The Women's Sharp Revenge: Five Pamphlets from the Renaissance*, London: Fourth Estate.

Shorter, Edward (1975) *The Making of the Modern Family*, New York: Collins.

Smith, A. Hassell (1989) 'Labourers in late sixteenth-century England: a case study from north Norfolk (Pt I)', *Continuity & Change* 4, 1: 11–52.

Smith, Bonnie G. (1984) 'The contributions of women to modern historiography in Great Britain, France and the United States, 1750–1940', *American Historical Review* 89: 709–32.

Smith, Lucy Toulmin (1870) introduction to Joshua Toulmin Smith (ed.) *English Gilds*, London: Trübner.

Snell, K. D. M. (1985) *Annals of the Labouring Poor: Social Change and Agrarian England 1660–1900*, Cambridge: Cambridge University Press.

Snell, K. D. M. and Millar, J. (1987) 'Lone-parent families and the welfare state', *Continuity & Change* 2, 3: 387–422.

Spring, Eileen (1983) 'The family, strict settlement, and historians', *Canadian Journal of History* 18, 3: 379–98.

——(1984) 'Law and the theory of the affective family', *Albion* 16, 1: 1–20.

Spufford, Margaret (1981) *Small Books and Pleasant Histories: Popular Fiction and its Readership in Seventeenth-Century England*, London: Methuen.

——(1984) *The Great Reclothing of Rural England: Petty Chapmen and their Wares in the Seventeenth Century*, London: Hambledon Press.

Staves, Susan (1990) *Married Women's Separate Property in England, 1660–1833*, Cambridge, Mass.: Harvard University Press.

Stetson (later Gilman), Charlotte Perkins (1899) *Women and Economics*, London: G. P. Putnam's Sons.

Stone, Lawrence (1977) *The Family, Sex and Marriage in England 1500–1800*, London: Weidenfeld & Nicolson.

Stopes, Charlotte Carmichael (1894) *British Freewomen: Their Historic Privileges*, London: Swan Sonnenschein.

Swanwick, H. M. (1913) *The Future of the Women's Movement*, London: G. Bell & Sons.

Swiney, Frances (1899) *The Awakening of Women or Woman's Part in Evolution*, London: George Redway.

Tawney, R. H. (1912) *The Agrarian Problem in the Sixteenth Century*, London: Longmans.

Thirsk, Joan (1985) foreword to Mary Prior (ed.) *Women in English Society 1500–1800*, London: Methuen.

Thomas, Janet (1988) 'Women and capitalism: oppression or emancipation?', *Comparative Studies in Society and History* 30, 3: 534–49.

Thorold Rogers, James E. (1866) *A History of Agriculture and Prices in England 1259–1793*, Oxford: Oxford University Press.

Thwaites, W. (1984) 'Women in the marketplace: Oxfordshire c.1690–1800', *Midland History* 9: 23–42.

Tilly, Louise A. and Scott, Joan W. (1978) *Women, Work and*

Family, New York: Holt, Rhinehart & Winston (2nd edn 1987, New York: Methuen).

Todd, Barbara (1985) 'The remarrying widow: a stereotype reconsidered', in Mary Prior (ed.) *Women in English Society 1500–1800*, London: Methuen.

——(1990) 'Freebench and free enterprise: widows and their property in two Berkshire villages', in John Chartres and David Hey (eds) *English Rural Society, 1500–1800: Essays in Honour of Joan Thirsk*, Cambridge: Cambridge University Press.

Todd, Janet (1989) *The Sign of Angellica: Women, Writing and Fiction, 1660–1800*, London: Virago.

Ulrich, Laurel Thatcher (1982) *Good Wives: Image and Reality in the Lives of Women in Northern New England 1650–1750*, New York: Knopf.

Valenze, Deborah (1991) 'The art of women and the business of men: women's work and the dairy industry c.1740–1840', *Past & Present* 130: 142–69.

Vanes, Jean (1986) *Apparelled in Red: The History of the Red Maids School*, Gloucester: Alan Sutton.

Vann, Richard (1979) 'Wills and the family in an English town: Banbury, 1550–1800', *Journal of Family History* 4, 3: 346–67.

Versluysen, Margaret Connor (1981) 'Midwives, medical men and "poor women labouring of child": lying-in hospitals in eighteenth-century London', in Helen Roberts (ed.) *Women, Health and Reproduction*, London: Routledge & Kegan Paul.

Vickery, Amanda (1991) 'Women and the world of goods: a Lancashire consumer and her possessions', in John Brewer and Roy Porter (eds) *Consumption and Society in the Seventeenth and Eighteenth Centuries*, London: Routledge.

Wabuda, Susan (1990) 'Shunamites and nurses of the English reformation: the activities of Mary Glover, niece of Hugh Latimer', in W. J. Sheils and Diana Wood (eds) *Women in the Church*, Studies in Church History 27, Oxford: Basil Blackwell.

Wales, Tim (1984) 'Poverty, poor relief and the life-cycle: some evidence from seventeenth-century Norfolk', in R. M. Smith (ed.) *Land, Kinship and Life-Cycle*, Cambridge: Cambridge University Press.

Wall, Richard (1981) 'Woman alone in English society', *Annales de Demographie Historique*: 303–17.

Wallas, Ada (1929) *Before the Bluestockings*, London: George Allen & Unwin.

Warnicke, Retha M. (1983) *Women of the English Renaissance and Reformation*, Westport, Conn.: Greenwood Press.

Weatherill, Lorna (1986) 'A possession of one's own: women and consumer behavior in England 1660–1740', *Journal of British Studies* 25, 2: 131–56.

——(1988) *Consumer Behaviour and Material Culture in Britain 1600–1760*, London: Routledge.

Weinstein, Helen (1992) *Catalogue of the Pepys Ballad Collection*, Suffolk: Boydell & Brewer.

Wiener, Carol Z. (1975) 'Sex roles and crime in late Elizabethan Hertfordshire', *Journal of Social History* 8: 38–60.

Wiesner, Merry E. (1986) *Working Women in Renaissance Germany*, New Brunswick, N.J.: Rutgers University Press.

Willen, Diane (1989) 'Women and religion in early modern England', in Sherrin Marshall (ed.) *Women in Reformation and Counter-Reformation Europe*, Bloomington: Indiana University Press.

Wilson, Adrian (1983) 'Ignorant midwives: a rejoinder', *Society for the Social History of Medicine Bulletin* 32: 46–9.

Wright, Sue (1985) ' "Churmaids, huswyfes and hucksters": the employment of women in Tudor and Stuart Salisbury', in Lindsey Charles and Lorna Duffin (eds) *Women and Work in Pre-Industrial England*, London: Croom Helm.

Wrightson, Keith (1982) *English Society 1580–1680*, London: Hutchinson.

——(1984) 'Kinship in an English village: Terling, Essex 1500–1700', in R. M. Smith (ed.) *Land, Kinship and Life-Cycle*, Cambridge: Cambridge University Press.

Wrightson, Keith and Levine, David (1979) *Poverty and Piety in an English Village: Terling, 1525–1700*, New York: Academic Press.

Wrigley, E. A. and Schofield, Roger (1981) *The Population History of England, 1541–1871: A Reconstruction*, London: Edward Arnold.

Wyman, A. L. (1984) 'The surgeoness: the female practitioner of surgery 1400–1800', *Medical History* 28: 22–41.

PREFACE

The investigation, whose conclusions are partly described in the following treatise, was undertaken with a view to discovering the actual circumstances of women's lives in the Seventeenth Century.

It is perhaps impossible to divest historical enquiry from all personal bias, but in this case the bias has simply consisted in a conviction that the conditions under which the obscure mass of women live and fulfil their duties as human beings, have a vital influence upon the destinies of the human race, and that a little knowledge of what these conditions have actually been in the past will be of more value to the sociologist than many volumes of carefully elaborated theory based on abstract ideas.

The theories with which I began this work of investigation as to the position occupied by women in a former social organization have been abandoned, and have been replaced by others, which though still only held tentatively have at least the merit of resting solely on ascertained fact. If these theories should in turn have to be discarded when a deeper understanding of history becomes possible, yet the picture of human life presented in the following pages will not entirely lose its value.

The picture cannot pretend to be complete. The Seventeenth Century provides such a wealth of historical material that only a small fraction could be examined, and though the selection has been as representative as possible, much that is of the greatest importance from the point of view from which the enquiry has been made, is not yet available. Many records of Gilds, Companies, Quarter Sessions and Boroughs which must be studied *in extenso* before a just idea can be formed of women's position, have up to the present been published only in an abbreviated form, if at all.

Another difficulty has been the absence of knowledge regarding women's position in the years preceding the Seventeenth

Century. This want has to some extent been supplied through the kindness of Miss Eileen Power, who has permitted me to use some of the material collected by her on this subject, but not yet published.

The Seventeenth Century itself forms a sort of watershed between two very widely differing eras in the history of Englishwomen – the Elizabethan and the Eighteenth Century. Thus characteristics of both can be studied in the women who move through its varied scenes, either in the pages of dramatists or as revealed by domestic papers or in more public records.

Only one aspect of their lives has been described in the present volume, namely their place in the economic organization of society. This has its own special bearing on the industrial problems of modern times; but Life is a whole and cannot safely be separated into watertight departments.

The productive activity which is here described was not the work of women who were separated from the companionship of married life and the joys and responsibilities of motherhood. These aspects of their life have not been forgotten, and will, I hope, be dealt with in a later volume, along with the whole question of girls' education.

How inseparably intertwined are these different threads of life will be shown by the fact that apprenticeship and service are left to be dealt with in the later volume as links in the educational chain, although in many respects they were essential features of women's economic position.

The conception of the sociological importance of past economic conditions for women I owe to Olive Schreiner, whose epoch-making book 'Women and Labour' first drew the attention of many workers in the emancipation of women to the difference between reality and the commonly received generalizations as to women's productive capacity. From my friend, Dr. K. A. Gerlach came the suggestion that I, myself, should attempt to supply further evidence along the lines so imaginatively outlined by Mrs. Schreiner. To Dr. Lilian Knowles I am indebted for the unwearied patience with which she has watched and directed my researches, and to Mrs. Bernard Shaw for the generous scholarship with which she assists those who wish to devote themselves to the investigation of women's historic past.

I should like here to express the deep sense of gratitude which I feel to those who have helped my work in these different ways, and to Mrs. George, whose understanding of Seventeenth Century conditions has rendered the material she collected for me particularly valuable. My thanks are also due to many other friends whose sympathy and interest have played a larger part than they know in the production of this book.

Mill Field,
   Street, Somerset.

CHAPTER I

INTRODUCTORY

Effect of environment on Women's development. Possible reaction on men's development—Importance of seventeenth century in historic development of English women—Influence of economic position—Division of Women's productive powers into Domestic, Industrial, and Professional—Three systems of Industrial Organisation—Domestic Industry—Family Industry—Capitalistic Industry or Industrialism—Definition of these terms—Historic sequence. Effect of Industrial Revolution on Women—in capitalistic class—in agriculture—in textile industries—in crafts and other trades. Transference of productive industry from married women to unmarried women—with consequent increase of economic independence for the latter and its loss for the former. Similar evolution in professions shows this was not due wholly to effect of capitalism.

HITHERTO the historian has paid little attention to the circumstances of women's lives, for women have been regarded as a static factor in social developments, a factor which, remaining itself essentially the same, might be expected to exercise a constant and unvarying influence on Society.

This assumption has however no basis in fact, for the most superficial consideration will show how profoundly women can be changed by their environment. Not only do the women of the same race exhibit great differences from time to time in regard to the complex social instincts and virtues, but even their more elemental sexual and maternal instincts are subject to modification. While in extreme cases the sexual impulses are liable to perversion, it sometimes happens that the maternal instinct disappears altogether, and women neglect or, like a tigress in captivity, may even destroy their young.

These variations deserve the most careful examination, for, owing to the indissoluble bond uniting the sexes, and the emotional power which women exert over men, the character of men's development is determined in some sort by the development which is achieved by women. In a society where women are highly developed men's characters are insensibly modified by association with them, and in a society where women are secluded and immature, men lack that stimulus which can only be supplied by the other sex.

It may be true, as Goethe said, that the eternal feminine leadeth us onwards, but whether this be upwards or downwards depends upon the characters of individual women.

Owing to the subtle reactions which exist between men and women and between the individual and the social organism in which he or she lives, accurate and detailed knowledge of the historic circumstances of human life becomes essential for the sciences of Sociology and Psychology. The investigation, of which the results are described in the following chapters, was undertaken with the object of discovering these circumstances as regards women in a limited field and during a short period.

The economic field has been chosen because, though woman no more than man lives by bread alone, yet without bread assuredly she cannot live at all, and without an abundant supply of it she cannot worthily perform her maternal and spiritual functions. These latter are therefore dependent upon the source of her food supply. The economic position has a further attraction to the student because it rests upon facts which can be elucidated with some degree of certainty. When these have once been made clear the way will have been prepared for the consideration of other aspects of women's lives.

The period under review, namely the seventeenth century, forms an important crisis in the historic development of Englishwomen. The gulf which separates the women of the Restoration period from those of the Elizabethan era can be perceived by the most casual reader of contemporary drama. To the objection that the heroines of Shakespeare on the one hand and of Congreve and Wycherley on the other are creations of the imagination, it must be replied that the dramatic poet can only present life as he knows it. It was part of Shakespeare's good fortune to live in a period so rich and vivid in its social life as was the reign of Elizabeth ; and the objective character of his portraits can be proved by the study of contemporary letters and domestic papers. Similarly the characters of the Restoration ladies described in the diary of Samuel Pepys and by other writers, confirm the picture of Society drawn by Congreve.

So profound a change occurring in the character of women indicates the seventeenth century as a period of special interest for social investigation, and consequently the economic position has been approached less from its direct effect upon the production of wealth than from its influence upon women's development. The mechanical aspect has in fact only been touched incidentally ; an attempt being rather made to discover how far the extent of women's productive capacity and the conditions under which it was exercised affected their maternal functions and reacted upon their social influence both within and beyond the limits of the family.

Generalisations are of little service for this purpose. Spinoza has said that the objects of God's knowledge are not universals but particulars, and it is in harmony with this idea that the following chapters consist chiefly of the record of small details in individual lives which indicate the actual relation of women to business and production, whether on a large scale or a small. The pictures given are widely representative, including not only the women of the upper classes, but still more important, those of the " common people," the husbandmen and tradesmen who formed the backbone of the English people, and also those of the

tragic class of wage earners, who, though comparatively
few in numbers, already constituted a serious problem
in the seventeenth century.

In the course of the investigation, comparison is
frequently made with the economic position of mediæval women on the one hand, and with women's
position under modern industrial conditions, on the
other.   It must be admitted, however, that comparisons with the middle ages rest chiefly on conjecture.

Owing to the greater complexity of a woman's life
her productive capacity must be classified on different
lines from those which are generally followed in
dealing with the economic life of men.

For the purposes of this essay, the highest, most
intense forms to which women's productive energy
is directed have been excluded ; that is to say, the
spiritual creaton of the home and the physical creation
of the child.   Though essentially productive, such
achievements of creative power transcend the limitations of economics and one instinctvely feels
that there would be something almost degrading
in any attempt to weigh them in the balance with
productions that are bought and sold in the market or
even with professional services.   Nevertheless it must
never be forgotten that the productive energy which
is described in the ensuing chapters was in no sense
alternative to the exercise of these higher forms of
creative power but was employed simultaneously with
them.   It may be suspected that the influences of
home life were stronger in the social life of the
seventeenth century than they are in modern England,
and certainly the birth-rate was much higher in every
class of the community except perhaps the very poorest.

But, leaving these two forms of creative power
aside, there remains another special factor complicating
women's economic position, namely, the extent of her
production for domestic purposes—as opposed to
industrial and professional purposes.   The domestic

category includes all goods and services, either material or spiritual, which are produced solely for the benefit of the family, while the industrial and professional are those which are produced either for sale or exchange.

In modern life the majority of Englishwomen devote the greater part of their lives to domestic occupations, while men are freed from domestic occupations of any sort, being generally engaged in industrial or professional pursuits and spending their leisure over public services or personal pleasure and amusement.

Under modern conditions the ordinary domestic occupations of Englishwomen consist in tending babies and young children, either as mothers or servants, in preparing household meals, and in keeping the house clean, while laundry work, preserving fruit, and the making of children's clothes are still often included in the domestic category. In the seventeenth century it embraced a much wider range of production ; for brewing, dairy-work, the care of poultry and pigs, the production of vegetables and fruit, spinning flax and wool, nursing and doctoring, all formed part of domestic industry. Therefore the part which women played in industrial and professional life was in addition to a much greater productive activity in the domestic sphere than is required of them under modern conditions.

On the other hand it may be urged that, if women were upon the whole more actively engaged in industrial work during the seventeenth century than they were in the first decade of the twentieth century, men were much more occupied with domestic affairs then than they are now. Men in all classes gave time and care to the education of their children, and the young unmarried men who generally occupied positions as apprentices and servants were partly employed over domestic work. Therefore, though now it is taken for granted that domestic work will be done by women, a considerable proportion of it in former days fell to the share of men.

These circumstances have led to a different use of terms in this essay from that which has generally been adopted ; a difference rendered necessary from the fact that other writers on industrial evolution have considered it only from the man's point of view, whereas this investigation is concerned primarily with its effect upon the position of women.

To facilitate the enquiry, organisation for production is divided into three types :

(a) Domestic Industry.
(b) Family Industry.
(c) Capitalistic Industry, or Industrialism.

No hard-and-fast line exists in practice between these three systems, which merge imperceptibly into one another. In the seventeenth century all three existed side by side, often obtaining at the same time in the same industries, but the underlying principles are quite distinct and may be defined as follows :

(a) *Domestic Industry* is the form of production in which the goods produced are for the exclusive use of the family and are not therefore subject to an exchange or money value.

(b) *Family Industry* is the form in which the family becomes the unit for the production of goods to be sold or exchanged.

The family consisted of father, mother, children, household servants and apprentices ; the apprentices and servants being children and young people of both sexes who earned their keep and in the latter case a nominal wage, but who did not expect to remain permanently as wage-earners, hoping on the contrary in due course to marry and set up in business on their own account. The profits of family industry belonged to the family and not to individual members of it. During his lifetime they were vested in the father who was regarded as the head of the family ; he was expected to provide from them marriage portions for his children as they reached maturity, and on his death the mother succeeded to his position as head of the family, his right of bestowal by will being strictly limited by custom and public opinion.

Two features are the main characteristics of Family Industry in its perfect form ;—first, the unity of capital and labour, for the family, whether that of a farmer or tradesman, owned stock and tools and themselves contributed the labour : second, the situation of the workshop within the precincts of the home.

These two conditions were rarely completely fulfilled in the seventeenth century, for the richer farmers and tradesmen often employed permanent wage-earners in addition to the members of their family, and in other cases craftsmen no longer owned their stock, but made goods to the order of the capitalist who supplied them with the necessary material. Nevertheless, the character of Family Industry was retained as long as father, mother, and children worked together, and the money earned was regarded as belonging to the family, not to the individual members of it.

From the point of view of the economic position of women a system can be classed as family industry while the father works at home, but when he leaves home to work on the capitalist's premises the last vestige of family industry disappears and industrialism takes its place.

(c) *Capitalistic Industry*, or *Industrialism*, is the system by which production is controlled by the owners of capital, and the labourers or producers, men, women and children receive individual wages.[1]

---

[1]The term " individual wages " is used here to denote wages paid either to men or women as individuals, and regarded as belonging to the individual person, while " family wages " are those which cover the services of the whole family and belong to the family as a whole. This definition differs from the common use of the terms, but is necessary for the explanation of some important points. In ordinary conversation " individual wages " indicate those which maintain an individual only, while " family wages " are those upon which a family lives. This does not imply a real

Domestic and family industry existed side by side
during the middle ages ; for example, brewing, baking,
spinning, cheese and butter making were conducted
both as domestic arts and for industrial purposes.
Both were gradually supplanted by capitalistic
industry, the germ of which was apparently introduced about the thirteenth century, and gradually
developed strength for a more rapid advance in the
seventeenth century.

While the development of capitalistic industry
will always be one of the most interesting subjects for
the student of political economy, its effect upon the
position and capacity of women becomes of paramount
importance to the sociologist.

This effect must be considered from three stand-
points :—

(1) Does the capitalistic organisation of industry
increase or diminish women's productive capacity ?

(2) Does it make them more or less successful in
their special function of motherhood ?

(3) Does it strengthen or weaken their influence over morals and their position in the general
organisation of human society ?

These three questions were not asked by the men
who were actors in the Industrial Revolution, and
apparently their importance has hitherto escaped the
notice of those who have written chapters of its
history.

Mankind, lulled by its faith in the " eternal feminine " has reposed in the belief that women remain
the same, however completely their environment may
alter, and having once named a place " the home "
thinks it makes no difference whether it consists of a
workshop or a boudoir.   But the effect of the

difference in the wages, as the same amount of money can be used to support one
individual in comfort or a family in penury.   In modern times the law recognises a
theoretic obligation on the part of a man to support his children, but has no power
to divert his wages to that purpose.   His wages are in fact recognised as his individual
property.   The position of the family was very different in the seventeenth century.

Industrial Revolution on home life, and through
that upon the development and characters of
women and upon their productive capacity, deeply
concerns the sociologist, for the increased productive
capacity of mankind may be dearly bought by the
disintegration of social organisation and a lowering
of women's capacity for motherhood.

The succeeding chapters will show how the spread
of capitalism affected the productive capacity of
women :—

(1) In the capitalist class where the energy and
hardiness of Elizabethan ladies gave way before
the idleness and pleasure which characterised the
Restoration period.

(2) In agriculture, where the wives of the richer
yeomen were withdrawing from farm work and where
there already existed a considerable number of labourers
dependent entirely on wages, whose wives having no
gardens or pastures were unable to supply the families'
food according to old custom. The wages of such
women were too irregular and too low to maintain
them and their children in a state of efficiency, and
through semi-starvation their productive powers and
their capacity for motherhood were greatly reduced.

(3) In the Textile Trades where the demand
for thread and yarn which could only be produced by women and children was expanding.
The convenience of spinning as an employment
for odd minutes and the mechanical character of its
movements which made no great tax on eye or brain,
rendered it the most adaptable of all domestic arts
to the necessities of the mother. [Spinning became
the chief resource for the married women who
were losing their hold on other industries, but its
return in money value was too low to render them
independent of other means of support.] There is
little evidence to suggest that women shared in
the capitalistic enterprises of the clothiers during

this period, and they had lost their earlier position as monopolists of the silk trade.

(4) In other crafts and trades where a tendency can be traced for women to withdraw from business as this developed on capitalistic lines. The history of the gilds shows a progressive weakening of their positions in these associations, though the corporations of the seventeenth century still regarded the wife as her husband's partner. In these corporations the effect of capitalism on the industrial position of the wage-earner's wife becomes visible.

Under family industry the wife of every master craftsman became free of his gild and could share his work. But as the crafts became capitalised many journeymen never qualified as masters, remaining in the outer courts of the companies all their lives, and actually forming separate organisations to protect their interests against their masters and to secure a privileged position for themselves by restricting the number of apprentices. As the journeymen worked on their masters' premises it naturally followed that their wives were not associated with them in their work, and that apprenticeship became the only entrance to their trade.

Though no written rules existed confining apprenticeship to the male sex, girls were seldom if ever admitted as apprentices in the gild trades, and therefore women were excluded from the ranks of journeymen. As the journeyman's wife could not work at her husband's trade, she must, if need be, find employment for herself as an individual. In some cases the journeyman's organisations were powerful enough to keep wages on a level which sufficed for the maintenance of their families ; then the wife became completely dependent on her husband, sinking to the position of his unpaid domestic servant.

In the Retail and Provision Trades which in some respects were peculiarly favourable for women, they experienced many difficulties owing to the restrictive rules of companies and corporations ; but where a man was engaged in this class of business, his wife shared his labours, and on his death generally retained the direction of the business as his widow.

The history of brewing is one of the most curious examples of the effect of capitalism on women's position in industry, for as the term " brewster " shows, originally it was a woman's trade but with the development of Capitalism it passed completely from the hands of women to those of men.

The tendency of capitalism to lessen the relative productive capacity of women might be overlooked if our understanding of the process was limited to the changes which had actually taken place by the end of the seventeenth century. No doubt the majority of the population at that time was still living under conditions governed by the traditions and habits formed during the period of Family and Domestic Industry. But the contrast which the life described in the following chapters presents to the life of women under modern conditions will be evident even to readers who have not closely followed the later historical developments of Capitalism.

In estimating the influence of economic changes on the position of women it must be remembered that Capitalism has not merely replaced Family Industry but has been equally destructive of Domestic Industry.

One unexpected effect has been the reversal of the parts which married and unmarried women play in productive enterprise. In the earlier stages of economic evolution that which we now call domestic work, viz., cooking, cleaning, mending, tending of children, etc., was performed by unmarried girls under the direction of the housewife, who was thus enabled to take an important position in the family industry. Under modern conditions this domestic work falls upon the mothers, who remain at home while the

unmarried girls go out to take their place in industrial
or professional life. [The young girls in modern life
have secured a position of economic independence,
while the mothers remain in a state of dependence
and subordination]—an order of things which would
have greatly astonished our ancestors.

In the seventeenth century the idea is seldom en-
countered that a man supports his wife ; husband and
wife were then mutually dependent and together
supported their children. At the back of people's
minds an instinctive feeling prevailed that the father
furnished rent, shelter, and protection while the mother
provided food ; an instinct surviving from a remote
past when the villein owed to his lord the labour of
three or four days per week throughout the year in
addition to the boon work at harvest or any other time
when labour was most wanted for his own crops ; surely
then it was largely the labour of the mother and the
children which won the family's food from the
yard-land.

The reality of the change which has been effected
in the position of wife and mother is shown by a letter
to *The Gentleman's Magazine* in 1834 criticising proposed alterations in the Poor Law. The writer defends
the system then in use of giving allowances from the
rates to labourers according to the number of their
children. He says that the people who animadvert
on the allowance system " never observe the cause
from which it proceeds. There are, we will say,
twenty able single labourers in a parish ; twenty
equally able married, with large families. One class
wants 12s. a week, one 20s. The farmer, who has his
choice of course takes the single." The allowance
system equalises the position of married and single.
Formerly this inequality did not exist " *because it was
of no importance to the farmer whether he employed the
single or married labourer, inasmuch as the labourer's
wife and family could provide for themselves.* They are

now dependent on the man's labour, or nearly so ; except in particular cases, as when women go out to wash, to nurse, or take in needlework, and so on. [The machinery and manufactures have destroyed cottage labour—spinning, the only resource formerly of the female poor, who thus were earning their bread at home, while their fathers and husbands were earning theirs abroad. . . . In agricultural parishes the men, the labourers, are not too numerous or more than are wanted ; but the families hang as a dead weight upon the rates for want of employment. The girls are now not brought up to *spin*—none of them know the art. They all handle when required, the hoe, and their business is weeding. Our partial remedy for this great and growing evil is allotments of land, which are to afford the occupation that the distaff formerly did ; and so the wife and daughters can be cultivating small portions of ground and raising potatoes and esculents, etc., the while the labourer is at his work."[1]

These far reaching changes coincided with the triumph of capitalistic organisation but they may not have been a necessary consequence of that triumph. They may have arisen from some deep-lying cause, some tendency in human evolution which was merely hastened by the economic cataclysm.

The fact that the evolution of women's position in the professions followed a course closely resembling that which was taking place in industry suggests the existence of an ultimate cause influencing the direction in each case.

---

[1] *Gentleman's Magazine*, 1834, Vol. I., p. 531. *A Letter to Lord Althorp on the Poor Laws*, by Equitas.

CHAPTER II

CAPITALISTS

Term includes aristocracy and *nouveau-riche*. Tendency of these two classes to approximate in manners—Activity of aristocratic women with affairs of household, estate and nation—Zeal for patents and monopolies—Money lenders —Shipping trade—Contractors—Joan Dant—Dorothy Petty—Association of wives in husbands' businesses—Decrease of women's business activity in upper classes—Contrast of Dutch women—Growing idleness of gentlewomen.

PERHAPS it is impossible to say what exactly constitutes a capitalist, and no attempt will be made to define the term, which is used here to include the aristocracy who had long been accustomed to the control of wealth, and also those families whose wealth had been newly acquired through trade or commerce. The second group conforms more nearly to the ideas generally understood by the term capitalist; but in English society the two groups are closely related.

The first group naturally represents the older traditional relation of women to affairs in the upper classes, while the second responded more quickly to the new spirit which was being manifested in English life. No rigid line of demarcation existed between them, because while the younger sons of the gentry engaged in trade, the daughters of wealthy tradesmen were eagerly sought as brides by an impoverished aristocracy. Therefore the manners and customs of the two groups gradually approximated to each other.

At the beginning of the seventeenth century it was usual for the women of the aristocracy to be very busy with affairs—affairs which concerned their household, their estates and even the Government.

Thus Lady Barrymore writes she is " a cuntry lady living in Ireland and convercing with none but masons and carpendors, for I am now finishing a house, so that if my govenour [Sir Edmund Verney] please to build a new house, that may be well seated and have a good prospect, I will give him my best advice gratis."[1]

Lady Gardiner's husband apologises for her not writing personally to Sir Ralph Verney, she " being almost melted with the double heat of the weather and her hotter employment, because the fruit is suddenly ripe and she is so busy preserving."[2]   Their household consisted of thirty persons.

Among the nobility the management of the estate was often left for months in the wife's care while the husband was detained at Court for business or pleasure. It was during her husband's absence that Brilliana, Lady Harley defended Brampton Castle from an attack by the Royalist forces who laid siege to it for six weeks, when her defence became famous for its determination and success.   Her difficulties in estate management are described in letters to her son :

" You know how your fathers biusnes is neglected ; and alas ! it is not speaking will sarue turne, wheare theare is not abilltise to doo other ways ; thearefore I could wisch, that your father had one of more vnderstanding to intrust, to looke to, if his rents are not payed, and I thinke it will be so. I could desire, if your father thought well of it, that Mr. Tomas Moore weare intrusted with it ; he knows your fathers estate, and is an honnest man, and not giuen to great expences, and thearefore I thinke he would goo the most frugally way.   I knowe it would be some charges to haue him and his wife in the howes ; but I thinke it would quite the chargess.   I should be loth to haue a stranger, nowe your father is away."[3]

---

[1] Verney Family, *Memoirs during the Civil War*, Vol. I., p. 210.

[2] Ibid, Vol. I., p. 12.

[3] Harley, *Letters of Brilliana, the Lady*, pp. 146-7, 1641.

" I loos the comfort of your fathers company, and am in but littell safety, but that my trust is in God ; and what is doun to your fathers estate pleases him not, so that I wisch meselfe, with all my hart, at Loundoun, and then your father might be a wittnes of what is spent; but if your father thinke it beest for me to be in the cuntry, I am every well pleased with what he shall thinke best."[1]

One gathers from these letters that in spite of her devotion and ability and his constant absence Sir E. Harley never gave his wife full control of the estate, and was always more ready to censure than to praise her arrangements ; but other men who were immersed in public matters thankfully placed the whole burthen of family affairs in the capable hands of their wives.

Lady Murray wrote of her father, Sir George Baillie, " He had no ambition but to be free of debt ; yet so great trust and confidence did he put in my mother, and so absolutely free of all jealousy and suspicion, that he left the management of his affairs entirely to her, without scarce asking a question about them ; except sometimes would say to her, ' Is my debt paid yet ? ' though often did she apply to him for direction and advice ; since he knew enough of the law for the management of his own affairs, when he would take the time or trouble or to prevent his being imposed upon by others."[2]

Mrs. Alice Thornton wrote of her mother : " Nor was she awanting to make a fare greatter improve-ment [than her dowery of £2000] of my father's estate through her wise and prudential government of his family, and by her care was a meanes to give oppor-tunity of increasing his patrimony."[3]

---

[1] Harley, *Letters of Brilliana, The Lady*, p. 167, 1642.

[2] Murray (Lady), *Memoirs of Lady Grisell Baillie*, p. 13.

[3] Thornton (Mrs. Alice), *Autobiography*, p. 101, (Surtees' Society Vol. lxii.)

In addition to the Household Accounts those of the whole of Judge Fell's estate at Swarthmore, Lancashire, were kept by his daughter Sarah. The following entries show that the family affairs included a farm, a forge, mines, some interest in shipping and something of the nature of a Bank.

July 11, 1676, is entered : " To m° Rec^d. of Tho : Greaves wife wch. I am to returne to London fo^r her, & is to bee p^d, to her sonn J^{no}. ffellp Walt^r. miers in London, 001. 00. 00.

Jan., 14, 1676-7, by money lent Willm Wilson our forge Clarke till hee gett money in for Ireon sold 10. 0. 0.

Aug. ye 9° 1677 by m° in expence at adgarley when wee went to chuse oare to send father 000. 00. 04."

Other payments are entered for horses to " lead oare."[1] &c., &c.

In addition to those of her family Sarah Fell kept the accounts for the local " Monthly Meeting " of the Society of Friends, making the payments on its behalf to various poor Friends.

One of the sisters after her marriage embarked upon speculations in salt ; of her, another sister, Margaret Rous, writes to their mother : " She kept me in the dark and had not you wrote me them few words about her I had not known she had been so bad. But I had a fear before how she would prove if I should meddle of her, and since I know her mind wrote to her, being she was so wickedly bent and resolved in her mind, I would not meddle of her but leave her to her husbands relations, and her salt concerns, since which I have heard nothing from her. But I understand by others she is still in the salt business. I know not what it will benefit her but she spends her time about it. I have left her at present."[2]

---

[1] Fell (Sarah), *Household Account Book*.

[2] Crosfield (H. G.), *Life of Margaret Fox, of Swarthmore Hall*, p. 232, 1699.

A granddaughter of Oliver Cromwell, the wife of
Thos. Bendish, was also interested in the salt business,
having property in salt works at Yarmouth in the management of which she was actively concerned. It was
said of her that " Her courage and presence of mind
were remarkable in one of her sex, . . . she
would sometimes, after a hard day of drudgery go to the
assembly at Yarmouth, and appear one of the most
brilliant there."[1]

Initiative and enterprise were shown by Lady
Falkland during her husband's term of office in
Ireland whither she accompanied him.

" The desire of the benefit and commodity of that
nation set her upon a great design : it was to bring
up the use of all trades in that country, which is fain to
be beholden to others for the smallest commodities ;
to this end she procured some of each kind to come from
those other places where those trades are exercised,
as several sorts of linen and woollen weavers, dyers, all
sorts of spinners and knitters, hatters, lace-makers,
and many other trades at the very beginning."

After a description of her methods for instruction
in these arts the biographer continues :   " She brought
it to that pass that they there made broad-cloth so
fine . . .   that her Lord being Deputy wore it.
Yet it came to nothing ; which she imputed to a
judgment of God on her, because the overseers made
all those poor children go to church ; . . . . and that
therefore her business did not succeed. But others
thought it rather that she was better at contriving than
executing, and that too many things were undertaken
at the very first ; and that she was fain (having little
choice) to employ either those that had little skill in the
matters they dealt in, or less honesty ; and so she was
extremely cozened . . .   but chiefly the ill order
she took for paying money in this . . .   having the

---

[1] Costello, *Eminent Englishwomen*, Vol. III, p. 55.

worst memory in such things in the world . . .
and never keeping any account of what she did, she
was most subject to pay the same things often (as
she hath had it confessed to her by some that they have
in a small matter made her pay them the same thing
five times in five days)."[1]

Lady Falkland received small sympathy from her
husband in her dealings with affairs—and though her
methods may have been exasperating, their unfortunate
differences were not wholly due to her temperament.
He had married her for her fortune and when this
was settled on their son and not placed in his control,
his disappointment was so great that his affections
were alienated from her.

Of her efforts to further his interests Lord Falkland
wrote to Lord Conway :

" My very good Lord,
        By all my wife's letters I understand my obli-
gations to your Lordship to be very many ; and she
takes upon her to have received so manifold and noble
demonstrations of your favour to herself, that she
begins to conceive herself some able body in court,
by your countenance to do me courtesies, if she had the
wit as she hath the will. She makes it appear she hath
done me some good offices in removing some infusions
which my great adversary here (Loftus) hath made
unto you . . . it was high time ; for many evil
consequences of the contrary have befallen me since
that infusion was first made, which I fear will not be
removed in haste ; and must thank her much for
her careful pains in it, though it was but an act of duty
in her to see me righted when she knew me wronged
. . and beseech your Lordship still to continue that
favour to us both ; —to her, as well in giving her
good counsel as good countenance within a new world
and court, at such a distance from her husband a poor

[1] *Falkland, (The Lady), Her Life,* pp. 18-20.

weak woman stands in the greatest need of to dispatch her suits," . . . etc., etc.

" Dublyn Castle this 26th of July, 1625."[1]

Later he continues in the same strain :

" . . . I am glad your Lordship doth approve my wife's good affection to her husband, which was a point I never doubted, but for her abilities in agency of affairs, as I was never taken with opinion of them, so I was never desirous to employ them if she had them, for I conceive women to be no fit solicitors of state affairs for though it sometimes happen that they have good wits, it then commonly falls out that they have over-busy natures withal. For my part I should take much more comfort to hear that she were quietly retired to her mother's in the country, than that she had obtained a great suit in the court."[2]

The sentiments expressed by Lord Falkland were not characteristic of his time, when husbands were generally thankful to avail themselves of their wives' services in such matters.

While Sir Ralph Verney was exiled in France, he proposed that his wife should return to England to attend to some urgent business. His friend, Dr. Denton replied to the suggestion :

" . . . not to touch upon inconveniences of y^r comminge, women were never soe usefull as now, and though y^u should be my agent and sollicitour of all the men I knowe (and therefore much more to be preferred in y^r own cause) yett I am confident if y^u were here, y^u would doe as our sages doe, instruct y^r wife, and leave her to act it wth committees, their sexe entitles them to many priviledges and we find the comfort of them more now than ever."[3]

---

[1] *Falkland (The Lady), Her Life*, pp. 131-132.

[2] *Ibid*, pp. 132-3.

[3] *Verney Family*, Vol. II., p. 240, 646.

There are innumerable accounts in contemporary
letters and papers of the brave and often successful
efforts of women to stem the flood of misfortune which
threatened ruin to their families.

Katharine Lady Bland treated with Captain Hotham
in 1642 on behalf of Lord Savile " and agreed with
him for the preservation of my lords estate and protection of his person for £1,000," £320 of which had
already been taken "from Lord Savile's trunk at
Kirkstall Abbey . . . and the Captain . . .
promised to procure a protection from the parliament . . . . for his lordships person and
estate."[1]

Lady Mary Heveningham, through her efforts
restored the estate to the family after her husband
had been convicted of high treason at the
Restoration.[2]

Of Mrs. Muriel Lyttelton the daughter of Lord
Chancellor Bromley, it was said that she " may be called
the second founder of the family, as she begged the
estate of King James when it was forfeited and lived
a pattern of a good wife, affectionate widow, and careful parent for thirty years, with the utmost prudence
and economy at Hagley to retrieve the estate and pay
off the debts ; the education of her children in virtue
and the protestant religion being her principal employ.
Her husband, Mr. John Lyttelton, a zealous papist,
was condemned, and his estates forfeited, for being
concern'd in Essex's plot."[3]

Charles Parker confessed, " Certainly I had starved
had I not left all to my wife to manage, who gets
something by living there and haunting some of her
kindred and what wayes I know not but I am sure

[1] *Calendar State Papers, Domestic*, April 8, 1646.

[2] *Hunter (Joseph), History and Topography of Ketteringham*, p, 46.

[3] Nash, *Hist. and Antiq. of Worcester*, Vol. I,, p. 492. It appears by depositions
in the Court of Chancery that she paid off £25,000 which was charged upon the
estate, and only sold lands to the value of £8,854, *Ibid*, p. 496.

such as noe way entangle me in conscience or loyalty
nor hinder me from serving the King."[1]

Lady Fanshawe said her husband " thought it
conveniente to send me into England again, ...
there to try what sums I could raise, both for his
subsistence abroad and mine at home. . . . I
. . . . embarked myself in a hoy for Dover, with
Mrs. Waller, and my sister Margaret Harrison and my
little girl Nan, ... I had . . . . .
the good fortune as I then thought it, to sell £300 a
year to him that is now Judge Archer in Essex, for
which he gave me £4,000 which at that time I thought
a vast sum ; . . . . five hundred pounds I
carried to my husband, the rest I left in my father's
agent's hands to be returned as we needed it."[2]

The Marquis of Ormonde wrote : " I have written
2 seuerall ways of late to my wife about our domestick
affaires, which are in great disorder betweext the want
of meanes to keepe my sonnes abroad and the danger
of leaueing them at home. . . . I thank you for
your continued care of my children. I haue written
twice to my wife to the effect you speake of. I pray
God shee be able to put it in execution either way."[3]

This letter does not breathe that spirit of confidence
in the wife's ability which was shown in some of the
others and it happened sometimes that the wife was
either overwhelmed by procedure beyond her understanding, or at least sought for special consideration
on the plea of her sex's weakness and ignorance.

Sarah, wife of Henry Burton, gives an account of
Burton's trial in the Star Chamber, his sentence and
punishment (fine, pillory, imprisonment for life)
and his subsequent transportation to Guernsey, "where

---

[1] *Nicholas Papers*, Vol. I., p. 97.   Charles Parker to Lord Hatton.

[2] *Fanshawe (Lady), Memoirs of*, pp. 80-81.

[3] *Nicholas Papers*, Vol. III., pp. 274-6.   Marquis of Ormonde to Sir Ed. Nicholas,
1656.

he now is but by what order your petitioner knoweth not and is kept in strict durance of exile and imprisonment, and utterly denied the society of your petitioner contrary to the liberties and privileges of this kingdome . . . debarred of the accesse of friends, the use of pen, inck and paper and other means to make knowne his just complaintes," and she petitions the House of Commons " to take her distressed condition into your serious consideracion and because your peticioner is a woman not knowing how to prosecute nor manage so great and weighty busines " begs that Burton may be sent over to prosecute his just complaint.[1]

Similarly, Bastwick's wife pleads that he is so closely imprisoned in the Isle of Scilly " that your petitioner is not permitted to have any access unto him, so that for this 3 yeares and upward hir husband hath been exiled from hir, and she in all this time could not obtayne leave, although she hath earnestly sued for it, neither to live with him nor so much as to see him, and whereas your peticioner hath many smale children depending uppon hir for there mauntenance, and she of hir selfe being every way unable to provide for them, she being thus separated from her deare and loving husband and hir tender babes from there carefull father (they are in) great straights want and miserie," and she begs that her husband may be sent to England," your Petitioner being a woman no way able to follow nor manage so great and weighty a cause . . ."[2]

The above efforts were all made in defence of family estates, but at this time women were also concerned with the affairs of the nation, in which they took an active part.

Mrs. Hutchinson describes how " When the Parliament sat again, the colonel [Hutchinson] sent up his

---

[1] *State Papers, Domestic*, cccclxxi. 36, Nov. 7, 1640.
[2] *S.P.D.*, cccclxxi. 37, 1640.

wife to solicit his business in the house, that the Lord
Lexington's bill might not pass the lower house . .
she notwithstanding many other discouragements
waited upon the business every day, when her
adversaries as diligently solicited against her " a
friend told her how " the laste statemen's wives came
and offered them all the information they had gathered
from their husbands, and how she could not but know
more than any of them ; and if yet she would impart
anything that might show her gratitude, she might
redeem her family from ruin, . . . but she discerned his drift and scorned to become an informer,
and made him believe she was ignorant, though she
could have enlightened him in the very thing he
sought for ; which they are now never likely to know
much of, it being locked up in the grave."[1]

Herbert Morley wrote to Sir William Campion in
1645 :

" I could impart more, but letters are subject to
miscarriage, therefore I reserve myself to a more fit
opportunity. . . . If a conference might be had,
I conceive it would be most for the satisfaction of us
both, to prevent of any possible hazard of your
person. If you please to let your lady meet me
at Watford . . . or come hither, I will procure
her a pass."[2]

Sir William replied : " For any business you have to
impart to me, I have that confidence in you, by reason
of our former acquaintance, that I should not make
any scruple to send my wife to the places mentioned ;
but the truth is, she is at present soe neare her time
for lying downe, for she expects to be brought to bed
within less than fourteen days, that she is altogether
unfit to take soe long a journey. . . ."[3]

[1] *Life of Colonel Hutchinson*, by his Wife, pp. 334-336.

[2] *Sussex Arch. Coll.*, Vol. x., p. 5. To Sir William Campion from Herbert Morley, July 23rd, 1645.

[3] *Ibid*, Vol. x., p. 6.

A book might be wholly filled with a story of the part taken by women in the political and religious struggles of this period. They were also active among the crowd who perpetually beseiged the Court for grants of wardships and monopolies or patents.

Ann Wallwyn writes to Salisbury soliciting the wardship of the son of James Tomkins who is likely to die.[1] The petition of Dame Anne Wigmore, widow of Sir Richard Wigmore, states that she has found out a suit which will rectify many abuses, bring in a yearly revenue to the Crown and give satisfaction to the Petitioner for the great losses of herself and her husband. Details follow for a scheme for a corporation of carriers and others.[2]

Dorothy Selkane reminds Salisbury that a patent has been promised her for the digging of coals upon a royal manor. The men who manage the business for her are content to undertake all charges for the discovery of the coal and to compensate the tenants of the manor according to impartial arbitrators. She begs Salisbury that as she has been promised a patent the matter may be brought to a final conclusion that she may not be forced to trouble him further "having alredie bestowed a yeres solicitinge therein."[3] In 1610 the same lady writes again:—"I have bene at gte toyle and charges this yere and a halfe past as also have bene put to extraordinarie sollicitacion manie and sundry waies for the Dispatching of my suite . . ." and begs that the grant may pass without delay.[4]

A grant was made in 1614 to Anne, Roger and James Wright of a licence to keep a tennis court at St. Edmund's Bury, co. Suffolk, for life.[5] Bessy

[1] *C.S.P.D.* lxvii, 129, 1611.
[2] *C.S.P.D.* clxii, 8. March 2, 1630.
[3] *S.P.D.*, xlviii. 119. 22nd October. 1609.
[4] *S.P.D.* liii, 131, April 1610.
[5] *C.S.P.D.* lxxvii, 5 April 5, 1614.

Welling, servant to the late Prince Henry, petitioned for the erecting of an office for enrolling the Apprentices of Westminster, etc. As this was not granted, she therefore begs for a lease of some concealed lands [manors for which no rent has been paid for a hundred years] for sixty-one years. The Petitioner hopes to recover them for the King at her own charges.[1] Lady Roxburgh craves a licence to assay all gold and silver wire " finished at the bar " before it is worked, showing that it is no infringement on the Earl of Holland's grant which is for assaying and sealing gold and silver after it is made. This, it is pointed out, will be a means for His Majesty to pay off the debt he owes to Lady Roxburgh which otherwise must be paid some other way.[2]

A petition from Katharine Elliot "wett nurse to the Duke of Yorke" shows that there is a moor waste or common in Somersetshire called West Sedge Moor which appears to be the King's but has been appropriated and encroached upon by bordering commoners. She begs for a grant of it for sixty years ; as an inducement the Petitioner offers to recover it at her own costs and charges and to pay a rent of one shilling per acre, the King never previously having received benefit therefrom.[3] The reference by Windebank notes that the king is willing to gratify the Petitioner. Another petition was received from this same lady declaring that " Divers persons being of no corporation prefers the trade of buying and selling silk stockings and silk waistcoats as well knit as woven uttering the Spanish or baser sort of silk at as dear rates as the first Naples and also frequently vending the woven for the knit, though in price and goodness there is almost half in half difference." She prays a grant for thirty-

---

[1] *S.P.D.* cxi, 121, 1619.

[2] *S.P.D.* clxxx, 66, 1624.

[3] *S.P.D.* cccxxiii, 109, 18th June, 1637.

one years for the selling of silk stockings, half stockings and waistcoats, to distinguish the woven from the knit receiving from the salesmen a shilling for every waistcoat, sixpence per pair of silk stockings and fourpence for every half pair.[1]

Elizabeth, Viscountess Savage, points out that Freemen of the city enter into bond on their admittance with two sureties of a hundred marks to the Chamberlain of London not to exercise any trade other than that of the Company they were admitted into. Of late years persons having used other trades and contrived not to have their bonds forfeited, and the penalty belonging to His Majesty, she begs a grant of such penalties to be recovered at her instance and charge.[2]

The petition of Margaret Cary, relict of Thomas Cary Esquire, one of the Grooms of the Chamber to the King on the behalf of herself and her daughters, begs for a grant to compound with offenders by engrossering and transporting of wool, wool fells, fuller's earth, lead, leather, corn and grain, she to receive a Privy Seal for two fourth-parts of the fines and compositions. Her reasons for desiring this grant are that her husband's expense in prosecuting like cases has reaped no benefit of his grant of seven-eighths of forfeited bonds for the like offences. She urges the usefulness of the scheme and the existence of similar grants.[3]

Mistress Dorothy Seymour petitions for a grant of the fines imposed on those who export raw hides contrary to the Proclamation and thereby make coaches, boots, etc., dearer. The reference to the Petition states : " It is His Majesty's gratious pleasure that the petitioner cause impoundr. to be given to the Attorney General touching the offences above mencioned . · . and as proffyt shall arise to His

---

[1] S.P.D. cccxxiii , 7. Bk. of Petitioners, Car. I.

[2] S.P.D. ccciii., 65, Dec. 6th, 1635.

[3] S.P.D. cccvi., 27, 1635.

Majesty . . . he will give her such part as shall fully satisfy her pains and good endeavours."[1]

The projecting of patents and monopolies was the favourite pursuit of fashionable people of both sexes. Ben Johnson satirises the Projectress in the person of Lady Tailebush, of whom the Projector, Meercraft says :

> . . . . . . " She and I now
> Are on a Project, for the fact, and venting
> Of a new kind of fucus (paint for Ladies)
> To serve the Kingdom ; wherein she herself
> Hath travel'd specially, by the way of service
> Unto her sex, and hopes to get the monopoly,
> As the Reward of her Invention."[2]

When Eitherside assures her mistress

> " I do hear
> You ha' cause madam, your suit goes on "

Lady Tailebush replies :

> " Yes faith, there's life in't now.   It is referr'd
> If we once see it under the seals, wench, then,
> Have with 'em, for the great caroch, six horses
> And the two coachmen, with my Ambler bare,
> And my three women ; we will live i' faith,
> The examples o' the Town, and govern it.
> I'll lead the fashion still." . . . . . . [3]

From the women who begged for monopolies which if granted must have involved much worry and labour if they were to be made profitable, we pass naturally to women who actually owned and managed businesses requiring a considerable amount of capital.   They not infrequently acted as pawn-brokers and money-lenders.   Thus, complaint is made that Elizabeth Pennell had stolen " two glazier's vices with the screws and appurtenances " and pawned them to

---

[1] S.P.D. cccxlvi, 2, Feb. 1st, 1637.

[2] Jonson, (Ben.) The Devil is an A ss, Act III, Scene iv.

[3] (Ibid), Act IV., Scene ii.

one Ellianor Troughton, wife of Samuel Troughton broker.[1]

Richard Braithwaite tells the following story of a " Useresse " as though this occupation were perfectly usual for women. " Wee reade in a booke entituled the *Gift of Feare*, how a Religious Divine comming to a certaine Vseresse to advise her of the state of her soule, and instruct her in the way to salvation at such time as she lay languishing in her bed of affliction ; told her how there were three things by her to be necessarily performed, if ever she hoped to be saved : She must become *contrite* in heart . . . *confesse* her sins . . . . make *restitution* according to her meanes whereto shee thus replyed, *Two of those first I will doe willingly : but to doe the last, I shall hold it a difficulty ; for should I make restitution, what would remaine to raise my children their portion ?* To which the Divine answered ; *Without these three you cannot be saved. Yea but*, quoth shee, *Doe our Learned Men and Scriptures say so ? Yes, surely* said the Divine. *And I will try*, (quoth shee) *whether they say true or no, for I will restore nothing.* And so resolving, fearefully dyed . . . for preferring the care of her posterity, before the honour of her Maker."[2]

The names of women often occur in connection with the shipping trade and with contracts. Some were engaged in business with their husbands as in the case of a fine remitted to Thomas Price and Collet his wife for shipping 200 dozen of old shoes, with intention to transport them beyond the seas contrary to a Statute (5th year Edward VI) on account of their poverty.[3] Others were widows like Anne Hodsall whose husband, a London merchant, traded for many

---

[1] *Middlesex Co. Rec. Sess. Books*, p. 18, 1690.

[2] Braithwaite, (Richd.), *The English Gentleman*, p. 300, 1641.

[3] Overall *Remembrancia, Analytical Index to*, p. 519, 1582.

years to the Canary Islands, the greatest part of his estate being there. He could not recover it in his lifetime owing to the war with Spain and therefore his wife was left in great distress with four children. Her estate in the Canary Islands is likely to be confiscated, there being no means of recovering it thence except by importing wines, and it would be necessary to take pipe-staves over there to make casks to bring back the wines. She begs the council therefore " in commiseration of her distressed estate to grant a licence to her and her assignes to lade one ship here with woollen commodities for Ireland, To lade Pipe staves in Ireland (notwithstanding the prohibition) and to send the same to the Canary Islands."[1]

Joseph Holroyd employed a woman as his shipping agent ; in a letter dated 1706 he writes re certain goods for Holland : that these " I presume must be marked as usual and forward to Madam Brown at Hull. . ." and he informs Madam Hannah Browne, that " By orders of Mr. John Whittle I have sent you one packe and have 2 packes more to send as und'. You are to follow Mr. Whittle's directions in shipping."[2]

In 1630 Margrett Greeneway, widow of Thos. Greeneway, baker, begged leave to finish carrying out a contract made by her husband notwithstanding the present restraint on the bringing of corn to London. The contract was to supply the East India Company with biscuit. Margrett Greeneway petitions to bring five hundred quarters of wheat to London—some are already bought and she asks for leave to buy the rest. The petition was granted.[3]

A Petition of " Emanuell Fynche, Wm. Lewis Merchantes and Anne Webber Widow on the behalfe

---

[1] *Council Register*, 8th August, 1628.

[2] Holroyd, Joseph (Cloth Factor) and Saml. Hill (clothier), *Letter Bks. of*, pp. 18-25.

[3] C.R., 3rd December, 1630.

of themselves and others owners of the shipp called the *Benediction* was presented to the Privy Council stating that the ship had been seized and detained by the French and kept at Dieppe where it was deteriorating. They asked to be allowed to sell her there.[1] The name of another woman ship-owner occurs in a case at Grimsby brought against Christopher Claton who " In the behalfe of his Mother An Alford, wid.,hath bought one wessell of Raffe of one Laurence Lamkey of Odwell in the kingdome of Norway, upon wch private bargane there appeares a breach of the priviledges of this Corporation."[2]

In 1636 upon the Petition of Susanna Angell " widowe, and Eliz. her daughter (an orphan) of the cittie of London humbly praying that they might by their Lordshipps warrant bee permitted to land 14 barrels of powder now arrived as also 38 barrells which is daily expected in the *Fortune* they paying custome and to sell the same within the kingdome or otherwise to give leave to transport it back againe into Holland from whence it came " the Officers of the customs were ordered to permit the Petitioners to export the powder.[3]

Women's names appear also in lists of contractors to the Army and Navy. Elizabeth Bennett and Thomas Berry contracted with the Commissioners to supply one hundred suits of apparel for the soldiers at Plymouth.[4]

Cuthbert Farlowe, Elizabeth Harper Widowe, Edward Sheldon and John Davis," poore Tradesmen of London " petition " to be paid the £180 yet unpaid of their accounts for furnishing the seamen for Rochelle with clothes and shoes " att the rates of ready money."[5]

[1] *S.P.D.* ccxxxvi., 45, 12th, April, 1633.

[2] *Hist. MSS. Com.*, 14 Rep., VIII., p. 284, 1655.

[3] *S.P.D.* ccxcii., 24. March 23, 1636/7., *Proceedings of Gunpowder Commissioners.*

[4] *S.P.D.* xx., 62, Feb. 9th, 1626.

[5] *S.P.D.* cxcvii., 64, July, 1631.

A warrant was issued " to pay to Alice Bearden £100 for certain cutworks furnished to the Queen for her own wearing."[1]

Edward Prince brought a case in the Star Chamber, v. Thomas Woodward, Ellenor Woodward, and Georg. Helliar defendants being Ironmongers for supposed selling of iron at false weights to undersell plaintiff. " Defendants respectively prove that they ever bought and sold by one sort of weight."[2]

For her tenancy of the Spy-law Paper Mill, Foulis " receaved from M^{rs}. lithgow by W^{m}. Douglas Hands 85 lib. for ye 1704 monie rent. She owes me 3 rim of paper for that yeir, besydes 4 rim she owes me for former yeirs."[3]

Joan Dant was one of the few women " capitalists " whose personal story is known in any detail. Her husband was a working weaver, living in New Paternoster Row, Spital Fields. On his death she became a pedlar, carrying an assortment of mercery, hosiery, and haberdashery on her back from house to house in the vicinity of London. Her conduct as a member of the Society of Friends was consistent and her manners agreeable, so that her periodic visits to the houses of Friends were welcomed and she was frequently entertained as a guest at their tables. After some years, her expenses being small and her diligence great, she had saved sufficient capital to engage in a more wholesale trade, debts due from her correspondents at Paris and Brussels appearing in her executor's accounts. In spite of her success in trade Joan Dant continued to live in her old frugal manner, and when she applied to a Friend for assistance in making her will, he was astonished to find her worth rather more than £9,000. He advised her to obtain the assistance

---

[1] S.P.D., clix., 27th Jan. 1630.

[2] S.P.D., dxxxi., 138, 1630.

[3] Foulis, Sir John, Account Book, 5th Jan., 1705.

of other Friends more experienced in such matters. On their enquiring how she wished to dispose of her property, she replied, " I got it by the rich and I mean to leave it to the poor."

Joan Dant died in 1715 at the age of eighty-four. In a letter to her executors she wrote, " It is the Lord that creates true industry in his people, and that blesseth their endeavours in obtaining things necessary and convenient for them, which are to be used in moderation by all his flock and family everywhere. . . And I, having been one that has taken pains to live, and have through the blessing of God, with honesty and industrious care, improved my little in the world to a pretty good degree ; find my heart open in that charity which comes from the Lord, in which the true disposal of all things ought to be, to do something for the poor,—the fatherless and the widows in the Church of Christ, according to the utmost of my ability."[1]

Another venture initiated and carried on by a woman, was an Insurance Office established by Dorothy Petty. An account of it written in 1710 states that :—
" The said *Dorothy* (who is the Daughter of a Divine of the Church of *England*, now deceas'd) did Set up an *Insurance Office* on *Births, Marriages, and Services*, in order thereby to serve the Publick, and get an honest Livelyhood for herself. . . . . The said *Dorothy* had such Success in her Undertaking, that more Claims were paid, and more Stamps us'd for Policies and Certificates in her Office than in all other the like Offices in *London* besides ; which good Fortune was chiefly owing to the Fairness and Justice of her Proceedings in the said Business : for all the Money paid into the Office was Entered in one Book, and all the Money paid out upon Claims was set down in another Book, and all People had Liberty to peruse

---

both, so that there could not possibly be the least Fraud in the Management thereof."[1]

In 1622 the names of Mary Hall, 450 coals, Barbara Riddell, 450 coals, Barbara Milburne, 60 coals, are included without comment among the brothers of the fellowship of Hostmen (coal owners) of Newcastle who have coals to rent.[2] The name of Barbara Milburne, widow, is given in the Subsidy Roll for 1621 as owning land.[3] That these women were equal to the management of their collieries is suggested by the fact that when in 1623 Christopher Mitford left besides property which he bequeathed direct to his nephews and nieces, five salt-pans and collieries to his sister Jane Legard he appointed her his executrix,[4] which he would hardly have done unless he had believed her equal to the management of a complicated business.

The frequency with which widows conducted capitalistic enterprises may be taken as evidence of the extent to which wives were associated with their husbands in business. The wife's part is sometimes shown in prosecutions, as in a case which was brought in the Star Chamber against Thomas Hellyard, Elizabeth his wife and John Goodenough and Hugh Nicholes for oppression in the country under a patent to Hellyard for digging saltpetre . . . " in pursuance of his direction leave and authority. . . Nicholes Powell, Defendants servant, and the said Hellyard's wife, did sell divers quantities of salt petre. More particularly the said Hellyard's wife did sell to Parker 400lbs. at Haden Wells, 300 or 400 lbs. at Salisbury and 300 or 400 lbs. at Winchester at £9 the hundred." Hellyard was sentenced to a fine of £1,000, pillory, whipping and imprisonment.

---

[1] *Case of Dorothy Petty*, 1710.

[2] *Newcastle and Gateshead, History of*, Vol. III., p. 242.

[3] *Ibid*, p. 237.

[4] *Ibid*, p. 252.

" As touching the other defendant Elizabeth Hellyard the courte was fully satisfyed with sufficient matter whereupon to ground a sentence against the defendant Eliz. but shee being a wyfe and subject to obey her husband theyr Lord ships did forbeare to sentence her."[1]

Three men, " artificers in glass making," beg that Lady Mansell may either be compelled to allow them such wages as they formerly received, or to discharge them from her service, her reduction of wages disabling them from maintaining their families, and driving many of them away.[2] Lady Mansell submits a financial statement and account of the rival glassmakers' attempts to ruin her husband's business, one of whom " hath in open audience vowed to spend 1000li, to ruine your petitioners husband joyninge with the Scottish pattentie taking the advantage of your petitioners husbands absence, thinckinge your petitioner a weake woman unable to followe the busines and determininge the utter ruine of your petitioner and her husband have inticed three of her workemen for windowe glasse, which shee had longe kepte att a weeklie chardge to her great prejudice to supplie the worke yf there should be anie necessitie in the Kingdome," etc., etc.," she begs justice upon the rivals, " your petitioner havinge noe other meanes nowe in his absence (neither hath he when he shall returne) but onelie this busines wherein he hath engaged his whole estate."[3]

Able business women might be found in every class of English society throughout the seventeenth century, but their contact with affairs became less habitual as the century wore away, and expressions of surprise occur at the prowess shown by Dutch women in

---

[1] *S.P.D.*, cclx., 21, 1634.

[2] *S.P.D.*, cxlviii., 52, 1623,

[3] *S.P.D.*; dxxi., 147. Addenda Charles I., 1625.

business. " At *Ostend*, *Newport*, and *Dunkirk*, where, and when, the *Holland* pinks come in, there daily the Merchants, that be but Women (but not such Women as the Fishwives of *Billingsgate* ; for these *Netherland* Women do lade many Waggons with fresh Fish daily, some for *Bruges*, and some for *Brussels*, etc., etc.) I have seen these Women-merchants I say, have their Aprons full of nothing but *English Jacobuses*, to make all their Payment of."[1]

Sir J. Child mentions " the Education of their Children as well Daughters as Sons ; all which, be they of never so great quality or estate, they always take care to bring up to write perfect good Hands, and to have the full knowledge and use of Arithmetick and Merchant Accounts," as one of the advantages which the Dutch possess over the English ; " the well understanding and practise whereof doth strangely infuse into most that are the owners of that Quality, of either Sex, not only an Ability for Commerce of all kinds, but a strong aptitude, love and delight in it ; and in regard the women are as knowing therein as the Men, it doth incourage their Husbands to hold on in their Trades to their dying days, knowing the capacity of their Wives to get in their Estates, and carry on their Trades after their Deaths : Whereas if a Merchant in England arrive at any considerable Estate, he commonly with-draws his Estate from Trade, before he comes near the confines of Old Age ; reckoning that if God should call him out of the World while the main of his Estate is engaged abroad in Trade, he must lose one third of it, through the un-experience and unaptness of his Wife to such Affairs, and so it usually falls out. Besides it hath been ob-served in the nature of Arithmetick, that like other parts of the Mathematicks, it doth not only improve the Rational Faculties, but inclines those that are expert

---

[1] *England's Way*, 1614. *Harleian Misc.*, Vol. III., p. 383.

in it to Thriftiness and good Husbandry, and prevents both Husbands and Wives in some measure from running out of their estates."[1]

This account is confirmed by Howell who writes of the Dutch in 1622 that they are " well versed in all sorts of languages . . . Nor are the Men only expert therein but the Women and Maids also in their common Hostries ; & in Holland the Wives are so well versed in Bargaining, Cyphering & Writing, that in the Absence of their Husbands in long sea voyages they beat the Trade at home & their Words will pass in equal Credit. These Women are wonderfully sober, tho' their Husbands make commonly their Bargains in Drink, & then are they more cautelous."[2]

This unnatural reversing of the positions of men and women was censured by the Spaniard Vives who wrote " In Hollande, women do exercise marchandise and the men do geue themselues to quafting, the which customes and maners I alowe not, for thei agre not with nature, ye which hath geuen unto man a noble, a high & a diligent minde to be busye and occupied abroade, to gayne & to bring home to their wiues & families to rule them and their children, ... and to ye woman nature hath geuen a feareful, a couetous & an humble mind to be subject unto man, & to kepe y^t he doeth gayne."[3]

The contrast which had arisen between Dutch and English customs in this respect was also noticed by Wycherley, one of whose characters, Monsieur Paris, a Francophile fop, describes his tour in Holland in the following terms : " I did visit, you must know, one of de Principal of de State General . . . and did find his Excellence weighing Sope, jarnie ha, ha, ha, weighing sope, ma foy, for he was a wholesale Chandeleer ; and

---

[1] Child, Sir J., *A New Discourse of Trade*, pp. 4-5. 1694,

[2] Howell, (Jas.), *Familiar Letters*, p. 103,

[3] Vives, *Office and Duties of a Husband*, trans. by Thos. Paynell.

his Lady was taking de Tale of Chandels wid her own witer Hands, ma foy ; and de young Lady, his Excellence Daughter, stringing Harring, jarnie . . . his Son, (for he had but one) was making the Tour of France, etc. in a Coach and six."[1]

The picture is obviously intended to throw ridicule on the neighbouring state, of whose navy and commercial progress England stood at that time in considerable fear.

How rapidly the active, hardy life of the Elizabethan gentlewoman was being transformed into the idleness and dependence which has characterised the lady of a later age may be judged by Mary Astell's comment on " Ladies of Quality." She says, " They are placed in a condition which makes that which is everyone's chief business to be their only employ. They have nothing to do but to glorify God and to benefit their neighbours."[2] After a study of the Restoration Drama it may be doubted whether the ladies of that period wished to employ their leisure over these praiseworthy objects. But had they the will, ignorance of life and inexperience in affairs are qualifications which perhaps would not have increased the effectiveness of their efforts in either direction.

The proof of the change which was taking place in the scope of upper class women's interests does not rest only upon individual examples such as those which have been quoted, though these instances have been selected for the most part on account of their representative character.

It is quite clear that the occupation of ladies with their husband's affairs was accepted as a matter of course throughout the earlier part of the century, and it is only after the Restoration that a change of fashion in this respect becomes evident. Pepys, whose milieu was

---

[1] Wycherley, *The Gentleman Dancing Master*, p. 21.

[2] Astell, (Mary), *A Serious Proposal*, p. 145, 1694.

typical of the new social order, after a call upon Mr. Bland, commented with surprised pleasure on Mrs. Bland's interest in her husband's affairs. " Then to eat a dish of anchovies," he says " and drink wine and syder and very merry, but above all things, pleased to hear Mrs. Bland talk like a merchant in her husband's business very well, and it seems she do understand it and perform a great deal."[1] The capacity of a woman to understand her husband's business seldom aroused comment earlier in the century, and would have passed unnoticed even by many of Pepys' contemporaries who lived in a different set. Further evidence of women's business capacity is found in the fact that men generally expected their wives would prove equal to the administration of their estates after their death, and thus the wife was habitually appointed executrix often even the sole executrix of wills. This custom was certainly declining in the latter part of the century. The winding up of a complicated estate and still more the prosecution of an extensive business, could not have been successfully undertaken by persons who hitherto had led lives of idleness, unacquainted with the direction of affairs.

That men did not at this time regard marriage as necessarily involving the assumption of a serious economic burden, but on the contrary, often considered it to be a step which was likely to strengthen them in life's battles, is also significant. This attitude was partly due to the provision of a dot by fathers of brides, but there were other ways in which the wife contributed to the support of her household. Thus in a wedding sermon woman is likened to a merchant's ship, for " She bringeth her food from far " . . . not meaning she is to be chosen for her dowry, " for the worst wives may have the best portions, . . . a good wife tho' she bring nothing in with her, yet,

---

[1] Pepys, (Sam.) *Diary*, Vol. II., p. 113, Dec. 31, 1662.

thro' her Wisdom and Diligence great things come in
by her ; she brings in with her hands, for, *She putteth her
hands to the wheel.* . . . . If she be too high to
stain her Hands with bodily Labour, yet she
bringeth in with her Eye, for, *She overseeth the
Ways of her Household,* . . . and eateth not the
Bread of *Idleness.*" She provides the necessities of
life. " If she will have Bread, she must not always
buy it, but she must sow it, and reap it and grind it,
. . . She must knead it, and make it into bread.
Or if she will have Cloth, she must not always run to
the Shop or to the score but she begins at the seed,
she carrieth her seed to the Ground, she gathereth Flax,
of her Flax she spinneth a Thread, of her Thread she
weaveth Cloth, and so she comes by her coat."[1]

The woman here described was the mistress of a
large household, who found scope for her productive
energy within the limits of domestic industry, but it
has been shown that the married woman often went
farther than this, and engaged in trade either as her
husband's assistant or even on her own account.

The effect of such work on the development of
women's characters was very great, for any sort of
productive, that is to say, creative work, provides a
discipline and stimulus to growth essentially different
from any which can be acquired in a life devoted
to spending money and the cultivation of ornamental
qualities.

The effect on social relations was also marked, for
their work implied an association of men and women
through a wide range of human interests and a consequent development of society along organic rather than
mechanical lines. The relation between husband and
wife which obtained most usually among the upper
classes in England at the opening of the seventeenth
century, appears indeed to have been that of partner-

---

[1] Wilkinson, (Robert), *Conjugal Duty*, pp. 13-17.

ship; the chief responsibility for the care of children and the management and provisioning of her household resting on the wife's shoulders, while in business matters she was her husband's lieutenant. The wife was subject to her husband, her life was generally an arduous one, but she was by no means regarded as his servant. A comradeship existed between them which was stimulating and inspiring to both. The ladies of the Elizabethan period possessed courage, initiative, resourcefulness and wit in a high degree. Society expected them to play a great part in the national life and they rose to the occasion ; perhaps it was partly the comradeship with their husbands in the struggle for existence which developed in them qualities which had otherwise atrophied.

Certainly the more circumscribed lives of the Restoration ladies show a marked contrast in this respect, for they appear but shadows of the vigorous personalities of their grandmothers. Prominent amongst the many influences which conspired together to produce so rapid a decline in the physique, efficiency and morale of upper class women, must be reckoned the spread of the capitalistic organisation of industry, which by the rapid growth of wealth made possible the idleness of growing numbers of women. Simultaneously the gradual perfecting by men of their separate organisations for trade purposes rendered them independent of the services of their wives and families for the prosecution of their undertakings. Though the stern hand of economic necessity was thus withdrawn from the control of women's development in the upper classes, it was still potent in determining their destiny amongst the " common people," whose circumstances will be examined in detail in the following chapters.

AGRICULTURE

ALTHOUGH the woollen trade loomed very large upon the political horizon because it was a chief source of revenue to the Crown and because rapidly acquired wealth gave an influence to clothiers and wool merchants out of proportion to their numbers, agriculture was still England's chief industry in the seventeenth century.

The town population has had a tendency to wear out and must be recruited from rural districts. The village communities which still persisted at this period in England, provided a vigorous stock, from which the men whose initiative, energy and courage have made England famous during the last two centuries were largely descended. Not only were the farming families prolific in numbers but they maintained a high standard of mental and moral virtue. It must be supposed therefore that the conditions in which they lived were upon the whole favourable to the development of their women-folk, but investigation will show that this was not the case for all members alike of the agricultural community, who may be roughly divided into three classes :

(a) Farmers. (b) Husbandmen. (c) Wage-earners.

(a) *Farmers* held sufficient land for the complete maintenance of the family. Their household often included hired servants and their methods on the larger farms were becoming capitalistic.

(b) *Husbandmen* were possessed of holdings insufficient for the complete maintenance of the family and their income was therefore supplemented by working for wages.

(c) *Wage-earners* had no land, not even a garden, and depended therefore completely on wages for the maintenance of their families.

In addition to the above, for whom agriculture was their chief business, the families of the gentry, professional men and tradesmen who lived in the country and smaller towns, generally grew sufficient dairy and garden produce for domestic consumption.

The above classification is arbitrary, for no hard and fast division existed. Farmers merged imperceptibly into husbandmen, and husbandmen into wage earners and yet there was a wide gulf separating their positions. As will be shown, it was the women of the first two classes who bore and reared the children who were destined to be the makers of England, while few children of the wage-earning class reached maturity.

A. *Farmers.*

However important the women who were the mothers of the race may appear to modern eyes, their history was unnoticed by their contemporaries and no analysis

was made of their development. The existence of
vigorous, able matrons was accepted as a matter of
course. They embodied the seventeenth century
idea of the " eternal feminine " and no one suspected
that they might change with a changing environment.
They themselves were too busy, too much absorbed
in the lives of others, to keep journals and they were
not sufficiently important to have their memoirs
written by other people.

Perhaps their most authentic portraits may be
found in the writings of the Quakers, who were largely
drawn from this class of the community. They
depict women with an exalted devotion, supporting
their families and strengthening their husbands
through the storms of persecution and amidst
the exacting claims of religion.

John Banks wrote from Carlisle Prison in 1648
to his wife, " No greater Joy and Comfort I have in
this world . . . than to know that thou and all
thine are well both in Body and Mind . . .
though I could be glad to see thee here, but do not
straiten thyself in any wise, for I am truly content to
bear it, if it were much more, considering thy Concerns
in this Season of the Year, being Harvest time and the
Journey so long."[1]   After her death he writes, " We
Lived Comfortably together many Years, and she was
a Careful Industrious Woman in bringing up of her
Children in good order, as did become the Truth, in
Speech, Behaviour and Habit ; a Meet-Help and a
good Support to me, upon the account of my Travels,
always ready and willing to fit me with Necessaries,
. . . and was never known to murmur, tho' I was
often Concerned, to leave her with a weak Family,
. . . She was well beloved amongst good Friends and
of her Neighbours, as witness the several hundreds that
were at her Burial. . . . our Separation by Death,

---

[1] Banks (John), *Journal*, p. 101, 1684.

was the greatest Trial that ever I met with, above any-thing here below. Now if any shall ask, Why I have writ so many Letters at large to be Printed . . . how can any think that I should do less than I have done, to use all Endeavours what in me lay, to Streng-then and Encourage my Dear Wife, whom I so often, and for so many Years was made to leave as aforesaid, having pretty much concerns to look after."[1]

Of another Quaker, Mary Batt, her father writes in her testimony that she was " Married to *Phillip Tyler* of *Waldon* in the County of *Somerset* before she attained the age of twenty years. . . . The Lord blessed her with Four Children, whereof two dyed in their Infancy, and two yet remain alive : at the Burial of her Husband, for being present, she had two Cows valued at Nine Pounds taken from her, which, with many other Tryals during her Widowhood, she bore with much Patience, . . . After she had remained a Widow about four Years, the Lord drew the affection of *James Taylor* . . . to seek her to be his Wife, and there being an answer in her, the Lord joyned them together. To her Husband her Love and Subjection was suitable to that Relation, being greatly delighted in his Company, and a Meet-Help, a faithful Yoak-fellow, . . . and in his Absence, not only carefully discharging the duty as her Place as a Wife, but diligent to supply his Place in those affairs that more immediately concerned him."[2] And her husband adds in his testimony, " My outward Affairs falling all under her charge (I, being absent, a Prisoner for my Testimony against Tythes) she did manage the same in such care and patience until the time she was grown big with Child, and as she thought near the time of her Travail (a condition much to be born with and pittyed) she then desired so much Liberty as to have my Company home

[1] Banks, (John), *Journal*, pp. 129-30.
[2] Batt (Mary), *Testimony of the Life and Death of*, pp. 1-3, 1683.

two Weeks, and went herself to request it, which
small matter she could not obtain, but was denied ;
and as I understood by her, it might be one of the
greatest occasions of her grief which ever happened
unto her, yet in much Meekness and true Patience
she stooped down, and quietly took up this her last
Cross also, and is gone with it and all the rest, out of the
reach of all her Enemies, . . . Three Nights and
Two Days before her Death, I was admitted to come
to her, though I may say (with grief) too late, yet it
was to her great joy to see me once more whom she
so dearly loved ; and would not willingly suffer me
any more to depart out of her sight until she had
finished her days, . . . Her Sufferings (in the
condition she was in) although I was a Prisoner, were
far greater then mine, for the whole time that she
became my Wife, which was some Weeks above Three
Years, notwithstanding there was never yet man,
woman, nor child, could justly say, she had given them
any offence . . . yet must . . . unreasonable men
cleanse our Fields of Cattle, rummage our House of
Goods, and make such havock as that my Dear Wife
had not wherewithal to dress or set Food before me
and her Children.[1]

The duties of a Farmer's wife were described a
hundred years earlier by Fitzherbert in the " Boke of
Husbandrie." He begins the " Prologue for the
wyves occupacyon," thus, " Now thou husbande that
hast done thy diligence and laboure that longeth to a
husband to get thy liuing, thy wyues, thy children,
and thy seruauntes, yet is there other thynges to be
doen that nedes must be done, or els thou shalt not
thryue. For there is an olde common saying, that
seldom doth ye husbande thriue without leue of his
wyf. By thys saying it shuld seem that ther be other
occupaciõs and labours that be most cõvenient

---

[1] Batt (Mary), *Testimony to Life and Death of*, pp. 5-7, 1683.

for the wyfes to do, and how be it that I haue not the
experience of all their occupacyions and workes as I
haue of husbandry, yet a lytel wil I speake what they
ought to do though I tel thẽ not how they should
do and excersyse their labour and occupacions.

A lesson for the wyfe . . . alway be doyng
of some good workes that the deuil may fynde the
alway occupied, for as in a standyng water are en-
gendred wormes, right so in an idel body are engendered
ydel thoughtes. Here maie thou see y^t of idelnes
commeth damnatiõ, & of good workes and labour
commeth saluacion. Now thou art at thy libertie to
chose whither waye thou wilte, wherein is great
diversite. And he is an unhappye man or woman that
god hath given both wit & reason and putteth him in
choise & he to chose the worst part. Nowe thou
wife I trust to shewe unto the diuers occupacions,
workes and labours that thou shalt not nede to be
ydel no tyme of ye yere. What thinges the wife is
bounde of right to do. Firste and principally the wyfe
is bound of right to loue her husband aboue father
and mother and al other men . . .

What workes a wyfe should do in generall. First
in the mornyng when thou art wakéd and purpose
to rise, lift up thy hãd & blis the & make a signe of
the holy crosse . . . and remembre thy maker
and thou shalte spede muche the better, & when thou
art up and readye, then firste swepe thy house ;
dresse up thy dyscheborde, & set al thynges in good
order within thy house, milke ye kie, socle thy calues,
sile up thy milke, take up thy children & aray thẽ,
& provide for thy husbandes breakefaste, diner,
souper, & for thy children & seruauntes, & take thy
parte wyth them. And to ordeyne corne & malt to
the myll, to bake and brue withall whẽ nede is.
And mete it to the myll and fro the myll, & se that
thou haue thy mesure agayne besides the tole or elles
the mylner dealeth not truly wyth the, or els thy corne

is not drye as it should be, thou must make butter and chese when thou may, serue thy swine both mornyng and eueninge, and giue thy polen meate in the mornynge, and when tyme of yeare cometh thou must take hede how thy henne, duckes, and geese do ley, and to gather up their egges and when they waxe broudy to set them there as no beastes, swyne, nor other vermyne hurte them, and thou must know that all hole foted foule wil syt a moneth and al clouen foted foule wyl syt but three wekes except a peyhen and suche other great foules as craynes, bustardes, and suche other. And when they haue brought forth theyr birdes to se that they be well kepte from the gleyd, crowes, fully martes and other vermyn, and in the begynyng of March, of a lytle before is time for a wife to make her garden and to get as manye good sedes and herbes as she can, and specyally such as be good for the pot and for to eate & as ofte as nede shall require it muste be weded, for els the wede wyll ouer grow the herbes, and also in Marche is time to sowe flaxe and hempe, for I haue heard olde huswyues say, that better is Marche hurdes then Apryll flaxe, the reason appereth, but howe it shoulde be sowen, weded, pulled, repealed, watred, washen, dried, beten, braked, tawed, hecheled, spon, wounden, wrapped, & ouen. It nedeth not for me to shewe for they be wyse ynough, and thereof may they make shetes, bord clothes, towels, shertes, smockes, and suche other necessaryes, and therfore lette thy dystaffe be alwaye redy for a pastyme, that thou be not ydell. And undoubted a woman cannot get her livinge honestly with spinning on the dystaffe, but it stoppeth a gap and must nedes be had. The bolles of flaxe whan they be rypled of, muste be rediled from the wedes and made dry with the sunne to get out the seedes. How be it one maner of linsede called lokensede wyll not open by the sunne, and therefore when they be drye they must be sore bruien and broken the wyves know how, & then

wynowed and kept dry til peretime cum againe.
Thy femell hempe must be pulled fro the chucle
hẽpe for this beareth no sede & thou muste doe by it
as thou didest by the flaxe. The chucle hempe doth
beare seed & thou must beware that birdes eate it not
as it groweth, the hempe thereof is not so good as
the femel hẽpe, but yet it wil do good seruice. It
may fortune sometime y^t thou shalte haue so many
thinges to do that thou shalte not wel know where is
best to begyn. Thẽ take hede whiche thinge should
be the greatest losse if it were not done & in what space
it would be done, and then thinke what is the greatest
loss & there begin. . . . It is cõvenient for a
husbande to haue shepe of his owne for many causes,
and then may his wife have part of the wooll to make
her husbande and her selfe sum clothes. And at the
least waye she may haue ye lockes of the shepe therwith
to make clothes or blankets, and couerlets, or both.
And if she haue no wol of her owne she maye take woll
to spynne of cloth makers, and by that meanes she
may have a conuenient liuing, and many tymes to do
other workes. It is a wiues occupacion to winow al
maner of cornes, to make malte wash and wring, to
make hey, to shere corne, and in time of nede to helpe
her husbande to fyll the mucke wayne or donge carte,
dryve the plough, to lode hey, corne & such other.
Also to go or ride to the market to sell butter, chese,
mylke, egges, chekens, kapons, hennes, pygges, gees,
and al maner of corne. And also to bye al maner of
necessary thinges belonging to a houshold, and to
make a true rekening & accompt to her husband
what she hath receyued and what she hathe payed.
And yf the husband go to the market to bye or sell
as they ofte do, he then to shew his wife in lyke maner.
For if one of them should use to disceiue the other,
he disceyveth him selfe, and he is not lyke to thryve,
& therfore they must be true ether to other.[1]

---

[1] Fitzherbert (Sir Anth.), *Boke of Husbandrye.*

Fitzherbert's description of the wife's occupation probably remained true in many districts during the seventeenth century. The dairy, poultry, garden and orchard were then regarded as peculiarly the domain of the mistress, but upon the larger farms she did not herself undertake the household drudgery. Her duty was to organise and train her servants, both men and women.

The wages assessments of the period give some idea of the size of farmers' households, fixing wages for the woman servant taking charge of maulting in great farms, every other maulster, the best mayde servant that can brewe, bake and dresse meate, the second mayd servant, the youngest mayd servant, a woman being skilful in ordering a house, dayry mayd, laundry mayd, and also for the men-servants living in the house, the bailiff of husbandry, the chief hinde, and the common man servant, the shepherd, and the carter.

That some women already aspired to a life of leisure is shown in an assessment for the East Riding of Yorkshire, which provides a special rate of wages for the woman servant " that taketh charge of brewing, baking, kitching, milk house or malting, that is hired with a gentleman or rich yeoman, whose wife doth not take the pains and charge upon her."[1]

In addition to the management of the dairy, etc., the farmer's wife often undertook the financial side of the business. Thus Josselin notes in his Diary : " This day was good wife Day with mee ; I perceive she is resolved to give mee my price for my farme of Mallories, and I intend to lett it goe." A few days later he enters " This day I surrendered Mallories and the appurtenances to Day of Halsted and his daughter."[2]

---

[1] Rogers (J. E. Thorold), *Hist. Agric. and Prices*, Vol. VI., pp. 686-9, assess. for Yorks, East Riding, Ap. 26, 1593.

[2] Josselin (R), *Diary*, p. 86, April 9th, and 30th, 1650.

The farmer's wife attended market with great
regularity, where she became thoroughly expert in the
art of buying and selling. The journey to market
often involved a long ride on horseback, not always
free from adventure as is shown by information given
to the Justices by Maud, wife of Thomas Collar of
Woolavington, who stated that as she was returning
home by herself from Bridgwater market on or about
7th July, Adrian Towes of Marke, overtook her and
calling her ugly toad demanded her name; he then
knocked her down and demanded her purse, to which,
hiding her purse, she replied that she had bestowed
all her money in the market. He then said, ' I think
you are a Quaker,' & she denied it, he compelled her
to kneel down on her bare knees and swear by
the Lord's blood that she was not, which to save her
life she did. Another woman then came up and
rebuked the said Towes, whereupon he struck her down
' atwhart ' her saddle into one of her panniers.[1]

Market was doubtless the occasion of much gossip,
but it may also have been the opportunity for a wide
interchange of views and opinions on subjects important to the well-being of the community. While
market was frequented by all the women of the
neighbourhood it must certainly have favoured
the formation of a feminine public opinion on current
events, which prevented individual women from
relying exclusively upon their husbands for information and advice.

The names of married women constantly appear in
money transactions, their receipt being valid for
debts due to their husbands. Thus Sarah Fell enters
in her Household Book, " Pd. Bridget Pind[r] in full
of her Husband's bills as appeares £3. 17s. 6d."[2] by m°
p[d] Anthony Towers wife in p[t] fo[r] manne[r] wee are to

---

[1] *Somerset Quarter Sessions Records*, Vol. III, pp. 370-1, 1659.

[2] *Fell (Sarah) Household Accounts*, p, 317, 1676.

have of he[r] 1.00[1] to m[o] Rec[d]. of Myles Gouth wife fo[r] ploughing for her 1.04 "[2]

Arithmetic was not considered a necessary item in the education of girls, though as the following incident shows, women habitually acted in financial matters.

Samuel Bownas had been sent to gaol for tithe, but the Parson could not rest and let him out, when he went to Bristol on business and spent two weeks visiting meetings in Wiltshire. After his return, while away from home a distant relation called and asked his wife to lend him ten pounds as he was going to a fair. She not thinking of tithe which was much more, lent it and he gave her a note, which action was approved by her husband on his return; but the relation returned again in Samuel Bownas's absence to repay, and tore the note as soon as he received it, giving her a quittance for the tithe instead. She was indignant, saying it would destroy her husband's confidence in her. The relation assured her that he would declare her innocence, but he could not· have persuaded her husband, for "he would have started so many questions that I could not possibly have affected it any other way than by ploughing with his heifer."[3]

Women's names frequently occur in presentments at Quarter Sessions for infringements of bye laws. The Salford Portmote "p' sent Isabell the wyef of Edmunde Howorthe for that she kept her swyne unlawfull, and did trespas to the corn of the said Raphe Byrom."[4]

Katharine Davie was presented " for not paving before her doore." Mrs. Elizabeth Parkhurst for

[1] *Fell (Sarah), Household Accounts*, p. 339, 1676.

[2] *Ibid*, p. 386, 1677.

[3] *Bownas (Samuel), Life*, pp. 116-17.

[4] *Salford Portmote Records*, Vol. I, p. 3, 1597.

" layinge a dunghill anenst her barne and not makinge the street cleane." Isabell Dawson and Edmund Cowper for the like and Mrs. Byrom and some men "for letting swyne go unringed and trespassinge into his neighbors corne & rescowinge them when they have beene sent to the fould."[1] " Charles Gregorie's wife complained that shee is distrained for 3s. for an amerciament for hoggs goeing in the Streete whereupon, upon her tendring of 3s. xijd is restored with her flaggon."[2] The owner of the pig appears very often to be a married woman. At Carlisle in 1619: ,' We amarye the wief of John Barwicke for keping of swine troughes in the hye streyt contrary the paine and therefore in amercyment according to the orders of this cyttie, xiid."[3]

Such women may often not have been farmers in the full sense of the word, but merely kept a few pigs to supplement the family income. Even the gentry were not too proud to sell farm and garden produce not needed for family consumption, and are alluded to as " . . . our Country Squires, who sell Calves and Runts, and their Wives perhaps Cheese and Apples."[4]

Many gentlewomen were proficient in dairy management. Richard Braithwaite writes of his wife :

> " Oft have I seen her from her Dayrey come
> Attended by her maids, and hasting home
> To entertain some Guests of Quality
> Shee would assume a state so modestly
> Sance affectation, as she struck the eye
> With admiration of the stander-by."

The whole management of the milch cows belonged to the wife, not only among farming people but also

---

[1] *Salford Portmote Records*, Vol. II., pp. 6-7, 1633.

[2] Guilding. *Reading Records*, Vol. IV., p. 512, 1653.

[3] Ferguson, *Municipal Records of Carlisle*, p. 278.

[4] Howell, *Familiar Letters*, p. 290, 1644.

among the gentry. The proceeds were regarded as
her pin-money, and her husband generally handed over
to her all receipts on this account, Sir John Foulis
for example entering in his account book : " June 30
1693. To my wife ye pryce of ye gaird kowes
Hyde, £4 0 0."[1]

Sometimes when the husband devoted himself to
good fellowship, the farm depended almost entirely
on his wife ; this was the case with Adam Eyre, a
retired Captain, who enters in his Dyurnall,
Feb. 10, 1647, " This morning Godfrey Bright
bought my horse of my wife, and gave her £5, and
promised to give her 20s. more, which I had all but
20s. and shee is to take in the corne sale £4." *May* 18,
1647, " I came home with Raph Wordsworth of the
Water hall who came to buy a bull on my wife, who
was gone into Holmefrith."[2]

The business capacity of married women was even
more valuable in families where the father wished to
devote his talents to science, politics, or religion, unencumbered by anxiety for his children's maintenance.
It is said in Peter Heylin's Life that " Being deprived
of Ecclesiastical preferments, he must think of some
honest way for a livelihood. Yet notwithstanding he
followed his studies, in which was his chief delight. . .
. . In which pleasing study while he spent his time, his
good wife, a discreet and active lady, looked both after
her Housewifery within doors, and the Husbandry
without ; thereby freeing him from that care and
trouble, which otherwise would have hindered his
laborious Pen from going through so great a work in
that short time. And yet he had several divertise-
ments by company, which continually resorted to his
house ; for having (God be thanked) his temporal
Estate cleared from Sequestration, by his Composition

[1] Foulis (Sir John, of Ravelston), *Acct. Bk*, p. 158.

[2] Eyre, (Capt. Adam), *A Dyurnall*, p. 16, p. 36.

with the Commissioners at *Goldsmith's Hall*, and this Estate which he Farmed besides, he was able to keep a good House, and relieve his poor brethren."[1]

Gregory King's father was a student of mathematics, " and practised surveying of land, and dyalling, as a profession ; but with more attention to *good-fellowship*, than mathematical studies generally allow : and, the care of the family devolved of course on the mother, who, if she had been less obscure, had emulated the-most eminent of the Roman matrons."[2]

Adam Martindale's wife was equally successful. He writes " about Michaelmas, 1662, I removed my family from the Vicarage to a little house at Camp-greene, . . . where we dwelt above three years and half . . . I was three score pounds in debt, . . . but (God be praised) while I staid there I paid off all that debt and bestowed £40 upon mareling part of my ground in Tatton. . . . If any aske how this could be without a Miracle, he may thus be satisfied. I had sent me . . . £41 . . . and the £10 my wife wrangled out of my successor, together with a table, formes and ceiling, sold him for about £4 more."[3] Later on he adds " My family finding themselves straitened for roome, and my wife being willing to keep a little stock of kine, as she had done formerly, and some inconvenience falling out (as is usual) by two families under a roofe, removed to a new house not completely furnished."[4]

That in the agricultural community women were generally supposed to be, from a business point of view, a help and not a hindrance to their husbands— that in fact the wife was not " kept " by him but helped him to support the family is shown by terms proposed

---

[1] *Heylin*, (*Peter*), pp. 18-19.

[2] King (Gregory), *Natural and Political Observations, etc.*

[3] *Martindale*, (*Adam*,) *Life*, p. 172.

[4] *Ibid*, p. 190.

for colonists in Virginia by the Merchant Taylors who offer "one hundred acres for every man's person that hath a trade, or a body able to endure day labour as much for his wief, as much for his child, that are of yeres to doe service to the Colony."[1]

B. *Husbandmen.*

Husbandmen were probably the most numerous class in the village community. Possessed of a small holding at a fixed customary rent and with rights of grazing on the common, they could maintain a position of independence.

Statute 31 Eliz., forbidding the erection of cottages without four acres of land attached, was framed with the intention of protecting the husbandman against the encroachments of capitalists, for a family which could grow its own supply of food on four acres of land would be largely independent of the farmer, as the father could earn the money for the rent, etc., by working only at harvest when wages were highest. As however this seasonal labour was not sufficient for the farmers' demands, such independence was not wholly to their mind, and they complained of the idleness of husbandmen who would not work for the wages offered. Thus it was said that " In all or most towns, where the fields lie open there is a new brood of upstart intruders or inmates . . . loiterers who will not work unless they may have such excessive wages as they themselves desire."[2] " There is with us now rather a scarcity than a superfluity of servants, their wages being advanced to such an extraordinary height, that they are likely ere long to be masters and their masters servants, many poor husbandmen being forced to pay near as much to their servants for wages as to their landlords for rent."[3]

---

[1] Clode, (C.M.) *Merchant Taylors*, Vol. I., p. 323.

[2] Pseudonismus, *Considerations concerning Common Fields and Enclosures,* 1654.

[3] Pseudonismus, *A Vindication of the Considerations concerning Common Fields and Enclosures,* 1656.

The holdings of the husbandmen varied fom seven acres or more to half an acre or even less of garden ground, in which as potatoes[1] were not yet grown in England the crop consisted of wheat, barley, rye, oats, or peas. Very likely there was a patch of hemp or flax and an apple-tree or two, a cherry tree and some elder-berries in the hedge, with a hive or two of bees in a warm corner. Common rights made it possible to keep sheep and pigs and poultry, and the possession of a cow definitely lifted the family above the poverty line.

Dorothy Osborne describing her own day to her lover, gives an idyllic picture of the maidens tending cows on the common : " The heat of the day is spent in reading or working, and about six or seven o'clock I walk out into a common that lies hard by the house, where a great many young wenches keep sheep and cows, and sit in the shade singing of ballads. I go to them and compare their voices and beauties to some ancient shepherdesses that I have read of, and find a vast difference there ; but trust me, I think these are as innocent as those could be. I talk to them and find they want nothing to make them the happiest people in the world but the knowledge that they are so. Most commonly, when we are in the midst of our discourse, one looks about her, and spies her cows going into the corn, and then away they all run as if they had wings at their heels. I, that am not so nimble, stay behind, and when I see them driving home their cattle, I think 'tis time for me to retire too."[2]

Husbandmen have been defined as a class who could not subsist entirely upon their holdings, but must to some extent work for wages. Their need for wages varied according to the size of their holding and according to the rent. For copy-holders the rent

---

[1] Potatoes were already in use in Ireland, but are scarcely referred to during this period by English writers.

[2] Osborne (Dorothy), Letters, pp. 103,4. 1652-1654.

was usually nominal,[1] but in other cases the husbandman was often forced to pay what was virtually a rack rent. Few other money payments were necessary and if the holding was large enough to produce sufficient food, the family had little cause to fear want.

Randall Taylor wrote complacently in 1689 that in comparison with the French peasants, " Our *English* husbandmen are both better fed and taught, and the poorest people here have so much of brown Bread, and the Gospel, that by the Calculations of our *Bills* of *Mortality* it appears, that for so many years past but One of Four Thousand is starved."[2]

The woman of the husbandman class was muscular and well nourished. Probably she had passed her girlhood in service on a farm, where hard work, largely in the open air, had sharpened her appetite for the abundant diet which characterised the English farmer's housekeeping. After marriage, much of her work was still out of doors, cultivating her garden and tending pigs or cows, while her husband did his day's work on neighbouring farms. Frugal and to the last degree laborious were her days, but food was still sufficient and her strength enabled her to bear healthy children and to suckle them. It was exactly this class of woman that the gentry chose as wet nurses for their babies. Their lives would seem incredibly

---

[1] 30s. Susanna Suffolke a young maid holds a customary cottage, . . . and renteth per annum 2d.

£28 Eliz. Filoll (widdow) holdeth one customary tenement. Rent per annum 26s. 8d.

£2 Mary Stanes holdeth one customary cottage (late of Robert Stanes) and renteth per annum 7d.

£12 Margaret Dowe (widdow) holdeth one customary tenement (her eldest son the next heir) rent 7s. 8d.

Among freeholders. Johan Mathew (widow) holdeth one free tenement and one croft of land thereto belonging . . . containing three acres and a half and renteth 3d.

(Stones, Jolley. 1628. From a List of Copyholders in West & S. Haningfield, Essex.)

[2] Taylor. (Randall), *Discourse of the Growth of England, etc.*, p. 96, 1689.

hard to the modern suburban woman, but they had their reward in the respect and love of their families and in the sense of duties worthily fulfilled.

The more prosperous husbandmen often added to their households an apprentice child, but in other cases the holdings were too small to occupy even the family's whole time.

At harvest in any case all the population of the village turned out to work ; men, women, and children, not only those belonging to the class of husbandmen, but the tradesmen as well, did their bit in a work so urgent ; for in those days each district depended on its own supply of corn, there being scarcely any means of transport.

Except during the harvest, wages were so low that a man who had a holding of his own was little tempted to work for them, though he might undertake some special and better-paid occupation, such as that of a shepherd. Pepys, describing a visit to Epsom, writes : " We found a shepherd and his little boy reading, far from any houses or sight of people, the Bible to him, I find he had been a servant in my Cozen Pepys's house . . . the most like one of the old patriarchs that ever I saw in my life . . . he values his dog mightily, . . . about eighteen score sheep in his flock, he hath four shillings a week the year round for keeping of them."[1]

Probably this picturesque shepherd belonged to the class of husbandmen, for the wages paid are higher than those of a household servant. Four shillings a week comes to £10. 8. o by the year, whereas a Wiltshire wages assessment for 1685 provided that a servant who was a chief shepherd looking after 1,500 sheep or more was not to receive more than £5 by the year.[2] On the other hand, four shillings a week would not

---

[1] Pepys, Vol. IV, p. 428. 14 July, 1667.

[2] *Hist. MSS. Miss. Com. Var. Coll.*, Vol. I. .p. 170.

maintain completely the shepherd, his boy and a dog, not to speak of a wife and other children. Thus, while the shepherd tended his sheep, we may imagine his wife and children were cultivating their allotment.

The wages for the harvest work of women as well as men, were fixed by the Quarter Sessions.[1] References to their work may be found in account books and diaries. Thus Dame Nicholson notes : " *Aug.* 13, 1690, I began to sher ye barin croft about 11 o'clock, ther was Gordi Bar and his wife—also Miler's son James and his sister Margit also a wife called Nieton— they sher 17 threv and 7 chivis."[2]

Best gives a detailed account of the division of work between men and women on a Yorkshire farm : " Wee have allwayes one man, or else one of the ablest of the women, to abide on the mowe, besides those that goe with the waines.[3] The best sort of men-shearers have usually 8d. a day and are to meate themselves ; the best sorte of women shearers have (most commonly) 6d. a day.[4] It is usuall in some places (wheare the furres of the landes are deepe worne with raines)

---

[1] A comparison of the assessments which have been preserved, in the different counties shows that men's earnings varied in the hay harvest from :—

  4d. and meat and drink, or 8d. without, to
8d. „ „ „ „ „ 1s. 4d. „
and in the corn harvest from :—

  5d. and meat and drink, or 10d. without, to
1s. „ „ „ „ „ 2s. „
Women's wages varied in the hay harvest from :—

  1d. and meat and drink, or 4d. without, to
6d. „ „ „ „ „ 1s. „
and in the corn harvest from :—

  2d. and meat and drink, or 6d. without, to
6d. „ „ „ „ „ 1s. „

The variations in these wages correspond with the price of corn in different parts of England and must not be regarded as necessarily representing differences in the real value of wages.

[2] Society of Antiquarians of Scotland, vol. xxxix, p. 125. *Dame Margaret Nicholson's Account Book.*

[3] Best, *Rural Economy*, p. 36.

[4] *Ibid*, p. 42.

to imploy women, with wain-rakes, to gather the corne
out of the said hollow furres after that the sweath-
rakes have done.[1] . . We use meanes allwayes to gett
eyther 18 or else 24 pease pullers, which wee sette
allways sixe on a lande, viz., a woman and a man, a
woman and a man, a woman or boy and a man, etc.,
the weakest couple in the fore furre. . . it is usuall
in most places after they gette all pease pulled, or the
last graine downe, to invite all the worke-folkes and
wives (that helped them that harvest) to supper, and
then have they puddinges, bacon, or boyled beefe,
flesh or apple pyes, and then creame brought in platters,
and every one a spoone ; then after all they have
hotte cakes and ale ; some will cutte theire cake
and putte into the creame and this feaste is called the
creame-potte or creame-kitte . . . wee send
allwayes, the daye before wee leade, [pease] two of our
boys, or a boy and one of our mayds with each of them a
shorte mowe forke to turn them."[2]

For thatching, Best continues : " Wee usually provide
two women for helpes in this kinde, viz, one to drawe
thacke, and the other to serve the thatcher ; she that
draweth thacke hath 3d. a day, and shee that serveth
the thatcher 4d. a day, because shee also is to temper
the morter, and to carry it up to the toppe of the
howse . . . Shee that draweth thatch shoulde
always have dry wheate strawe . . . whearewith
to make her bandes for her bottles. She that serveth
will usually carry up 4 bottles at a time, and sometimes but 3 if the thatch bee longe and very wette."[3]

---

[1] Best, *Rural Economy*, p.59.

[2] *Ibid*, pp. 93-4.

[3] *Ibid*, pp. 138-9. " The thatchers," Best says, " have in most places 6d. a day
& theire meate in Summer time, . . . yett we neaver use to give them above 4d . . .
. . . because their dyett is not as in other places ; for they are to have three meale
a day, *viz*. theire breakfaste att eight of the clocke, . . . theire dinner about twelve and
theire supper about seaven or after when they leave worke ; and att each meale.
fower services, viz. butter, milke, cheese, and either egges, pyes, or bacon, and sometimes porridge insteade of milke : if they meate themselves they have usually 10d.
a day."

" Spreaders of mucke and molehills are (for the
most parte) women, boyes and girles, the bigger and
abler sorte of which have usually 3d. a day, and the
lesser sorte of them 2d. a day."[1] " Men that pull
pease have 8d. women 6d. a day."[2]

A picture of hay-harvesting in the West of England
given by Celia Fiennes suggests that in other parts of
England to which she was accustomed, the labour,
especially that of women, was not quite so heavy.
All over Devon and Cornwall she says, hay is carried
on the horses' backs and the people " are forced to
support it wth their hands, so to a horse they have
two people, and the women leads and supports them,
as well as y[e] men and goe through thick and thinn.
. . . I wondred at their Labour in this kind, for
the men and the women themselves toiled Like their
horses."[3]

There was hardly any kind of agricultural work from
which women were excluded. Everenden " payed
1s. 2d. to the wife of Geo. Baker for shearing 28 sheep."[4]
In Norfolk the wages for a " woman clipper of sheepe "
were assessed at 6d. per day with meat and drink, 1s.
without, while a man clipper was paid 7d. and 14d.
It is noteworthy that only 4d. per day was allowed in the
same assessment for the diet of " women and such
impotent persons that weed corn and other such like
Laborers " and 2d. per day for their wages.[5] Pepys
on his visit to Stonehenge " gave the shepherd-
woman, for leading our horses, 4d.,"[6] while Foulis
enters, " Jan. 25, 1699 to tonie to give ye women at

---

[1] Best, *Rural Economy*, p. 140.

[2] *Ibid*, p. 142.

[3] Fiennes (Celia), *Through England on a Side-saddle*, p. 225.

[4] Suss. Arch. Coll. Vol. IV., p. 24. *Everendon Account Book*

[5] Tingye (J. C.) *Eng. Hist. Rev*, Vol. XIII., pp. 525-6.

[6] Pepys, Vol. V., p. 302. (11th June, 1668).

restalrig for making good wailings of strae, 4s. (Scots money)."[1]

But the wives of husbandmen were not confined to agricultural work as is shown by many payments entered to them in account books :[2] Thus the church wardens at Strood, in Kent, paid the widow Cable for washing the surplices 1s.[3] ; and at Barnsley they gave " To Ricard Hodgaris wife for whipping dogs " (out of the Church) 2s.[4] while " Eustace Lowson of Salton (a carrier of lettres and a verie forward, wicked woman in that folly) and Isabell her daughter are included in a Yorkshire list of recusants.[5]

No doubt the mother with young children brought them with her to the harvest field, where they played as safely through the long summer day as if they and she had been at home. But at other times she chose work which did not separate her from her children, spinning being her unfailing resource. It is difficult living in the age of machinery to imagine the labour which clothing a family by hand-spinning involved, though the hand-spun thread was durable and fashions did not change.

In spite of the large demand the price paid was very low, but when not obliged to spin for sale,

---

[1] Foulis (Sir John) *Acct. Bk.*, p. 246.

[2] " Aug. 7th. 1701 to my wife, to a Bleicher wife at bonaley for bleitching 1. 3. 4." (Scots)

" Jan. 28th, 1703 to my good douchter jennie to give tibbie tomsome for her attendance on my wife the time of her sickness 5.16.0 (Scots). (*Foulis (Sir John) Acct. Bk.* p. 295, 314.)

" Sep. 11th, 1676, pd. her (Mary Taylor) more for bakeing four days. Mothers Acct. 8d. (*Fell, (Sarah) Household Accts.* p. 309.)

" Pd. Widow Lewis for gathering herbs two daies 6d. (Sussex, Arch. Coll. xlviii. p. 120. *Extracts from the Household Account Book of Herstmonceux Castle.*)

Paid to goodwife Stopinge for 2 bundles of Rushes at Whitsuntide for the Church, iiijd. (*Churchwarden's Account Book, Strood*, p. 95, 1612.

[3] *Churchwarden's Account Book, Strood*, p. 197. 1666.

[4] Cox (J. C.) *Churchwarden's Accts.*, p. 309.

[5] *Yorks. North Riding, Q. S. Rec.*, Vol. I,, p. 62, Jan. 8. 1606-7.

time was well spent in spinning for the family.
The flax or hemp grown on the allotment, was
stored up for shirts and house-linen. If the husbandman had no sheep, the children gathered scraps of
wool from the brambles on the common, and thus
the only money cost of the stuff worn by the
husbandman's household was the price paid to the
weaver.

The more prosperous the family, the less the mother
went outside to work, but this did not mean, as under
modern conditions, that her share in the productive
life of the country was less. Her productive energy
remained as great, but was directed into channels
from which her family gained the whole profit. In
her humble way she fed and clothed them, like the
wise woman described by Solomon.

The more she was obliged to work for wages, the
poorer was her family.

C. *Wage-earners.*

In some respects it is less difficult to visualise the
lives of women in the wage-earning class than in the
class of farmers and husbandmen. The narrowness
of their circumstances and the fact that their destitution brought them continually under the notice
of the magistrates at Quarter Sessions have preserved
data in greater completeness from which to reconstruct
the picture. Had this information been wanting
such a reconstruction would have demanded no vivid
imagination, because the results of the semi-
starvation of mothers and small children are very
similar whether it takes place in the seventeenth or
the twentieth century ; the circumstances of the
wives of casual labourers and men who are out of work
and " unemployable " in modern England may
be taken as representing those of almost the whole
wage-earning class in the seventeenth century.

The most important factors governing the lives of
wage-earning women admit of no dispute. First

among these was their income, for wage-earners have already been defined as the class of persons depending wholly upon wages for the support of their families.

Throughout the greater part of the seventeenth century the rate of wages was not left to be adjusted by the laws of supply and demand, but was regulated for each locality by the magistrates at Quarter Sessions. Assessments fixing the maximum rates were published annually and were supposed to vary according to the price of corn. Certainly they did vary from district to district according to the price of corn in that district, but they were not often changed from year to year.

Prosecutions of persons for offering and receiving wages in excess of the maximum rates frequently occurred in the North Riding of Yorkshire, but it is extremely rare to find a presentment for this in other Quarter Sessions. The Assessments were generally accepted as publishing a rate that public opinion considered fair towards master and man, and outside Yorkshire steps were seldom taken to prevent masters from paying more to valued servants. That upon the whole the Assessments represent the rate ordinarily paid can be shown by a comparison with entries in contemporary account-books.

The Assessments deal largely with the wages of unmarried farm servants and with special wages for the seasons of harvest, intended for the occasional labour of husbandmen, but in addition there are generally rates quoted by the day for the common labourer in the summer and winter months. Even when meat and drink is supplied, the day-rates for these common labourers are higher than the wages paid to servants living in the house and are evidently intended for married men with families.

In one Assessment different rates are expressly given for the married and unmarried who are doing the same work,[1] a married miller receiving with his meat and drink, 4d. a day which after deducting holidays would amount to £5 0 0 by the year, while the unmarried miller has only 46s. 8d. and a pair of boots.

Assessments generally show a similar difference between the day-wages of a common labourer and the wages of the best man-servant living in the house, and it may therefore be assumed that day labourers were generally married persons.

Day rates were only quoted for women on seasonal jobs, such as harvest and weeding. It was not expected that married women would work all the year round for wages, and almost all single women were employed as servants.

The average wage of the common agricultural labourer as assessed at Quarter Sessions was 3½d. per day in winter, and 4½d. per day in summer, in addition to his meat and drink. Actual wages paid confirm

---

[1] " A shoemaker servant of the best sorte being married, to have without m-ate and drinke for every dosin of shoes   xxijd.
ditto unmarried to have by the yeare with meat and drink and withowte a leverye
                                                                                                                        liijs.
Millers and drivers of horses beinge batchelors then with meate and drinke and without a liverye and a payre of boots   xlvis viijd.
Millers and drivers of horses beinge married men shall not take more by the daye then with meate and drinke   ivd. and without viijd.
a man servant of the best sorte shall not have more by the yeare then with a levereye   xls. and without xlvjs viiid.
the same, of the thirde sorte has only with a leverye
                                                                        xxvjs viiid. and without xxxiijs iiijd.
while any sort of labourer, from the Annunciation of our Ladye until Michellmas has with meat and drink by the day   ivd. and without viijd.
From Michellmas to the Annunciation   iiid. and without vijd.
The best sorte of women servants shall not have more by the yeare than with a liverye   xxjs. and without xxvjs viiid.
while " a woman reaping of corne " shall not have " more by the daye then vd with meat and drink."
                                                        (*Hertfordshire Assessment*, 1591).
Every man-servant serving with any person as a Comber of Wooll to have by the yeare 40s.
Every such servant being a single man and working by ye pound to have by ye pound 1^d.
Every such servant being a marryed man and having served as an apprentice thereto according to the statute to have by ye pound 2^d.
                                                        (*Assessment for Suffolk*, 1630).

the truth of these figures, though it is not always clear whether the payments include meat and drink.[1]

If we accept the Assessments as representing the actual wages earned by the ordinary labourer we can estimate with approximate accuracy the total income of a labourer's family, for we have defined the wage earner as a person who depended wholly upon wages and excluded from this class families who possessed gardens. Taking a figure considerably higher then the one at which the Assessment averages work out, namely 5d. per day instead of 4d. per day, to be the actual earnings of a labouring man in addition to his meat and drink, and doubling that figure for the three months which include the hay and corn harvests, his average weekly earnings will amount to 3s. 2d.

---

[1] Paid to a shovele man for 2 days to shovell in the cart rakes, 2s. (*Hertford Co. Rec.*, Vol. I, p. 233, 1672.) 2¼ days' work of a labourer, 2s. 6d. (*ibid*, p. 130, 1659).

For one daies work for one labourer, 1s. (*Stro.d Churchwarden's Acc.* p. 182, 1662.)

Pd. to James Smith for one days' work thatching about Widow Barber's house, she being in great distress by reason she could not lie down in her bed and could get no help to do the same. 1s. 2d. (*Cratford Parish Papers*, p. 152, 1622.) Thatchers were paid more than ordinary labourers, being generally assessed at the same rate as a carpenter, or a mower in the harvest.

July 15, 1676. Tho. Scott for workeinge hay 2 dayes, 4d.

Tho. Greaves younger for workeinge hay 2 dayes, 4d.

May 5, 1678, Will Braithwt for threshing 6 dayes 1.00

April 27, 1676, by mo. pd. him for thatching 2 days at Petties Tenemt, 8d.

August 2. 1676. pd. Margt Dodgson for workinge at hay & other worke 5 weekes 03.06.

pd. Mary Ashbrner for workinge at hay & other worke 4 weekes & 3 dayes, 03. 0.0.

Sept 4. pd. Will Nicholson wife for weedinge in ye garden & pullinge hempe 12 dayes 01. 0. 0.

Oct. 2. pd. Issa. Atkinson for her daughtr Swingleinge 6 dayes 01. 0. 0.

May. 7, 1677. pd.Will Ashbrner for his daughter harrowing here 2 weekes 01. 0. 0. (*Fell (Sarah), House Acct.*)

Labourers' wages 4d. per day.

(*Hist. MSS. Comm. Var. Coll.* Vol. IV. 133, 1686. Sir Jno. Earl's Inventory of goods.

Weeks' work common labourer, 3s. Thos. West, 1 week's haying 2s. (*Sussex Arch. Coll.*, Vol. IV, p. 24, *Everendon Acc. Book*, 1618.)

Paid for a labourer 3 dayes to hoult the alees and carrying away the weedes, 1s. 6d. (*Cromwell Family, Bills and Receipts*, Vol. II, p. 233, 1635.)

Jan. 26. 1649. Payd. to John Wainwright for 5 days worke 1s. 8d. [Yorkshire]. (*Eyre (Capt. Adam) Dyurnall*, p. 117.)

Thos. Hutton, xiiij days work ijs. iiijd, his wyfe xij dayes iiijs. Thos. Hutton xiiij dayes at hay vid, his wyfe 4 dayes xvjd. Leonell Bell, xiij dayes about hay, vjs. vjd. Tho. Bullman the lyke. iiijs. iiijd, Thos. Hutton 4 dayes at mowing corne, xvjd. *Howard Household Book*, p. 40-41).

Except in exeptional circumstances his wife's earnings would not amount to more than 1s. a week and her meat and drink. The more young children there were, the less often could the wife work for wages, and when not doing so her food as well as the chidren's must be paid for out of the family income.

In a family with three small children it is unlikely that the mother's earnings were more than what would balance days lost by the father for holidays or illness, and the cost of his food on Sundays, but allowing for a small margin we may assume that 3s. 6d. was the weekly income of a labourer's family, and that this sum must provide rent and clothing for the whole family and food for the mother and children.

A careful investigation of the cost of living is necessary before we can test whether this amount was adequate for the family's maintenance.

There is no reason to suppose that a diet inferior to present standards could maintain efficiency in the seventeenth century. On the contrary, the English race at that time attributed their alleged superiority over other nations to a higher standard of living.[1]

---

[1] The dietary in charitable institutions gives an idea of what was considered bare necessity.

(*Children's Diet in Christ Church Hospital*, 1704.)

For breakfast, Bread and Beer. For dinner, Sunday, Tuesday, and Thursday, boiled beef and pottage. Monday, milk pottage, Wednesday, furmity. Friday old pease & pottage. Saturday water gruel. For supper bread and cheese or butter for those that cannot eat cheese. Sunday supper, legs of mutton. Wednesday and Friday, pudding pies.

(*Stow, London, Book* I, p. 182.)

Diet for Workhouse, Bishopsgate Street, London.

They have Breakfasts, dinners, and suppers every day in the week. For each mea 4 oz. bread, 1½ oz. cheese, 1 oz. butter, 1 pint of beer. Breakfast, four days, bread and cheese or butter and beer. Mondays a pint of Pease Pottage, with Bread and Beer. Tuesdays a Plumb Pudding Pye 9 oz. and beer. Wednesdays a pint of Furmity. On Friday a pint of Barley Broth and bread. On Saturdays, a plain Flower Sewet Dumpling with Beer. Their supper always the same, 4 oz. bread, 1½ of cheese or 1 oz. of butter, and beer sufficient. (Stow, *London*, Book I, p. 199).

Lady Grisell Baillie gives her servant's diet:

Sunday they have boild beef and broth made in the great pot, and always the broth made to serve two days. Monday, broth made on Sunday, and a Herring. Tuesday, broth and beef. Wednesday, broth and two eggs each. Thursday, broth and beef. Friday, Broth and herring. Saturday, broth without meat, and cheese, or a pudden

A comparison between the purchasing power of money in the seventeenth and twentieth centuries is unsatisfactory for our purpose, because the relative values of goods have changed so enormously. Thus, though rent, furniture and clothes were much cheaper in the seventeenth century, there was less difference in the price of food. Sixpence per day is often given in Assessments as the cost of a labourer's meat and drink and this is not much below the amount spent per head on these items in wage-earners' families during the first decade of the twentieth century.

One fact alone is almost sufficient to prove the inadequacy of a labourer's wage for the maintenance of his family. His money wages seldom exceeded the estimated cost of his own meat and drink as supplied by the farmer, and yet these wages were to supply all the necessaries of life for his whole family. Some idea of the bare cost of living in a humble household may be gained by the rates fixed for pensions and by allowances made for Poor Relief. From these it appears that four shillings to five shillings a week was considered necessary for an adult's maintenance.

The Cromwell family paid four shillings weekly " to the widd. Bottom for her bord."[1] Pensions for maimed soldiers and widows were fixed at four shillings per week " or else work to be provided which will make their income up to 4s. per week. Sick and wounded soldiers under cure for their wounds to have 4s. 8d per week."[2]

---

or blood-pudens, or a hagish, or what is most convenient. Breakfast and super, ha an oat loaf or a proportion of broun bread, but better set down the loaf, and see non is taken or wasted, and a muchkin of beer or milk whenever there is any. At dinner a mutchkin of beer for each. *Baillie (Lady Grisell). Household Book* pp. 277-8. 1743.

[1] *Cromwell Family, Bills and Receipts*, Vol. II., p. 233, 1635.

[2] *Acts and Ordinances of the Interregnum*, II., p. 536. (For Maimed Soldiers and Widows of Scotland and Ireland, Sept 30, 1651.

The Justices in the North Riding of Yorkshire drew up a scale of reasonable prices for billeted soldiers by which each trooper was to pay for his own meat for each night—6d ; dragoon, 4½d ; foot soldier, 4d.[1]

" Edward Malin, blacksmith, now fourscore and three past and his wife fourscore, wanting a quarter " very poor and unable " to gett anything whereby to live," complained to the Hertfordshire Quarter Sessions that they receive only 1s. 6d. a week between them ; " others have eighteen pence apiece single persons " and desire that an order be made for them to have 3s. together which is but the allowance made to other persons.[2]

In cases of Poor Relief where payments were generally intended to be supplementary to other sources of income, the grants to widows towards the maintenance of their children were often absurdly small ; In Yorkshire, Parish officers were ordered to " provide convenient habitation for a poor woman as they shall think fit and pay her 4d. weekly for the maintenance of herself and child."[3] In another case to pay a very poor widow 6d. weekly for the maintenance of herself and her three children.[4] The allowance of 12d. weekly to a woman and her small children was reduced to 6d., " because the said woman is of able body, and other of her children are able to work."[5] On the other hand when an orphan child was given to strangers to bring up, amounts varying from 1s. to 5s. per week were paid for its maintenance.[6]

---

[1] *Yorks. North Riding, Q. S. Rec.*, Vol. VII., p. 106, 1690.

[2] *Hertfordshire, Co. Rec.*, Vol. I., p. 258, 1675.

[3] *Yorks. N.R. Q.S. Rec.*, Vol. VI., p. 242, 1675.

[4] *Ibid*, p. 217, 1674.

[5] *Ibid*, p. 260, 1674

[6] Joane Weekes . . . " hadd a maide childe placed to her to bee kept & brought upp, the mother of which Childe was executed at the Assizes, six pounds per ann, proporconed toward the keepinge of the said childe . . . besides she

Thus the amount paid by the Justices for maintaining one pauper child sometimes exceeded the total earnings of a labourer and his wife. Other pauper children were maintained in institutions. The girls at a particularly successful Industrial School in Bristol were given an excellent and abundant diet

---

desireth some allowance extraordinary for bringinge the said Childe to bee fitt to gett her livinge." (*Somerset*, Q.S. *Rec.*, Vol. III, p. 28-9, 1647).

In 1663 a woman who was committed to the Castle of Yorke for felony and afterwards executed, was while there delivered of a male child, which was left in the gaol, and as it was not known where the woman was last an inhabitant the child could not be sent to the place of her settlement, Sir Tho. Gower was desired by Justices of Assize to take a course for present maintenance of the child. He caused it to be put unto the wife of John Boswell to be nursed and provided for with other necessaries. John Boswell and his wife have maintained the child ever since and have hitherto received no manner of allowance for the same. Ordered that the several Ridings shall pay their proportions to the maintenance past and present, after the rate of £5 per annum. (*Yorks. N.R. Q.S.Rec.*, Vol. VI, pp. 102-3, 1666.)

Marmaduke Vye was only to have £4 a year for keeping the child born in the gaol of Ivelchester whose mother was hanged for cutting of purses. (*Somerset Q.S. Rec.*, Vol. I, p. 101., 1613.)

Item payd to the said widowe Elkyns for Dyett and keeping of a poore child leafte upon the chardge of the parish at 11d. the weecke from the 14th of August, 1599, till this secound of Sept., 1601, every Saturday, being two yeres and three weeckes, videlicet 107 weeckes in toto v^{li} vijs. (*Ch. Accs.*, St. *Michael's in Bedwendine, Worcester*, p. 147.)

Itm pd. to Batrome's wife of Linstead for keeping of Wright's child 52 weeks £3. 0s. 8d. (Cratfield *Parish Papers*, p. 129, 1602.)

Pd to Geo. Cole to take and bring up Eliz. Wright, the daughter of Ann Wright according to his bond, £4. 0s. 0d. More towards her apparell 5s. (*Ibid*, p. 137. 1609.)

Item paide Chart's Child's keeping by the week £4. 11s. 8d. Item for apparrell £1. 18s. 2d. Item paid to the surgeon for her. 3s. 6d. (*Suss. Arch. Coll.*, Vol. xx., p. 101, *Acct. Bk of Cowden*. 1627.)

for apparrelling Wm. Uridge and for his keeping this yeare £5. 12s. 9d. (*Ibid*, p. 103, 1632.)

For the keep of William Kemsing 14 weeks £1. 2s.8d and 23 weeks at 2s per week, £2. 6s. 0d. and for apparrelling of him; and for his indentures; and for money given with him to put him out apprentice; and expended in placing him out £11. 17s. 9d. (*Ibid*, p. 107, 1650.)

John Mercies wief for keeping Buckles child, weekly,	1s. 6d.
John Albaes wief for keeping Partickes child	1s. 4d.

(*S.P.D.* cccxlvii, 67, 1. Feb, 1637. Answer of Churchwardens to Articles given by J.P's for St. Albans).

George Arnold and Jas. Michell late overseers of the poore of the parishe of Othery . . . had committed a poore child to the custody, keepinge and maintenance of . . . Robert Harris promising him xijd. weekly. (*Somerset*, Q.S. *Rec.*, Vol. III, p. 1, 1646.) Order for Thos. Scott, a poor, lame, impotent child, to be placed with Joanna Brandon; She to be paid 5s. a week for his maintenance. (*Middlesex Co. Rec.*, p. 180, *Sess. Book*, 1698).

at a cost of 1s. 4d. per head per week.[1]   At Stepney, the poor were maintained at 2s. 10d or 3s. per week, including all incidental expenses, firing and lodging. At Strood in Kent, 2s. was paid for children boarded out in poor families, while the inmates of the workhouse at Hanstope, Bucks, were supposed not to cost the parish more than 1s. 6d. a week per head.[2]   At Reading it was agreed " that Clayton's wief shall have xiiiid. a weeke for every poore childe in the hospitall accomptinge each childe's worke in parte of payment.[3]

These and many other similar figures show that a child must have cost from 1s. to 1s. 6d. a week for food alone, the amount varying according to age.   Above seven years of age, children began to contribute towards their own support, but they were not completely self-supporting before the age of thirteen or fourteen.

According to the wages assessments, a woman's diet was reckoned at a lower figure than a man's, but whenever they are engaged on heavy work such as reaping corn or shearing sheep, 6d. or 8d. a day is allowed for their " meate and drinke." On other work, such as weeding or spinning, where only 2d. a day is reckoned for wages, their food also is only estimated as costing 2d. to 4d.   As in such cases they are classed with " other impotent persons " it must not be supposed that 2d. or 3d. represents the cost of the food needed by a young active woman ; it may even have been prolonged semi-starvation that had reduced the woman to the level of impotency.   Unfortunately, there is often a wide difference between the cost of what a woman actually eats and what is necessary to

---

[1] Cary, *Acc. Proceedings of the Corporation of Bristol.* 1700.   " Their diets were made up of such provisions as were very wholesome, viz. Beef, Pease, Potatoes, Broath, Pease-porridge, Milk-porridge, Bread and Cheese, good Beer, Cabage, Carrots, Turnips, etc. it stood us (with soap to wash) in about sixteen pence per week for each of the one hundred girls."

[2] *Account Workhouses,* 1725, p. 13, p. 37, p. 79.

[3] Guilding, *Reading,* Vol. II., p. 273, Jan. 16, 1625-6.

maintain her in efficiency. Probably the woman who was doing ordinary work while pregnant or suckling a baby may have needed as much food as the woman who was reaping corn ; but in the wage-earner's family she certainly did not get it ; thus when a writer[1] alleges that a man's diet costs 5d. a day and a woman's 1s. 6d per week, his statement may be correct as to fact, though the babies have perished for want of nourishment and the mother has been reduced to invalidism.

Another writer gives 2s. as being sufficient to " keep a poor man or woman (with good husbandry) one whole week."[2] Certainly 2s. is the very lowest figure that can have sufficed to keep up the mother's strength. The bare cost of food for a mother and three children must have amounted to at least 5s. 6d. per week, but there were other necessaries to be provided from the scanty wages. The poorest family required some clothes, and though these may have been given by charitable persons, rent remained to be paid. Building was cheap. In Scotland, the " new house " with windows glazed with " ches losens " only cost £4 12s. 3d. to build, while a " cothouse " built for Liddas " the merchant " cost only £1 0 0 ;[3] other cots were built for 4s., 11s. 1d, 5s. and 14s. 4d. These Scottish dwellings were mud hovels, but in England the labourers' dwellings were not much better.

Celia Fiennes describes the houses at the Land's End as being " poor Cottages, Like Barns to Look on, much Like those in Scotland, but to doe my own country its right y[e] Inside of their Little Cottages are Clean and plaister'd and such as you might Comfortably Eat and drink in, and for curiosity sake I dranck there and met with very good bottled ale."[4]

---

[1] Dunning, R. *Plain and Easie Method*, p. 5, 1686.

[2] *Trade of England*, p. 10, 1681.

[3] Baillie (Lady Grisel), *House Book*, Introd. lxiv.

[4] Fiennes (Celia), *Through England on a Side-saddle*, p. 224.

In some places the labourers made themselves habitations on the waste, but this was strictly against the law, such houses being only allowed for the impotent poor.

Many fines are entered in Quarter Sessions Records for building houses without the necessary quantity of land. By 39 Eliz. churchwardens and overseers were ordered, for the relief of the impotent poor, to build convenient houses at the charges of the Parish, but only with the consent of the Lord of the Manor. 43 Eliz. added that such buildings were not at any time after to be used for other inhabitants but only for the impotent poor, placed there by churchwardens and overseers.

The housing problem was so acute that many orders were made by the justices sanctioning or ordering the erection of these cottages. " Rob. Thompson of Brompton and Eliz. Thompson of Aymonderby widow, stand indicted for building a cottage in Aymonderby against the statute, etc., upon a piece of ground, parcell of the Rectorie of Appleton-on-the street, and in which the said Eliz. doth dwell by the permission of John Heslerton, fermour of the said Rectorie, and that the same was so erected for the habitation of the said Eliz[th]. being a poore old woman and otherwise destitute of harbour and succour . . ordered that the said cottage shall continue . . for the space of twelve yeares, if the said Eliz[th]. live so long, or that the said Heslerton's lease do so long endure."[1] In another case, Nicholas Russell, the wife of Thomas Waterton, and Robert Arundell, were presented for erecting cottages upon the Lord's waste . . . at the suit of parishioners these cottages are allowed by Mr. Coningsby, lord of the manor.[2]

It was often necessary to compel unwilling over-

---

[1] *Yorks. N.R. Q.S. Rec.*, Vol. I., p. 29. 1605-6.

Hertfordshire Co. Rec., Vol. I., p. 63, 1639,-41.

seers to build cottages for the impotent poor, and for
widows. " A woman with three children prays leave
for the erection of a cottage in East Bedwyn, she having
no habitation, but depending upon alms ; from lying
in the street she was conveyed into the church where
she remained some small time, but was then ejected by
the parish." The overseers are ordered to provide for
her.[1]

The overseers at Shipley were ordered to build a
house on the waste there for Archelaus Braylsford, to
contain " two chambers floored fit for lodgings " or in
default 5s. a week. At the following sessions his house
was further ordered to be " a convenient habitation
12 feet high upon the side walls soe as to make 2
convenient chambers."[2]

The housing problem however could not be settled
by orders instructing the overseers to build cottages

---

[1] *Hist., MSS. Com. Var. Coll.*, Vol. I, p. 113, *Wilts. Q.S.Rec.* 1646.

[2] Cox. *Derbyshire Annals*, Vol. II, p. 176, 1693.
The following cases are representative of an immense number of petitions from
widows and the impotent poor :

1608. Margaret Johns having dwelt in Naunton Beauchamp for 55 years has now
no house or room but dwells in a barn, she desires to have house room and will not
charge the parish so long as she is able to work.

1620. Eleanor Williams charged with keeping of young child is now unprovided
with house room for herself and her poor child, her husband having left the soile
where they lately dwelled and is gone to some place to her unknown. She is
willing " to relieve her child by her painful labour but wanteth a place for abode "
prays to be provided with house room.
(Bund, J. W. Willis, *Worcestershire Co. Records*, Vol. I., pp. 116-7, 337).

1621. Overseers of Uggliebarbie to provide a suitable dwelling for 2 women
(sisters) if they refuse them a warrant, etc. (*Yorks. North Riding Q.S. Recs.*, Vol.
III., p. 118.)

1672. Parish Officers of Scruton to provide a convenient habitation for Mary
Hutchinson and to set her on work, and provide for her, etc., until she shall recover
the possession of certain lands in Scruton. (*Ibid*, Vol. VI., p. 175).

1684. Mary Marchant . . . livinge in good estimation And repute for many years
together ; being very Carefull to maintaine herself And family for being prejudice
to ye sd. Towne ; ye petitioners husbande beinge abrpad and driven Away ; and
returninge not backe Againe to her leaveinge ye petitioner with a little girle ; being
In want was put into a little cottage by & with ye consent of ye sd. Towne ; ye sd.
Owner of ye sd. Tenement comeinge when ye petitioner was gon forth to worke
leavinge her little girle in ye sd. house ; ye sd. Owner get a locke And Key upp on ye
door, where as your petitioner cannot Injoy her habitation wth peace and quietness ;
soe yt your petitioner is likely to starve for want of A habitation and child, etc.
(Cox. J. C., *Derbyshire Annals*, Vol. II., pp. 175-6, *Q.S. Recs.*, 1684).

for the impotent poor alone. Petitions were received as often from able-bodied labourers and for them the law forbade the erection of a cottage without four acres of land attached. The magistrates had no power to compel the provision of the land and thus they were faced with the alternatives of breaking the law and sanctioning the erection of a landless cottage on the waste or else leaving the labourer's family to lie under hedges. The following petitions illustrate the way in which this situation was faced :

George Grinham, Norton-under-Hambton, " in ye behalfe of himselfe, his poore wife and famelye " begged for permission " for my building y^{er}, of a little poor house for ye comfort of my selfe, my poore wife and children betwixt those other 2 poore houses erected on the glebe . . . being a towne borne childe y^{er} myselfe."[1]

Another from William Dench, " a very poor man and having a wife and seven children all born at Longdon," who was destitute of any habitation, states that he was given by William Parsons of Longdon, yeoman, in charity, " a little sheep-cote which sheep cote petitioner, with the consent of the church-wardens and overseers converted to a dwelling. Afterwards he having no licence from Quarter Sessions, nor under the hands of the Lord of the Manor so to do, and the sheepcote being on the yeoman's freehold and not on the waste or common, contrary to Acts 43 Eliz. c. 2 and 31 Eliz. c. 7 he was indicted upon the Statute against cottages and sued to an outlawry. He prays the benefit of the King's pardon and for licence in open session for continuance of his habitation." [2]

Eliz. Shepperd of Windley alleged she " was in possession of a Certayne cottage situate in Chevin, which was pulled downe and taken away by the

---

[1] *Somerset, Q.S. Rec.*, Vol. I., p. 41, 1609.

[2] *Hist. MSS. Com. Var. Coll.*, Vol. I., p. 296, *Worcestershire, Q.S. Rec.*, 1617.

Inhabitants of Dooeffield, shee left without habitation and hath soe Continued Twelve months at the least, shee being borne in Windley, and hath two small children " prayed the inhabitants should find her a homestead—the case was adjourned because the overseers raised a technical objection ; that Eliz. Shepherd was married, & a woman's petition could only proceed from a spinster or widow—meanwhile another child was born, and at the Michaelmas Sessions a joint petition was presented by Ralph Shepherd and Eliz. his wife, with the result that " the overseers are to find him habitation or show cause."[1]

Joseph Lange of Queene Camell " being an honest poore laborer and havinge a wife and 2 smale Children " prayed that he " might haue libertie to erect a Cottage uppon a wast ground " . . . This was assented to " for the habitacon of himselfe for his wife and afterwards the same shall be converted to the use of such other poore people etc."

Order that Robert Morris of Overstowey, husbandman, a very poor man having a wife and children, and no place of habitation " soe that hee is like to fall into greate misery for want thereof " may erect and build him a cottage on some part of the " wast " of the manor of Overstowey . . . (subject to the approbation of the Lord of the said Manor)."[2]

The predicament of married labourers is shown again in the following report to the Hertfordshire Quarterly Sessions : " John Hawkins hath erected a cottage on the waste of my mannour of Benington, in consideration of the great charge of his wife and children that the said Hawkins is to provide for, I do hereby grant and give leave to him to continue the said cottage during his life and good behaviour."[3]

---

[1] Cox, J. C. *Derbyshire Annals*, Vol. II., pp. 173-4, 1649.

[2] *Somerset Q.S. Rec.*, Vol. III., pp. 29, 58.

[3] *Hertford Co. Rec.*, Vol. I., p. 100, 1652.

Labourers naturally were unwilling to hire cottages while there was a possibility of inducing the justices to provide one on the waste rent free. The church-wardens of Great Wymondley forwarded a certificate stating " that the poor people of the said parish that are old and not able to work are all provided for and none of the poor people of the said parish have been driven to wander into other unions to beg or ask relief, for this thirty years last past. This Nathaniel Thrussel, which now complains, is a lusty young man, able to work and always brought up to husbandry, his wife, a young woman, always brought up to work, and know both how to perform their work they are hired to do, and have at present but one child, but did not care to pay rent for a hired house when he had one nor endeavour to hire a house for himself when he wants."[1]

The scarcity of cottages resulted in extortionate rents for those that existed ; Best noted that in his district " Mary Goodale and Richard Miller have a cottage betwixt them ; Mary Goodale hath two roomes, and the orchard and payeth 6s. per annum ; and Richard Miller, hayth one roomestead and payeth 4s. per annum. . . . They usually lette their cottages hereaboutes, for 10s. a piece, although they have not soe much as a yard, or any backe side belonging to them."[2]

The rents paid elsewhere are shown in the returns made in 1635 by the Justices of the Peace for the Hundreds of Blofield and Walsham in Norfolk concerning cottages and inmates :

Thos. Waters hath 3 inmates :

Wm. Wyley   pays £1. per annum
Anthony Smith „   £1. per annum
Roger Goat   „   12s. per annum

" which are all poore labourers and have wifes and

---

[1] *Hertford Co. Rec.*, Vol. I., p. 370, 1687.

[2] Best, *Rural Econ.*, p. 125.

severall children and if they be put out cannot be
provided in this towne and by reason of their charge
and poverty are not likely to be taken elsewhere."
" Wm. Browne hath 2 inmates :
    Edmund Pitt   14s. per annum
    Wm. Jostling   14s. per annum
that are very poor and impotent and take colleccion.
Wm. Reynoldes hath 2 inmates :
    Anthony Durrant   £1 16s. per annum
    Wm. Yurely   16s. per annum
both are very poore labourers and have wifes and small
children. Jas. Candle owner of a cottage [has] Robert
Fenn, 13s. a poore man. Anne Linckhorne 1 inmate
Philip Blunt that pay £1. 17. 0 that is a poore man and
hath wife and children."[1]

Thus it appears that while a labourer who obtained
a cottage on the waste lived rent free, twenty or
thirty shillings might be demanded from those who
were less fortunate.

Whatever money was extorted for rent meant
so much less food for the mother and children, for it
has been shown that the family income was insufficient for food alone, and left no margin for rent or
clothes.

The relation of wages to the cost of living is seldom
alluded to by contemporary writers, but a pamphlet
published in 1706 says of a labourer's family, " a poor
Man and his Wife may have 4 or 5 children, 2 of them
able to work, and 3 not able, and the Father and Mother
not able to maintain themselves and Families in
Meat, Drink, Cloaths and House Rent under 10s.
a week."[2]

A similar statement is made by Sir Matthew Hale,
who adds " and so much they might probably get if
employed."[3] But no evidence has been found from

[1] *S.P.D.*, cccx., 104. 1635. Returns made by Justices of the Peace.
[2] Haynes, (John.), *Present State of Clothing*, p. 5. 1706.
[3] Hale, (Sir Matt). *Discourse touching Provision for the Poor*, p. 6, 1683

which we can imagine that an agricultural labourer's family could possibly earn as much as 10s. a week in the seventeenth century. Our lower estimate is confirmed by a report made by the Justices of the Peace for the half hundred of Hitching concerning the poor in their district ; " when they have worke the wages geven them is soe small that it hardlye sufficeth to buy the poore man and his familye breed, for they pay 6s. for one bushell of mycelyn grayne and receive but 8d. for their days work. It is not possible to procure mayntenance for all these poore people and their famylyes by almes nor yet by taxes."[1]

The insolvency of the wage-earning class is recognized by Gregory King in his calculations of the income and expense of the several Families of England, for the year 1680. All other classes, including artisans and handicrafts show a balance of income over expenditure but the families of seamen, labourers and soldiers show an actual yearly deficit.[2]

A still more convincing proof of the universal destitution of wage earners is shown in the efforts made by churchwardens and overseers in every county throughout England to prevent the settlement within the borders of their parish of families which depended solely on wages.

Their objection is not based generally upon the ground that the labourer or his wife were infirm, or idle, or vicious ; they merely state that the family is likely to become chargeable to the parish. Each parish was responsible for the maintenance of its own

---

[1] *S.P.D.* ccclxxxv., 43. Mar. 8, 1638.

[2] King (Gregory). *Nat. and Political Observations*, pp. 48-9.

NO. OF FAMILIES.	PERSONS.	YEARLY INCOME PER HEAD.	EXPENSE PER HEAD.	LOSS PER HEAD
50,000 Common Seamen	150,000	£7.	£7. 10s.	10s.
364,000 Labouring people & outservants	1,275,000	£4. 10s.	£4. 12s.	2s.
400,000 Cottagers & Paupers	1,300,000	£2.	£2. 5s.	5s.
35,000 Common soldiers	70,000	£7.	£7. 10s.	10s.

poor, and thus though farmers might be needing more labourers, the parish would not tolerate the settlement of families which could not be self-supporting.

The disputes which arose concerning these settlements contain many pitiful stories.

" Anthony addams " tells the justices that he was born in Stockton and bred up in the same Parish, most of his time in service and has " taken great pains for my living all my time since I was able and of late I fortuned to marry with an honest young woman, and my parishioners not willing I should. bring her in the parish, saying we should breed a charge amongst them. Then I took a house in Bewdley and there my wife doth yet dwell and I myself do work in Stockton . . . and send or bring my wife the best relief I am able, and now the parish of Bewdley will not suffer her to dwell there for doubt of further charge. . . . I most humbly crave your good aid and help in this my distress or else my poor wife and child are like to perish without the doors : . . . that by your good help and order to the parish of Stockton I may have a house there to bring my wife & child unto that I may help them the best I can."[1]

Another petition was brought by Josias Stone of Kilmington . . . " shewinge that he hath binn an Inhabitant and yet is in Kilmington aforesaid and hath there continued to and fro these five yeares past and hath donn service for the said parishe and hath lately married a wife in the said parish intendinge there to liue and reside yet since his marriage is by the said parishe debarred of any abidinge for him and his said wife there in any howse or lodginge for his mony."[2]

Another dispute occurred over the case of Zachary Wannell and his wife who came lately from Wilton " into the towne of Taunton where they haue been

---

[1] *Hist. MSS. Com. Var. Coll.*, Vol. I., p. 298, *Worcestershire Q.S. Rec.*, 1618.

[2] *Somerset, Q.S. Rec.*, Vol. III., p. 15, 1647.

denyed a residence and they ly upp and downe in barnes and hay lofts, the said Wannell's wife being great with child; the said Wannell and his wife to be forthwith set to Wilton and there to continue until the next General Sessions. The being of the said Wannell and his wife at Wilton not to be interpreted as a settlement of them there."[1]

There were endless examples of these conflicts often attended as in the above case with great cruelty.[2]

---

[1] *Somerset Q.S. Rec.*, Vol. III., p. 246, 1654.

[2] One Humfrey Naysh, a poore man hath ben remayning and dwellinge within the pish of Newton St. Lowe by the space of five years or thereabouts and now being maryed and like to haue charge of children, the pishioners Do endeuor to put the said Naishe out of their pish by setting of amcents and paynes in their Courts on such as shall give him house-roome, or suffer him to liue in their houses which he doth or offereth to rent for his money which the court conceiveth to be vnjust and not accordinge to lawe." Overseers ordered to provide him a house for his money. *Ibid.*, Vol. II, p. 19, 1626.)

The petition of the "overseer of the poore of the parishe of East Quantoxhead . . . that one Richard Kamplyn late of Kilve with his wife and three small children are late come as Inmates into the Parish of East Quantoxhead which may hereafter become very burdensome and chargeable to the said parish if tymley prevention bee not taken therein." *Ibid.*, Vol. III, p. 9, 1646.

"John Tankens, his wife and three children . . . had lived twoe yeares in Chewstoake undisturbed and from thence came to Chew Magna and there took part of a Cottage for their habitation for one yeare . . . whereof the parishe of Chew Magna taking notice found themselves aggrieved thereatt, and brought the same in question both before the next Justice of the peace of Chew Magna and att the Leete or Lawday, and yett neither the said Tankens, his wife or children, had beene actually chardgeable to the said parishe of Chew Magna. This Court in that respect thinketh not fitt to disturbe the said Tankens, his wife or children duringe the said terme, but doth leave them to thend of the same terme to bee settled accordinge by lawe they ought. And because the parishioners of Chew Magna haue been for the most parte of the tyme since the said Tankens, his wife and Children came to Chew Magna complayninge against them, This court doth declare that the beinge of them att Chew Magna aforesaid duringe the said terme shall not bee interpreted to bee a settlement there. (*Ibid.*, Vol. III, pp. 94-5, 1649).

"Pet. of Richard Cookesley of Ashbrettle shewing that he is married in the said parish and the said parish endeavour to haue him removed from thence although hee is no way chargeable, this court doth see noe cause but that the said Cookesley may remaine att Ashbrittle aforesaid; provided that his being there shall not be interpretted to bee a settlement of him there." (*Ibid.*, Vol. III., p. 248, 1654).

James Hurde a poor labourer stated that for these two years last past he had dwelt in the parish of Westernemore "In a house wch he hired for his monie" and had taken great pains to maintain himself, his wife and two children, wherewith he never yet charged the said parish nor hopeth ever to do. And yet the parishioners and church-wardens there, do "indeavour" and threaten to turn him out of the parish unless he will put in sufficient sureties not to charge the said parish which he cannot by reason he is but a poor labourer; he humbly requests that he may quietly inhabit in the said parish so long as he doth not charge the same, otherwise he and his family are like to perish. (*Ibid.*, Vol. I, p. 94, 1612.)

The Justices were shocked at the consequent demoralization and generally supported the demands of the labourers as regards their settlement and housing. One writes to the clerk of the Peace : " I have sent you enclosed the recognizance of William Worster and William Smith, of Bovindon, for contempt of an order of sessions . . . in the behalfe of one, John Yorke, formerly a vagrant, but now parishionir of Bovingdon. Yet I believe the rest of the inhabitants will doe their utmost to gett him thence though they force him to turn vagrant againe. Yorke will be with you to prove that he was in the parish halfe-a-year or more before they gave him any disturbance, and that not privately, for he worked for severall substantiall men and was at church, and paid rent."[1]

But the Justices never suspected that the rate of wages which they themselves had fixed below subsistence level was at the root of the settlement difficulty. The overseers believed that all the troubles might be solved if only young people would not marry imprudently, and they petitioned the Justices begging that overseers of parishes might not be compelled to provide houses for such young persons " as will marry before they have provided themselves with a settling."[2]

While the overseers were seeking to exclude all wage earners from the parish, individual farmers, perchance the overseers themselves wanted more labourers. To meet this difficulty, the overseers discovered an ingenious device. Before granting a settlement, they required the labourer to find sureties to save the parish harmless from his becoming chargeable to it. Obviously a labourer could not himself find sureties, but the farmer who wished to employ him was in a position to do so, and thus the responsibility for the wage-earner's family would be laid upon the person who profited

---

[1] *Hertford Co. Rec.*, Vol. I., p. 321. 1681. Letter from Francis Leigh to Clerk of Peace.

[2] *Hist. MSS. Com, Var. Coll.* Vol. I., p. 322 *Worcestershire Q. S. Rec.*, 1661.

by his services. Petitions against this demand for sureties came before the Quarter Sessions. One from Robert Vawter stated that he was " a poore Day labourer about a quarter of a yere sithence came into the said parish of Clutton, and there marryed with a poore Almesmans Daughter, now liveing with her said father in the Almeshouse of Clutton aforesaid, and would there settle himselfe with his said wife." He was ordered to find sureties or to go to gaol.[1]

It was reported at Salford " Whereas Rich. Hudson is come lately into the towne with his wife and ffoure children to Remaine that the Burrow-reeve and Constables of this towne shall give notice unto Henry Wrigley, Esq., upon whose land he still remaynes that hee remove him and his wife and children out of this Towne within this moneth unlesse hee give sufficient security upon the paine of ffive pounds."[2]

Similar orders were made re Nathan Cauliffe, his wife and three children, Robert Billingham with wife and two children, Peter ffarrant and his wife, & Roger Marland and wife. Later the record continues, " and yet the said parties are not removed " order was therefore made " that this order shalbee put in execution."[3] Another step in the proceedings is recorded in the entry, " Whereas James Moores, George Moores and Adam Warmeingham stand bound unto Henry Wrigling Esq. in £20 for the secureinge the Towne from any poverty or disability which should or might befall unto the said James, his wife, children, or family or any of them. And whereas it appeares that the said James Moores hath been Chargeable whereby the said bond is become forfeit yet this Jury doth give the said George Moores and Adam Warmeingham this

---

[1] *Somerset Q.S. Rec.*, Vol. II., p. 292, 1637-8.

[2] *Salford Portmote Records*, Vol. II., p. 144, 1655.

[3] *Ibid.*, p. 151, 1656.

libtie that the said James shall remove out of this towne before the next Court Leet.''[1]

Fines were exacted from those who harboured unfortunate strangers without having first given security for them, and no exception was made on the score of relationship. James Meeke of Myddleton was presented " for keeping of his daughter Ellen Meeke, having a husband dwelling in another place, and having two children borne forth of the parishe.''[2]

Rules made at Steeple Ashton by the Churchwardens declare : " There hath much povertie happened unto this p'ish by receiving of strangers to inhabit there and not first securing them ag'st such contingencies and avoyding the like occasions in tyme to come, It is ordered by this vestrie that ev'ry p'son or p'sons whatsoev'r w'ch shall lett or sett any houseinge or dwellinge to any stranger and shall not first give good securite for defending and saving harmeless the said inhabitants from the future charge as may happen by such stranger comeing to inhabite w'thin the said p'ish and if any p'son shall doe to the contrary Its agreed that such p'son soe receiving such stranger shal be rated to the poor to 20s. monethlie over and above his monethlie tax.''[3]

The penalties at Reading were higher. " At this daye Wm. Porter, th'elder was questioned for harboringe a straunger woman, and a childe, viz[t], the wief of John Taplyn ; he worketh at Mr. Ed. Blagrave's in Early : Confesseth. The woman saith she hath byn there ever syns Michaellmas last, and payed rent to goodman Porter, xxs a yeare ; her kinsman Faringdon did take the house for them. Wm. Porter was required to paye xs a weeke accordinge to the orders and was willed to ridd his tenant with all speed upon

---

[1] *Salford Portmote Rec.*, Vol. II., p. 150.

[2] *Yorks. N.R. Q.S. Rec.*, Vol. I., p. 170, 1609.

[3] *Wilts. Notes and Queries*, Vol. VII., p. 281, 1664. *Churchwarden's Acct. Book. Steeple Ashton.*

payne of xs a weeke and to provide suretyes to discharge the towne of the childe."[1]

The starvation and misery described in Quarter Sessions Records were not exceptional calamities, but represent the ordinary life of women in the wage earning class. The lives of men were drab and monotonous, lacking pleasure and consumed by unending toil, but they did not often suffer hunger. The labourer while employed was well fed, for the farmer did not grudge him food, though he did not wish to feed his family. There was seldom want of employment for agricultural labourers, and when their homes sank into depths of wretchedness and the wife's attractiveness was lost through slow starvation, the men could depart and begin life anew elsewhere.

The full misery of the labourer's lot was only felt by the women ; if unencumbered they could have returned, like the men, to the comfortable conditions of service, but the cases of mothers who deserted their children are rare.

The hardships suffered by the women of the wage-earning class proved fatal to their children. Gregory King estimated that there were on an average only $3\frac{1}{2}$ persons, including father and mother in a labourer's family though he gives 4.8 as the average number of children for each family in villages and hamlets.[2] Another writer gives 3 persons as the average number for a labourer's family.[3] The cases of disputed settlements which are brought before Quarter Sessions confirm the substantial truth of these estimates. It is remarkable that where the father is living seldom more than two or three children are mentioned, often only one, though in cases of widows where the poverty is recent and caused as it were by the accidental effect of

[1] Guilding, *Reading Records*, Vol. II., p. 181, 1624.

[2] King (Gregory) *Natural and Political Observations and Conclusions*, p. 44, pp. 48-9.

[3] *Grasier's Complaint*, p. 60.

the husband's premature death, there are often five to ten children. In Nottingham, of seventeen families, who had recently come to the town and been taken in as tenants, and which the Council wanted to eject for fear of overcrowding, only one had four children, one three, and the rest only two or one child apiece.[1]

In fact, however large the birth rate may have been, and this we have no means of ascertaining, few children in the wage-earning class were reared. Of those who reached maturity many were crippled in mind or body, forming a large class of unemployables destined to be a burthen instead of strength to the community.

This appalling loss and suffering was not due to the excessive work of married women but to their under-feeding and bad housing. Probably the women of the wage-earning class actually accomplished less work than the women of the husbandman class ; but the latter worked under better conditions and were well nourished, with the result that their sons and daughters have been the backbone of the English nation.

The sacrifice of the wage-earners' children was caused by the mother's starvation ; vainly she gave her own food to the children for then she was unable to suckle the baby and grew too feeble for her former work. Probably she had herself been the daughter of a husbandman and was inured to labour from child hood. " Sent abroad into service and hardship when but 10 years old " as Oliver Heywood wrote of a faithful servant, she met the chances which decide a servant's life. The work on farms was rough, but generally healthy. At first the child herded the pigs or the geese and followed the harrow and as she grew older the poultry yard and the cows divided her attention with the housework. Sometimes she was brutally treated and often received little training in

---

[1] *Nottingham, Records of the Borough of,* Vol. IV., pp. 312-5. 1613.

her work, but generosity in meat and drink has always
been characteristic of the English farmer, and during
the hungry years of adolescence the average girl who
was a servant in husbandry was amply nourished. Then
came marriage. The more provident waited long in
the hope of securing independence, and one of those
desirable cottages with four acres of land, but to
some the prospect seemed endless and at last they
married hoping something would turn up ; or perhaps
they were carried away by natural impulses and
married young without any thought for the future.
Such folly was the despair of Churchwardens and
Overseers, yet the folly need not seem so surprising
when we consider that delay brought the young
people no assurance of improvement in their position.
Church and State alike taught that it was the duty
of men and women to marry and bring forth children,
and if for a large class the organisation of Society
made it impossible for them to rear their children,
who is to blame for the fate of those children, their
parents or the community ?

After one of these imprudent marriages the husband
sometimes continued to work on a farm as a servant,
visiting his wife and children on Sundays and holidays.
By this means he, at least, was well fed and well
housed. The woman with a baby to care for and
feed, could not leave her home every day to work and
must share the children's food. In consequence
she soon began to practise starvation. Her settlement was disputed, and therefore her dwelling was
precarious. Nominally she was transferred on marriage
to the parish where her husband was bound as servant
for the term of one year, but the parish objected to
the settlement of a married man lest his children
became a burden on them.

No one doubted that it was somebody's duty to
care for the poor, but arrangements for relief were
strictly parochial and the fear of incurring unlimited

future responsibilities led English parishioners to strange lengths of cruelty and callousness. The fact that a woman was soon to have a baby, instead of appealing to their chivalry, seemed to them the best reason for turning her out of her house and driving her from the village, even when a hedge was her only refuge.

The once lusty young woman who had formerly done a hard day's work with the men at harvesting was broken by this life. It is said of an army that it fights upon its stomach. These women faced the grim battle of life, laden with the heavy burden of child-bearing, seldom knowing what it meant to have enough to eat. Is it surprising that courage often failed and they sank into the spiritless, dismal ranks of miserable beings met in the pages of Quarter Sessions Records, who are constantly being forwarded from one parish to another.

Such women, enfeebled in mind and body, could not hope to earn more than the twopence a day and their food which is assessed as the maximum rate for women workers in the hay harvest. On the contrary, judging from the account books of the period, they often received only one penny a day for their labour. Significant of their feebleness is the Norfolk assessment which reads, " Women and such impotent persons that weed corne, or other such like Labourers 2d with meate and drinke, 6d without."[1] Such wages may have sufficed for the infirm and old, but they meant starvation for the woman with a young family depending on her for food. And what chance of health and virtue existed for the children of these enfeebled starving women ?

On the death or desertion of her husband the labouring woman became wholly dependent on the Parish for support.

---

[1] *Eng. Hist. Rev.*, Vol. xiii., p. 522.

The conduct of the magistrates in fixing maximum wages at a rate which they knew to be below subsistence level seems inexplicable ; is in fact inexplicable until it is understood that these wages were never intended to be sufficient for the support of a family. Statute 31 Eliz. and others, show that the whole influence of the Government and administration was directed to prevent the creation of a class of wage-earners. It was an essential feature of Tudor policy to foster the Yeomanry, from whose ranks were recruited the defenders of the realm. Husbandmen were recognised as " the body and stay " of the kingdom.[1] They made the best infantry when bred " not in a servile or indigent fashion, but in some free and plentiful manner."[2] If the depopulation of the country-side went on unchecked, there would come to pass " a mere sollitude and vtter desolation to the whole Realme, furnished only with shepe and shepherdes instead of good men ; wheareby it might be a prey to oure enymies that first would sett vppon it."[3]

Probably the consideration of whether a family could be fed by a labourer's wage, seldom entered the Justices' heads. They wished the family to win its food from a croft and regarded the wages as merely supplementary. The Justices would like to have exterminated wage-earners, who were an undesirable class in the community, and they might have succeeded as the conditions imposed upon the women made the rearing of children almost impossible, had not economic forces constantly recruited the ranks of wage-earners from the class above them.

The demands of capital however for labour already exceeded the supply available from the ranks of husbandmen, and could only be met by the establish-

---

[1] Lipson, *Economic Hist. of England*, p. 153.

[2] Bacon, *Works*, Vol. VI., p. 95.

[3] Lamond (Eliz.) *Discourse of the Common weal*, 1581.

ment of a class of persons depending wholly on wages. The strangest feature of the situation was the fact that the magistrates who were trying to exterminate wage-earners were often themselves capitalists creating the demand.

'The actual proportion of wage-earners in the seventeenth century can only be guessed at. The statement of a contemporary[1] that Labourers and Cottagers numbered 2,000,000 persons, out of a population of only 5,000,000 must be regarded as an exaggeration ; in any case their distribution was uneven.

Complaints are not infrequently brought before Quarter Sessions from parishes which say they are burdened with so great a charge of poor that they cannot support it ; to other parishes the Justices are sometimes driven to issue orders on the lines of a warrant commanding " the Churchwardens of the townes of Screwton and Aynderby to be more diligent in relieving their poore, that the court be not troubled with any further claymours therein."[2]

On the other hand there were many districts where the wage earner was hardly known and the authorities, like the Tithing men of Fisherton Delamere could report that they " have (thanks to the Almighty God theirfor) no popish recusants ; no occasion to levy twelvepence, for none for bear to repair to divine service; no inns or alehouses licensed or unlicensed, no drunken person, no unlawful weights or measures, no neglect of hues and cries, no roads out of repair, no wandering rogues or idle persons, and no inmates of whom they desire information."[3] Or the Constable of Tredington who declared that " the poor are weekly relieved, felons none known. Recusants one Bridget Lyne, the

---

[1] *Grasier's Complaint*, p. 60.

[2] *Yorks. N.R. Q.S. Rec.*, Vol. I., p. 22-3, 1605.

[3] *Hist. MSS. Com.Var. Coll.*,Vol. I., p, 93. *Wilts Q.S. Rec.*, 1621. A similar detailed return was made from the Hundred of Wilton in 1691. Many often return ' omnia bene ' and the like in brief.

wife of Thos. Lyne. Tobacco none planted. Vagrants Mary How, an Irish woman and her sister were taken and punished according to the Statute and sent away by pass with a guide towards Ireland in the County of Cork."[1] or as in another report " We have no bakers or alehouses within our parish. We cannot find by our searches at night or other time that any rogues or vagabonds are harboured saving Mr. Edward Hall who lodged a poor woman and her daughter. We do not suffer any vagrants which we see begging in our parish but we give them punishment according as we ought."[2]

A review of the whole position of women in Agriculture at this time, shows the existence of Family Industry at its best, and of Capitalism at its worst. The smaller farmers and more prosperous husbandmen led a life of industry and independence in which every capacity of the women, mental, moral and physical had scope for development and in which they could secure the most favourable conditions for their children —while among capitalistic farmers a tendency can already be perceived for the women to withdraw from the management of business and devote themselves to pleasure. At the other end of the scale Capitalism fed the man whom it needed for the production of wealth but made no provision for his children; and the married woman, handicapped by her family ties, when she lost the economic position which enabled her through Family Industry to support herself and her children, became virtually a pauper.

---

[1] Bund (J. W. Willis) *Worcestershire Co. Rec.*, Vol. I., p. 564, 1634.

[2] *Ibid*, Vol. I, p. 571, 1634.

CHAPTER IV.

TEXTILES.

(A) *Introductory.* Historical importance in women's economic development —Predominance of women's labour—Significance in development of Industrialism—Low wages.

(B) *Woollen Trade.* Historical importance—Proportions of men and women employed—Early experiments in factory system abandoned—Declining employment of women in management and control—Women Weavers—Burling—Spinning—Organization of spinning industry—Women who bought wool and sold yarn made more profit than those who worked for wages—Methods of spinning—Class of women who span for wages—Rates of wages—Disputes between spinsters and employers—Demoralisation of seasons of depression—Association of men and women in trade disputes.

(C) *Linen.* Chiefly a domestic industry—Introduction of Capitalism—Increased demand caused by printing linens—Attempt to establish a company—Part taken by women—weaving—bleaching—spinning—Wages below subsistence level—Encouragement of spinning by local authorities to lessen poor relief—Firmin.

(D) *Silk. Gold and Silver.* Silk formerly a monopoly of gentlewomen—In seventeenth century virtually one of the pauper trades. Gold and Silver furnished employment to the poorest class of women—Factory system already in use.

(E) *Conclusion.*

FROM the general economic standpoint, the textile industries rank second in importance to agriculture during the seventeenth century, but in the history of women's economic development they hold a position which is quite unique. If the food supply of the country depended largely on the work of women in agriculture, their labour was absolutely indispensable to the textile industries, for in all ages and in all countries spinning has been a monopoly of women. This monopoly is so nearly universal that we may suspect some physiological inability on the part of men to spin a fine even thread at the requisite speed, and spinning forms the greater part of the labour in the production of hand-made textile fabrics.

It requires some effort of the imagination in this mechanical age to realize the incessant industry which the duty of clothing her own family imposed on every woman, to say nothing of the yarn required for the famous Woollen Trade. The service rendered by women in spinning for the community was compared by contemporaries to the service rendered by the men who ploughed. " Like men that would lay no hand to the plough, and women that would set no hand to the wheele, deserving the censure of wise Solomon, Hee that would not labour should not eat."[1]

Textile industries fall into three groups : Woollen, Linen, and Miscellaneous, comprising silk, etc. Cotton is seldom mentioned although imported at this time in small quantities for mixture with linen.

The predominance of women's labour in the textile trades makes their history specially significant in tracing the evolution of women's industrial position under the influences of capitalism ; for the woollen trade was one of the first fields in which capitalistic organization achieved conspicuous success.

The importance of the woollen trade as a source of revenue to the Crown drew to it so much attention that many details have been preserved concerning its development ; showing with a greater distinctness than in other and more obscure trades, the steps by which Capitalistic Organization ousted Family Industry and the Domestic Arts. It is surely not altogether accidental that Industrialism developed so remarkably in two trades where the labour of women predominated —in the woollen trade which in the seventeenth century was already organized on capitalistic lines, and, one hundred years later, in the cotton trade.

Some characteristic features of modern Industrialism were absent from the woollen trade in the seventeenth century. The work of men and women alike was carried

---

[1] *Declaration of the Estate of Clothing*, p. 2, 1613.

on chiefly at home, and thus the employment of married women and children was unimpeded ; nor are there any signs of industrial jealousy between men and women, who on the contrary, stand by each other during this period in all trade disputes.   Nevertheless, the position of the woman wage-earner in the textile trades was extraordinarily bad, and this in spite of the fact that the demand for her labour appears nearly always to have exceeded the supply.   The evidence contained in the following chapter shows that the wages paid to women in the seventeenth century for spinning linen were insufficient, and those paid for spinning wool, barely sufficient, for their individual maintenance, and yet out of them women were expected to support, or partly support, their children.

Possibly the persistence of such low wages throughout the country was due in a measure to the convenience of spinning as a tertiary occupation for married women.   She who was employed by day in the intervals of household duties with her husband's business or her dairy and garden, could spin through the long winter evenings when the light was too bad for other work.   The mechanical character of the movements, and the small demand they make on eye or thought, renders spinning wonderfully adapted to women whose serious attention is engrossed by the care or training of their children.   A comparison of spinster's wages with those of agricultural labourers, which were also below subsistence level, will show however that such an explanation does not altogether meet the cse.

The fact is that far from underselling the spinsters[1] who were wholly dependent on wages for their living, it seems probable that the women who only span for sale after the needs of their own households had been supplied, received the highest rates of pay, just as the husbandman, who only worked occasionally for wages,

---

[1] Spinster in the seventeenth century is used in its technical sense and refers equally to women who are married, unmarried or widows.

was paid better than the labourer who worked for them all the year round, and whose family depended exclusively on him. Disorganization and lack of bargaining power, coupled with traditions founded upon an earlier social organization, were responsible for the low wages of the spinsters. The agricultural labourer was crippled in his individual efforts for a decent wage because society persisted in regarding him as a household servant. The spinster was handicapped because in a society which began to assert the individual's right to freedom, she had from her infancy been trained to subjection.

It must however be remembered that though a large part of the ensuing chapter is concerned with spinsters and their wages, much, perhaps most, of the thread spun never came into the market, but was produced for domestic consumption. Thus we find all three forms of industrial organisation existing simultaneously in these trades—Domestic Industry, Family Industry, and Capitalistic Industry.

Domestic Industry lingered especially in the Linen Trade until machinery made the spinning wheel obsolete, and Family Industry was still extensively practised in the seventeenth century; but Capitalistic Industry, already established in the Woollen Trade, was making rapid inroads on the other branches of the Textile Trades.

Although Capitalism undermined the position of considerable economic independence enjoyed by married women and widows in the tradesman and farming classes, possibly its intoduction may have improved the position of unmarried women, and others who were already dependent on wages; but such improvements belong to a later date. Their only indication in the seventeenth century is the clearly proved fact that wages for spinning were higher in the more thoroughly capitalistic woollen trade, than in the linen trade. Further evidence is a suggestion by Defoe that wages for spinning in the woollen trade were doubled, or even trebled, in the first decade of the eighteenth century, but no sign of this advance can be detected in our period.

(B.) *Woollen Trade.*

The interest of the Government and of all those who studied financial and economic questions, was focussed upon the Woollen Trade, owing to the fact that it formed one of the chief sources of revenue for the Crown. At the close of the seventeenth century woollen goods formed a third of the English exports.[1]

Historically the Woollen Trade has a further importance, due to the part which it played in the development of capitalism. The manufacture of woollen materials had existed in the remote past as a family industry, and even in the twentieth century this method still survives in the remoter parts of the British Isles ; but the manufacture of cloth for Foreign trade was from its beginning organized on Capitalistic lines, and the copious records which have been preserved of its development, illustrate the history of Capitalism itself.

It was estimated that about one million men, women and children were exclusively employed in the clothing trade,—" all have their dependence solely and wholly upon the said *Manufacture*, without intermixing themselves in the labours of *Hedging*, *Ditching*, *Quicksetting*, and others the works belonging to Husbandry."[2]

In 1612 eight thousand persons, men, women and

---

[1] Davenant (Inspector-General of Exports and Imports). *An account of the trade between Greate Britain, France, Holland, Spain, Portug: :, Italy, Africa, Newfoundland etc., with the importations and exportations of all Commodities, particularly of the Woollen Manufactures, delivered in his reports made to the Commissioners for Publick Accounts.* 1715, p. 71. Our general exports for the year 1699 are valued at £6, 788,166, 17s. 6¼d. Whereof the Woollen Manufacture for the same year are valued at £2,932,292, 17s. 6¼d.

[2] *Proverb Crossed*, p. 8, 1677. See also *Case of the Woollen Manufacturers of Great Britain* which states that they are " the subsistance of more than a Million of Poor of both sexes, who are employed therein."

children were said to be employed in the clothing trade in Tiverton alone.[1] While giving 933,966 hands as the number properly employed in woollen manufacture, another writer says that women and children (girls and boys) were employed in the proportion of about eight to one man.[2]

Such figures must be taken with reserve, for the proportions of men and women employed varied according to the quality of the stuff woven, and pamphleteers of the seventeenth century handled figures with little regard to scientific accuracy.[3] But the uncertainty only refers to the exact proportion ; there can be no doubt that the Woollen Trade depended chiefly upon women and children for its labour supply.

For the student of social organization it is noteworthy that in the two textile trades through which capitalism made in England its most striking advances —the woollen trade, and in later years, the cotton trade, the labour of women predominated,—a fact which suggests obscure actions and reactions between capitalism and the economic position of women, worthy of more careful investigation than they have as yet received.

The woollen trade passed through a period of rapid progress and development in the sixteenth century. It was then that the Clothiers of Wiltshire and Somerset acquired wealth and fame, building as a memorial for posterity the Tudor houses and churches which

---

[1] Dunsford. *Hist. Tiverton*, p. 408.

[2] *Short Essay upon Trade*, p. 18, 1741.

[3] The following estimates were made by different writers : out of 1187 persons supposed to be employed for one week in making up 1200 lbs. weight of wool, 900 are given as spinners. (*Weavers True Case*, p. 42, 1714.)

One pack of short wool finds employment for 63 persons for one week, viz : 28 men and boys : 35 women and girls who are only expected to do the carding and spinning.

A similar pack made into stockings would provide work for 82 men and 102 spinners and if made up for the Spanish trade, a pack of wool would employ 52 men and 250 women.

(Haynes (John) *Great Britain's Glory*, p. 6, p. 8. 1715.)

still adorn these counties. Leland, writing of a typical
clothier and his successful enterprises and ambitions,
describes at Malmesbury, Wiltshire " a litle chirch
joining to the South side of the *Transeptum* of thabby
chirch, . . . Wevers hath now lomes in this litle
chirch, but it stondith . . . the hole logginges
of thabbay be now longging to one Stumpe, an exceding
riche clothiar that boute them of the king. This
Stumpes sunne hath maried Sir Edward Baynton's
doughter. This Stumpe was the chef causer and
contributer to have thabbay chirch made a paroch
chirch. At this present tyme every corner of the vaste
houses of office that belongid to thabbay be fulle
of lumbes to weve clooth yn, and this Stumpe entendith
to make a stret or 2 for clothier in the bak vacant
ground of the abbay that is withyn the toune waulles."[1]

There must have been a marked tendency at this time
to bring the wage-earners of the woollen industry
under factory control, for a description which is given
of John Winchcombe's household says that

> " Within one room being large and long
> There stood two hundred Looms full strong,
> Two hundred men the truth is so
> Wrought in these looms all in a row,
> By evry one a pretty boy
> Sate making quills with mickle joy.
> And in another place hard by,
> An hundred women merrily,
> Were carding hard with joyful cheer
> Who singing sate with voices clear.
> And in a chamber close beside,
> Two hundred maidens did abide,
> In petticoats of Stammell red,
> And milk-white kerchers on their head." [2]

These experiments were discontinued, partly because
they were discountenanced by the Government, which
considered the factory system rendered the wage-earners
too dependent on the clothiers ; and also because
the collection of large numbers of workpeople under one

---

[1] Leland (John) *Itinerary*, 1535-1543 ; Part II, pp. 131-2.

[2] Lipson, *Econ. Hist. of England*, p. 420.

roof provided them with the opportunity for combination and insubordination.[1] Moreover the factory system was not really advantageous to the manufacturer before the introduction of power, because he could pay lower wages to the women who worked at home than to those who left their families in order to work on his premises. Thus the practice was dropped. In 1603 the Wiltshire Quarter Sessions published regulations to the effect that "Noe Clotheman shall keepe above one lombe in his house, neither any weaver that hath a ploughland shall keepe more than one lombe in his house. Noe person or persons shall keepe any lombe or lombs goeinge in any other house or houses beside their owne, or mayntayne any to doe the same."[2]

Few references occur to the wives of successful clothiers or wool-merchants who were actively interested in their husband's business, though no doubt their help was often enlisted in the smaller or more struggling concerns. Thus the names of three widows are given in a list of eleven persons who were using handicrafts at Maidstone. "The better sorte of these we take to bee but of meane ability and most of them poore but by theire trade the poore both of the towne and country adjoyning are ymploied to spynnyng."[3]

A pamphlet published in 1692 describes how in former days " the Clothier that made the cloth, sold it to the merchant, and heard the faults of his own cloth ; and forc'd sometimes not only to promise amendment himself, but to go home and tell *Joan*, to have the Wool better pick'd, and the Yarn better spun."[4]

A certain Rachel Thiery applied for a monopoly

---

[1] See *Weavers' Act,* 1555.

[2] *Hist. MSS. Com. Var. Coll.,* Vol. I., p. 75, *Wilts. Q.S. Rec.,* 1603.

[3] *S.P.D.,* cxxix, 45, Ap. 10, 1622, *Return of the Mayor.*

[4] *Clothier's Complaint, etc.,* p. 7, 1692.

in Southampton for the pressing of serges, and having heard that the suit had been referred by the Queen to Sir J. Cæsar, the Mayor and Aldermen wrote, July 2, 1599, to let him know how inconvenient the granting of the suit would be to the town of Southampton.

I. Those strangers who have presses already would be ruined.

II. Many of their men servants (English and strangers) bred up to the trade would be idle.

III. " The woeman verie poore and beggarlie, altogether unable to performe it in workmanshipp or otherwise. . . . Againe she is verie idle, a prattling gossipp, unfitt to undertake a matter of so great a charge, her husband a poore man being departed from her and comorant in Rochell these 11 yeres at least. She is verie untrustie and approoved to have engaged mens clothes which in times past have been putt to her for pressinge. Verie insufficient to answer of herself men's goodes and unable to procure anie good Caution to render the owners there goodes againe, havinge not so much as a howse to putt her head in, insomuch as (marvellinge under what coullour she doth seeke to attaine to a matter of such weight) we . . . should hold them worsse than madd that would hazzard or comitt there goodes into her handes. And to conclude she is generallie held amongest us an unfitt woeman to dwell in a well governed Commonwealth."[1]

An incident showing the wife as virtual manager of her husband's business is described in a letter from Thomas Cocks of Crowle to Sir Robert Berkely, Kt., in 1633. He writes complaining of a certain Careless who obtained a licence to sell ale " because he was a surgeon and had many patients come to him for help, and found it a great inconvenience for them to go to remote places for their diet and drink, and in that

---

[1] Lansdowne, 161, fo. 127, 2nd July, 1599.

respect obtained a licence with a limitation to sell ale
to none but his patients. . . . but now of late
especially he far exceeds his bounds. . . . A poor
fellow who professed himself an extraordinary carder
and spinner . . . was of late set a work by my
wife to card and spin coarse wool for blankets and when
he had gotten some money for his work to Careless
he goes." Having got drunk there and coming back in
the early hours of the morning he made such a noise
in the churchyard "being near my chamber I woke
my wife who called up all my men to go into the
churchyard and see what the matter was."[1]

That Mrs. Cocks should engage and direct her husband's workpeople would not be surprising to seventeenth century minds, for women did so naturally in
family industry; but when capitalized, business tended
to drift away beyond the wife's sphere, and thus even
then it was unusual to find women connected with
the clothing trade, except as wage-earners.

Of the processes involved in making cloth, weaving
was generally done by men, while the spinning, which
was equally essential to its production, was exclusively
done by women and children.

In earlier days weaving had certainly been to some
extent a woman's trade. "Webster" which is the
feminine form of the old term "Webber" is used in
old documents, and in these women are also specifically
named as following this trade; thus on the Suffolk Poll
Tax Roll are entered the names of

> "John Wros, shepherd.
> Agneta his wife, webster.
> Margery, his daughter, webster.
> Thomas his servant and
> Beatrice his servant."

It appears also that there were women among the
weavers who came from abroad to establish the cloth
making in England, for a Statute in 1271 provides that

" all workers of woollen cloths, male and female,
as well of Flanders as of other lands, may safely come
into our realm there to make cloths . . . upon the
understanding that those who shall so come and make
such cloths, shall be quit of toll and tallage, and of
payment of other customs for their work until the end
of five years."[1]

Later however, women were excluded from cloth
weaving on the ground that their strength was insufficient to work the wide and heavy looms in use ; thus
orders were issued for Norwich Worsted Weavers in
1511 forbidding women and maids to weave worsteds
because " thei bee nott of sufficient powre to werke
the said worsteddes as thei owte to be wrought."[2]

Complaint was made in Bristol in 1461 that weavers
" puttyn, occupien, and hiren ther wyfes, doughters,
and maidens, some to weve in ther owne lombes and
some to hire them to wirche with othour persons of
the said crafte by the which many and divers of the
king's liege people, likely men to do the king service
in his wars and in defence of this his land, and sufficiently learned in the said craft, goeth vagrant and
unoccupied, and may not have their labour to their
living."[3]

At Kingston upon-Hull, the weavers Composition
in 1490, ordained that " ther shall no woman worke
in any warke concernyng this occupacon wtin the
towne of Hull, uppon payn of xls. to be devyded in
forme by fore reherced."[4]

A prohibition of this character could not resist the
force of public opinion which upheld the woman's
claim to continue in her husband's trade. Widow's
rights are sustained in the Weaver's Ordinances

[1] Riley. *Chronicles of London*, p. 142.

[2] Tingye, *Norwich Records*, Vol. II., p, 378.

[3] *Little Red Book of Bristol*, Vol. II., p. 127.

[4] Lambert, 2000 *years of Gild Life*, p. 6.

formulated by 25 Charles II. which declare that " it shall be lawfull for the Widow of any Weaver (who at the time of his death was a free Burgesse of the said Town, and a free Brother of the said Company) to use and occupy the said trade by herselfe, her Apprentices and Servants, so long as shee continues a Widow and observeth such Orders as are or shalbe made to be used amongst the Company of Weavers within this Town of Kingston upon Hull.[1]

Even when virtually excluded from the weaving of " cloaths " women continued to be habitually employed in the weaving of other materials. A petition was presented on their behalf against an invention which threatened a number with unemployment : " Also wee most humbly desire your worship that you would have in remembrance that same develishe invention which was invented by strangers and brought into this land by them, which hath beene the utter overthrowe of many poore people which heretofore have lived very well by their handy laboure which nowe are forced to goe a begginge and wilbe the utter Destruccion of the trade of weaving if some speedy course be not taken therein. Wee meane those looms with 12, 15, 20, 18, 20, 24, shuttles which make tape, ribbon, stript garteringe and the like, which heretofore was made by poore aged woemen and children, but none nowe to be seene."[2]

The Rules of the Society of Weavers of the " Stuffs called Kiddirminster Stuffes" required that care should be taken to have apprentices " bound according to ye Lawes of ye Realme . . . for which they shall be allowed 2s. 6d and not above, to be payd by him or her that shall procure the same Apprentice to be bound as aforesayd."[3]

---

[1] Lambert, 2000 *Years of Gild Life*, p. 210.

[2] *S.P.D.*, cxxi, 155, 1621.

[3] Burton, J. R., *Hist. of Kidderminster.*, p. 175, *Borough Ordinances*, 1650.

John Grove w as bound about the year 1655 to " the said George and Mary to bee taught and instructed in the trade of a serge-weaver," and a lamentable account is given of the inordinate manner in which the said Mary did beat him.[1]

It is impossible from the scanty information available to arrive at a final conclusion concerning the position of women weavers. Clearly an attempt had been made to exclude them from the more highly skilled branches of the trade, but it is also evident that this had not been successful in depriving widows of their rights in this respect. Nor does the absence of information concerning women weavers prove that they were rarely employed in such work. The division of work between women and men was a question which aroused little interest at this time and therefore references to the part taken by women are accidental. They may have been extensively engaged in weaving for they are mentioned as still numerous among the hand-loom weavers of the nineteenth century.[2] Another process in the manufacture of cloth which gave employment to women was " Burling." The minister and Mayor of Westbury presented a petition to the Wiltshire Quarter Sessions in 1657 on behalf of certain poor

[1] *Somerset Q.S. Rec.*, Vol. III., pp. 268-9. 1655.

[2] *Report of the Commissioners on the condition of the Handloom Weavers*, 1841. x p. 323, Mr. Chapman's report.

" The young weaver just out of his apprenticeship is perhaps as well able to earn as he will be at any future period setting aside the domestic comforts incidental to the married state, his pecuniary condition is in the first instance improved by uniting himself with a woman capable of earning perhaps nearly as much as himself, and performing for him various offices involving an actual pecuniary saving. A married man with an income, the result of the earnings of himself and wife of 20s. will enjoy more substantial comfort in every way than he alone would enjoy with an income of 15s. a week. This alone is an inducement to early marriage. In obedience to this primary inducement the weaver almost invariably marries soon after he is out of his apprenticeship. But the improvement of comfort which marriage brings is of short duration ; . . About the tenth year the labour of the eldest child becomes available. . . . Many men have depended on their wives & their children to support themselves by their own earnings, independent of his wages. The wives and children consequently took to the loom, or sought work in the factories ; and now that there is little or no work in the district, the evil is felt, and the husband is obliged to maintain them out of his wages."

people who had obtained their living by the " Burling
of broad medley clothes," three of whose daughters
had now been indicted by certain persons desirous
to appropriate the said employment to themselves ;
they show " that the said employment of Burling
hath not been known to be practised among us
as any prentice trade, neither hath any been apprentice to it as to such, but clothiers have ever putt theyr
clothes to Burling to any who would undertake the
same, as they doe theyr woolles to spinning. Also that
the said imployment of Burling is a common good to
this poore town and parish, conducing to the reliefe
of many poore families therein and the setting of
many poore children on work. And if the said imployment of Burling should be appropriated by any particular persons to themselves it would redound much to
the hurt of clothing, and to the undoing of many
poore families there whoe have theyre cheife main-
teynance therefrom."[1]

It was not however the uncertain part they played
in the processes of weaving, burling or carding, which
constituted the importance of the woollen trade in
regard to women's industrial position. Their employment in these directions was insignificant compared
with the unceasing and never satisfied demand which
the production of yarn made upon their labour. It is
impossible to give any estimate of the quantity of wool
spun for domestic purposes. That this was considerable
is shown by a recommendation from the Commission
appointed to enquire into the decay of the
Cloth Trade in 1622, who advise " that huswyves
may not make cloth to sell agayne, but for the provision
of themselves and their famylie that the clothiers
and Drapers be not dis-coraged."[2]

The housewife span both wool and flax for domestic

---

[1] *Hist. MSS. Com. Var. Coll.*, Vol. I., p. 135, *Wilts. Q.S. Rec.*, 1657.

[2] *Report of Commission of Decay of Clothing Trade*, 1622, Stowe, 554, fo. 48b.

use, but this aspect of her industry will be considered
more fully in connection with the linen trade, attention
here being concentrated on the condition of the
spinsters in the woollen trade. Their organization
varied widely in different parts of the country. Sometimes the spinster bought the wool, span it, and then
sold the yarn, thus securing all the profit of the tran-
saction for herself. In other cases she was supplied
with the wool by the clothier, or a " market spinner "
and only received piece wages for her labour. The
system in vogue was partly decided by the custom
of the locality, but there was everywhere a
tendency to substitute the latter for the former
method.

Statute I. Edward VI. chap. 6 recites that " the
greatest and almost the whole number of the
poor inhabitants of the county of Norfolk and the
city of Norwich be, and have been heretofore for a
great time maintained and gotten their living, by
spinning of the wool growing in the said county of
Norfolk, upon the rock [distaff] into yarn, and by all
the said time have used to have their access to common
markets within the said county and city, to buy their
wools, there to be spun as is aforesaid, of certain persons
called retailers of the said wool by eight penny worth
and twelve penny worth at one time, or thereabouts,
and selling the same again in yarn, and have not used to
buy, ne can buy the said wools of the breeders of the
said wools by such small parcels, as well as for that
the said breeders of the said wools will not sell their
said wools by such small parcels, as also for that the
most part of the said poor persons dwell far off from
the said breeders of the said wools."[1]

During a scarcity of wool the Corporation at Norwich compelled the butchers to offer their wool fells
exclusively to the spinsters during the morning hours

[1] James (John) *Hist. of Worsted*, p. 98.

until the next sheep-shearing season, so that the tawers and others might not be able to outbid them.[1]

It is suggested that nearly half the yarn used in the great clothing counties at the beginning of the seventeenth century was produced in this way : " Yarn is weekly broughte into the market by a great number of poor people that will not spin to the clothier for small wages, but have stock enough to set themselves on work, and do weekly buy their wool in the market by very small parcels according to their use, and weekly return it in yarn and make good profit, having the benefit both of their labour and of their merchandize and live exceeding well. . . . So many that it is supposed that more than half the cloth of Wilts., Gloucester and Somersetshire is made by means of these yarnmakers and poor clothiers that depend wholly on the wool chapman which serves them weekly for wools either for money or credit."[2]

Apparently this custom by which the spinsters retained in their own hands the merchandize of their goods still prevailed in some counties at the beginning of the following century, for it is said in a pamphlet which was published in 1741 " that poor People, chiefly Day Labourers, ... whilst they are employed abroad themselves, get forty or fifty Pounds of Wool at a Time, to employ their Wives and Children at home in Carding and Spinning, of which when they have 10 or 20 pounds ready for the Clothier, they go to Market with it and there sell it, and so return home as fast as they can. . . . the common way the poor women in *Hampshire*, *Wiltshire*, and *Dorsetshire*, and I believe in other counties, have of getting to Market (especially in the Winter-time) is, by the Help of some Farmers' Waggons, which carry them and their yarn ; and as soon as the Farmers have set down their

---

[1] Tingye. *Norwich*, Vol II. xcvii, 1532.

[2] *S.P.D.* lxxx., 13., Jan. 1615. *General Conditions of Wool and Cloth Trade,*

corn in the Market, and baited their Horses, they return home. . . . During the Time the waggons stop, the poor Women carry their Yarn to the Clothiers for whom they work ; then they get the few Things they want, and return to the Inn to be carried home again. . . . Many of them ten or twelve miles . . . there will be in Market time 3 or 400 poor People (chiefly Women) who will sell their Goods in about an Hour."[1]

According to this writer other women worked for the " rich clothier" who " makes his whole year's provision of wool beforehand . . . in the winter time has it spun by his own spinsters . . . at the lowest rate for wages," or they worked for the " market spinner " or middleman who supplied them with wool mixed in the right proportions and sold their yarn to the clothiers. In either case the return for their labour was less than that secured by the spinsters who had sufficient capital to buy their wool and sell the yarn in the dearest market. When the Staplers tried to secure a monopoly for selling wool, the Growers of wool, or Chapmen petitioned in self-defence explaining " that the clothier's poor are all servants working for small wages that doth but keepe them alive, whereas the number of people required to work up the same amount of wool in the new Drapery is much larger. Moreover, all sorts of these people are masters in their trade and work for themselves, they buy and sell their materials that they work upon, so that by their merchandize and honest labour they live very well. These are served of their wools weekly by the wool-buyer."[2]

Opinion was divided as to whether the spinster found it more advantageous to work direct for the Clothier or for the Market Spinner. A proposal in

---

[1] *Remarks upon Mr. Webber's scheme*, pp. 21-2, 1741.

[2] *S.P.D.*, lxxx., 15-16., Jan, 1615.

1693 to put down the middle man, was advised against by the Justices of Assize for Wiltshire, on the ground that it was " likely to cause great reduction of wages and employment to the spinners and the poor, and a loss to the growers of wool, and no advantage in the quality of the yarn."

The Justices say in their report : " We finde the markett spinner who setts many spinners on worke spinnes not the falce yarn, but the poorer sorte of people (who spinne theyr wool in theyr owne howses) for if the markett spinners who spinne greate quantitys and sell it in the markett should make bad yarne, they should thereby disable themselves to maynetayne theyre creditt and livelyhood. And that the more spinners there are, the more cloth will be made and the better vent for Woolls (which is the staple commodity of the kingdome) and more poor will be set on worke. The markett spinners (as is conceived) are as well to be regulated by the lawe, for any falcity in mixing of theyr woolles as the Clothier is, who is a great markett spinner himselfe and doth both make and sell as falce yarne as any market spinner . . . We finde the markett spinner gives better wages than the Clothier, not for that reason the Clothier gives for the falcity of the yarne, but rather in that the markett spinners vent much of their yarne to those that make the dyed and dressed clothes who give greater prizes than the white men do."[1]

The fine yarn used by the Clothiers required considerable skill in spinning, and the demand for it was so great in years of expansion that large sums of money were paid to persons able to teach the mysteries of the craft in a new district. Thus the Earl of Salisbury made an agreement in 1608 with Walter Morrell that he should instruct fifty persons of the parish of Hatfield, chosen by the Earl of Salisbury, in

---

[1] S.P.D.,ccxliii., 23, July 23, 1633.

the art of clothing, weaving, etc. He will provide
work for all these persons to avoid idleness and for the
teaching of skill and knowledge in clothing will pay
for the work at the current rates, except those who are
apprentices. The Earl of Salisbury on his part will
allow Walter Morrell a house rent free and will pay
him £100 per annum "for instructing the fifty persons,
to be employed in :—the buying of wool, sorting it,
picking it, dying it, combing it, both white and
mingle colour worsted, weaving and warping and
quilling both worsted of all sorts, dressing both
woollen and stuffes, spinning woollen (wofe and
warpe), spinning all sortes of Kersey both high
wheel and low wheel, knitting both woollen and
worsted."[1]

A similar agreement is recorded in 1661-2 between
the Bailiffs and Burgesses of Aldeburgh and " Edmund
Buxton of Stowmarket, for his coming to set up his
trade of spinning wool in the town and to employ the
poor therein, paying him £50—for 5 years and £12—
for expense of removing, with a house rent free and the
freedom of the town."[2]

The finest thread was produced on the distaff, but
this was a slow process, and for commoner work
spinning wheels were in habitual use —

> " There are, to speed their labor, who prefer
> " Wheels double spol'd, which yield to either hand
> " A sev'ral line ; and many, yet adhere
> " To th' ancient distaff, at the bosom fix'd,
> " Casting the whirling spindle as they walk."[3]

The demands made on spinning by this ever expanding
trade were supplied from three sources : (1) the wives
of farmers and other well to do people, (b) the wives of
husbandmen and (c) women who depended wholly

---

[1] *S.P.D.*, xxxviii., 72, 73, Dec. 1608.

[2] *Hist. MSS. Com. Var. Coll.*, Vol. IV., p. 311.

[3] Dyer John., *The Fleece*, 1757.

on spinning for their living, and who are therefore
called here spinsters. The first care of the farmers'
wives was to provide woollen stuffs for the use of
their families, but a certain proportion of their yarn
found its way to the market. The clothiers at Salisbury
who made the better grades of cloth were said to
" buy their yarn of the finer kinds that come to the
market at from 17d the lb. to 2s. 4d, made all of the
finer sortes of our owne Welshire wool, and is spun by
farmers' wives and other of the better sorte of people
within their owne houses, of whose names wee keep
due Register and do write down with what cardes they
promise us their several bundles of yarne are carded, and
do find such people just in what they tell us, or can
otherwise controule them when wee see the proofe
of our cloth in the mill, . . . and also some very
few farmers' wives who maie peradventure spinne
sometimes a little of those sortes in their own houses
and sell the same in the markett and is verie current
without mixture of false wooll grease, etc."[1]
　　Probably a larger supply of yarn came from the
families of husbandmen where wife and children
devoted themselves to spinning through the long
winter evenings. Children became proficient in the
art at an early age, and could often spin a good thread
when seven or eight years old. This subsidiary employment was not sufficient to supply the demand for
yarn, and in the clothing counties numbers of women
were withdrawn from agricultural occupations to
depend wholly upon their earnings as spinsters.
　　The demand made by the woollen trade on the labour
of children is shown by a report from the Justices
of the Peace of the Boulton Division of the Hundred
of Salford, . . . "for apprentices there hath
beene few found since our last cerdificate by reason
of the greate tradeing of fustians and woollen cloth

---

[1] *S.P.D.*, cclxvii., 17, May 2, 1634. Certificate from Anthony Wither, Commissioner
or reformation of clothing.

within the said division, by reason whereof the inhabitants have continuall employment for their children in spinning and other necessary labour about the same."[1]

Those who gave out the wool and collected the yarn were called market spinners, but the qualifying term " market " is sometimes omitted, and when men are referred to as spinners it may be assumed that they are organising the work of the spinsters, and not engaged themselves in the process of spinning.[2] Though the demand for yarn generally exceeded the supply, wages for spinning remained low throughout the seventeenth century. A writer in the first half of the eighteenth century who urges the establishment of a nursery of spinners on the estate of an Irish landlord admits that their labour is " of all labour on wools the most sparingly paid for."[3]

Wages for spinning are mentioned in only three of the extant Quarter Sessions' Assessments, and it is not specified whether the material is wool or flax :

1654. Devon. 6d. per week with meat and drink, or 1s. 4d. without them.

1688. Bucks. Spinners shall not have by the day more than 4d. without meat and drink.

1714. Devon. 1s. per week with meat and drink, 2s. 6d. without them.

These rates are confirmed by entries in account

---

[1] *S.P.D.*, ccclxiv., 122, July, 1637.

[2] *Somerset Q.S. Rec.*, Vol. III., p. 56, 1648. *Complaint . . . by . . . Thos Chambers, Randall Carde, Dorothy Palmer, Stephen Hodges and Wm. Hurman, persons ymployed by Henry Denmeade servant to Mr. Thos. Cooke, Clothier for the spinning of certen wool and convertinge it into yarne and twistinge it thereof for the benefitt of the said Mr. Cooke that theire wages for the same spinninge and twistinge had been deteyned from them by the said Mr Cooke . . . it is ordered that the said Mr. C. doe forthwith pay to the said Thos. Chambers the some of ffowerteene shillings to the said Randall Carde the some of nyne shillings and fower pence, to the said Dorothy Palmer the some of eighteen shillings and one penny to the said Stephen Hodges the some of nyne shillings and four pence and to the said Wm. Hurman the some of nyne shillings.*

[3] *Scheme to prevent the running of Irish wools to France,* p. 19.

books,[1] but it was more usual to pay by the piece.
Though it is always more difficult to discover the
possible earnings per day of women who are working
by a piece rate in their own homes, it so happens that
several of the writers who discuss labour questions
in the woollen trade specially state that their estimates
of the wages of spinners are based on full time.
John Haynes quoted figures in 1715 which work out at
nearly 1s. 6d. per week for the spinners of wool into stuffs
for the Spanish Trade, and about 2s. 11d. for stockings,[2]
another pamphlet gives 24s. as the wages of
9 spinsters for a week,[3] while in 1763 the author of
the "Golden Fleece" quotes 2s. 3d. a week for
Spanish wools.[4] Another pamphlet says that the
wages in the fine woollen trade " being chiefly
women and children, may amount, one with another
to £6 per annum."[5] A petition from the weavers,
undated, but evidently presented during a season of
bad trade, declares that " there are not less than a
Million of poor unhappy objects, *women and children
only*, who . . . are employed in Spinning Yarn
for the Woollen Manufacturers ; Thousands of these
have now no work at all, and all of them have suffered
an Abatement of Wages ; so that now a Poor Woman,
perhaps a Mother of many Children, must work very
hard to gain Three Pence or Three Pence Farthing per
Day."[6]

---

[1] (*Howard Household Book*, p. 63, 1613.) " Widow Grame for spinning ij stone and
5ˡ of wooll vjs.   To the wench that brought it iijd.   To Ellen for winding yarn iij
weekes xviijd.

(Fell, Sarah ; *Household Accounts*, Nov. 28, 1677, p. 439.) Pd. Agnes Holme of
Hawkshead foᵗ spininge woole here 7 weeks 02.04

[2] Haynes, *Great Britain's Glory*, pp. 8, 9.

[3] *Weavers' True Case*, p. 43, 1719.

[4] James, John, *Hist of the Worsted Manufacture*, p. 239.

[5] *Further considerations for encouraging the Woollen Manufactures.*

[6] *Second Humble Address from the Poor Weavers.*

Though these wages provided no margin for the support of children, or other dependants, it was possible for a woman who could spin the better quality yarns to maintain herself in independence.

John Evelyn describes " a maiden of primitive life, the daughter of a poore labouring man, who had sustain'd her parents (some time since dead) by her labour, and has for many years refus'd marriage, or to receive any assistance from the parish, besides ye little hermitage my lady gives her rent free : she lives on fourepence a day, which she gets by spinning; says she abounds and can give almes to others, living in greate humility and content, without any apparent affectation or singularity ; she is continualy working, praying, or reading, gives a good account of her knowledge in religion, visites the sick ; is not in the least given to talke ; very modest, of a simple not unseemly be- haviour, of a comely countenance, clad very plaine, but cleane and tight. In sum she appeares a saint of an extraordinary sort, in so religious a life as is seldom met with in villages now-a-daies."[1]

It is probable that the wages for spinning were advanced soon after this date, for Defoe writes in 1728 that " the rate for spinning, weaving and all other Manufactory-work, I mean in Wool, is so risen, that the Poor all over *England* can now earn or gain near twice as much in a Day, and in some Places, more than twice as much as they could get for the same work two or three Years ago . . . the poor women now get 12d. to 15d. a Day for spinning, the men more in proportion, and are full of work."[2] " The Wenches . . . . wont go to service at 12d. or 18d. a week while they can get 7s. to 8s. a Week at spinning ; the Men won't drudge at the Plow and Cart &c., and per- haps get £6 a year . . . . when they can sit

---

[1] Evelyn (John) *Diary*, Vol. III., p. 7, 1685

[2] Defoe, *Behaviour*, p. 83.

still and dry within Doors, and get 9s. or 10s. a Week at Wool-combing or at Carding.[1] "Would the poor Maid-Servants who choose rather to spin, while they can gain 9s. per Week by their Labour than go to Service at 12d. a week to the Farmers Houses as before; I say would they sit close to their work, live near and close, as labouring and poor People ought to do, and by their Frugality lay up six or seven shillings per Week, none could object or blame them for their Choice."[2] Defoe's statement as to the high rate of wages for spinning is supported by an account of the workhouse at Colchester where the children's "Work is Carding & Spinning Wool for the Bay-makers; some of them will earn 6d. or 7d. a Day."[3] But there is no sign of these higher wages in the seventeenth century.

Continual recriminations took place between clothiers and spinsters, who accused one another of dishonesty in their dealings. A petition of the Worsted Weavers of Norwich and Norfolk, and the Bayes and Sayes makers of Essex and Suffolk, to the Council proposes: "That no spinster shall winde or reele theire yarne upon shorter reeles (nor fewer thriddes) than have bene accustomed, nor ymbessell away their masters' goodes to be punished by the next Justices of the Peace."[4]

And again in 1622 the Justices of the Peace of Essex inform the Council: "Moreover wee under-stand that the clothiers who put forthe their woolle to spinne doe much complaine of the spinsters that they use great deceit by reason they doe wynde their yarne into knottes upon shorter reeles and fewer threedes by a fifth part than hath beene accustomed.

---

[1] Defoe, *Behaviour*, pp. 84-5.

[2] *Ibid*, p. 88.

[3] *Acc. of several Workhouses*, p. 59, 1725.

[4] *S.P.D.*, civ. 97, 1618. *Petition for regulation.*

The which reeles ought to be two yardes about and the knottes to containe fowerscore threedes apeece."[1]

On the other hand in Wiltshire the weavers, spinners and others complained that they " are not able by their diligent labours to gett their livinges, by reason that the Clothiers at their will have made their workes extreme hard, and abated wages what they please. And some of them make such their workfolkes to doe their houshold businesses, to trudge in their errands, spoole their chains, twist their list, doe every command without giving them bread, drinke or money for many days labours."[2]

Report was made to the Council in 1631-2 that the reele-staffe in the Eastern Counties " was enlarged by a fift or sixt part longer than have bene accustomed and the poores wages never the more encreased." Whereupon the magistrates in Cambridge agreed " that all spinsters shall have for the spinning and reeling of six duble knots on the duble reele or 12 on the single reele, a penny, which is more by 2d. in the shilling than they have had, and all labourers and other artificers have the like increase. Essex and Suffolk are ready to make the same increase provided that the same reel and rate of increase is used in all other counties where the trade of clothing and yarn-making is made, otherwise one county will undersell another to the ruin of the clothiers and the poor dependent on them. Therefore the Council order that a proportional increase of wages is paid according to the increase of the reel and the officers employed for keeping a constant reel to give their accounts to the Justices of the Assize."[3]

Other complaints were made of clothiers who forced their work-people to take goods instead of

---

[1] *S.P.D.*, cxxx., 65, May 13, 1662.

[2] *Hist. MSS. Com. Var. Coll.*, Vol., I., p. 94, *Wilts. Q.S. Rec.*, 1623.

[3] *Council Register*, 2nd March, 1631-2.

money in payment of wages. At Southampton in
1666 thirty-two clothiers, beginning with Joseph
Delamot, Alderman, were presented for forcing their
spinners " to take goods for their work whereby the
poor were much wronged, being contrary to the statute,
for all which they were amerced severally." The
records however do not state that the fine was exacted.[1]

Low as were the spinster's wages even in seasons of
prosperity, they, in common with the better paid
weavers endured the seasons of depression, which were
characteristic of the woollen industry. The English
community was as helpless before a period of trade
depression as before a season of drought or flood.
Employment ceased, the masters who had no sale for
their goods, gave out no material to their workers,
and men and women alike, who were without land as a
resource in this time of need, were faced with starvation and despair.[2] The utmost social demoralisation ensued, and family life with all its valuable
traditions was in many cases destroyed.

Complaints from the clothing counties state
" That the Poor's Rates are doubled, and in some
Places trebbled by the Multitude of Poor Perishing and
Starving Women and Children being come to the
Parishes, while their Husbands and Fathers *not able
to bear the cries which they could not relieve*, are fled
into *France* . . . to seek their Bread."[3]

These conditions caused grave anxiety to the

---

[1] Davies (J. S.) *Southampton*, p. 272.

[2] A report to the council from the High Sheriff of Somerset says : " Yet I thincke
it my duty to acquaynt your Lordshipps that there are such a multytude of poore
cottages builte upon the highwaies and odd corners in every countrie parishe
within this countye, and soe stufte with poore people that in many of those parishes
there are three or fower hundred poore of men and women and children that did gett
most of their lyvinge by spinnyng, carding and such imployments aboute wooll and
cloath.   And the deadness of that trade and want of money is such that they are for
the most parte without worke, and knowe not how to live.   This *is* a great grievance
amongst us and tendeth much to mutinye."
    (*S.P.D.*, cxxx., 73, May 14, 1622, High Sheriff of Somersershire to the Council.)

[3] *Second Humble Address from the poor Weavers.*

Government who attempted to force the clothiers
to provide for their work-people.[1]

Locke reported to Carleton, Feb. 16th, 1622 : " In
the cloathing counties there have bin lately some
poore people (such chieflie as gott their living by
working to Clothiers) that have gathered themselves
together by Fourty or Fifty in a company and gone
to the houses of those they thought fittest to relieve
them for meate and money which hath bin given more
of feare than charitie. And they have taken meate
openly in the markett without paying for it. The
Lords have written letters to ten Counties where
cloathing is most used, that the Clothier shall not put
off his workemen without acquainting the Councill,
signifying that order is taken for the buying off their
cloathes, and that the wooll grower shall afford them
his wooll better cheape but yet the cloathiers still
complaine that they can not sell their cloath in Blackwell Hall. . . ."[2]

The Justices of Assize for Gloucester reported
March 13, 1622, that they have interviewed the
Clothiers who have been forced to put down looms
through the want of sale for their cloth. The Clothiers
maintain that this is due to the regulations and practices
of the Company of Merchant Adventurers. They
say that they, the Clothiers, have been working at a
loss since the deadness of trade about a year ago,
" their stocks and credits are out in cloth lying upon
their hands unsold, and that albeit they have bought
their woolles at very moderate prices, being such as do
very much impoverish the grower, yet they cannot sell

---

[1] The Council ordered the Justices of the Peace for the counties of Wilts, Somerset
Dorset, Devon, Glocester, Worcester, Oxford, Kent and Suffolk, to summon
clothiers and " deale effectually with them for the employment of such weavers,
spinners and other persons, as are now out of work. . . . We may not indure
that the cloathiers . . . should att their pleasure, and without giving knowledge
thereof unto this Boarde, dismisse their workefolkes, who being many in number
and most of them of the poorer sort are in such cases likely by their clamour to disturb
the quiet and government of those partes wherein they live." (C.R., 9th Feb., 1621-2.)

[2] S.P.D., cxxvii., 102, Feb. 16, 1622.

the cloth made thereof but to their intolerable losses, and are enforced to pawne theire clothes to keepe theire people in work, which they are not able to indure. . . . that there are at the least 1500 loomes within the County of Gloucester and in . . . the Citie and that xxs. in money and sixteene working persons and upwards doe but weekly mainteyne one loome, which doe require 1500li. in money, by the weeke to mainteyne in that trade 24000 working people besides all others that are releeved thereby, and so the wages of a labouring person is little above xiid. the week being much too little."[1]

In June of the same year the Justices of Gloucester wrote to the Council : " The distress of those depending on the Cloth trade grows worse and worse. Our County is thereby and through want of money and means in these late tymes growne poore, and unable to releeve the infynite nomber of poore people residinge within the same (drawne hither by meanes of clothing) . . . therefore very many of them doe wander, begg and steale and are in case to starve as their faces (to our great greefes) doe manifest. . . . The peace is in danger of being broken."[2]

The distress was not limited to the rural districts ; the records of the Borough of Reading describe efforts made there for its alleviation. " At this daye the complainte of the poore Spynners and Carders was agayne heard etc. The Overseers and Clothiers apoynted to provide and assigne them worke apeared and shewed their dilligence therein, yett the complaint for lacke of worke increaseth ; for a remedye is agreed to be thus, viz : every Clothier according to his proportion of . . . shall weekly assigne and put to spynning in the towne his ordinarye and course wooffe wooll, and shall not send it unto the country and if

---

[1] *S.P.D.*, cxxviii., 49, March 13, 1622.

[2] *S.P.D.*, cxxxi., 4., June 1, 1622.

sufficient be in the towne to doe it[1]." At another
time it is recorded that " In regard of the great
clamour of divers poore people lackinge worke and
employment in spynninge and cardinge in this Towne,
yt was this daye thought fitt to convent all the undertakers of the stocke given by Mr. Kendricke, and uppon
their appearaunce it was ordered, and by themselves
agreed, that every undertaker, for every 300li. shall
put a woowf a weeke to spyninge within the Towne,
as Mr. Mayour shall apoynt, and to such spynners as
Mr. Mayour shall send to them[2]."

In these times of distress and in all disputes concerning wages and the exactions of the employers,
men and women stood together, supporting each other
in their efforts for the improvement of their lot.
Thus the Justices of the Peace of Devonshire reported
that " complaints were made by the most parte of
the clothiers weavers, spinsters and fullers between
Plymouth and Teignmouth."[3] and the Council is
informed that at the last Quarter Sessions in Wilts,
many " weavers, spinners, and fullers for themselves
and for manie hundreds more . . . complained
of distress by increasing want of work. . . .
Clothiers giving up their trade, etc."[4]

Sometimes the petitions, though presented on behalf
of spinners as well as weavers, were actually signed
only by men. This was the case with the Weavers,
Fullers and Spinners of Leonard Stanley and King
Stanley in Gloucestershire, who petitioned on behalf
of themselves and others, 800 at the least, young and
old, of the said parishes, " Whereas your poore petitioners have heretofore bene well wrought and imployed in our sayd occupations belonging to the trade of

---

[1] Guilding, *Reading*, Vol. II., p. 159, 1623.

[2] *Ibid*, Vol. III., p. 7, Mar. 3, 1629-30.

[3] *S.P.D.*, xcvii., 85, May 25, 1618. J.P.s of Devonshire to Council.

[4] *Ibid*, cxv., 20, May 11, 1620. J.P.s of Wiltshire to Council.

clothing whereby we were able in some poore measure and at a very lowe rate to maintaine ourselves and families soe as hitherto they have not suffered any extreme want. But now soe it is that we are likely for the time to come never to be imployed againe in our callinges and to have our trades become noe trades, whereunto we have bene trained up and served as apprentices according to the lawe, and wherein we have always spent our whole time and are now unfitt for . . . other occupations, neither can we be received into worke by any clothiers in the whole countrey."[1]

At other times women took the lead in demanding the redress of grievances from which all were suffering. When the case of the say-makers abating the wages of the spinsters, weavers and combers of Sudbury was examined by the Justices, the Saymakers alleged that all others did the same, but that they were content to give the wages paid by them if these were extended by proclamation or otherwise throughout the kingdom. " But if the order is not general it will be their undoing . . ." Whereupon the Justices ordered the Saymakers to pay spinsters " for every seaven knottes one penny, the reel whereon the yarne is reeled to be a yard in length—no longer," and to pay weavers " 12d. a lb. for weaving thereof for white sayes under 5 lbs. weight."[2]

Shortly afterwards the Council received a petition from the Mayor asking to be heard by the Council or Commissioners to answer the complaint made against them. " by Silvia Harber widow set on worke by Richard Skinnir of Sudbury gent . . . for abridging and wronging of the spinsters and weavers of the said borough in their wages and for some other wrongs supposed to bee done to the said Silvia Harber,"

---

[1] S.P.D., ccxliv., 1. Aug. 1, 1633.

[2] S.P.D., clxxxix., 40, Ap. 27, 1631. J.P.s of Essex to Council.

followed by an an affidavit stating "Wee whose names are hereunder written doe testifye as followeth with our severell handes to our testification.

1. That one Silvia Harber of our Towne of Sudbury comonly called Luce Harbor did say that shee had never undertaken to peticion the Lordes of the Counsell in the Behalfe of the Spinsters of Sudbury aforesaid but by the inducement of Richard Skinner gentleman of the Towne aforesaid who sent for her twoe or three times before shee would goe unto him for that purpose, and when shee came to him hee sent her to London and bare her charges. Witness, Daniel Biat Clement Shelley.

2. That having conference with Richard Skinner aforesaid Gentleman, hee did confesse that hee would never have made any stir of complaint against the saymakers in behalf of weavers and spinsters, but that one Thomas Woodes of the towne abovesaid had given him Distaystfull wordes." Witness, Vincent Cocke.[1]

No organisation appears to have been formed by the wage-earners in the woollen Trade. Their demonstrations against employers were as yet local and sporadic. The very nature of their industry and the requirements of its capitalistic organisation would have rendered abortive on their part the attempt to raise wages by restricting the numbers of persons admitted into the trade; but the co-operation in trade disputes between the men and women engaged in this industry, forms a marked contrast to the conditions which were now beginning to prevail in the apprentice trades and which will be described later. Though without immediate result in the woollen trade, it may be assumed that it was this habit of standing shoulder to shoulder, regardless of sex jealousy, which ensured that when Industrialism attained a further development

---

[1] *S.P.D.*, cxcvii., 72, July, 1631. Affidavit about Saymakers in County of Suffolk.

in the closely allied cotton trade, the union which was
then called into being embraced men and women on
almost equal terms.

The broad outline of the position of women in the
woollen trade as it was established in the seventeenth
century shows them taking little, if any, part in the
management of the large and profitable undertakings
of Clothiers and Wool-merchants. Their industrial
position was that of wage-earners, and though the
demand for their labour generally exceeded the supply,
yet the wages they received were barely sufficient for
their individual maintenance, regardless of the fact that
in most cases they were wholly or partly supporting
children or other dependants.

The higher rates of pay for spinning appear to have
been secured by the women who did not depend
wholly upon it for their living, but could buy
wool, spin it at their leisure, and sell the yarn in the
dearest market ; while those who worked all the
year round for clothiers or middlemen, were often
beaten down in their wages and were subject to
exactions and oppression.

C. *Linen.*

While the woollen trade had for centuries been developing under the direction of capitalism, it was only
in the seventeenth century that this influence begins
to show itself in the production of linen. Following the
example of the clothiers, attempts were then made to
manufacture linen on a large scale. For example,
Celia Fiennes describes Malton as a " pretty large
town built of Stone but poor ; . . . there was one
Mr. Paumes that marry'd a relation of mine, Lord
Ewers' Coeheiress who is landlady of almost all y^e
town. She has a pretty house in the place. There is
the ruins of a very great house wh^{ch} belonged to y^e
family but they not agreeing about it Caused ye deface-
ing of it. She now makes use of ye roomes off y^e
out-buildings and gate house for weaving and Linning

Cloth, haveing set up a manuffactory for Linnen wh[ch] does Employ many poor people."[1]

In spite of such innovations the production of linen retained for the most part its character as one of the crafts " yet left of that innocent old world." The housewife, assisted by servants and children span flax and hemp for household linen, underclothes, children's frocks and other purposes, and then took her thread to the local weaver who wove it to her order. Thus Richard Stapley, Gent., enters in his Diary : " A weaver fetched 11 pounds of flaxen yarn to make a bedticke ; and he brought me ten yds of ticking for y[e] bed, 3 yds and $\frac{3}{4}$ of narrow ticking for y[e] bolster & for y[e] weaving of which I paid him 10s. and ye flax cost 8d. per pound. My mother spun it for me, and I had it made into a bed by John Dennit, a tailor, of Twineham for 8d. on Wednesday, July 18th, and it was filled on Saturday, August 4th by Jonas Humphrey of Twineham for 6d. The weaver brought it home July 6th.[2] Similarly Sarah Fell enters in her Household book : " Nov. 18th, 1675, by m[o]. p[d]. Geo. ffell weaver fo[r] workeinge 32 : ells of hempe tow cloth of Mothrs. at 1d$\frac{1}{4}$ ell. 000.04.00 "[3]

By the industry and foresight of its female members the ordinary household was supplied with all its necessary linen without any need for entering the market, the expenses of middlemen and salesmen being so avoided. Nevertheless, it is evident that a considerable sale for linen had always existed, for the linen drapers were an important corporation in many towns. This sale was increased through an invention made about the middle of the century : By printing patterns on linen a material was produced which

[1] Fiennes (Celia) p. 74. *Through England on a Side-saddle.*

[2] *Suss. Arch. Coll.*, Vol. II., p. 121. *Extracts from the Diary of Richard Stapley, Gent.*, 1682-1724.

[3] Fell (Sarah) *Household Accts.*, p. 233.

closely imitated the costly muslins, or calicoes as they were then called, imported from India ; but at so reasonable a price that they were within the reach of a servant's purse. Servants were therefore able to go out in dresses scarcely distinguishable from their mistresses', and the sale of woollen and silk goods was seriously affected. The woollen trade became alarmed ; riots took place ; weavers assaulted women who were wearing printed linens in the streets, and finally, Parliament, always tender to the woollen trade, which furnished so large a part of the national revenue, prohibited their use altogether. The linen printers recognising that " the Reason why the *English* Manufacture of linnen is not so much taken notice of as the *Scotch* or *Irish*, is this, the *English* is mostly consumed in the Country, . . . whereas the *Scotch* and *Irish* must come by sea and make a Figure at our custom's house,"[1] urged in their defence that " the linens printed are chiefly the Growth and Manufacture of *North Britain* pay 3d. per Yard to the Crown, . . . and Employ so many Thousands of *British* poor, as will undoubtedly entitle them to the Care of a British Parliament."[2]

But even this argument was unavailing against the political influence of the woollen trade. The spirit of the time favouring the spread of capitalistic enterprise from the woollen trade into other fields of action, an attempt was now made to form a Linen Company. Pamphlets written for and against this project furnish many details of the conditions then prevailing in the manufacture of linen. " How," it was said, will the establishment of a Linnen Company " affect the Kingdom in the two Pillars that support it, that of the Rents of Land and the imploying our Ships and Men at Sea, which are thought the Walls of the

---

[1] *Case of British and Irish Manufacture of Linnen.*

[2] *Case of the Linen Drapers.*

Nation. For the Rents of Land they must certainly
fall, for that one Acre of Flax will imploy as many
Hands the year round, as the Wooll of Sheep that
graze twenty Acres of Ground. The Linnen Manufactory imploys few men, the Woollen most, Weaving,
Combing, Dressing, Shearing, Dying, etc. These Eat
and Drink more than Women and Children ; and so
as the Land that the Sheep graze on raiseth the Rent,
so will the Arable and Pasture that bears Corn, and
breeds Cattle for their Subsistence. Then for the
Employment of our Shipping, it will never be preten-
dedthat we can arrive to Exportation of Linnen ; there
are others and too many before us in that. . . . That
Projectors and Courtiers should be inspired with
New Lights, and out of love to the Nation, create
new Methods in Trades, that none before found out ;
and by inclosing Commons the Liberty of Trade into
Shares, in the first place for themselves, and then for
such others as will pay for both, is, I must confess,
to me, a Mystery I desire to be a Stranger unto. . . .
The very Name of a Company and Joint-Stock in
Trade, is a spell to drive away, and keep out of that
place where they reside, all men of Industry. . . .
The great motive to Labour and Incouragement of
Trade, is an equal Freedom, and that none may be
secluded from the delightful Walks of Liberty . . .
a Subjection in Manufactories where a People are
obliged to one Master, tho' they have the full Value
of their Labour, is not pleasing, they think themselves
in perpetual Servitude, and so it is observed in *Ireland*,
where the *Irish* made a Trade of Linnen Yarn, no
Man could ingage them, but they would go to the
Market and be better satisfied with a less price, than
to be obliged to one master. . . . There was
much more Reason for a Company and Joint-stock
to set up the Woollen Manufactory, in that ignorant
Age, than there is for this of the Linnen Manufactory ;
that of the Woollen was a new Art not known in this

Kingdom, it required a great Stock to manage, there
was required Foreign as well as Native Commodities
to carry it on. . . . and when the Manufactory
was made, there must be Skill and Interest abroad to
introduce the Commodity where others had the Trade
before them ; but there is nothing of all this in the
Linnen Manufactory ; Nature seems to design it
for the weaker Sex. The best of Linnen for Service
is called House Wife's Cloth, here then is no need
of the Broad Seal, or Joint-Stock to establish the
Methods for the good Wife's weeding her Flax-garden,
or how soon her Maid shall sit to her Wheel after
washing her Dishes ; the good Woman is Lady of
the Soil, and holds a Court within herself, throws
the Seed into the Ground, and works it till she brings
it there again, I mean her Web to the bleaching
Ground. . . . To appropriate this which the
poorest Family may by Labour arrive unto, that is,
finish and bring to Market a Piece of Cloth, to me
seems an infallible Expedient to discourage universal
Industry. . . . . The Linnen Manufactory above
any Trade I know, if (which I must confess I doubt)
it be for the Good of the Nation, requires more Charity
than Grandeur to carry it on, the poor Spinner comes
as often to her Master for Charity to a sick Child, or
a Plaister for a Sore, as for Wages ; and this she cannot
have of a Company, but rather less for her labour,
when they have beat all private Undertakers out.
These poor Spinners can now come to their Master's
Doors at a good time, and eat of their good tho' poor
master's Chear ; they can reason with him, if any
mistake, or hardship be put upon them, and this
poor People love to do, and not be at the Dispose of
Servants, as they must be where their Access can only
be by Doorkeepers, Clerks, etc., to the Governors
of the Company."*

---

* Linnen and Woollen Manufactory, p. 4-8, 1691.

On the other side it was urged that " All the Arguments that can be offer'd for Encouraging the woollen manufacture in *England* conclude as strongly in proportion for Encouraging the linnen manufacture in *Scotland*. 'Tis the ancient Staple Commodity there, as the Woollen is here."[1]

The part taken by women in the production of linen resembled their share in woollen manufactures. Some were weavers ; thus Oliver Heywood says that his brother-in-law, who afterwards traded in fustians, was brought up in Halifax with Elizabeth Roberts, a linen weaver.[2] Entries in the Foulis Account Book show that they were sometimes employed in bleaching but spinning was the only process which depended exclusively on their labour.

The rates of pay for spinning flax and hemp were even lower than those for spinning wool. Fitzherbert expressly says that in his time no woman could get her living by spinning linen.[3] The market price was of little moment to well-to-do women who span thread for their family's use and who valued the product of their labour by its utility and not by its return in money value ; but the women who depended on spinning for their living were virtually paupers, as is shown by the terms in which reference is made to them :—" shee beeinge very poore, gettinge her livinge by spinninge and in the nature of a widowe, her husband beeinge in the service of His Majesty."[4]

Yet the demand for yarn and thread was so great that if spinners had been paid a living wage there would have been scarcely any need for poor relief.

The relation between low wages and pauperism was hardly even suspected at this time, and though the

---

[1] *True case of the Scots Linen Manufacture.*
[2] Heywood (Rev. Oliver) *Autobiography*, Vol. I., p. 36.
[3] Ante, p. 48.
[4] *S.P.D.*, cccclvii., 3. June 13, 1640.

spinsters' maximum wages were settled at Quarter
Sessions, no effort was made to raise them to a subsistence level Instead of attempting to do so Parish
Authorities accepted pauperism as "the act of God," and
concentrated their attention on the task of reducing
rates as far as possible by forcing the pauper women
and children, who had become impotent or vicious
through neglect and underfeeding, to spin the thread
needed by the community. Schemes for this
purpose were started all over the country; a few
examples will show their general scope. At Nottingham
it was arranged for Robert Hassard to "Receave pore
children to the number of viij. or more, . . and to
haue the benefitt of theire workes and labours for
the first Moneth, and the towne to allowe him towards
their dyett, for everie one xijd. a Weeke, and theire
parents to fynde them lodginge ; and Robert Hassard
to be carefull to teache and instructe them speedyly
in the spyninge and workinge heare, to be fitt to make
heare-cloth, and allsoe in cardinge and spyninge of
hards to make candle weeke, and hee to geue them
correccion, when need ys, and the greate wheeles
to be called in, and to be delivered for the vse of
these ymployments.[1]

A few years later in the scheme "for setting the
poore on worke" the following rates of pay were
established :—

6d. per pound for cardinge and spinning finest wool.
5d. „ - „   for ye second sort.
4d.ob. (= *obolus,*½d.) for ye third sorte.
1d. per Ley [skein] for ye onely spinninge all sortes
     of linen, the reele beeing 4 yards.
ob per pound for cardinge candleweake.
1d. „   „   for pulling midling [coarser part] out
     of it.
1d. „   „   for spininge candleweake.[2]

---

[1] *Nottingham Records*, Vol. V., pp. 174-5, 1636.
[2] *Ibid*, pp. 259-60, 1649.

Orders for the Workhouse at Westminster in 1560, read that "old Women or middle-Aged that might work, and went a Gooding, should be Hatchilers of the Flax; and one Matron over them. That common Hedges, and such-like lusty naughty Packs, should be set to spinning; and one according to be set over them. Children that were above Six and not twelve Years of Age should be sent to winde Quills to the Weavers."[1]

At a later date in London " Besides the relieving and educating of poor friendless harborless children in Learning and in Arts, many hundreds of poor Families are imployed and relieved by the said Corporation in the Manufactory of Spinning and Weaving : and whosoever doth repair either to the Wardrobe near Black-friars, or to Heiden-house in the Minories, may have materials of Flax, Hemp, or Towe to spin at their own houses. . . . leaving so much money as the said materials cost, until it be brought again in Yarn ; at which time they shall receive money for their work. . . . every one is paid according to the fineness or coarseness of the Yarn they spin. . . . so that none are necessitated to live idly that are desirous or willing to work. And it is to be wished and desired, that the Magistrates of this city would assist this Corporation. . . . in supressing of Vagrants and common Beggars . . . . that so abound to the hindrance of the Charity of many pious people towards this good work."[2]

The Cowden overseers carried out a scheme of work for the poor from 1600 to 1627, buying flax and having it spun and woven into canvas. The work generally paid for itself ; only one year is a loss of 7s. 8d. entered, and during the first seventeen years the amount expended yearly in cash and relief did

---

[1] Stow, *London*, Book VI., p. 60.

[2] *Poor Out-cast Children's Song and Cry.*

not exceed £6 11s. rising then in 1620 to £28 5s. 10d., after which it fell again. The scheme was finally abandoned in 1627, the relief immediately rising to £43 7s. 6d.[1]

Richard Dunning describes how in Devon " for Employing Women, . . . We agreed with one Person, who usually Employed several *Spinsters*, . . . he was to employ in *Spinning, Carding*, etc., all such Women as by direction of the Overseers should apply to him for Work, to pay them such Wages as they should deserve."[2]

" Mary Harrison, daughter of Henry Harrison, was comited to the hospitall at Reading to be taught to spyn and earne her livinge."[3] Similarly at Dorchester " Sarah Handcock of this Borough having this day been complayned of for her disorderly carriage and scolding in the work house . . . . among the spinsters, is now ordered to come no more to the work house to work there, but is to work elsewhere and follow her work, or to be further delt withall according to the lawe."[4]

At Dorchester a school was maintained for some years in which poor children were taught spinning : " This day John Tarrenton . . . . . is agreed withall to vndertake charge and to be master of the Hospitall to employ halfe the children at present at burlinge,[5] and afterwards the others as they are willing and able, To have the howse and Tenne per annum : wages for the presente, and yf all the Children come into burlinge, and ther be no need of the women that doe now teach them to spinne, then the Towne

---

[1] *Suss. Arch. Coll.*, Vol. xx., pp. 99-100, *Acct. Book of Cowdon.*

[2] Dunning, *Plain and Easie Method*, p. 8, 1686.

[3] Guilding, *Reading*, Vol. II., p. 294.

[4] Mayo (C.H) *Municipal Records of Dorchester*, p. 667, 1635.

[5] To burl, " to dress cloth as fullers do."

to consyder of Tarrington to giue him either part
or all, that is ix pownd, the women now hath.[1] . . .

Another entry, February 3rd, 1644–5, records that
" Mr. Speering doth agree to provide spinning work
for such poore persons that shall spin with those
turnes as are now there [in the hospital house] . . .
and to pay the poore for their spinning after the vsual
rates for the worke they doe.[2]

In 1649 it is entered " This day Thos. Clench
was here, and demanded 10 *li.* per ann. more
than the stocke of the Hospital, which is 150 *li.*
lent him for the furnishing of the house with worke
for spinners, and for the overlooking to the children
. . . the spinners shall have all the yeare 3½d. a *li.*
for yearne . . . . and that there be as many
children kept aworke as the roomes will hold . . .
wee shall take into consideracion the setting of the
poore on worke in spinning of worsted, and knitting
of stockins, and also of setting vp a trade of making
sackcloth.[3]

Schemes for teaching spinning were welcomed
with enthusiasm by the economists of the period,
because in many districts the poor rates had risen to
an alarming height. They believed that if only
the poor would work all would be well. One writer
urged " That if the Poor of the Place do not know how
to spin, or to do the Manufacture of that Place, that
then there be Dames hired at the Parish-Charge to
teach them ; and Men may learn to spin as well as
Women, and Earn as much money at it as they can
at many other employments."[4] Another writer calculated that if so employed " ixcl children wh^{ch} daielie
was ydle may earne one w^t another vjd. a weke wh^{ch}

[1] Mayo (C. H.), *Municipal Records of Dorchester*, p. 515, 1638.

[2] *Ibid*, p. 521.

[3] *Ibid*, pp. 517–8.

[4] *Trade of England*, p. 10, 1681.

a mownte in the yere t o jMiijcxxxv[li]. Also that jciiijxx women . . ar hable to earne at lest some xijd., some xxd., and some ijs. vjd. a weeke."[1]

This zest for teaching spinning was partly due to the fact that the clothiers were represented on the local authorities, and often the extending of their business was hampered by the shortage of spinsters. But the flaw in all these arrangements was the fact that spinning remained in most cases a grant in aid, and could not, owing to the low wages paid, maintain a family, scarcely even an individual, on the level of independence.

Children could not live on 6d. a week, or grown women on 1s. or 1s. 8d. a week. And so the women, when they depended wholly upon spinning flax for their living, became paupers, suffering the degradation and loss of power by malnutrition which that condition implies.

In a few cases this unsatisfactory aspect of spinning was perceived by those who were charged with relieving the poor. Thus, when a workhouse was opened in Bristol in 1654, the spinning scheme was soon abandoned as unprofitable.[2] Later, when girls were again taught spinning, the managers of the school " soon found that the great cause of begging did proceed from the low wages for Labour ; for after about eight months time our children could not get half so much as we expended in their provisions. The manufacturers . . . . were always complaining the Yarn was spun couarse, but would not advance above eightpence per pound for spinning, and we must either take this or have no work." Finally the Governor took pains therefore to teach them to produce a finer yarn at 2s. to 3s. 6d. per pound. This paid better, and would have been more profitable still if

[1] Tingey, *Norwich*, Vol. II, p. 355.

[2] Latimer, *Annals of Bristol*, p. 249.

the girls as they grew older had not been sent to
service or put into the kitchen.[1]

Thomas Firmin, after a prolonged effort to help
the poor in London, came to a similar conclusion.
He explains that " the Poor of this Parish, tho' many,
are yet not so many as in some others ; yet, even
here there are many poor people, who receive Flax
to spin, tho' they are not all Pensioners to the Parish,
nor, I hope, ever will be, it being my design to prevent
that as much as may be ; . . . . there are above
500 more out of other Parishes in and about the
City of *London* ; some of which do constantly follow
this Employment, and others only when they have
no better ; As, suppose a poor Woman that goes
three dayes a Week to Wash or Scoure abroad, or one
that is employed in Nurse-keeping three or four
Months in a Year, or a poor Market-woman, who
attends three or four Mornings in a Week with her
Basket, and all the rest of the time these folks
have little or nothing to do ; but by means of this
spinning are not only kept within doors . . . .
but made much more happy and chearful."[2]

Firmin began his benevolent work in an optimistic
spirit, " had you seen, as I have done many a time,
with what joy and satisfaction, many Poor People
have brought home their Work, and received their
money for it, you would think no Charity in the World
like unto it. Do not imagine that all the Poor People
in *England,* are like unto those Vagrants you find up
and down in the Streets. No, there are many Thousands whose necessities are very great, and yet do what
they can by their Honest Labour to help themselves ;
and many times they would do more than they do
but for want of Employment. Several that I have
now working to me do spin, some fifteen, some sixteen,

---

[1] Cary,(John) *Proceedings of Corporation of Bristol*, p. 13, 1700.

[2] Firmin, *Some Proposals*, p. 19, 1678.

hours in four and twenty, and had much rather do it than be idle.[1]

The work developed until " He employed in this manufacture some times 1600, some times 1700 Spinners, besides Dressers of flax, Weavers and others. Because he found that his Poor must work sixteen hours in the day to earn sixpence, and thought their necessities and labour were not sufficiently supplied or recompensed by these earnings ; therefore he was wont to distribute Charity among them . . . without which Charity some of them had perished for want, when either they or their children fell ill . . . . Whoever of the Spinners brought in two pound of Yarn might take away with 'em a Peck of Coals. Because they soiled themselves by carrying away Coals in their Aprons or Skirts . . . . he gave 'em canvass bags. By the assistance and order of his Friends he gave to Men, Women and Children 3,000 Shirts and Shifts in two years."[2]

" In above £4000, laid out the last Year, reckning House-rent, Servants wages, Loss by Learners, with the interest of the Money, there was not above £200 lost, one chief reason of which was the kindness of several Persons, who took off good quantities . . at the price they cost me to spin and weave . . . . and . . . . the East India Co., gave encouragement to make their bags." But the loss increased as time went on . . . . " In 1690 his design of employing the poor to spin flax was taken up by the Patentees of the Linen Manufacture, who made the Poor and others, whom they employed, to work cheaper ; yet that was not sufficient to encourage them to continue the manufacture . . . The poor spinners, being thus deserted, Mr. *Firmin* returned to 'em again ; and managed that trade as

---

[1] Firmin, Thomas, *Life*, pp. 31-32, 1698.

[2] *Ibid*, pp 31-2, 1698.

he was wont; But so, that he made it bear almost its own Charges. But that their smaller Wages might be comfortable to them he was more Charitable to 'em, and begged for 'em of almost all Persons of Rank with whom he had intimacy, or so much as Friendship. He would also carry his Cloth to divers, with whom he scarce had any acquaintance, telling 'em *it was the Poor's cloth, which in conscience they ought to buy at the Price it could be afforded.*[1] . . . Finally, " he was persuaded by some, to make trial of the *Woollen Manufacture ;* because at this, the Poor might make better wages, than at Linen-work. But the price of wool advancing very much, and the *London*-Spinsters being almost wholly unskilful at Drawing a Woollen-Thread, after a considerable loss . . . . and 29 months trial he gave off the project."[2]

Firmin's experiment, corroborating as it does the results of other efforts at poor relief, shows that at this time women could not maintain themselves by the wages of flax spinning ; still less could they, when widows, provide for their children by this means.

But though the spinster, when working for wages received so small a return for her labour, it must not be forgotten that flax spinning was chiefly a domestic art, in which the whole value of the woman's labour was secured to her family, unaffected by the rate of wages. Therefore the value of women's labour in spinning flax must not be judged only according to the wages which they received, but was more truly represented by the quantity of linen which they produced for household use.

---

[1] Firmin (Thomas) *Life*, pp. 33-6.

[2] *Ibid*, pp. 39-40.

D.   *Silk, and Gold and Silver.*

THE history of the Silk Trade differs widely from
that of either the Woollen or Linen Trades. The conditions of its manufacture during the fifteenth century
are described with great clearness in a petition presented
to Henry VI. by the silk weavers in 1455, which
" Sheweth unto youre grete wisdoms, and also prayen
and besechen the Silkewymmen and Throwestres of
the Craftes and occupation of Silkewerk within the
Citee of London, which be and have been Craftes
of wymmen within the same Citee of tyme that noo
mynde renneth unto the contrarie. That where
it is pleasyng to God that all his Creatures be set in
vertueux occupation and labour accordyng to their
degrees, and convenient for thoo places where their
abode is, to the nourishing of virtue and eschewyng
of vices and ydelness. And where upon the same Craftes,
before this tyme, many a wurshipfull woman within
the seid Citee have lyved full hounourably, and therwith
many good Housholdes kept, and many Gentilwymmen
and other in grete noumbre like as there nowe be
moo than a M., have been drawen under theym in
lernyng the same Craftes and occupation full vertueusly,
unto the plesaunce of God, whereby afterward they
have growe to grete wurship, and never any thing
of Silke brought into yis lande concerning the same
Craftes and occupation in eny wise wrought, but in
rawe Silk allone unwrought "; but now wrought goods
are introduced and it is impossible any longer to obtain
rawe material except of the worst quality . . . .
" the sufferaunce whereof, hath caused and is like to
cause, grete ydelness amongs yonge Gentilwymmen
and oyer apprentices of the same Craftes within ye
said Citee, and also leying doun of many good and not-
able Housholdes of them that have occupied the same
Craftes, which be convenient, worshipfull and accordyng
for Gentilwymmen, and oyer wymmen of wurship, aswele

within ye same Citee as all oyer places within this Reaume." The petitioners assumed that " Every wele disposed persone of this land, by reason and naturall favour, wold rather that wymmen of their nation born and owen blode hadde the occupation thereof, than strange people of oyer landes."[1]

The petition received due attention, Statute 33, Henry VI enacting that " Whereas it is shewed to our Sovereign Lord the King in his said parliament, by the grevous complaint of the silk women and spinners of the mystery and occupation of silk-working, within the city of London, how that divers Lombards and other strangers, imagining to destroy the said mystery, and all such virtuous occupations of women in the said Realm, to enrich themselves . . . . have brought . . . . such silk so made, wrought, twined, ribbands, and chains falsely and deceitfully wrought, all manner girdels and other things concerning the said mystery and occupation, in no manner wise bringing any good silk unwrought, as they were wont." Therefore the importation of " any merchandise . . . . . . touching or concerning the mystery of silk women, (girdels which come from Genoa only excepted,)" is forbidden.[2]

This statute was re-enacted in succeeding reigns with the further explanation that " as well men as women " gained their living by this trade.

Few incidents reveal more clearly than do these petitions the gulf separating the conception of women's sphere in life which prevailed in mediæval London, from that which governed society in the first decade of the twentieth century. The contrast is so great that it becomes difficult to adjust one's vision to the implications which the former contains. Other incidents

---

[1] *Rolls of Parliament*, V., 325. *A Petition of Silk Weavers*, 34 Henry VI., c. 55.

[2] *Statutes*, II., p. 374, 33 Henry VI., c. 5.

can be quoted of the independence, enterprise, and capacity manifested by the prosperous women of the merchant class in London during the Middle Ages. Thus Rose de Burford, the wife of a wealthy London merchant, engaged in trading transactions on a large scale both before and after her husband's death. She lent money to the Bishop in 1318, and received 100 Marks for a cope embroidered with coral. She petitioned for the repayment of a loan made by her husband for the Scottish wars, finally proposing that this should be allowed her off the customs which she would be liable to pay on account of wool about to be shipped from the Port of London.[1]

It is, however, a long cry from the days of Rose de Burford to the seventeenth century, when "gentilwymmen and other wymmen of worship" no longer made an honourable living by the silk trade; which trade, in spite of protecting statutes, had become the refuge of paupers. To obviate the difficulties of an exclusive reliance on foreign supplies for the raw material of the silk trade, James I. ordered the planting of 10,000 mulberry trees so that "multitudes of persons of both sexes and all ages, such as in regard of impotence are unfitted for other labour, may bee set on worke, comforted and releved."[2]

The unsatisfactory state of the trade is shown in a petition from the merchants, silk men, and others trading for silk, asking for a charter of incorporation because "the trade of silke is now become great whereby . . . . customes are increased and many thousands of poore men, women and children sett on worke and mayntayned. And forasmuch as the first beginning of this trade did take its being from women then called silkwomen who brought

---

[1] By kind permission of Miss Eileen Power.

[2] *S.P.D.*, xxvi., 6.   Jan. 1607.

upp men servants, that since have become free of all or moste of the severall guilds and corporacions of London, whose ordinances beeing for other particular trades, meet not with, nor have power to reprove such abuses and deceipts as either have or are likely still to growe upon the silk trade."[1]

A petition from the Master, Wardens and Assistants of the Company of Silk Throwers, shows that by this " Trade between Forty and Fifty thousand poor Men, Women and Children, are constantly Imployed and Relieved, in and about the City of *London* . . . . divers unskilful Persons, who never were bred as Apprentices to the said Trade of *Silk-throwing*, have of *Late years* intruded into the said Trade, and have Set up the same ; and dwelling in Places beyond the Bounds and Circuit of the Petitioners Search by their Charter, do use Divers Deceits in the *Throwing* and *Working* of the Manufacture of Silk, to the great Wrong and Injury of the Commonwealth, and the great Discouragement of the Artists of the said Trade."[2]

An act of Charles II. provided that men, women and children, if native subjects, though not apprentices, might be employed to turn the mill, tie threads, and double and wind silk, " as formerly."[3]

" There are here and there," it was said " a Silk Weaver or two (of late years) crept into some cities and Market Towns in *England*, who do employ such people that were never bound to the Trade . . . . in all other Trades that do employ the poor, they cannot effect their business without employing such as were never apprentice to the Trade . . . the Clothier must employ the Spinner and Stockcarder, that peradventure were never apprentices to any trade, else they could never accomplish their

---

[1] *S.P.D.*, clxxv., 102, Nov. 25, 1630.

[2] *Humble Petition of the Master, Wardens and Assistants of the Company of Silk Throwers.*

[3] Statutes 13 and 14, Charles II., c. 15.

end. And it is the same in making of Buttons and Bone lace, and the like. But it is not so in this Trade ; for they that have been apprentices to the Silk-weaving Trade, are able to make more commodities than can be easily disposed of . . . . because there hath not been for a long time any other but this, to place forth poor men's Children, and Parish Boyes unto ; by which means the poor of this Trade have been very numerous."[1]

During this period all the references to silk-spinning confirm the impression that it had become a pauper trade. A pamphlet calling for the imposition of a duty on the importation of wrought silks explains that " The Throwsters, by reason of this extraordinary Importation of raw Silk, will employ several hundred persons more than they did before, as Winders, Doublers, and others belonging to the throwing Trade, who for the greatest part are poor Seamen and Soldier's wives, which by this Increase of Work will find a comfortable Subsistence for themselves and Families, and thereby take off a Burthen that now lies upon several Parishes, which are at a great charge for their Support."[2] The " comfortable subsistence " of these poor seamen's wives amounted to no more than 1s. 6d. or 1s. 8d. per week.[3]

There seems here no clue to explain the transition from a monopoly of gentlewomen conducting a profitable business on the lines of Family Industry to a disorganised Capitalistic Trade, resting on the basis of women's sweated labour. The earlier monopoly was, however, probably favoured by the expensive nature of the materials used, and the necessity

---

[1] *Trade of England*, p. 18.

[2] *Answer to a Paper of Reflections, on the Project for laying a Dnty on English Wrought Silks.*

[3] *Case of the Manufacturers of Gilt and Silver Wire*, 1714.

for keeping in touch with the merchants who imported them, while social customs secured an equitable distribution of the profits. With the destruction of these social customs and traditions, competition asserted its sway unchecked, till it appeared as though there might even be a relation between the costliness of the material and the wretchedness of the women employed in its manufacture ; for the women who span gold and silver thread were in the same stage of misery.

Formerly women had been mistresses in this class of business as well as in the Silk Trade, but a Proclamation of June 11th, 1622, forbade the exercise of the craft by all except members of the Company of Gold Wire Drawers.

Under this proclamation the Silver thread of one Anne Twiseltor was confiscated by Thomas Stockwood, a constable, who entered her house and found her and others spinning gold and silver thread. " The said Anne being since married to one John Bagshawe hath arrested Stockwood for the said silver upon an action of £10, on the Saboth day going from Church, and still prosecuteth the suite against him in Guild Hall with much clamor."[1] Bagshawe and his wife maintained that the silver was sterling, and therefore not contrary to the Proclamation. Stockwood refused to return it unless he might have some of it. Therefore they commenced the suit against him.

Probably few, if any, women became members of the Company of Gold Wire Drawers, and henceforward they were employed only as spinners. Their poverty is shown by the frequency with which they are mentioned as inmates of tenement houses, which through overcrowding became dangerous to the public health. It was reported to the Council for example, that Katherine Barnaby " entertayns in her house in Great

---

[1] *C.R.*, June 16, 1624.

Wood Streate, divers women kinde silver spinners."[1]

These poor women worked in the spinning sheds of their masters, and thus the factory system prevailed already in this branch of the textile industry; the costliness of the fabrics produced forbade any great expansion of the trade, and therefore the Masters were not obliged to seek for labour outside the pauper class.

The Curate, Churchwardens, Overseers and Vestrymen of the parish of St. Giles, Cripplegate, drew up the following statement : " There are in the said Parish, eighty five sheds for the spinning Gilt and Silver Thread, in which are 255 pair of wheels.

The Masters with their Families amount unto	581
These imploy poor Parish-Boys and Girls to the number of	1275
There are 118 master Wire-Drawers, who with their wives, Children and Apprentices, make	826
Master weavers of Gold and Silver Lace and Fringes 106 Their Wives, Children, Apprentices and Journey Men amount unto	2120
Silver and Gold Bone-Lace makers, and Silver and Gold Button makers with their Families	1000
Windsters, Flatters of Gold and Silver and Engine Spinners with their Families	300
Total	6208

They continue : " The Poor's Rate of the Parish amounts to near Four Thousand Pounds per annum. . . . The Parish . . . . at this present are indebted One Thousand Six Hundred and Fifty Pounds. Persons are daily removing out of the Parish, by Reason of this heavy Burthen, empty Houses increasing. If a Duty be laid on the manufacture of Gold and Silver wyres the Poor must necessarily be increased."[2]

---

[1] *S.P.D.*, ccclix., Returns to Council . . . of houses, etc, 1637.

[2] *Case of the Parish of St. Giles, Cripplegate.*

Such a statement is in itself proof that Gold and Silver Thread making ranked among the pauper trades in which the wages paid must needs be suplemented out of the poor rates.

E. Conclusion.

It has been shown that in textile industries all spinning was done exclusively by women and children, while they were also engaged to some extent in other processes, such as weaving, burling, bleaching, fulling, etc. The fact that the nation depended entirely upon women for the thread from which its clothing and household linen was made must be remembered in estimating their economic position. Even if no other work had fallen to their share, they can hardly have been regarded as mere dependants on their husbands when the clothing for the whole family was spun by their hands ; but it has been explained in the previous chapter that in many cases the mother, in addition to spinning, provided a large proportion of the food consumed by her family. If the father earned enough money to pay the rent and a few other necessary expenses, the mother could and did, feed and clothe herself and her children by her own labours when she possessed enough capital to confine herself wholly to domestic industry. The value of a woman's productive capacity to her family was, however, greatly reduced when, through poverty, she was obliged to work for wages, because then, far from being able to feed and clothe her family, her wages were barely adequate to feed herself.

This fact indicates the weakness of women's position in the labour market, into which they were being forced in increasing numbers by the capitalistic organisation of industry. In consequence of this weakness, a large proportion of the produce of a woman's labour was diverted from her family to the profit of the capitalist or the consumer ; except in the most skilled branches of the woollen industry, spinning was a pauper trade, a " sweated industry," which did not provide its workers with the means for keeping themselves and their families in a state of efficiency, but left them to some extent dependent on other sources for their maintenance.

Comparing the various branches of textile industry together, an interesting light is thrown upon the reactions between capitalistic organisation of labour and women's economic position.

Upper class women had lost their unique position in the silk trade, and the wives of wealthy clothiers and wool merchants appear to have seldom taken an active interest in business matters. Thus it was only as wage-earners that women were extensively employed in the textile trades.

Their wages were lowest in the luxury trades i.e., silk, silver and gold, and in the linen trade. The former were now wholly capitalistic, but the demand for luxuries being limited and capable of little expansion, the labour available in the pauper classes was sufficient to satisfy it. The situation was different in the linen and allied trades, where the demand for thread, either of flax or hemp, appears generally to have been in excess of the supply. Although the larger part of the linen manufactured in England was still produced under the conditions of domestic industry, the demand for thread for trade purposes was steady enough to suggest to Parish Authorities the value of spinning as a means of reducing the poor rates. It did not occur to them, however, that if the wages paid for spinning were higher the poor would have been as eager to learn spinning as to gain apprenticeship in the skilled trades, and thus the problem of an adequate supply of yarn might have been solved at one stroke with the problem of poverty itself ; no attempt was made to raise the wages, and the production of thread for trade purposes continued to be subsidised out of the poor rates. The consequent pauperisation of large numbers of women was a greater disaster than even the burthen of the poor rates. Instead of the independence and self-reliance which might have been secured through adequate wages, mothers were not only humiliated and degraded, but their physical efficiency and that of their children was lowered owing to the inadequacy of the grudging assistance given by the Churchwardens and Overseers.

The woollen trade, in which capitalistic organisation had attained its largest development, presents a more favourable aspect as regards women's wages. Already in the seventeenth century a spinster could earn sufficient money to maintain her individual self. In spite of periodic seasons of depression, the woollen trade was rapidly expanding; often the scope of the clothiers was limited by the quantity of yarn available, and so perforce they must seek for labour outside the pauper class. Possibly a rise was already taking place in the spinsters' wages at the close of the century, and it is interesting to note that during this period the highest wages were earned, not by the women whose need for them was greatest, that is to say the women who had children depending exclusively on their wages, but rather by the well-to-do women who could afford to buy the wool for their spinning, and hold the yarn over till an advantageous opportunity arose for selling it.

Spinning did not present itself to such women as a means of filling up vacant hours which they would otherwise have spent in idleness, but as an alternative to some other profitable occupation, so numerous were the opportunities offered to women for productive industry within the precincts of the home. Therefore to induce women of independent position to work for him, the Clothier was obliged to offer higher wages than would have been accepted by those whose children were suffering from hunger.

Somewhat apart from economics and the rate of wages, is the influence which the developments of the woollen trade exercised on women's social position, through the disintegration of the social organisation known as the village community. The English village had formed a social unit almost self-contained, embracing considerable varieties of wealth, culture and occupation, and finding self-expression in a public opinion which provided adequate sanction for its customs, and determined all the details of manners and morals. In the formation of this public opinion women took an active part.

The seasons of depression in the Woollen Trade brought to such communities in the " Clothing Counties " a desolation which could only be rivalled by Pestilence or Famine. Work came to a standstill, and wholesale migrations followed. Many fathers left their starving families, in search of work elsewhere and were never heard of again. The traditions of family life and the customs which ruled the affairs of the village were lost, never to be again restored, and with them disappeared, to a great extent, the recognised importance of women in the life of the community.

The social problems introduced by the wages system in its early days are described in a contemporary pamphlet. It must be remembered that the term " the poor " as used at this time signified the pauper class, hard-working, industrious families who were independent of charity or assistance from the poor rates being all included among the " common people." " I cannot acknowledge," the writer says, " that a Manufacture maketh fewer poor, but rather the contrary. For tho' it sets the poor on work where it finds them, yet it draws still more to the place ; and their Masters allow wages so mean, that they are only preserved from starving whilst they can work ; when Age, Sickness, or Death comes, themselves, their wives or their children are most commonly left upon the Parish; which is the reason why those Towns (as in the *Weald of Kent*) whence the clothing is departed, have fewer poor than they had before."[1]

---

[1] *Reasons for a Limited Exportation of Wooll,* 1677

CHAPTER V.

CRAFTS AND TRADES.

(A) *Crafts.* Influence of Gilds—Inclusion of women—Position of craftsman's wife—Purposes of Gilds—The share of women in religious, social and trading privileges—Admission chiefly by marriage—Stationer's Company—Carpenter's Company—Rules of other Gilds and Companies—Apprenticeship to women—Exclusion of women did not originate in sex jealousy—Position of women in open trades—Women's trades.

(B) *Retail Trades.* Want of technical training inclined women towards retailing—Impediments in their way—Apprenticeship of girls to shopkeepers—Prosecution of unauthorised traders—Street and market trading—Pedlars, Regraters, Badgers—Opposition of shopkeepers.

(C) *Provision Trades.*

　　1. *Bakers.* Never specially a woman's trade—Widows—Share of married women.

　　2. *Millers.* Occasionally followed by women.

　　3. *Butchers.* Carried on by women as widows and by married women—also independently—Regrating.

　　4. *Fishwives.* Generally very poor.

　　5. *Brewers.* Originally a special women's trade—Use of feminine form Brewster—Creation of monopoly—Exclusion of women by the trade when capitalised—retailing still largely in hands of women.

　　6. *Vintners.*

AGRICULTURE and the textile industries having been considered separately, owing to their importance and the very special conditions obtaining in both, the other forms of industry in which women were employed may be roughly divided into three classes, according to certain influences which made them more or less suitable for women's employment.—(*a*) Skilled Trades. (*b*) Retail Trades. (*c*) Provision Trades.

(*a*) *The Skilled Trades.* Most characteristic of the skilled trades are those crafts which became more or less highly organised and specialised by means of Gilds ; though girls were seldom apprenticed to the gild trades, yet her marriage to a member of the Gild conferred upon a woman her husband's rights and privileges ; and as she retained these after his

death, she could, as a widow, continue to control
and direct the business which she inherited from
her husband. In many trades the gild organisation
broke down, and though the form of apprenticeship
was retained its observance secured few, if any,
privileges. Some skilled trades were chiefly if not
wholly, in the hands of women, and these appear
never to have been organised, though long appren-
ticeships were served by the girls who entered them.

(b) *The Retail Trades.* The classification of retail
trades as a group distinct from the Skilled Trades and
the Provision Trades is somewhat arbitrary, because
under the system of Family Industry, the maker of
the goods was often his own salesman, or the middlemen who sold the goods to the consumers were
themselves organised into gilds. Nevertheless, from
the woman's point of view retailing deserves separate
consideration, because, whether as a branch of Family
Industry or as a trade in itself, the employment of
selling was so singularly adapted to the circumstances
of women, that among their resources it may almost
take rank with agriculture and spinning.

(c) *The Provision Trades* also, whether concerned
with the production or only with the sale of Provisions,
occupy a special position, because the provisioning
of their households has been regarded from time
immemorial as one of the elementary duties falling
to the share of women, and it is interesting to note
how far skill acquired by women in such domestic
work was useful to them in trade.

In all three classes of industry women were employed
as their husbands' assistants or partners, but in the
middle ages married women also engaged in business
frequently on their own account. This was so
usual that almost all the early Customs of the Boroughs
enable a woman, when so trading, to go to law
as though though she were a femme sole, and provide
that her husband shall not be responsible for her

debts. For example, the Customs of the City of London declare that: " Where a woman coverte de baron follows any craft within the said city by herself apart, with which the husband in no way intermeddles, such woman shall be bound as a single woman in all that concerns her said craft. And if the wife shall plead as a single woman in a Court of Record, she shall have her law and other advantages by way of plea just as a single woman. And if she is condemned she shall be committed to prison until she shall have made satisfaction; and neither the husband nor his goods shall in such case be charged or interfered with. If a wife, as though a single woman, rents any house or shop within the said city, she shall be bound to pay the rent of the said house or shop, and shall be impleaded and sued as a single woman, by way of debt if necessary, notwithstanding that she was coverte de baron, at the time of such letting, supposing that the lessor did not know thereof. . . . Where plaint of debt is made against the husband, and the plaintiff declares that the husband made the contract with the plaintiff by the hand of the wife of such defendant, in such case the said defendant shall have the aid of his wife, and shall have a day until the next Court, for taking counsel with his wife."[1]

The Customal of the Town and Port of Sandwich provides that " if a woman who deals publickly in fish, fruit, cloth or the like, be sued to the amount of goods delivered to her, she ought to answer either with or without her husband, as the plaintiff pleases. But in every personal plea of trespass, she can neither recover nor plead against any body, without her husband. If she be not a public dealer, she cannot answer, being a covert baron."[2]   Similarly at Rye,

---

[1] *Liber Albus*, pp. 181-2. 1419.

[2] Lyon. *Dover*, Vol. II., p. 295.

" if any woman that is covert baron be impleaded in plea of debt, covenant broken, or chattels withheld, and she be known for sole merchant, she ought to answer without the presence of her baron."[1]

In Carlisle it was said that " where a wife that haith a husband use any craft with[in] this citie or the liberties of the same besides her husband crafte or occupation and that he mel not wth her sayd craft this wife shalbe charged as woman sole. And if the husband and the wife be impledit in such case the wife shall plead as woman sole. And if she be condempned she shall goe to ward unto she haue mayd agrement. And the husband nor his guds shal not in this case be charged. And if the woman refuse to appeare and answere the husband or servand to bryng her in to answer."[2]

Though examples of the separate trading of women occur frequently in the seventeenth century, no doubt the more usual course was for her to assist her husband in his business. When this was transacted at home her knowledge of it was so intimate that she could successfully carry on the management during her husband's absence. How complete was the reliance which men placed upon their wives under these circumstances is illustrated by the story of John Adams, a Quaker from Yorkshire, who took a long journey " in the service of Truth " to Holland and Germany. He describes how a fearful being visited him by night in a vision, telling him that he had been deceived, and not for the first time, in undertaking this service, and that all was in confusion at home. " The main reason why things are so is, thy wife, that used to be at the helm in thy business, is dead." Thoroughly alarmed, he was preparing to hurry home when a letter arrived, saying that all was well,

---

[1] Lyon, *Dover*, Vol. II., p. 359.

[2] Ferguson, *Carlisle* p. 79 ; from *Dormont Book*.

" whereby I was relieved in mind, and confirmed I was in my place, and that it was Satan, by his transformation, who had deceived and disturbed me."[1]

The understanding and good sense which enabled women to assume control during the temporary absence of their husbands, fitted them also to bear the burden alone when widowed. Her capacity was so much taken for granted that public opinion regarded the wife as being virtually her husband's partner, leases or indentures were made out in their joint names, and on the husband's death the wife was left in undisturbed possession of the stock, apprentices and goodwill of the business.

A. *Skilled Trades or Crafts.*

The origin of the Craft Gilds is obscure. They were preceded by Religious Gilds in which men and women who were associated in certain trades united for religious and social purposes. Whether these Religious Gilds developed naturally into organisations concerned with the purpose of trade, or whether they were superseded by new associations whose first object was the regulation and improvement of the craft and with whom the religious and social ceremonies were of secondary importance is a disputed point, which, if elucidated, might throw some light on the industrial history of women. In the obscurity which envelopes this subject one certain fact emerges; the earlier Gilds included sisters as well as brothers, the two sexes being equally concerned with the religious and social observances which constituted their chief functions.

As the Gilds become more definitely trade organisations the importance of the sisters diminishes, and in some, the Carpenters for example, they appear to be virtually excluded from membership though

---

[1] *Irish Friend*, Vol. IV., p. 150.

this exclusion is only tacitly arrived at by custom, and is not enforced by rules. In other Gilds, such as the Girdlers and Pewterers, it is evident that though women's names do not occur in lists of wardens or assistants, yet they were actively engaged in these crafts and, like men, were subject to and protected by the regulations of their Gild or Company.

Very little is yet known of the industrial position of Englishwomen in the middle ages. Poll-tax returns show, however, that they were engaged in many miscellaneous occupations. Thus the return for Oxford in 1380 mentions six trades followed by women, viz.—37 spinsters, 11 shapesters (tailors), 9 tapsters (inn keepers), 3 sutrices (shoemakers,) 3 hucksters, 5 washerwomen, while in six others both men and women were employed, namely butchers, brewers, chandlers, ironmongers, netmakers and kempsters (wool combers). 148 women were enrolled as ancillæ or servants, and 81 trades were followed by only men.

A similar return for the West Riding of Yorks in 1379 declares the women employed in different trades to be as follows :—6 chapmen, 11 inn keepers, 1 farrier, 1 shoemaker, 2 nurses, 39 brewsters, 2 farmers, 1 smith, 1 merchant, 114 domestic servants and farm labourers, 66 websters, (30 with that surname), 2 listers or dyers, 2 fullers or walkers, and 22 seamstresses.[1] In every case these would be women who were carrying on their trade separately from their husbands, or as widows. During the following centuries women's names are given in the returns made of the tradesmen working in different Boroughs, occurring sometimes in trades which would seem to modern ideas most unlikely for them. Thus 5 widows and 35 men's names are given in a list of the smiths at Chester for the year 1574.[2]

---

[1] By kind permission of Miss Eileen Power.

[2] Harl. MSS., 2054. fo. 22., *The Smiths Book of Accts.* Chester, 1574.

It must be remembered that, except those who are classed as servants, all grown-up women were either married or widows. It was quite usual for a married woman to carry on a separate business from her husband as sole merchant, but it was still more customary for her to share in his enterprise, and only after his death for the whole burden to fall upon her shoulders. How natural it was for a woman to regard herself as her husband's partner will be seen when the conditions of family industry are considered. Before the encroachments of capitalism the members of the Craft Gilds were masters, not of other men, but of their craft. The workshop was part of the home, and in it, the master, who in the course of a long apprenticeship had acquired the technical mastery of his trade, worked with his apprentices, one or two journeymen and his wife and children. The number of journeymen and apprentices was strictly limited by the Gild rules ; the men did not expect to remain permanently in the position of wage-earners, but hoped in course of time to marry and establish themselves as masters in their craft. Apart from the apprentices and journeymen no labour might be employed, except that of the master's wife and children ; but there are in every trade processes which do not require a long technical training for their performance, and thus the assistance of the mistress became important to her husband, whether she was skilled in the trade or not, for the work if not done by her must fall upon him. Sometimes her part was manual, but more often she appears to have taken charge of the financial side of the business, and is seen in the role of salesman, receiving payments for which her receipt was always accepted as valid, or even acting as buyer. In either case her services were so essential to the business that she usually engaged a servant for household matters, and was thus freed from the routine of domestic drudgery. Defoe, writing in

the first decades of the eighteenth century, notes that
" women servants are now so scarce that from thirty
and forty shillings a Year, their Wages are increased
of late to six, seven and eight pounds *per Annum*,
and upwards. . . . an ordinary Tradesman cannot
well keep one ; but his Wife, who might be useful
in his Shop, or Business, must do the Drudgery of
Household Affairs ; And all this, because our
Servant Wenches are so puff'd up with Pride
now-a-Days that they never think they go fine
enough."[1]

The position of a married woman in the tradesman
class was far removed from that of her husband's
domestic servant. She was in very truth mistress of
the household in that which related to trade as well as
in domestic matters, and the more menial domestic
duties were performed by young unmarried persons
of either sex. To quote Defoe again, " it is but
few Years ago, and in the Memory of many now living,
that all the Apprentices of the Shop-keepers and Ware-
house-keepers. . . . submitted to the most servile
Employments of the Families in which they serv'd ;
such as the *young Gentry*, their Successors in the
same Station, scorn so much as the Name of now ;
such as *cleaning* their Masters' Shoes, bringing *Water*
into the Houses from *the Conduits* in the Street,
which they carried on their Shoulders in long Vessels
call'd Tankards ; also waiting at Table, ... but
their Masters are oblig'd to keep Porters or Footmen
to wait upon the apprentices."[2]

The rules of the early Gilds furnish abundant
evidence that women then took an active part in
their husbands's trades ; thus in 1297 the Craft of
Fullers at Lincoln ordered that " none [of the craft]
shall work at the wooden bar with a woman, unless

---

[1] Defoe, *Everybody's Business is No-Body's Business*, p. 6, 1725.

[2] Defoe, *Behaviour of Servants*, p. 12, . 1724.

with the wife of a master or her handmaid,"[1] and
in 1372, when articles were drawn up for the Leathersellers and Pouch-makers of London, and for Dyers
serving those trades, the wives of the dyers of
leather were sworn together with their husbands
" to do their calling, and, to the best of their power,
faithfully to observe the things in the said petition
contained ; namely John Blakthorne, and Agnes,
his wife ; John Whitynge, and Lucy, his wife ; and
Richard Westone, dier, and Katherine, his wife."[2]

The craft Gilds had either disappeared before the
seventeenth century or had developed into Companies,
wealthy corporations differing widely from the earlier
associations of craftsmen. But though the Companies
were capitalistic in their tendencies, they retained
many traditions and customs which were characteristic of the Gilds. The master's place of business
was still in many instances within the precincts of
his home, and when this was the case his wife retained
her position as mistress. Incidental references often
show the wife by her husband's side in his shop
Thus Thomas Symonds, Stationer, when called as a
witness to an inquest in 1514 describes how " within
a quarter of an hower after VII. a clock in the morning,
Charles Joseph came before him at his stall and said
' good morow, goship Simondes,' and the said Simonds
said ' good morow ' to hym againe, and the wife of
the said Simons was by him, and because of the
deadly countenance and hasty goinge of Charles,
the said Thomas bad his wife looke whether Charles
goeth, and as she could perceue, Charles went into
an ale house."[3]

Decker describes a craftsman's household in " A
Shoemaker's Holiday." The mistress goes in and out

---

[1] Smith (Toulmin), *English Gilds*, p. 180.

[2] Riley (H. T.), *Memorials of London*, p. 365.

[3] Arber, *Stationers*, Vol. III., Intro, p. 19.

of the workshop, giving advice, whether it is wanted
or not.

Firk : " Mum, here comes my dame and my master.
　　　She'll scold, on my life, for loitering this
　　　Monday ; . . . . "

Hodge : " Master, I hope you will not suffer my
　　　dame to take down your journeyman. . . "

Eyre : " Peace, Firk ; not I, Hodge ; . . . she
　　　shall not meddle with you . . . away,
　　　queen of clubs ; quarrel not with me and
　　　my men, with me and my fine Firk ; I'll
　　　firk you, if you do."[1]

But the meddling continues to the end of the play.

The same sort of scene is again described in " The
Honest Whore," where Viola, the Linen Draper's
wife, comes into his shop, and says to the two Prentices
and George the servant, who are at work,

　　　" Come, you put up your wares in good order,
　　　here, do you not, think you : One piece
　　　cast this way, another that way ! You had
　　　need have a patient master indeed."

George replies (aside) " Ay, I'll be sworn, for we
　　　have a curst mistress."[2]

Comedy is concerned with the foibles of humanity,
and so here the faults of the mistress are reflected,
but in real life she is often alluded to as her husband's
invaluable lieutenant. There can be no doubt that
admission to the world of business and the responsibilities which rested on their shoulders, often developed
qualities in seventeenth century women which the
narrower opportunities afforded them in modern society
have left dormant. The wide knowledge of life
acquired by close association with their husbands' affairs,
qualified mothers for the task of training their children ;
but it was not only the mother who benefited by the

---

[1] Decker (Thos.), *Best Plays*, p. 29.

[2] *Ibid*, p. 108.

incorporation of business with domestic affairs, for
while she shared her husband's experiences he became
acquainted with family life in a way which is impossible
for men under modern conditions. The father was
not separated from his children, but they played around
him while he worked, and his spare moments could be
devoted to their education. Thus the association
of husband and wife brought to each a wider, deeper
understanding of human life.

Returning to the position of women in the Craft
Gilds and the later Companies, it must be remembered
that originally these associations had a three-fold
purpose, (a) the performance of religious ceremonies,
(b) social functions, (c) the protection of trade interests and the maintenance of a high standard of
technical efficiency.

Women are not excluded from membership by
any of the earlier charters, which, in most cases
expressly mention sisters as well as brothers, but references to them are more frequent in the provisions
relating to the social and religious functions of the
Gild than in those concerning technical matters.
Though after the Reformation the performance
of religious ceremonies fell into abeyance, social
functions continued to be an important feature of
the Companies.

Entrance was obtained by apprenticeship, patrimony,
redemption or, in the case of women, by marriage.
The three former methods though open to women,
were seldom used by them, and the vast majority
of the sisters obtained their freedom through marriage.
During the husband's life time their position is not
very evident, but on his death they were possessed
of all his trade privileges. The extent to which
widows availed themselves of these privileges varied
in different trades, but custom appears always to
have secured to the widow, rather than to the son
the possession of her husband's business.

Hitherto few records of the Gilds and Companies have been printed *in extenso*; possibly when others are published more light may be shed on the position which they accorded to women. The Stationers and the Carpenters are selected here, not because they are typical in their dealings with women, but merely because their records are available in a more complete form than the others.

The Stationers' Company included Stationers, Booksellers, Binders and Printers; apprenticeship to either of these trades conferred the right of freedom in the company, but the position of printer was a prize which could not be attained purely by apprenticeship; before the Long Parliament this privilege was confined to twenty-two Printing Houses only besides the Royal Printers, vacancies being filled up by the Court of Assistants, with the approval of the Archbishop of Canterbury. Any stationer who had been made free of his Company might publish books, but printing was strictly limited to these twenty-two houses. A vacancy seldom occurred, because, according to the old English custom, on the printer's death his rights were retained by his widow, and in this Company they were not even alienated when she married again, but were shared by her second husband; thus a printer's widow, whatever her age might be, was regarded as a most desirable " partie." The widow Francis Simson married in succession Richard Read and George Elde, the business following her, and Anne Barton married a second, third and fourth time,[1] none of the later husbands being printers.

Though amongst the printers the line of descent appears to have been more often from husband to wife and wife to husband than from father to son, a list, giving the names of the master printers as they

[1] Arber, *Stationers*, Vol. V., Intro. xxix-xxx.

succeeded each other from 1575 to 1635 shows that
the business was acquired by marrying the printer's
widow, by purchase from her, and also by descent.
Four women are mentioned : —William Ellis bound
to Mrs. East, a printer's widow who, having left the
trade many years was brought up in the art of printing
by Mr. Fletcher upon composition. Mrs. Griffyn
had two apprentices, Mrs. Dawson had three apprentices and Mrs. Purslow two apprentices.[1] Another
list made in 1630 of the names of the Master Printers
of London gives twenty-one men and three women,
namely—Widdow Alde, Widdow Griffin,and " Widdow
Sherleaker lives by printing of pictures."[2] In 1634
the names of twenty-two printers are given, among
whom are the following women—" Mr. William
Jones succeeded Rafe Blore and paies a stipend to
his wife . . . . neuer admitted.

Mistris [ ] Alde, widdowe of Edward Alde
[who] deceased about 10 yeeres since, (but she
keepes her trade by her sonne who was Ra[lph]
joyners sonne) neuer Admitted, neither capable of
Admittance.

Mistris [ ] Dawson widow of John Dawson
deceased about a yeere since [he] succeeded his vnkle
Thomas Dawson about 26 yeers since . . . never
admitted neither capeable, (she hath a sonne about
19 yeares old, bredd to ye trade).

Mistris [ ] Pursloe widdow of George Pursloe
who succeeded Simon Stafford about 5 yeeres since
[she was] never admitted neither capeable. (haviland,
Yo[u]ng and fletcher haue this.)

Mistris [ ] Griffin widdow of Edward Griffin
[who] succeeded Master [Melchisedeck] Bradwood
about 18 yeeres since [she was] never admitted neither

1 S.P.D., cccxiv., 127., Feb. 1636.

2 Ibid, clxxv., 45., Nov. 12, 1630.

capable. (she hath a sonne.) (haviland, Yo[u]ng and fletcher have this yet).[1]

Men as well as women in the list are noted as " never admitted neither capable of admittance."

Whether these women took an active part in the management of the business which they thus acquired or whether they merely drew the profits, leaving the management to others, is not clear. From the notes to the above list it would appear that they often followed the latter course, but elsewhere women are mentioned who are evidently taking an active part in the printing business. For example, an entry in the Stationers Register states at a time when Marsh and Vautrollier had the sole printing of school books " It is agreed that Thomas Vautrollier his wife shall finish this present impression which shee is in hand withall in her husband's absence, of Tullie's Epistles with Lambini's annotations."[2]

After his death Vautrollier's widow printed one book but immediately after, on March 4th, 1587-8, the Court of Assistants ordered that " Mrs. Vautrollier, late wife of Thomas Vautrollier deceased, shall not hereafter print any manner of book or books whatsoever, as well by reason that her husband was noe printer at the time of his decease, as alsoe by the decrees sette downe in the Starre Chamber she is debarred from the same." This order is inexplicable, as other printers' widows exercised their husbands' business, and Thomas Vautrollier's name is duly given in the order of succession from Master Printers. Possibly the business had been transferred to her daughter, who married Field, their apprentice. Field died in 1625, his widow continuing the business.[3]

---

[1] Arber, *Transcript*, Vol. III, add, 701.

[2] Stopes (Mrs. C. C.) *Shakespeare's Warwickshire Contemporaries*, p. 7.

[3] *Ibid*, p. 8. (Some authorities state that Field married the widow, others the daughter of Vautrollier.)

Among thirty-nine printing patents issued by
James I. and Charles II. is one to " Hester Ogden,
als ffulke Henr. Sibbald *et* Tho. Kenithorpe for
printing a book called The Sincire and True Translation of the Holy Scripture into the Englishe tounge."
It appears as though Hester Ogden was no mere
figure head, for His Majesty's Printers appealed
against this licence on the grounds that it infringed
their rights, protesting that " Mistris Ogden a maried
woman one of Dr. Fulkes daughters did lately [sue]
his Majesie to haue ye printing of her fathers workes,
which his [Majestie] not knowing ye premises
granted, and ye same being first referred [to the]
Archbishop of Canterbury . . . their lordships
. . . . deliuered their opinion against her,
since which she hath gotten a new reference to
the Lord Chancellor and Master Secretary Nanton,
who not examining ye title vpon oath and the Stationers
being not then able to produce those materiall proofes
which now they can their honors certified for her,
wherevpon her friends hath his Majestie's grant
for ye printing and selling of the sayed book for
xxi. years to her vse . . . . Mistris Ogden
hath gotten by begging from ye clergy and others
diuers great somes of money towards ye printing
of her fathers workes. Master Norton and myself
haue for many £1000 bought ye office of his
Majesties printer to which ye printing of ye translacons
of the Bible or any parts thereof sett furth by the
State belongs. Now the greatest parte of Dr.
Fulkes worke is the new testament in English sett
forth by authoritie."[1]

Another patent was granted to Helen Mason
for " printing and selling the abridgment of
the book of martyres,"[1] while Jane, wife
of Sir Thomas Bludder, petitions Archbishop

---

[1] Arber, *Transcript*, Vol. III., p. 39.

Laud, showing that " She with John Bill an infant have by grant from the King the moiety of the office of King's Printer and amongst other things the printing of Bibles. This is infringed by a printer in Scotland, who printed many Bibles there and imported them into England . . . . she prays the Archbishop to hear the case himself."[2]

Many of the books printed at this time bear the names of women printers,[3] but though women might own and direct the printing houses, there is no indication that they were ever engaged in the manual processes of printing. The printers' trade does in fact furnish rather a good example of the effect upon women's economic position of the transition from family industry to capitalistic organisation. It is true that many links in the evolution must be supplied by the imagination. We can imagine the master printer with his press, working at home with the help of his apprentice, his wife and children ; then as his trade prospered he employed journeymen printers who were the real craftsmen, and it became possible for the owner of the business to be a man or woman who had never been bred up to the trade.

Apprenticeship was still exacted for the journeymen. A Star Chamber decree in 1637 provides that no " master printer shall imploy either to worke at the Case, or the Presse, or otherwise about his printing, any other person or persons, then such only as are Free-men, or Apprentices to the Trade or mystery of Printing."[1] While in 1676 the Stationers' Company ordained that " no master-printer, or

---

[1] Arber, *Transcript*, Vol. V., lviii.

[2] *S.P.D.*, cccxxxix., p. 89.

[3] e.g. *An Essay of Drapery* . . . by William Scott, printed by Eliz. Alde for S. Pennell, London, 1635. Calvin, *Institution of Christian Religion*. Printed by the widowe of R. Wolfe, London, 1574. The fourthe edition of *Porta Linguarum* is printed by E. Griffin for M. Sparke. London, 1639.

other printer or workman . . . . shall teach, direct or instruct any person or persons whatsoever, other than his or their own legitimate son or sons, in this Art or Mystery of Printing, who is not actually bound as an Apprentice to some lawful authorised Printer."[2]

From the omission here of any mention of daughters it is clear that the Master Printers' women folk did not concern themselves with the technical side of his trade ; but some attempt was evidently made to use other girls in the unskilled processes, for on a petition being presented in 1635 by the younger printers, concerning abuses which they wished removed, the Stationers' Company adopted the following recommendation, " That no Master Printer shall hereafter permit or suffer by themselves or their journeyman any Girles, Boyes, or others to take off anie sheets from the tinpin of the presse, but hee that pulleth at the presse shall take off every sheete himself."[3]

The young printers were successful in their efforts to preserve the monopoly value of their position, and formed an organisation amongst themselves to protect their interests against the masters; but in this association the wives of the young printers found no place. They could no longer help their husbands who were working, not at home, but on the master's premises ; and as girls were not usually apprenticed to the printing trade women were now virtually excluded from it.

Some imagination is needed to realise the social results of the change thus effected by capitalistic organisation on the economic position of married women, for no details have been discovered of the

[1] Arber, *Transcript*, Vol. IV., p. 534.

[2] *Ibid*, Vol. I, p. 16.

[3] *S.P.D.*, ccci., 105, Nov. 16, 1635.

printers' domestic circumstances; but as the wife was clearly unable to occupy herself with her husband's trade, neither she nor her daughters could share the economic privileges which he won for himself and his fellows by his organising ability. If his wages were sufficiently high for her to devote herself to household affairs, she became his unpaid domestic servant, depending entirely on his goodwill for the living of herself and her children; otherwise she must have conducted a business on her own account, or obtained work as a wage earner, in neither case receiving any protection from her husband in the competition of the labour market.

The wives and widows of the Masters were meanwhile actively engaged in other branches of the Stationers' Company. In a list of Publishers covering the years 1553–1640, nearly ten per cent. of the names given are those of women, probably all of whom were widows.[1] One of these, the widow of Francis Coldock, married in 1603 Isaac Binge, the Master of the Company. " She had three husbands, all Bachelors and Stationers, and died 1616, and is buried in St. Andrew Undershaft in a vault with Symon Burton her father.[2] The names of these women can be found also in the books they published. For example " The True Watch and Rule of Life " by John Brinsley the elder, printed by H. Lownes for Joyce Macham, *7th ed.* 1615, the eighth edition being printed for her by T. Beale in 1619, and " an Epistle . . . . upon the present pestilence " by Henoch Clapham, was printed by T.C. for the Widow Newbery, London, 1603. A woman who was a Binder is referred to in an order made by the Bishop of London in 1685 " to damask . . . . counterfeit Primmirs' seized at Mrs. Harris's Binder, "[1] and Women are

---

[1] Arber, *Transcript*, Vol. V., p. lxxxi-cxi.

[2] *Ibid*, Vol. V., p. lxiii.

also met with as booksellers. Anne Bowler
sold the book " Catoes Morall Distichs " . . . .
printed by Annes Griffin. The Quakers at Horsley
Down paid to Eliz. ffoulkes 3s. for their minute book,[2]
while Pepys' bookseller was a certain Mrs. Nicholls.[3]
The death of Edward Croft, Bookseller, is recorded
in Smyth's *Obituary*, " his relict, remarried since
to Mr. Blagrave, an honest bookseller, who live
hapily in her house in Little Britain."[4]
The trade of a bookseller was followed by women
in the provinces as well as in London, the Howards
paying " For books bought of Eliz. Sturton iijs.[5]
and Sir John Foulis enters in his account book
" To Ard. Hissops relict and hir husband for 3 paper
bookes at 10 gr. p. peice and binding other 4 bookes,
18. 14. o [Scots money], to them for a gramer and
a salust to the bairns, 1.2.o. She owes me 6/8. of
change."[6]
Presumably all the women who were engaged
in either of these allied trades in London were free
of the Stationers' Company, and in most cases they
were widows. Many apprentices were made free
on the testimony of a woman,[7] and though these

[1] Arber, *Transcript*, Vol. V., p. lv.

[2] Monthly Meeting Minutes. Horsleydown, 13 1mo 167⅞.

[3] Pepys, *Diary*, Vol. I., p. 26.

[4] Smyth's *Obituary*, p. 77.

[5] Howard, *Household Books*, p. 161, 1622.

[6] Foulis, Sir John, *Acct. Book*, p. 22, 1680.

[7] " Mistres Gosson. Stephan Coxe, Sworne and Admytted a Freeman of this
Companie iijs, iiijd. Note that master Warden White Dothe Reporte, for mistres
Gosson's Consent to the makinge of this prentice free. (Arbers, *Transcript*, Vol. II.,
p. 727, 1600.) Alice Gosson Late wyfe of Thomas Gosson. Henry Gosson sworne and
admitted A ffreeman of this company per patrimonium iijs. iiijd, (*Ibid*, p. 730, 1601.)
Mistries Woolff. John Barnes sworne and admitted A freeman (*Ibid*, p. 730,
1601. Jane proctor, Wydowe of William proctor. Humfrey Lympenny sworne
and admitted A ffreeman of this Companye iijs. iiijd. (*Ibid*, p. 730,
1601.) Mystris Conneway Nicholas Davyes sworn and admitted A freeman of,
this company per patrimonium iijs. iiijd, (*Ibid*, p. 7?2, 1602.)

in some cases may have almost completed their servitude before the death of their master, " Mistris Woolff " gives testimony for one apprentice in 1601, and for another in 1603, showing that she at least continued the management of her husband's business for some years, and as she received a new apprentice during this time,[1] it is evident that she had no intention of relinquishing it.

When on her husband's death the widow transferred an apprentice to some other master we may infer that she felt unable to take the charge of business upon her. This happened not infrequently, " Robert Jackson late apprentise with Raffe Jackson is putt ouer by consent of his mystres unto master Burby to serve out the Residue of his terms of apprentishood with him, the Last yere excepted. . . . Anthony Tomson . . . . hath putt him self an apprentice to master Gregorie Seton . . . . for 8 yeres . . . . . Eliz. Hawes shall haue the services and benefit of this Apprentise during her wydohed or marrying one of the Company capable of him."[2] " John leonard apprentise to Edmond Bolifant deceased is putt ouer by the consent of the said mary Bolyfant unto Richard Bradocke . . . . to serue out the residue of his apprentiship."[3] But whether the widow wished to continue the business as a " going concern " or not, she, and she only, was in possession of the privileges connected therewith, for she was virtually her husband's partner, and his death did not disturb her possession. The old rule of copyright recognised her position, providing " that copies

---

[1] Johne Adams of London (stationer's son) apprenticed to Alice Woolff of citie of London widowe for 8 years 2s. 6d. (Arber, *Transcript*, Vol. II, p. 253, 1601.) Other instances of apprentices being bound to women occur as for example " Wm. Walle apprenticed to Elizabeth Hawes Widow for 8 years (*Ibid*, Vol. II., p. 287, 1604.) " Thomas Richardson of York apprenticed to Alice Gosson, of citie of London wydowe for 7 years, 2s. 6d. (*Ibid*, Vol. II., p. 249, 1600).

[2] *Ibid*, p. 260, 1602.)

[3] *Ibid*, p. 262, 1602.

peculiar for life to any person should not be granted
to any other but the Widow of the deceased, she
certifying the title of the book to the Master and
Wardens, and entering the book in the " bookes
of thys Company."[1]

The history of the Carpenters' Company resembles
that of the Staticners' in some respects, though
the character of a carpenter's employment, which was
so often concerned with building operations, carried
on away from his shop, did not favour the continuance
of his wife in the business after his death. The
" Boke " of the ordinances of the Brotherhood of the
Carpenters of London, dated 1333, shows the Society
to have been at that time a Brotherhood formed "of
good men carpenters of men and women" for common
religious observances and mutual help in poverty
and sickness, partaking of the nature of a Benefit
Society rather than a Trade Union. The Brotherhood was at the same time a Sisterhood, and Brethren
and Sisters are mentioned together in all but two of
its articles. In the later code of ordinances, of which
a copy has been preserved dated 1487, sisters are but
twice mentioned, when tapers are prescribed at the
burying of their bodies and prayers for the resting
of their souls.[2] Women's names seldom occur in
the Records, apart from entries connected with those
who were tenants, or charitable grants to widows
fallen into poverty, or with payments to the Bedell's
wife for washing tablecloths and napkins.[3] In one
instance considerable trouble was experienced because
the Bedell's wife would not turn out of their house after

---

[1] Arber *Transcript*, Vol. V., p. 11, 1560.

[2] *Records of the Worshipful Company of Carpenters*, Vol. II., Intro., p. ix.

[3] For example " Itm payd to the bedells wyffe for kepyng of the gardyn vijs.
Ibid, Vol. IV., p. 2. *Warden's Acct. Book*, 1546. She had besides iiijs. "for her
hole yeres wasschyng the clothes " (p. 11) and iiijd. "for skoryng of the vessell,"
(p. 13) this payment was later increased to xijd. and she had "for bromes for Or
Hall every quarter a jd. (p. 33) in Reward for her attendance ijs, (p. 114). Burdons
wyffe for dressing your dinner xiiijd. (p. 129).

the Bedell's death. In September, 1567, "it is agreed and fullie determyned by the M[r] wardeins & assystaunce of this company that Syslie burdon wydowe late wife of Richard burdon dwelling w[th]in this house at the will & pleasure of the foresaid M[r] & wardeins shall quyetlye & peaceablye dept out of & from her now dwellinge at Xpistmas next or before & at her departure to have the some of Twentie six shillinges & eight pence of Lawfull money of England in reward."[1] Syslie Burdon however did not wish to move, and in the following February another entry occurs " at this courte it is agreed further that Cysley burdon wydowe at the feast daye of thannunciacon of o[r] Ladie S[t] marye the virgin next ensueng the date abovesayd shall dept. & goe from her nowe dwellinge house wherein she now dwelleth w[th] in this hall & at the same tyme shall have at her deptur if she doethe of her owne voyd w[th]out anye further troublynge of the M[r] and wardeins of this house at that p'sent tyme the some of Twentie six shillinges eight-pense in reward."[2] Cyslie Burdon may have believed that as a widow she had a just claim to the house, for leases granted by the Company at this time were usually for the life of the tenant and his wife.[3]

Women accompanied their husbands to the Company dinners as a matter of course. In 1556 " the clothyng " are ordered to pay for " ther dynner at

---

[1] *Records of the Worshipful Company of Carpenters*, Vol. III., *Court Book*, p. 97.

[2] *Ibid*, p. 103.

[3] *Ibid*, Vol. III., pp. 10-11, March 15, 1544-5. " agreyed and codyssendyd thatt frances pope and hys wyffe schall have and hold a gardyn plott lyeng be oure hall in the prysche of alhallouns at london Wall for the tyme of the longer lever of them bothe payeing viijs: be the yere . . . the sayd [ ]pope nor hys wyffe schall not take dowene no palles nor pale postes nor Raylles In the garden nor no tres nor bussches schall nott plucke upe be the Rootes nor cutte theme downe nor no maner of erbys . . . w[t]owt the lycens of the Master and Wardyns of the mystery of Carpenters Aug. 10, 1564, " agreed and condissendid that Robart masckall and Elyzabeth his wiffe shall have and hold the Howse which He now occupieth duryng his lyffe and after the deseese of the said Robart to Remayne to Elizabeth his wyffe duryng her wyddohed paying yerlye x[l]s of lawfull mony of England " etc, *Ibid*, Vol. III., p. 78.

the Dynner day ijs. vjd. a man whether ther wyffes or they themselves come or no."[1] But the entries do not suggest that the position of equal sisters which they held in the days of the old " Boke " was maintained. Women made presents to the Company. " Mistrys ellis," the wife of one of the masters of the Company, presented " a sylv̄ pott psell gylt the q̄ter daye at candylmas wayeing viij ozes & a qter."[2] This apparently was in memory of her deceased husband, for in the same year she "turned over" an apprentice, and in 1564 a fine was paid by Richard Smarte " for not comyng at yᵉ owre appoynted to mistris Ellis beriall—xijd."[3] Neither the existence of these two instances, which show a lively interest in the Company, nor the absence of other references can be taken as conclusive evidence one way or another concerning the social position of the sisters in the Company. Among the many judgments passed on brothers for reviling each other, using " ondecent words," etc., etc., only once is a woman fined for this offence, when in 1556 the warden enters in his account book " Resd of frances stelecrag a fyne for yll wordes that his wyffe gave to John Dorrant ijˢ—Resd of John Dorrant for yll wordes that he gave to Mystris frances xvjᵈ—Resd of Wyllam Mortym̄ a fyne for callyng of Mystris frances best ijˢ ."[4]

It is certain that the wives of carpenters, like the wives of other tradesmen, shared the business anxieties of their husbands, the help they rendered being most often in buying and selling. This activity is reflected in some rules drawn up to regulate

[1] *Records of Worshipful Company of Carpenters*, Vol. III., p. 58.

[2] *Ibid*, Vol. IV., p. 99, *Wardens Acct. Book*, 1558.

[3] In 1563 xxs. was " Resd of Wyllym barnewell at yᵉ buryall of his wiffe yᵗ she dyd wyll to be gyven to yᵉ Cōpany. (*Ibid*, Vol. IV., p. 147) Payd at the buryall of barnewell's wyffe at yᵉ kyges hedd. xiiijs. iiijd. Paid to the bedle for Redyng of yᵉ wyll viijd. (*Ibid*, Vol. IV., p. 149.)

[4] *Ibid*, Vol. IV., p. 84.

the purchase of timber. In 1554 " y^t was agreyd be the Master & wardyns and the moste parte of the assestens that no woman shall come to the waters to by tymber bourde lath q̄ters ponchons gystes & Raffters ther husbandes beyng in the town uppon payne to forfyt at ëvry tyme so fownd."[1] The Company's decision was not readily obeyed, for on March 8th, 1547, " the Master and the Wardyns w^t partt of the Assestens went to the gyldehall to have had a Redresse for the women that came to the watersyde to by stuffe,"[2] and on March 10th " was called in John Armestrong, Wyllyam boner, Wyllyam Watson, John Gryffyn and Henry Wrest there having amonyssion to warne ther wyffes that they schulde not by no stuffe at the waters syd upone payne of a fyne."[3]

On her husband's death the carpenter's wife generally retired from business, transferring her apprentices for a consideration to another master. That this practice was not universal is shown in the case of a boy who had been apprenticed to Joseph Hutchinson and was " turned over to Anne Hayward, widow, relict of Richard Hayward Carpentar."[4] Mrs. Hayward must clearly have been actively prosecuting her late husband's business. The women who " make free " apprentices seem generally to have done so within a few months of their husband's deaths. That the Company recognised the right of women to retain apprentices if they chose is shown by the following provision in Statutes dated November 10th, 1607. " If any Apprentice or Apprentices Marry or Absent themselves from their Master or Mistress During their Apprenticehood, then within

---

[1] *Records of Worshipful Company of Carpenters*, Vol. III., p. 15, *Court Book*.

[2] *Ibid*, Vol. III., p. 30.

[3] *Ibid*, Vol. III., p. 31.

[4] *Ibid*, Vol. I., p. 136.

one month the Master or Mistress is to Bring their
Indentures to the hall to be Registered and Entered,
etc " " None to Receive or take into their service
or house any Man or Woman's Apprentice Covenant
Servant or Journeyman within the limits aforesaid,
etc."[1]

When a carpenter's widow could keep her husband's
business together, no one disputed her right to
receive apprentices. Several instances of their doing
so are recorded towards the end of the century.[2] The
right to succeed her husband in his position as carpenter
and member of the worshipful company was immediately allowed when claimed by a widow ; thus the
court " agreed . . . . that Johan burton wydowe
late wife of [ ] burton citezein and Carpenter of
London for that warninge hathe not ben goven unto
her from tyme to tyme at the Quarterdaies heretofore
From henseforthe shall have due warninge goven unto
her everye Quarterdaye and at the next Quarterdaie

[1] *Records of the Worshipful Company of Carpenters*, Vol. 1., Intro. vii-viii.

[2] *Ibid*, p. 137, May 2, 1671. Richardus Read filius Thome Read de Chart
Magna in Com. Kanc. Shoemaker po : se appren Josepho Hutchinson Bedello Hujus
Societat pro Septem Ann a die dat Indre Dat die et ann ult pred (Assign immediate
Susanne Catlin vid nuper uxor. Johannis Catlin nuper Civis et Carpenter London
defunct uten etc).

Ibid, p. 153. Dec. 5, 1676. Johannes Keyes filius Willi. Keyes nuper de
Hampsted in Com. Middx. Milwright ed Elizabetham Davis vid. willi Davis nuper
Civi & Carpentar de London a die date pred etc (sic)

Ibid, p. 158. July 1, 1679. Samuell Goodfellow filius Johanni of Rowell in
Com. Northton Corwayner pon se Martha Wildey relict of Robert pro septem annis
a dat etc.

Ibid, p. 161. Ap. 5, 1681. Georg Thomas filius Thome nuper de Carlyon in Com
Monmouth gent pon se Apprenticum Elizabeth Whitehorne of Aldermanbury
vid. Johis. pro septem Annis a dat.

Ibid, p. 164. Oct. 4, 1681. Richard Lynn sonn of William Lynn decd. pon se
Apprenticum Marie Lynn widdow Relict of the said William C : C: pro septem
annis a dat.

Ibid, p. 165. March 7, 1681-2. John Whitehorne son of John Whitehorne C : C :
Ld, pon se apprenticum Elizabethe Relict. ejusdem Joh's Whitehorne pro septem
annis a dat.

Ibid, p. 171. Apr. 5. 1686. Richard S'evenson sonne of Rob' Stevenson late of
Dublin in the Kingedome of Ireland Pavier bound to Anne Nicholson Widowe the
Relict of Anthony Nicholson, for eight yeares.

Ibid, p. 189. June 7, 1692. Robert Harper sonne of William Harper of
Notchford in the county of Chesheire, bound to Abigail Taylor for Seaven Yeares.

she shall paye in discharge of tharrerages behind Twelve pence & so shall paye her Quateridge (p^d xijd.) "[1]; a year later " burtons widow " makes free an apprentice Mighell Pattinson.[2]

Curiously enough, during the period 1654 to 1670, twenty-one girls were bound apprentice at Carpenters' Hall. Probably none of these expected to learn the trade of a carpenter.[3] Nine were apprenticed to Richard Hill and his wife, who lived first near St. Michael's, Cornehill,[4] and afterwards against Trinity Minories.[5] They were apprenticed for seven years to learn the trade of a sempstress, and probably in each case a heavy premium was paid, a note being made against the name of Prudentia Cooper, who was bound in 1664 "(obligatur Pater in 50^l pro ventute apprenticij)."[6]

Richard Hill's wife's name is included in the Indentures three times, and in 1672 a boy was apprenticed to " Ric. Hill Civi *et* Carpenter London necnon de little Minories Silk Winder."[7] We may infer that Mrs. Hill had founded the business before or after her marriage with the carpenter, and that hers proving profitable the husband had been satisfied with working for wages, while retaining the freedom of the Company, or had transferred his services to his wife's business, adding that of a Silk winder to it. One girl originally apprenticed to Henry Joyse was " turned over to Anne Joyse sempstress & sole merchant without Thomas Joyse her husband,"[8] five were apprenticed

---

[1] *Records of Worshipful Company of Carpenters*, Vol. III., p. 102, *Court Book*, 1567.

[2] *Ibid*, Vol. III., p. 200.

[3] *Ibid*, Vol. I., Intro. p. x-xi. Apprentice Entry Book.

[4] *Ibid*, Vol. I., p. 62.

[5] *Ibid*, Vol. I., p. 125.

[6] *Ibid*, Vol. I., p. 78.

[7] *Ibid*, Vol. I., p. 145.

[8] *Ibid*, Vol. I., p. 136

to Henry Joyce to learn the trade of a milliner. No
mention is made of his wife, but as he received boy
apprentices also,[1] it may be supposed that in fact
the two trades of a carpenter and a milliner were
carried on in this case simultaneously by him and his
wife. The blending of these two trades is noted
again in the case of Samuel Joyce ;[2] the trade the
other girls were to learn is not generally specified,
but Rebecca Perry was definitely apprenticed to
William Addington " to learne the Art of a Sempstress
of his wife."[3] Two girls were apprenticed to " Thome
Clarke . . . . London Civi et Carpenter ad
discend artem de Child's Coate seller existen. art.
uxoris sue pro septem annis."[4]

Elizabeth Lambert, the daughter of Thomas Lambert, formerly of London, silkeman, was apprenticed
in 1678 to Rebecca Cooper, widow of Thomas Cooper,
" Civis Carpenter London," for seven years.[5] Another
girl who had been apprenticed to this same woman
in 1668 applied for her freedom in 1679, which was
granted, though apparently her request was an unusual one, the records stating that " Certaine Indentures of Apprentiship were made whereby Rebecca
Gyles, daughter of James Gyles of Staines, ...
was bound Apprentice to Rebecca Cooper of the
parish of St. Buttolph without Aldgate widdow for
seaven yeares . . . . this day att a Court of
assistants then holden for this Company came Rebecca
Gylles Spinster sometime servant to Rebecca Cooper
a free servant of this Company, and complained that

---

[1] *Records of the Worshipful Company of Carpenters*, Vol. 1., p. 65, e.g. Brewin
Radford (obligatur Maria Radford de Perpole in Com Dorsett vid. in 100^l pro
ventut apprentice).

[2] *Ibid*, Vol. I., p. 149, 1674. " Edmundus Wilstead filius Henrici Wilstead de Thet-
ford in Com Norfolcie yeoman po : se appren. Samueli Joyse Civi et Carpenter London necnon de Exambia Regali London miliner pro septem annis " etc.

[3] *Ibid*, Vol. I., p. 162.

[4] *Ibid*, Vol. I., p. 148.

[5] *Ibid*, Vol. I., p. 156.

haveing served her said Mistres faithfully a Terme of seaven years wh^ch expired the twenty-fourth day of June, 1675, and often desired of her said Mistris Testimony of her service to the end shee might bee made free, her said Mistres had hitherto denyed the same ; & then presented credible persons within this Citty to testifie the truth of her said service, desireing to bee admitted to the freedome of this Company, which this Table thought reasonable, vnlesse the said Rebecca Cooper, her said Mistres on notice hereof to bee given, shall shew reasonable cause to the contrary, etc."[1] Encouraged by the success of this application, two other girls followed Rebecca Gyles' example, one being presented for her freedom at Carpenters' Hall by Thomas Clarke in 1683 and another by Henry Curtis in 1684.[2]

Thus it may be presumed that apprenticeship to a brother or sister of the Carpenters' Company conferred the right of freedom upon any girls who chose to avail themselves of the privilege, even when the trade actually learnt was not that of carpentry. Amongst the girl apprentices only one other was directly bound to a woman, namely " Elizabetha filia Hester Eitchus ux. Geo. Eitchus nuper Civi et Carpentar. pon se dict Hester matri pro septem ann a dat etc."[3] Although Hester Eitchus is here called " uxor " she must really have been a widow, for her name would not have appeared alone on the indenture during her husband's lifetime ; boy apprentices had previously been bound to him, and no doubt as in the other cases husband and wife had been prosecuting their several trades simultaneously, the wife retaining her membership in the Carpenters' Company when left a widow. An independent

---

[1] Jupp. *Carpenters*, p. 161, 1679.

[2] *Records of Worshipful Company of Carpenters*, Vol. I., p. 198.

[3] *Ibid*, Vol. I., *App. Entry Book*, p. 159, Feb. 3, 1679.

business must have been very necessary for the wife
in cases where the husband worked for wages, and not
on his own account, for in 1563 carpenter's wages
were fixed "be my lorde mayors commandement. . .
yf they dyd fynde themselves meat and drynke
at xiiij^d the day and their servants xij^d. Itm otherwises
the sayd carpynters to have viij^d the day wayges
meat & drynke & their servants vj^d meat & drynke."[1]
These wages would have been inadequate for the
maintenance of a family in London, and therefore
unless the carpenter was in a position to employ
apprentices and enter into contracts, in which case
he could find employment also for his wife, she must
have traded in some way on her own account.

It is difficult to say how far the position of women
in the Stationers' and Carpenters' Companies was
typical of their position in the other great London
Companies and in the Gilds and Companies which
flourished or decayed in the provinces. All these
organisations resembled each other in certain broad
outlines, but varied considerably in details. All
seem to have agreed in the early association of brothers
and sisters on equal terms for social and religious
purposes. Thus the Carpenters' was "established
one perpetual brotherhood, or guild . . . . to
consist of one master, three wardens, and commonalty
of freemen, of the Mystery of Carpentry . . . .
and of the brethren and sisters of freemen of the
said mystery."[2] The charter granted by Henry VI.
to the Armourers and Braziers provided "that the
brethren and sisters of that ffraternity or guild, . . .
should be of itself one perpetual community . . . .
and have perpetual sucession. And that the brothers
and sisters of the same ffraternity or guild, ...
might choose and make one Master and two Wardens

---

[1] *Records of the Worshipful Company of Carpenters*, Vol. III., p. 75, *Court Book*.

[2] Jupp. *Carpenters*, p. 12.

from among themselves; and also elect and make another
Master and other Wardens into the office aforesaid,
according to the ordinances of the better and worthier
part of the same brethren and sisters . . . . . ."[1] In
this case the sisters were regarded as active and
responsible members but of the Merchant Taylors
Clode says " It is clear that women were originally
admitted as members and took apprentices ; that it
was customary in later years for women to dine or be
present at the quarterly meetings is evidenced by a
notice of their absence in 1603, ' the upper table near
to the garden, commonly called the *Mistris Table*,
was furnished with sword bearer and gentlemen
strangers, there being no gentlewomen at this Quarter
Day.' In many of the wills of early benefactors,
sisters as well as brethren are named as ' devisees.'
Thus in Sibsay's (1404) the devise is ' to the Master
and Wardens and brethren and sisters ' . . . . .
When an Almsman of the Livery married with the
Company's consent his widow remained during her
life an almswoman, and was buried by the Company.
In that sense she was treated as a sister of the
fraternity, but she probably exercised no rights as a
member of it."[2]

The sisters are often referred to in the rules relating to
the dinners, which were such an important feature
of gild life. The " Grocers " provided that " Every
one of the Fraternity from thenceforward, that has
a wife or companion, shall come to the feast, and bring
with him a lady if he pleases ; [et ameyne avec luy
une demoiselle si luy plest] if they cannot come, for
the reasons hereafter named, that is to say, sick,
big with child, and near deliverance, without any
other exception ; and that every man shall pay for
his wife 20d. ; also, that each shall pay 5s., that is

---

[1] *Armourers and Braziers. Charter and By-laws of the Company*, p. 4.

[2] Clode. *History of the Merchant Taylors*, London, Vol. I., p. 42.

to say, 20d. for himself, 20d. for his companion, and 20d. for the priest. And that all women who are not of the Fraternity, and afterwards should be married to any of the Fraternity, shall be entered and looked upon as of the Fraternity for ever, and shall be assisted and made as one of us ; and after the death of her husband, the widow shall come to the dinner, and pay 40d. if she is able. And if the said widow marries any one not of the Fraternity, she shall not be admitted to the said feast, nor have any assistance given her, as long as she remains so married, be whom she will ; nor none of us ought to meddle or interfere in anything with her on account of the Fraternity, as long as she remains unmarried."[1]

The Wardens of the Merchant Gild at Beverley were directed to make in turn yearly " one dinner for all his bretherne and theire wieves."[2] The Pewterers decided that " every man and wif that comyth to the yemandries dynner sholde paye xvjd. And every Jorneyman that hath a wif . . . . xvj^d. And every lone man beinge a howsholder that comyth to dynner shall paye xij^d. and every Jorneyman having no wif and comyth to dynner shall paye viij^d. . . . . every man that hath bynne maryed wthin the same ij years shall geve his cocke or elle paye xij^d . . . . Provided always that none bringe his gest wth him wthowt he paye for his dynner as moch as he paith for hymself and that they bring no childerne wth them passing one & no more."[3] In 1605 it was agreed that " ther shalbe called all the whole clothyng and ther wyves and the wydowes whose husbandes have byne of the clothynge and that shalbe payed ijs. man & wyffe and the wydowes xijd. a peece."[4] In 1672, the expense

---

[1] Heath, *Acct. of the Worshipful Company of Grocers*, p. 53, memo. 1348.

[2] Leach, *Beverley Town Documents*, p. 95, 1582.

[3] Welch, *History of Pewterers Company*, Vol. I., p. 201, 1559.

[4] *Ibid*, Vol. II., p. 47.

of entertaining becoming irksome, " an order of Co^{rt} for ye abateing extrao^rdinary Feasting " was made, requiring the " Master & Wardens . . . . to deposit each 12li & spend ye one half thereof upon the Masters & Wardens ffeast this day held, and the Other moyety to be and remain to ye Comp^a use. Now this day the s^d Feast was kept but by reason of the women being invited ye Charge of ye Feast was soe extream that nothing could be cleered to ye house according to ye s^d order. There being Spent near 90li."[1]

Sisters are also remembered in the provisions made for religious observances and assistance in times of sickness. The ordinances of the Craft of the Glovers at Kingston-upon-Hull required that " every brother and syster of ye same craff^{tt} be at every offeryng within the sayd town with every brother or syster of the same crafftt as well at weddynges as at beryalles." Brethren and sisters were to have lights at their decease, and if in poverty to have them freely.[2] The " yoman taillours " made application " that they and others of their fraternity of yomen yearly may assemble . . . . near to Smithfield and make offerings for the souls of brethren and sister etc."[3] In the city of Chester, when a charter wa given to joiners, carvers and turners to become a separate Company, not part of the Carpenters' as formerly, to be called the Company of the Joiners, it is said " Every brother of the said occupacions shall bee ready att all times . . . . to come unto . . . . the burial of every brother and sister of the said occupacions."[4]

Sisters must have played an important part in the

---

[1] Welch, *Hist. of Pewterers'Company*, Vol. II., p. 145.

[2] Lambert, *Two Thousand Years of Gild Life*, p. 217, 1499.

[3] *Ibid*, p. 229, 1415.

[4] Harl. MSS., 2054, fo.5. *Charter of the Joiner's Co.*

functions of the Merchant Taylors of Bristol, for an order was made in 1401 that " the said maister and iiii wardeyns schall ordeyne every yere good and convenient cloth of oon suyt for all brothers and sisters of the said fraternity . . . ."[1] The Charter of this Company provided that " ne man ne woman be underfange into the fraternite abovesaid withoute assent of the Keper and maister etc. . . . . and also that hit be a man or woman y knowe of good conversation and honeste . . . . Also y^t eny brother other soster of thys fraternite above sayde that have trewly y payed hys deutes yat longeth to ye fraternite falle into poverte other into myschef and maie note travalle for to he be releved, he schal have of ye comune goodes every weke xxi^d of monei . . . . and yf he be a man yat hath wyfe and chylde he schal trewly departe alle hys goodes bytwyne heir and hys wyfe and children; and ye partie that falleth to hym he schal trewly yeld up to ye mayster and to ye wardynes of the fraternite obove sayde, in ye maner to fore seide. . . . . " The brothers and sisters shall share in the funeral ceremonies, etc., " also gif eny soster chyde with other openly in the strete, yat eyther schalle paye a pounde wex to ye lighte of the fraternite; and gif they feygte eyther schall paie twenty pounde wex to ye same lyte upon perryle of hir oth gif thei be in power. And gif eny soster by y proved a commune chider among her neygbourys after ones warnyng other tweies at the (delit) ye thridde tyme ye maister and ye wardeynes of ye fraternite schulle pute her out of ye compaynye for ever more."[2]

Chiding and reviling were failings common to all gilds, and were by no means confined to the sisters. The punishments appointed by the Merchant

---

[1] Fox (F. F.) *Merchant Taylors, Bristol*, p. 31.

[2] *Ibid*, p. 26-9.

Gild at Beverley for those " who set up detractions, or rehearse past disputes, or unduly abuse "[1] are for brothers only.   And though it was " Agreed by the M[r] Wardens and Assystaunce " of the Pewterers that " Robert west sholde bringe in his wif vpon ffrydaye next to reconsile her self to M[r] Cacher and others of the Company for her naughty mysdemeano[r] of her tonge towarde them, "[2] the quarrelling among the Carpenters seems to have been almost confined to the men.

There can be no doubt that the sisters shared fully in the social and religious life of the Gilds ; it is also perfectly clear that the wife was regarded by the Gild or Company as her husband's partner, and that, after his death she was confirmed in the possession of his business with his leases and apprentices at least during the term of her widowhood.

But the extent to which she really worked with him in his trade and was qualified to carry it on as a going concern after his death is much more difficult to determine, varying as it did from trade to trade and depending so largely in each case upon the natural capacity of the individual woman concerned.   The extent to which a married woman could work with her husband depended partly upon whether his trade was carried on at home or abroad.   It has been suggested that the carpenters who often were engaged in building operations could not profit much by their wives' assistance, but many trades which in later times have become entirely closed to women were then so dependent on their labour that sisters are mentioned specifically in rules concerning the conditions of manufacture.   Thus the charter of the Armourers and Brasiers was granted in the seventeenth year of James I. " to the Master and

---

[1] Leaeh, *Beverley Town Documents*, p. 78, 1494.

[2] Welch, Charles, *Hist. of Pewterers Company*, Vol. I., p. 200, 1558.

Wardens and Brothers and Sisters of the ffraternity
. . . . that from thenceforth All & all manner
of brass and copper works . . . . edged tools
. . . . small guns . . . . wrought by any
person or persons being of the same ffraternity . . .
should be searched and approved . . . . by
skilful Artificers of the said ffraternity."[1] Rules
which were drawn up at Salisbury in 1612 provide that
no free brother or sister shall " rack, set, or cause
to be racked or set, any cloth upon any tenter, on the
Sabbath day, under the forfeiture of 2s." The Wardens
of the Company of Merchants, Mercers, Grocers,
Apothecaries, Goldsmiths, Drapers, Upholsterers, and
Embroiderers were ordered to search the wares,
merchandise, weights and measures of sisters as well
as brothers.[2] " No free brother or sister is at any time
to put any horse leather into boots or shoes or any
liquored calves leather into boots or shoes, to be
sold between the feast of St. Bartholomew the Apostle
and the Annunciation of the Virgin Mary . . . .
No free brother or sister is to keep or set up any standing in the market place, except in fair times. No
brother or sister is to set open his or her shop, or to
do any work, in making or mending of boots and
shoes on the Sabbath day, on pain of twelve pence
forfeit."[3]

Rules which specifically permit the employment
of the master's wife or daughter in his trade while
excluding other unapprenticed persons, are in themselves evidence that they were often so employed.

---

[1] *Armourers and Brasiers, Charter and Bye laws of Company of.* p. 5. See also
Johnson, *Ordinances of the Drapers of London*, Vol. I., p. 280, 1524).
" (it shall not be lawful unto any brother or sister freed in this fellyship
to take mo. apprentices than may stand in good order for their degree) . . .
every brother being in the master's livery shall pay 6s. 8d. and every sister whose
husband has been of the aforesaid livery shall pay for every apprentice 6s. 8d. and
every other brother or sister not being of the master's livery shall pay for every
apprentice 3s. 4d.

[2] Hoare, Sir R. C., *Hist. of Modern Wilts*, Vol. VI., p. 340.

[3] *Ibid*, Vol. VI., p. 343.

Thus the Glovers allowed " noe brother of this ffraternity " to " take an apprentice vnder the full end and tearme of seaven years ffuly to be compleat . . . . excepting brothers son or daughter . ."[1] No leatherseller might " put man, child or woman to work in the same mistery, if they be not bound apprentice, and inrolled in the same mistery ; excepting their wives and children."[2] Similarly the Girdlers in 1344 ordered that " no one of the trade shall get any woman to work other than his wedded wife or daughter "[3] while by a rule of the Merchant Taylors, Bristol " no person . . . shall cutt make or sell any kynde of garment, garments, hose or breeches within ye saide cittie . . . unles he be franchised and made free of the saide crafte (widdowes whose husbandes were free of ye saide crafte duringe the tyme of their wyddowhedd vsinge ye same with one Jorneyman and one apprentice only excepted) "[4]

The association of women with their husbands in business matters is often suggested by the presence of both their names on indentures. Walter Beemer, for example, was apprenticed to John Castle of Marke and Johane his wife to be instructed and brought up in the trade of a tanner.[5] Sometimes it is shown by the indifference with which money transactions are conducted either with husband or with wife. When the Corporation at Dorchester purchased a new mace in 1660, Mr. Sam White's wife appears to have acted throughout in the matter. An entry in the records for 1660 states that " the silver

---

[1] Ferguson, *Carlisle*, p. 212, *Glover's Gild*, 1665.

[2] Black, W. H., *Articles of the Leathersellers*, p. 21, 1398.

[3] Smythe, W. D., *Hist. of Worshipful Co. of Girdlers, London*, p. 63.

[4] Fox, F. F., *Merchant Taylors, Bristol*, pp. 64-65.

[5] *Somerset Quarter Sessions Records*, Vol. III., p. 165, 1652.

upon the old maces . . . . comes unto iij^{li}. xviij^s. iij^d, which was intended to bee delivered to Mr. Sam: White's wife towards payment for the new Maces . . . . Mr. White hath it the 18th of January, 1660. (Inserted later).

July 3rd, 1661.—pd. Mrs. White as appeareth forward   5   0   0

October 4th, 1661.—pd. Mrs. White more as appeareth forward   4   10   0

About Michaelmas, Mr. Sauage pd Mrs. White in dollers   7   7   0

April 26th, 1661.—It is ordered and agreed that twenty shillings a man, which shall be lent and advanced to Mr. Samuel White's wife by any of this Company towards payment for the Maces shall be repayed back to them."[1]

An equal indifference is shown by the Carpenters' Company in making payments for their ale. Sometimes these are entered to William Whytte, but quite as often to " his wyffe." For example in 1556 " Itm payd for Yest to Whytte's wyffe iiij^d "[2] " Resd óf Whytte's wyffe her hole yere's Rent in ale xxix^s iiij^d "[3] " Itm payd to whytte's wyffe for ale above the rent of hyr howsse iij^s.vj^d." " Itm payd to whytte's wyff for hopyng of tobbis xvj^d."[4] Finally, in 1559, when perhaps William Whytte had departed this life, it is entered " Resd of Mother whytte hole yeres rent xxix^s.vij^d."[5]

The Pewterers, in order to check stealing, ordered that " none of the sayde Crafte shall bye anye Leade of Tylers, Laborers, Masons, boyes, nor of women Nor of none such as shall seme to be a Suspect pson," adding

---

[1] Mayo, G. H., *Municipal Records, Dorchester*, p. 466.

[2] *Rec. of Worshipful Co. of Carpenters*, Vol. IV., p. 56, *Warden's Acct. Book*, 1556.

[3] *Ibid*, Vol. IV., p. 86.

[4] *Ibid*, Vol. IV., p. 88.

[5] *Ibid*, Vol. IV., p. 101.

"that none of the sayde companye shalbe excusyd by his wif or servannte nor none other suche lyk excuse."[1]

Gild rules recognise the authority of the mistress over apprentices, the Clockmakers ordaining that "no servant or apprentice that . . . . hath without just and reasonable cause, departed from his master, mistress or dame, ... shall be admitted to work for himself,"[2] while the charter of the Glass-sellers provides suitable punishment "if any apprentice . . . . shall misbehave himself towards his master or mistress . . . . or shall lie out of his master or mistress's house without his or her privity."[3]

When a man who belonged to Gild or Company died, his wife was free to continue his business under her own management, retaining her position as a free sister, or she might withdraw from trade and transfer her apprentices to another brother. In the Carpenters' and some other trades the latter was the more usual course to follow; thus Thomas Mycock, a cutler, on taking over an apprentice who had served John Kay, deceased, six years, covenanted to pay Kay's widow 20s. a year for the three remaining years,[4] but on the other hand the widow Poynton was paid 15s. 7d. "for glass worke" by the Burgery of Sheffield;[5] showing that she had not withdrawn from business on her husband's death. It is clear that widows often lost their rights as sisters, if they took, as a second husband, a man who was not and did not become a brother of the same Gild. Thus there is an entry in the "Pewterers' Records," 1678, concerning "Mrs. Sicily Moore, formerly the wife of

[1] Welch, *Hist. of Pewterers' Company*, Vol. I., pp. 180-181.

[2] Overall, *Company of Clockmakers*, London, p. 43, 1632.

[3] Ramsay, Wm., *Hist. of the Glass-Sellers*, p. 125.

[4] Leader, *Hist. of Company of Cutlers*, Vol. I., p. 47, 1696.

[5] Leader, *Records of the Burgery of Sheffield*, p. 227, 1685.

Edward Fish, late member of this Comp^a decd, and since marryed to one Moore, a fforeignir, now also decd, desired to be admitted into the ffreedome of this Comp^a. After some debate the Court agreed and soe Ordered that she shall be received into the ffreedom of the Comp^a Gratis, onely paying usuall ffees and this Condition that she shall not bind any app'ntice by virtue of the s^d Freedom."[1]

Instances occur in which an apprentice was discharged because " the wife, after the death of her Husband, taught him not."[2] The apprentice naturally brought forward this claim if by so doing there was a chance of shortening the term of his service, but he was not always successful. The Justices dismissed a case brought by Edward Steel, ordering him to serve Elizabeth Apprice, widow, the remainder of his term. He was apprenticed in 1684 to John Apprice Painter-Stainer for nine years ; he had served seven years when his master died, and he now declares that Elizabeth, the widow, refuses to instruct him. She insists that since her husband's death she has provided able workmen to instruct this apprentice, and that he was now capable of doing her good service.[3] When the " widowe Holton prayed that she [being executor to her husband] maye have the benefitt of the service of Roger Jakes, her husband's apprentice by Indenture, for the residue of the years to come, which he denyeth to performe, it was ordered that th'apprentice shall dwell and serve his dame duringe the residue of his terme, she providing for him as well work as other things fitt for him."[4] The Girdlers having accused Richard Northy of having more than the just number of apprentices, he stated

---

[1] Welch, *Hist. of Pewterers' Company*, Vol. II., p. 153.

[2] Stow, *London*, Book V., p. 335.

[3] *Middlesex Sessions Book*, p. 47, 1691.

[4] Guilding, *Reading Records*, Vol. II., p. 362.

in his defence that the apprentice " was not any
that was taken or bound by him, but was left unto
him by express words in the will of his deceased
mother-in-law wh[ch] will, wth the probate thereof,
he now produced in court."[1]

The occurrence of widows' names among the cases
which came before the Courts for infringements
of the Company's rules is further evidence that they
were actively engaged in business. " Two bundles
of unmade girdles were taken from widows Maybury
and Bliss, young widows " they were ordered to
pay 5s. each by way of fine for making and selling unlawful wares."[2]   Richard Hewatt, of Northover in
Glastonbury, fuller, when summoned to appear before
the Somerset Quarter Sessions as a witness, refers
to his dame Ursula Lance who had " lost 2 larrows
worth five shillings and that Robert Marsh, one of
the constables of Somerton Hundred, found in the
house of William Wilmat the Larrows cloven in pieces
and put in the oven, and the Rack-hookes that were
in the larrows were found in the fire in the said house."[3]

Widows were very dependent upon the assistance
of journeymen, and often chose a relation for this
responsible position.   At Reading " All the freman
Blacksmiths in this Towne complayne that one Edward
Nitingale, a smith, beinge a forreynour, useth the trade
of a blacksmith in this Corporacion to the great
dammage of the freemen :   it was answered that he is a
journey-man to the Widowe Parker, late wife to
Humfrey Parker, a blacksmith, deceassed, and worketh
as her servant at 5s. a weeke, she being his aunt, and
was advised to worke in noe other manner but as a
journey-man."[4]   The connection often ended in

---

[1] Smythe, *Company of Girdlers*, p. 133, 1635.

[2] *Ibid*, p. 87, 1627.

[3] *Somerset Q.S. Rec.*, Vol. III., pp. 365-6, 1659.

[4] Guilding, *Reading Records*, Vol. III., p. 502, 1640.

marriage; it was brought to the notice of one of the Quaker's Meetings in London that one of their Members, "Will Townsend . . . card maker proposes to take to wife Elizabeth Doshell of ye same place to be his wife, and ye same Elizabeth doth propose to take ye said Will to be her husband, the yonge man liveing with her as a journey-man had thought and a beliefe that she would come to owne ye truth and did propose to her his Intentions towards her as to marige before she did come to owne the truth which thinge being minded to him by ffriends. . . . he has acknowledged it soe and sayes it had been beter that he had waited till he had had his hope in some measure answered."[1]

Such marriages, though obviously offering many advantages, were not always satisfactory. A lamentable picture of an unfortunate one is given in the petition of Sarah Westwood, wife of Robert Westwood, Feltmaker, presented to Laud in 1639, showing that "your petitioner was (formerly) the wife of one John Davys, alsoe a Feltmaker, who dying left her a howse furnished with goodes sufficient for her use therein and charged with one childe, as yet but an infant, and two apprentices, who, for the residue of their termes . . . could well have atchieved sufficient for the maynetenance of themselves and alsoe of your petitioner and her child. That being thus left in good estate for livelyhood, her nowe husband became a suitor unto her in the way of marriage, being then a journeyman feltmaker. . . ."

Soon after their marriage, "Westwood following lewde courses, often beate and abused your petitioner, sold and consumed what her former husband left her, threatened to kill her and her child, turned them out of dores, refusing to afford them any means of subsistance, but on the contrary seekes the utter ruin of them both and most scandelously has traduced

---

[1] *Horsleydown Monthly Meeting Minute Book*, 19 11mo., 1675.

your petitioner giving out in speeches that she would have poysoned him thereby to bring a generall disgrace upon her, . . . and forbiddes all people where she resortes to afford her entertaignment, and will not suffer her to worke for the livelyhood of her and her child, but will have accompt of the same. . . . Albeit he can get by his labour 20/- a weeke, yet he consumes the same in idle company . . . having lewdlie spent all he had with your petitioner."[1]

Though their entrance to the Gilds and Companies was most often obtained by women through marriage, it has already been shown that their admission by apprenticeship was not unknown, and they also occasionally acquired freedom by patrimony; thus " Katherine Wetwood, daughter of Humphrey Wetwood, of London, Pewterer, was sworn and made free by the Testimony of the Master and Wardens of the Merchant Taylors' Co., and of two Silk Weavers, that she was a virgin and twenty-one years of age. She paid the usual patrimony fine of 9s.2d."[2] More than one hundred years later Mary Temple was made free of the Girdlers' Company by patrimony.[3] No jealousy is expressed of the women who were members of the Companies, but all others were rigorously excluded from employment. Complaints were brought before the Girdlers' that certain Girdlers in London " set on worke such as had not served 7 years at the art, and also for setting forreigners and maids on worke."[4] Rules were made in Bristol in 1606, forbidding women to work at the trades of the whitawers (white leather dressers), Point makers and Glovers.[5]

---

[1] S.P.D., ccccxxxv. 42, Dec. 6, 1639.

[2] Welch, Pewterers, Vol. II., p. 92, 1633-4.

[3] Smythe, Company of Girdlers, p. 128, 1747.

[4] Ibid, p. 88, 1628.

[5] Latimer, Annals of Bristol, p. 26, 1606.

In the unprotected trades where the Gild organisation had broken down, and the profits of the small
tradesmen had been reduced to a minimum by unlimited competition, the family depended upon the
labour of mother and children as well as the father for
its support. Petitions presented to the King concerning grievances under which they suffer, generally
include wives and children in the number of those
engaged in the trade in question. On a proposal
to tax tobacco pipes, the makers show " that all
the poorer sort of the Trade must be compelled to
lay it down, for want of Stock or Credit to carry it
on ; and so their Wives and Children, who help to
get their Bread, must of necessity perish, or become
a Charge to their respective Parishes. That when
a Gross of Pipes are made, they sell them for 1s. 6d.
and 1s. 10d., out of which 2d. or 3d. is their greatest
Profit. And they not already having Stock, or can
make Pipes fast enough to maintain their Families,
how much less can they be capable, when half the
Stock they have, must be paid down to pay the
King his Duty ? "[1]

The Glovers prepared a memorandum showing
the great grievances there would be if a Duty be laid
on Sheep and Lamb Skins, Drest in Oyl etc. " The
Glovers," they say, " are many Thousands in Number,
in the Counties of England, City of London and
Liberties thereof, and generally so Poor (the said
Trade being so bad and Gloves so plenty) that mear
Necessity doth compel them to Sell their Goods daily
to the Glove-sellers, and to take what Prises they will
give them, to keep them and their Children and Families at Work to maintain them, or else they must
perrish for want of Bred."[2]

---

[1] *Humble Petition and Case of the Tobacco Pipe Makers of the Citys of London and Westminster*, 1695.

[2] *Reasons humbly offered by the Leather-Dressers and Glovers, &c.*

The Pin-makers say that their company "consists for the most part of poor and indigent People, who have neither Credit nor Money to purchase Wyre of the Merchant at the best hand, but are forced for want thereof, to buy only small Parcels of the second or third Buyer, as they have occasion to use it, and to sell off the Pins they make of the same from Week to Week, as soon as they are made, for ready money, to feed themselves, their Wives, and Children, whom they are constrained to imploy to go up and down every Saturday Night from Shop to Shop to offer their Pins for Sale, otherwise cannot have mony to buy bread."[2]

A similar picture is given in the " Mournfull Cryes of many thousand Poore tradesmen, who are ready to famish through decay of Trade." " Oh that the cravings of our Stomacks could bee heard by the Parliament and City ! Oh that the Teares of our poore famishing Babes were botled ! Oh that their tender Mothers Cryes for bread to feed them were in-graven in brasse . . . . O you Members of Parliament and rich men in the City, that are at ease, and drink Wine in Bowles . . . . you that grind our faces and Flay off our skins . . . . is there none to Pity . . . . Its your Taxes Customes and Excize, that compels the Country to raise the price of Food and to buy nothing from us but meere absolute necessaries ; and then you of the City that buy our Worke, must have your Tables furnished . . . . and therefore will give us little or nothing for our Worke, even what you please, because you know wee must sell for Monyes to set our Families on worke, or else wee famish . . . . and since the late Lord Mayor Adams, you have put into execution an illegall, wicked Decree of the Common Counsell ; whereby you have

---

[2] *Case or Petition of the Corporation of Pin-makers.*

taken our goods from us, if we have gone to the Innes
to sell them to the Countrimen; and you have mur-
dered some of our poor wives, that have gone to Innes
to find countrimen to buie them."[1]

In each case it will be noticed that the wife's
activity is specially mentioned in connection with
the sale of the goods. Women were so closely connected with industrial life in London that when the Queen
proposed to leave London in 1641 it was the women
who petitioned Parliament, declaring, " that your
Petitioners, their Husbands, their Children and their
Families, amounting to many thousand soules; have
lived in plentifull and good fashion, by the exercise
of severall Trades and venting of divers workes . . .
All depending wholly for the sale of their commodities,
(which is the maintenance and very existence and
beeing of themselves, their husbands, and families)
upon the splendour and glory of the English Court,
and principally upon that of the Queenes Majesty."[2]

In addition to these Trades, skilled and semi-
skilled, in which men and women worked together,
certain skilled women's trades existed in London which
were sufficiently profitable for considerable premiums
to be paid with the girls who were apprenticed to
them.[3] These girls probably continued to exercise
their own trade after marriage, their skill serving them
instead of dowry, the Customs of London providing
that " married women who practise certain crafts
in the city alone and without their husbands, may
take girls as apprentices to serve them and learn their
trade, and these apprentices shall be bound by their
indentures of apprenticeship to both husband and
wife, to learn the wife's trade as is aforesaid, and such

---

[1] *Mournfull Cryes of many Thousand Poore Tradesmen,* 1647.

[2] *Humble Petition of many thousands of Courtiers, Citizens, Gentlemens and
Tradesmens Wives, &c.*

[3] Ante. p. 175.

indentures shall be enrolled as well for women as for men."[1] The girls who were apprenticed to Carpenters were evidently on this footing.

References in contemporary documents to women who were following skilled or semi-skilled trades in London are very frequent. Thus Thomas Swan is reported to have committed thefts " on his mistress Alice Fox, Wax-chandler of Old Bailey."[2] Mrs. Cellier speaks of " one Mrs. Phillips, an uphol- sterer,"[3] while the Rev. Giles Moore notes in his diary " payed Mistress Cooke, in Shoe Lane, for a new trusse, and for mending the old one and altering the plate thereof, £1 5 0 ; should shee dye, I am in future to inquire for her daughter Barbara, who may do the like for mee."[4] Isaac Derston was "put an app. to Anthony Watts for the term of seven years, but turned over to the widow—dwelling near : palls : who bottoms cane chaires, £2 10 0."[5] That the bottoming of cane chairs was a poor trade is witnessed by the meagreness of the premium paid in this case.

No traces can be found of any organisation existing in the skilled women's trades, such as upholstery, millinery, mantua-making, but a Gild existed among the women who sorted and packed wool at Southampton. A Sisterhood consisting of twelve women of good and honest demeanour was formed there as a company to serve the merchants in the occupation of covering pokes or baloes [bales]. Two of the sisters acted as wardens. In 1554 a court was held to adjudicate on the irregular attendance of some of the sisters. The names of two wardens

---

[1] Eileen Power, by kind permission, 1419.

[2] *C.S.P.D.* cv. 53, Jan. 19, 1619.

[3] Cellier (Mrs.) *Malice Defeated.* p. 25.

[4] *Suss. Arch. Coll.*, Vol. I., p. 123, *Journal Rev.*, 1676.

[5] *Monthly Meeting Minute Book, Peele,* Nov. 24, 1687.

and eleven sisters are given ; no one who was absent from her duties for more than three months was permitted to return to the Sisterhood without the Mayor's licence. " Item, y^t is ordered by the sayde Maior and his bretherne that all suche as shall be nomynated and appoynted to be of the systeryd shall make a brekefaste at their entrye for a knowlege and shal bestowe at the least xx^d or ij^s, or more as they lyste."[1]

Possibly when more records of the Gilds and Companies have been published in a complete form, some of the gaps which are left in this account of the position of women in the skilled and semi-skilled trades may be filled in ; but the extent to which married women were engaged in them must always remain largely a matter of conjecture, and unfortunately it is precisely this point which is most interesting to the sociologist. Practically all adult women were married, and the character of the productive work which an economic organisation allots to married women and the conditions of their labour decide very largely the position of the mother in society, and therefore, ultimately, the fate of her children. The fragmentary evidence which has been examined shows that, while the system of family industry lasted, it was so usual in the skilled and semi-skilled trades for women to share in the business life of their husbands that they were regarded as partners. Though the wife had rarely, if ever, served an apprenticeship to his trade, there were many branches in which her assistance was of great value, and husband and wife naturally divided the industry between them in the way which was most advantageous to the family, while unmarried servants, either men or women, performed the domestic drudgery. As capitalistic organisation developed, many avenues of industry were, however, gradually closed to married women. The masters no longer

[1] Davies. (J., S.) *Hist of Southampton*, p. 279.

depended upon the assistance of their wives, while
the journeyman's position became very similar to
that of the modern artisan ; he was employed on the
premises of his master, and thus, though his association
with his fellows gave him opportunity for combination,
his wife and daughters, who remained at home, did
not share in the improvements which he effected in
his own economic position. The alternatives before
the women of this class were either to withdraw
altogether from productive activity, and so become
entirely dependent upon their husband's goodwill,
or else to enter the labour market independently and
fight their battles alone, in competition not only with
other women, but with men.

Probably the latter alternative was still most often
followed by married women, although at this time the
idea that men " keep " their wives begins to prevail :
but the force of the old tradition maintained amongst
women a desire for the feeling of independence which
can only be gained through productive activity, and
thus married women, even when unable to work with
their husbands, generally occupied themselves with
some industry, however badly it might be paid.

B. *Retail Trades.*

The want of technical skill and knowledge which so
often hampered the position of women in the Skilled
Trades, was a smaller handicap in Retail Trades,
where manual dexterity and technical knowledge
are less important than general intelligence and a
lively understanding of human nature. Quick per-
ception and social tact, which are generally supposed
to be feminine characteristics, often proved useful
even to the craftsman, when his wife assumed the
charge of the financial side of his business ; it is
therefore not surprising to find women taking a
prominent part in every branch of Retail Trade.
In fact the woman who was left without other

resources turned naturally to keeping a shop, or to the sale of goods in the street, as the most likely means for maintaining her children, and thus the woman shopkeeper is no infrequent figure in contemporary writings.   For example, in one of the many pamphlets describing the incidents of the Civil War, we read that " Mistresse Phillips was sent for, who was found playing the good housewife at home (a thing much out of fashion) . . . . and committed close prisoner to castle."   Her husband having been driven before from town, " She was to care for ten children, the most of them being small, one whereof she at the same time suckled, her shop (which enabled her to keep all those) was ransacked," £14 was taken, and the house plundered, horse and men billetted with her when she could scarce get bread enough for herself and her family without charity.   She was tried, and condemned to death, when, the account continues, " Mistress Phillips not knowing but her turne was next, standing all the while with a halter about her neck over against the Gallowes, a Souldier would have put the halter under her Handkerchiefe, but she would not suffer him, speaking with a very audible voice, ' I am not ashamed to suffer reproach and shame in this cause,' a brave resolution, beseeming a nobler sex, and not unfit to be registered in the Book of Martyrs."

The woman shop-keeper is found also among the stock characters of the drama.   In " The Old Batchelor " Belinda relates that " a Country Squire, with the Equipage of a Wife and two Daughters, came to Mrs. Snipwel's Shop while I was there . . . . the Father bought a Powder-Horn, and an Almanack, and a Comb-Case ; the Mother, a great Fruz-Towr, and a fat Amber-Necklace ; the Daughters only tore two Pair of Kid-leather Gloves, with trying 'em on."[1]

Amongst the Quakers, shop-keeping was a usual employment for women.   Thomas Chalkley, soon

---

[1] Congreve (Wm.).   *The Old Batchelor*, Act iv., Sc., viii.

after his marriage " had a Concern to visit Friends in the counties of Surrey, Sussex and Kent, which I performed in about two Weeks Time, and came home and followed my calling, and was industrious therein ; and when I had gotten something to bear my expenses, and settled my Wife in some little Business I found an Exercise on my Spirit to go over to *Ireland*."[1] Another Quaker describes how he applied himself " to assist my Wife in her Business as well as I could, attending General, Monthly and other Meetings on public Occasions for three Years."[2] The provision of the little stock needed for a shop was a favourite method of assisting widows.

The frequency with which payments to women are entered in account books[3] is further evidence of the extent to which they were engaged in Retail Trades, but this occupation was not freely open to all and any who needed it. It was, on the contrary, hedged about with almost as many restrictions as the gild trades. The craftsman was generally free to dispose of his own goods, but many restrictions hampered the Retailer, that is to say the person who bought to sell again. The community regarded this class with some jealousy, and limited their numbers. Hence, the poor woman who sought to improve her position by opening

---

[1] Chalkley, *Journal*, pp. 30-31, 1690.

[2] Bownas, Samuel, *Life of*, p. 135.

[3] The Churchwardens of St. Margaret's, Westminster, paid 6d. to " Goodwyfe Wells for salt to destroy the fleas in the Churchwarden's pew." (Cox. Churchwardens Accts., p. 321, 1610.). Among the Cromwell family receipts is one in 1624 " from ye Right wor⁰ ye Lady Carr by the hands of Henry Hanby, the somme of twenty and one pounds in full payment of all Reckonings from the beginninge of the world . . . . . by me ellen Sadler X (*Cromwell Family Bills and Receipts*, p. 15.) " A bill for Mrs. Willie of Ramsie the 14 of April 1636 for material and making your daughter petecoate

,,	,,	your silk grogram coate
,,	,,	your daughter's gasson shute
,,	,,	your daughter's silke moheare wascote
,,	,,	your damask coate

Total 7. 17. 9. (*Ibid*, p. 26c).

a little shop, did not always find her course clear. In fact there were many towns in which the barriers between her and an honest independence were insurmountable. Girls were, however, apprenticed to shop-keepers oftener than to the gild trades, and licences to sell were granted to freewomen as well as to freemen. At Dorchester, girls who had served an apprenticeship to shopkeepers were duly admitted to the freedom of the Borough; we find entered in the Minute Book the names of Celina Hilson, apprenticed to Mat. Hilson, Governor, haberdasher, and Mary Goodredge, spinster, haberdasher of small wares; also of James Bun (who had married Elizabeth Williams a freewoman) haberdasher of small wares; Elizabeth Williams, apprenticed seven years to her Mother, Mary W., tallow chaundler, and of William Weare, apprenticed to Grace Lacy, widow, woolen draper.[1] An order was granted by the Middlesex Quarter Sessions to discharge Mary Jemmett from apprenticeship to Jane Tyllard, widow, from whom she was to learn " the trade of keeping a linen shop,"[2] and an account is given of a difference between Susanna Shippey, of Mile End, Stepney, widow, and Ann Taylor, her apprentice, touching the discharge of the said apprentice. It appears that Ann has

---

The Rev. Giles Moore bought " of Widdow Langley 2 more fine sheets, of Goodwyfe Seamer 9 ells. and a halfe of hempen cloath. (*Suss. Arch Coll.* Vol., I. p. 68 1656. Rev. Giles Moore's Journal).

Foulis paid, in Scots money, Jan. 22, 1692 "to Mrs. Pouries lad for aniseed, carthamums &c. 11s." (p. 144), and on Aug. 3, 1696 he "received from Eliz. Ludgate last Whits mail' for ye shop at fosters Wyndhead 25 lib." (p. 195). Jan. 14, 1704 " to my douchter Jean be Mrs. Cuthbertsons paym^t for 4 ell & ¾ flowered calico to lyne my nightgowne 7. 13. o. (p. 339) May 23, 1704 "receaved from Agnes philp Whitsun. maill for the shop at fosters wyndhead and ye key therof, and given it to the Candlemakers wife who has taken the shop 25 lib (p. 346). (Foulis *Acct Book*). Similar entries are in the *Howard Household Book*, 1619. To Mrs. Smith for lining [linen] for my Lord, had in Easter tearm, 5^li x^s. Mrs. Smith for napry had in May vj^li ii^s (*Howard Household Book, pp.* 105 and 161.).

[1] Mayo, *Municipal Records of Dorchester*, p. 428-9.

[2] *Middlesex County Records*, p. 180, 1698.

often defrauded her mistress of her goods and sold them for less than cost price.[1]

Little mercy was shown to either man or woman who engaged in the Retail Trade without having served an apprenticeship. A warrant was only issued to release " Elizabeth Beaseley from the Hospital of Bridewell on her brother John Beaseley's having entered into bond that she shall leave off selling tobacco in the town of Wigan."[2] Mary Keeling was presented at Nottingham " for falowing ye Treaid of a Grocer and Mercer and kepping open shope for on month last past, *contra Statum*, not being *aprentice*."[3] At Carlisle it was ordered that " Isaack Tully shall submit himself to pay a fine to this trade if they shall think it fitting for taking his sister to keep & sell waires for him contrary to our order,"[4] and when it was reported that " Mrs. Studholme hath employed James Moorehead Scotsman to vend and sell goods in her shop contrary to an order of this company wee doe order that the wardens of our company shall fourthwith acquaint Mrs. Studholme yt. she must not be admitted to entertain him any long^r in her employmt but that before our next quarter day she take some other course for keeping her shop and yt. he be noe longer employed therein till yt. time."[5] At a later date Mrs. Sybil Hetherington, Mrs. Mary Nixon, Mrs. Jane Jackson, widow, and four men, were dealt with for having shops or retailery of goods contrary to the statute.[6]

---

[1] *Middlesex County Records*, p. 2, 1690.

[2] *C. R.* 18th, August, 1640.

[3] *Nottingham Records*, Vol. V., p. 331, 1686.

[4] Ferguson, *Municipal Records, Carlisle*, p. 110, 1651.

[5] *Ibid*, p. 112, 1668.

[6] *Ibid*, p. 115, 1719.

There were fewer restrictions on retailing in London
than in the provinces, and trading was virtually free
in the streets of London. An act of the Common
Council, passed in 1631, deals with abuses rising from
this freedom, declaring " that of late it is come to
passe that divers unruly people, as Butchers, Bakers,
Poulters, Chandlers, Fruiterers, Sempsters, sellers
of Grocery wares, Oyster wives, Herbe wives, Tripe
wives, and the like ; who not contented to enjoy the
benefit and common right of Citizens, by holding
their market and continual Trades in their several
Shops & houses where they dwell, doe . . . . by
themselves, wives, children and seruants enter into,
and take up their standings in the said streets and
places appointed for the common Markets, unto
which the country people only have in former times
used to resort to vend and utter their victuall and
other commodities ; in which Markets the said Freemen doe abide for the most part of the day and that
not only upon Market dayes, but all the weeke long
with multitudes of Baskets, Tubs, Chaires, Boards
& Stooles, ... the common Market places
by these disordered people be so taken up, that country people when they come with victual and provision
have no roome left them to set down their . . . .
baskets."[1]

In provincial towns, stalls in the market place
were leased to tradesmen by the Corporation, the
rents forming a valuable revenue for the town ; infringements of the monopoly were summarily dealt
with and often the privilege was reserved for " free "
men and women. Thus at St. Albans Richard
Morton's wife was presented because she " doth
ordinarilie sell shirt bands and cuffes, hankerchers,
coifes, and other small lynenn wares openlie in the
markett,"[2] not being free. It was as a special favour

---

[1] *Act of Common Council for reformation, etc.*

[2] Gibbs, *Corporation Records of St. Albans*, p. 62, 1613.

that leave was given to a poor woman to sell shoes in Carlisle market. The conditions are explained as follows :—" Whereas Ann Barrow the wife of Richard Barrow formerly one that by virtue of the Coldstream Act brought shoes and exposed them to sell in Carlisle market he being long abroad and his said wife poor the trade is willing to permit the said Ann to bring and sell shoes provided always they be the work of one former servant and noe more and for this permission she owns the trades favour and is thankful for it . . . . agreed and ordered that every yeare she shall pay 2s."[1]

The Corporation at Reading was occupied for a whole year with the case of the " Aperne woman." The first entry in the records states that " Steven Foord of Newbery the aperne woman's husband, exhibited a lettre from the Lord of Wallingford for his sellerman to shewe and sell aperninge [2] in towne, in Mr. Mayor's handes, etc. And thereupon tollerated to doe as formerly she had done, payeing yerely 10s. to the Hall."[3] Next year there is another entry to the effect that " it was agreed that Steven Foorde's wief shall contynue sellinge of aperninge, as heretofore, and that the other woman usinge to sell suche stuffes at William Bagley's. dore shalbe forbidden, and shall not hencefourth be permitted to sell in the boroughe etc., and William Bagley shall be warned."[4] The other woman proving recalcitrant, " at Steven Foorde's wive's request and complaynte it was grannted that William Bagley's stranger, selling aperninge in contempt of the government, shalbe questioned."[5] Finally

---

[1] Ferguson, *Carlisle*, p. 187, 1669.

[2] Stuff for Aprons.

[3] Guilding, *Reading Records*, Vol. II., p. 171, 1624.

[4] *Ibid*, Vol. II., p. 240, 1625.

[5] *Ibid*, Vol. II., p. 252.

it was " agreed that Steven Foorde's wife shall hence-
forth keepe Markett and sell onely linsey woolsey
of their own making in this markett, according to
the Lord Wallingforde's lettre, she payeing xs. per
annum, and that noe other stranger shall hence-
forth keepe markett or sell lynsey and woolsey in this
markett."[1]

At this time, when most roads were mere bridle
tracks, and few conveniences for travel existed, when
even in towns the streets were so ill-paved that in
bad weather the goodwife hesitated before going to
the market, the dwellers in villages and hamlets were
often fain to buy from pedlars who brought goods
to their door and to sell butter and eggs to anyone who
would undertake the trouble of collection. Their
need was recognised by the authorities, who granted
a certain number of licences to Badgers, Pedlars and
Regraters, and probably many others succeeded in
trading unlicensed. This class of Dealers was
naturally regarded with suspicion by shopkeepers. A
pamphlet demanding their suppression, points out that
" the poor decaying Shopkeeper has a large Rent to
pay, and Family to Support ; he maintains not
his own Children only, but all the poor Orphans and
Widows in his Parish ; nay, sometimes the Widows
and Orphans of the very Pedlar or Hawker, who has
thus fatally laboured to starve him." As for the
Hawkers, " we know they pretend they are shut out
of the great Trading Cities, Towns and Corporations
by the respective Charters and all other settled Privileges of those Places, but we answer that tho' for
want of legal Introduction they may not be able to set
up in Cities, Corporations, etc., yet there are very many
Places of very great Trade, where no Corporation
Privileges would obstruct them . . . . if any
of them should be reduc'd and . . . . be brought
to the Parish to keep ; that is to say, their Wives and

---

[1] *Guilding, Reading Records*, Vol. II., p. 267.

Children, the Manufacturers, the Shopkeepers who confessedly make up the principal Numbers of those corporations, and are the chief Supporters of the Parishes, will be much more willing to maintain them, than to be ruin'd by them."[1]

The terms Badging, Peddling, Hawking and Regrating are not very clearly defined, and were used in senses which somewhat overlap each other ; but the Badger seems to have been a person who " dealt ' in a wholesale way. A licence was granted in 1630 to " Edith Doddington of Hilbishopps, widdowe, to be a badger of butter and cheese and to carry the same into the Counties of Wiltes, Hamsher, Dors[tt] and Devon, and to retourne againe with corne and to sell it againe in any faire or markett within this County during one whole yeare now next ensueing ; and she is not to travell with above three horses, mares or geldings at the most part."[2] The authorities, fearing lest corners and profiteering should result from interference with the supply of necessaries, made " ingrossing " or anything resembling an attempt to buy up the supply of wheat, salt, etc., an offence. Amongst the prosecutions which were made on this account are presentments of " John Whaydon and John Preist of Watchett, partners, for ingross of salt, Julia Stone, Richard Miles, Joane Miles als. Stone of Bridgwater for ingross of salte." [3] of " Johann Stedie of Fifehead, widdow, ... for ingrossinge of corne contrary etc,"[4] of " Edith Bruer and Katherine Bruer, Spinsters, of Halse . . . . for ingrossinge of corne,"[5] and of " Johann Thorne

---

[1] *Brief State of the Inland and Home Trade.* pp. 59 and 63, 1730.

[2] *Somerset Q. S. Records*, Vol. II., p. 119, 1630.

[3] *Ibid*, Vol. II., p. 153, 1631.

[4] *Ibid*, Vol. II., p. 161.

[5] *Ibid*, Vol. II., p. 165.

. . . . widow . . . . for ingrossinge of wheate, Barley, Butter and Cheese."[1]

Pedlars and hawkers carried on an extensive trade all over the country. At first sight this would seem a business ill suited to women, for it involved carrying a heavy pack of goods on the back over long distances ; and yet it appears as though in some districts the trade was almost their monopoly. The success that attended Joan Dant's efforts as a pedlar has been told elsewhere.[2] How complete was the ascendency which women had established in certain districts over this class of trade is shown by the following definition of the term " Hawkers " :—" those that profer their Wares by Wholesale which are called Hawkers, and which are not only the Manufacturers themselves, but others besides them, viz. the Women in *London*, in *Exceter* and in *Manchester*, who do not only Profer Commodities at the Shops and Ware houses, but also at Inns to Countrey-Chapmen. Likewise the *Manchester*-men, the *Sherborn* —men, and many others, that do Travel from one Market-Town to another ; and there at some Inn do profer their Wares to sell to the Shopkeepers of the place."[3]

Though peddling might in some cases be developed into a large and profitable concern, more often it afforded a bare subsistence. The character of a woman engaged in it is given in a certificate brought before the Hertford Quarter Sessions in 1683 by the inhabitants of Epping, which states that " Sarah, wife of Richard Young, of Epping, cooper, who was accused of pocket-picking when she was about her lawfull and honest imploy of buying small wares and wallnuts " at Sabridgworth fair, is " a very honest and well-behaved woman, not given to pilfer or

---

[1] *Somerset Q. S. Records*, Vol. II., p. 223.

[2] *Ante*, p. 33.

[3] *Trade of England.* p. 21, 1681.

steale," and that they believe her to be falsely accused.[1]

While the Pedlar dealt chiefly in small wares and haberdashery, Regraters were concerned with the more perishable articles of food. In this they were seriously hampered by bye-laws forbidding the buying and selling of such articles in one day. The laws had been framed with the object of preventing a few persons buying up all the supplies in the market and selling them at exorbitant prices, but their application seems to have been chiefly directed in the interests of the shopkeepers, to whom the competition of women who hawked provisions from door to door was a serious matter, the women being contented with very small profits, and the housewives finding it so convenient to have goods brought to their very doorstep. The injustice of the persecution of these poor women is protested against by the writer of a pamphlet, who points out that " We provide Men shall not be cheated in buying a pennyworth of Eggs, but make no provision to secure them from the same Abuse in a hundred pounds laid out in Cloaths. The poor Artizan shall not be oppressed in laying out his penny to one poorer than himself, but is without Remedy, shortened by a Company in his Penny as it comes in. I have heard Complaints of this Nature in greater matters of the publik Sales of the *East India Company*, perhaps if due consideration were had of these great Ingrossers, there would be found more Reason to restrain them, than a poor Woman that travels in the Country to buy up and sell in a Market a few Hens and Chickens."[2]

Even in the Middle Ages the trade of Regrating was almost regarded as the prerogative of women. Gower wrote " But to say the truth in this instance, the trade of regratery belongeth by right rather to women.

---

[1] *Hertfordshire County Records*, Vol. I., pp. 347-8.

[2] *Linnen and Woollen Manufactury*, p. 7, 168ᵗ.

But if a woman be at it she in stinginess useth much
more machination and deceit than a man ; for she
never alloweth the profit on a single crumb to escape
her, nor faileth to hold her neighbour to paying his
price ; all who beseech her do but lose their time, for
nothing doth she by courtesy, as anyone who drinketh
in her house knoweth well."[1]

In later times the feminine form of the word is
used in the ordinances of the City of London, clearly
showing that the persons who were then carrying on
the trade were women ; thus it was said "Let no
Regrateress pass *London Bridge* towards *Suthwerk*,
nor elsewhere, to buy Bread, to carry it into the
City of *London* to sell ; because the Bakers of *Suthwerk*,
nor of any other Place, are not subject to the Justice
of the City." And again "Whereas it is common for
merchants to give Credit, and especially for Bakers
commonly to do the same with Regrateresses . . . .
. . . . we forbid, that no Baker make the benefit
of any Credit to a Regrateress, as long as he shall
know her to be involved in her Neighbour's Debt."[2]
Moreover a very large proportion of the prosecutions
for this offence were against women. "We Amerce
Thomas Bardsley for his wife buyinge Butter Contrary
to the orders of the towne in xijd."[3] "Katherine
Birch for buyinge and selling pullen [chicken] both of
one day 3s. Thos. Ravald wife of Assheton of Mercy
bancke for sellinge butter short of waight."[4] "Thomas
Massey wife for buyinge a load of pease and sellinge
them the same day. Amerced in 1s."[5] "Katharine
Hall for buyinge and sellinge Cheese both of one day

---

[1] Gower. *Le mirour de l'omme* (trans. from French verse by Eileen Power).

[2] Stow, *London*, Book V., p. 343. Assize of Bread.

Manchester Court Leet Records, Vol. IV., p. 110, 1653.

[4] *Ibid*, p. 212, 1657

[5] *Ibid*. p. 244, 1658.

6d. Anne Rishton for buyinge and sellinge butter the same day Amercd in 3. o."[1]

As the Regrater dealt chiefly in food, her business is closely connected with the provision trades, but enough has been said here to indicate that of all retailing this was the form which most appealed to poor women, who were excluded from skilled trades and whose only other resource was spinning. The number of women in this unfortunate position was large, including as it did not only widows, whose families depended entirely upon their exertions, but also the wives of most of the men who were in receipt of day wages and had no garden or grazing rights. It has already been shown that wages, except perhaps in some skilled trades, were insufficient for the maintenance of a family. Therefore, when the mother of a young family could neither work in her husband's trade nor provide her children with food by cultivating her garden or tending cows and poultry, she must find some other means to earn a little money. By wages she could seldom earn more than a penny or twopence a day and her food. Selling perishable articles of food from door to door presented greater chances of profit, and to this expedient poor women most often turned. In proportion as the trade was a convenience to the busy housewife, it became an unwelcome form of competition to the established shopkeepers, who, being influential in the Boroughs, could persecute and suppress the helpless, disorganised women who undersold them.

(C) *Provision Trades.*

Under this head are grouped the Bakers, Millers, Butchers and Fishwives, together with the Brewers, Innkeepers and Vintners, the category embracing both those who produced and those who retailed the provisions in question.

---

[1] *Manchester Court Test Records*, p. 243, 1658.

A large proportion both of the bread and beer consumed at this time was produced by women in domestic industry. The wages assessments show that on the larger farms the chief woman servant was expected both to brew and to bake, but the cottage folk in many cases cannot have possessed the necessary capital for brewing, and perhaps were wanting ovens in which to bake. Certainly in the towns both brewing and baking existed as trades from the earliest times. Though in many countries the grinding of corn has been one of the domestic occupations performed by women and slaves, in England women were saved this drudgery, for the toll of corn ground at the mill was an important item in the feudal lord's revenue, and severe punishments were inflicted on those who ground corn elsewhere. The common bakehouse was also a monopoly of the feudal lord's,[1] but his rights in this case were not carried so far as to penalize baking for domestic purposes.

It might be supposed that industries such as brewing and baking, which were so closely connected with the domestic arts pertaining to women, would be more extensively occupied by women than trades such as those of blacksmith or pewterer or butcher ; but it will be shown that skill acquired domestically was not sufficient to establish a woman's position in the world of trade, and that actually in the seventeenth century it was as difficult for her to become a baker as a butcher.

Baking.—After the decay of feudal privileges the trade of baking was controlled on lines similar to those governing other trades, but subject to an even closer supervision by the local authorities, owing to the

---

[1] Petronilla, Countess of Leicester, granted to Petronilla, daughter of Richard Roger's son of Leicester and her heirs " all the suit of the men outside the Southgate aforesaid to bake at her bakehouse with all the liberties and free customs, saving my customary tenants who are bound to my bakehouses within the town of Leicester." Bateson, (M.) *Records, Leicester*, Vol. l., p. 10.

fact that bread is a prime necessity of life. On this
account its price was fixed by " the assize of bread."
The position of women in regard to the trade was
also somewhat different, because while in other
trades they possessed fewer facilities than men for
acquiring technical experience, in this they learnt
the art of baking as part of their domestic duties.
Nevertheless, in the returns which give the names of
authorised bakers, those of women do not greatly
exceed in number the names which are given for
other trades ; of lists for the City of Chester, one
gives thirty names of bakers, six being women, all
widows, while another gives thirty-nine men and no
women,[1] and a third twenty-six men and three women.
The assistance which the Baker's wife gave to her
husband, however, was taken for granted.   At Carlisle,
the bye-laws provide that " noe Persons .   .   .   .
shall brew or bayk to sell but only freemen and thare
wifes."[2] and a rule at Beverley laid down that " no
common baker or other baker called boule baker,
their wives, servants, or apprentices, shall enter the
cornmarket any Saturday for the future before 1 p.m.
to buy any grain, nor buy wheat coming on Saturdays
to market beyond 2 bushels for stock for their own
house after the hour aforesaid."[3]

A writer, who was appealing for an increase in the
assize of bread, includes the wife's work among the
necessary costs of making a loaf ; " Two shillings was
allowed by the assize for all maner of charges in baking
a quarter of wheate over and above the second price
of wheate in the market," but the writer declares
that in Henry VII.'s time " the bakers .   .   .   .   .
might farre better cheape and with lesse charge of
seruantes haue baked a quarter of Wheate, then now

---

[1] *Harl. MSS.*, 2054, fo. 44 and 45, 2105, fo. 301.

[2] Ferguson, *Carlisle, Dormont Book*, p. 69, 1561.

[3] *Beverley Town Documents*, pp. 39–40.

they can." It was then allowed for " everie quarter
of wheate baking, for furnace and wood vid. the Miller
foure pence, for two journymen and two pages five-
pence, for salt, yest, candle & sandbandes two pence,
for himselfe, his house, his wife, his dog & his catte
seven pence, and the branne to his advantage."[1]

The baker's wife figures also in account books, as
transacting business for her husband. Thus the
Carpenters' Company " Resd of Lewes davys wyffe
the baker a fyne for a license for John Pasmore the
forren to sette upe a lytyll shed on his backsyde."[2]

Although conforming in general to the regulations
for other trades, certain Boroughs retained the rights
over baking which had been enjoyed by the Feudal
Lord, the Portmote at Salford ordering that " Samell
Mort shall surcease from beakinge sale bread by the
first of May next upon the forfeit of 5ls except hee
beake at the Comon beakehouse in Salford."[3] In
other towns the bakers were sufficiently powerful
to enforce their own terms on the Borough. In York,
for instance, the Corporation of Bakers, which became
very rich, succeeded in excluding the country, or
" boule bakers, " from the market, undertaking to
sell bread at the same rates ; but the monopoly once
secured they declared it was impossible to produce
bread at this price, and the magistrates allowed an
advance.[4] In some cases bakers were required to
take out licences, these being granted only to freemen
and freewomen ; in others they were formed into
Companies, with rules of apprenticeship. " They
shall receive no man into their saide company of
bakeres, nor woman unles her husband have bene
a free burges, and compound with Mr. Maior and

[1] Powell. *Assize of Bread.* 1600.

[2] *Records of Worshipful Company of Carpenters,* Vol. IV., p. 69, 1554.

[3] *Salford Portmote Records,* Vol. II., p. 188.

[4] *S.P.D.* cxxxiv., 36. November 27, 1622.

the warden of the company."[1]   At Reading in 1624,
" the bakers, vizt., William Hill, Abram Paise, Alexander Pether, complayne against bakers not freemen,
vizt., Izaak Wracke useth the trade his wief did use
when he marryed. Michaell Ebson saith he was
an apprentice in towne ard having noe worke doth a
little to gett bread. James Arnold will surceasse
. . . . Wydowe Bradbury alwayes hath used
to bake."[2]

That women were members of the Bakers' Companies
is shown by rules which refer to sisters as well as
brothers. In 1622 the Corporation at Salisbury
ordained that " no free brother or free sister shall at
any time hereafter make, utter, or sell bread, made
with butter, or milk, spice cakes, etc . . . . except it be before spoken for funerals, or upon the
Friday before Easter, or at Christmas . . . No
free brother or free sister shall sell any bread in the
market. No free brother or free sister shall hereafter
lend any money to an innholder or victualler, to the
intent or purpose of getting his or their custom"[3]
It is not likely that many women served an apprenticeship, but the frequency with which they are
charged with offences against the Bye-Laws is some
clue to the numbers engaged in the trade. For
instance, in Manchester, Martha Wrigley and nine
men were presented in 1648 " for makeinge bread
above & vnder the size & spice bread."[4] In 1650,
twenty-five men and no women were charged with
a similar offence,[5] in 1651 eleven men and no women[6]

---

[1] Lambert, *Two Thousand Years of Gild Life*, p. 307.   *Composicion of Bakers*, *Hull.*, 1598.

[2] Guilding, *Reading Records*, Vol. II., p. 181.

[3] Hoare, (Sir. R. C.). *Hist. of Wiltshire*, Vol. VI., p. 342.

[4] *Manchester Court Leet Records*, Vol. IV., p. 31.

[5] *Ibid*, p. 47.

[6] *Ibid*, p. 51.

and in 1652 are entered the names of five men and ten women[1],

The constant complaints brought against people who were using the trade " unlawfully " show how difficult it was to enforce rules of apprenticeship in a trade which was so habitually used by women for domestic purposes. Information was brought that " divers of the inhab[ts] of Thirsk do use the trade of baking, not having been apprentices thereof, but their wives being brought up and exercised therein many yeares have therefore used it . . . . and the matter referred to the Justices in Q[r] Sessions to limitt a certain number to use that trade without future trouble of any informers and that such as are allowed by the said Justices, to have a tolleration to take apprentices . . . . the eight persons, viz., Ja[s]. Pibus, Anth. Gamble. John Harrison, Widow Watson, Jane Skales, Jane Rutter, Tho. Carter and John Bell, shall onlie use and occupie the said trade of baking, and the rest to be restrayned."[2] The insistence upon apprenticeship must have been singularly exasperating to women who had learnt to bake excellent bread from their mothers, or mistresses, and it was natural for them to evade, when possible, a rule which seemed so arbitrary ; but they could not do so with impunity. Thus the Hertfordshire Quarter Session was informed " One Andrew Tomson's wife doth bake, and William Everite's wife doth bake bread to sell being not apprenticed nor licensed."[3] How heavily prosecutions of this character weighed upon the poor, is shown by a certificate brought to the same Quarter Sessions nearly a hundred years later, stating that " William Pepper, of Sabridgworth, is of honest and industrious behaviour, but

---

[1] *Manchester Court Leet Records*, p. 70.

[2] Atkinson, (J. C.), *Yorks. N. R. Q. S. Records*, Vol. I., p. 81. July 8, 1607.

[3] *Hertford Co. Records*, Vol. I, p, 32, 1600.

in a poor and low condition, and so not able to support the charge of defending an indictment against him for baking for hire (he having once taken a halfpenny for baking a neighbour's loaf) and has a great charge of children whom he has hitherto brought up to hard work and industrious labour, who otherwise might have been a charge to the parish, and will be forced to crave the relief of the parish, to defray the charge that may ensue upon this trouble given him by a presentment."[1]

The line taken by the authorities was evidently intended to keep the trade of baking in a few hands. The object may have been partly to facilitate inspection and thereby check short measure and adulteration; whatever the motive the effect must certainly have tended to discourage women from developing the domestic art of baking into a trade. Consequently in this, as in other trades, the woman's contribution to the industry generally took the form of a wife helping her husband, or a widow carrying on her late husband's business.

Millers :—It was probably only as the wife or widow of a miller that women took part in the business of milling. An entry in the Carlisle Records states " we amercye Archilles Armstronge for keeping his wief to play the Milner, contrary the orders of this cyttie."[2] But it is not unusual to come across references to corn mills which were in the hands of women; a place in Yorkshire is described as being " near to Mistress Lovell's Milne."[3] " Margaret Page, of Hertingfordbury, widow," was indicted for " erecting a mill house in the common way there,"[4] and at Stockton " One water corne milne . . . .

[1] *Hertford County Records*, Vol. I., p. 365, 1686.

[2] Ferguson, *Carlisle.* p. 278. April 21, 1619.

[3] J. C. Atkinson, *Yorks. N. R. Q. S. Records*, Vol. II., p. 8, 1612.

Hertford County Records, Vol. II., p. 25, 1698.

is lett by lease unto Alice Armstrong for 3 lives."[1]

Such instances are merely a further proof of the activity shown by married women in the family business whenever this was carried on within their reach.

Butchers :—The position which women took in the Butchers' trade resembled very closely their position as bakers, for, as has been shown, the special advantages which women, by virtue of their domestic training, might have enjoyed when trading as bakers, were cancelled by the statutes and bye-laws limiting the numbers of those engaged in this trade. As wife or widow women were able to enter either trade equally. Both trades were subject to minute supervision in the interests of the public, and as a matter of fact, from the references which happen to have been preserved, it might even appear that the wives of butchers were more often interested in the family business than the wives of bakers. An Act of Henry VIII. " lycensyng all bochers for a tyme to sell vytell in grosse at theyr pleasure " makes it lawful for any person "to whom any complaynt shuld be made upon any Boucher his wyff servaunte or other his mynysters refusing to sell the said vitayles by true and lawfull weight . . . . to comytt evry such Boucher to warde,"[2] shows an expectation that the wife would act as her husband's agent. But the wife's position was that of partner, not servant. During the first half of the century, certainly, leases were generally made conjointly to husband and wife ; for example, "Phillip Smith and Elizabeth, his wife" appeared before the Corporation at Reading " desiringe a new lease of the Butcher's Shambles, which was granted."[3]

---

[1] Brewster, *Stockton-on-Tees*, p. 42.

[2] Statutes 27 Henry VIII. c. 9.

[3] Guilding, *Reading Records*, Vol. IV., p. 122.

Customs at Nottingham secured the widow's possession of her husband's business premises even without a lease, providing that " when anie Butcher shall dye thatt holds a stall or shopp from the towne, thatt then his wyefe or sonne shall hould the same stall or shopp, they vsinge the same trade, otherwaies the towne to dispose thereof to him or them thatt will give moste for the stall or shopp : this order to bee lykewise to them thatt houlds a stall in the Spice-chambers."[1]

The names of women appear in lists of butchers in very similar proportions to the lists of bakers. Thus one for Chester gives the names of twenty men followed by three women,[2] and in a return of sixteen butchers licensed to sell meat in London during Lent, there is one woman, Mary Wright, and her partner, William Woodfield.[3]   Bye-laws which control the sale of meat use the feminine as well as the masculine pronouns, showing that the trade was habitually used by both sexes. The " Act for the Settlement and well ordering of the several Public Markets within the City of London " provides that " all and every Country butcher . . . . Poulterer . . . . Country Farmers, Victuallers Laders or Kidders . . . . may there sell, utter and put to open shew or sale his, her or their Beef, Mutton, etc., etc.[4] It may be supposed that these provisions relate only to the sale of meat, and that women would not often be associated with the businesses which included slaughtering the beasts, but this is not the case. Elizabeth Clarke is mentioned in the Dorchester Records as " apprenticed 7 years to her father a

[1] *Nottingham Records*, Vol. V., p. 284, 1654.

[2] *Harl. MSS.*, 2105 fo., 300 b.,1565.

[3] *S. P. D.* cxix. 107. February 24. 1621.

[4] *Act for the Settlement and well Ordering of the Several Publick Markets within the City of London*, 1674.

butcher,"[1] and other references occur to women who were clearly engaged in the genuine butcher's trade. For example, a licence was granted " to Jane Fouches of the Parish of St. Clement Danes, Butcher to kill and sell flesh during Lent,"[2] and among eighteen persons who were presented at the Court Leet, Manchester, " for Cuttinge & gnashing of Rawhides for their seuerall Gnashinge of evry Hyde," two were women, " Ellen Jaques of Ratchdale, one hyde, Widdow namely Stott of Ratchdale, two hydes."[3]

Beside these women, who by marriage or apprenticeship had acquired the full rights of butchers and were acknowledged as such by the Corporation under whose governance they lived, a multitude of poor women tried to keep their families from starvation by hawking meat from door to door. They are often mentioned in the Council Records, because the very nature of their business rendered them continually liable to a prosecution for regrating. Thus at the Court Leet, Manchester, Anne Costerdyne was fined 1s. " for buyinge 4 quarters of Mutton of W^m. Walmersley & 1 Lamb of Thomas Hulme both wch shee shold the one & same day."[4] Their position was the more difficult, because if they did not sell the meat the same day sometimes it went bad, and they were then prosecuted on another score. Elizabeth Chorlton, a butcher's widow, was presented in 1648 " for bueing and sellinge both on one day " and was fined 3s. 4d.[5] She was again fined with Mary Shalcross and various men in 1650 for selling unlawful meat and buying and selling on one day.[6]

---

[1] Mayo, *Municipal Records of Dorchester*, p. 428, 1698.

[2] *S P. D.* 1. clxxxviii. James I., undated.

[3] *Manchester Court Leet Records*, Vol. V., p. 236, 1674.

[4] *Ibid*, p. 221, 1674.

[5] *Manchester Court Leet Records*, Vol. IV., p. 31.

[6] *Ibid*, p. 40.

She was presented yet again in 1653 for selling "stinking meate," and fined 5s.[1]   Evidently Elizabeth Chorlton was an undesirable character, for she had previously been convicted of selling by false weights ;[2] nevertheless it seems hard that when it was illegal to sell stinking meat women should also be fined for selling it on the same day they bought it, and though this particular woman was dishonest no fault is imputed to the character of many of the others who were similarly presented for regrating.

There remains yet another class of women who were connected with the Butchers' trade, namely the wives of men who were either employed by the master butchers, or who perhaps earned a precarious living by slaughtering pigs and other beasts destined for domestic consumption.   In such work there was no place for the wife's assistance, and, like other wage-earners, in spite of any efforts she might make in other directions, the family remained below the poverty line.   An instance may be quoted from the Norwich Records where, in a census of the poor (i.e. persons needing Parish Relief) taken in 1570, are given the names of " John Hubbard of the age of 38 yeres, butcher, that occupie slaughterie, and Margarit his wyfe of the age of 30 yeres that sell souce, and 2 young children, and have dwelt here ever."[3]

Fishwives.—There is no reason to suppose that women were often engaged in the larger transactions of fishmongers.   Indeed an English writer, describing the Dutchwomen who were merchants of fish, expressly says that they were a very different class from the women who sold fish in England, and who were commonly known as fisherwives.[4]   Nevertheless that

---

[1] *Manchester Court Leet Records*, Vol. IV., p. 68.

[2] *Ibid*, p. 15, 1648.

[3] Tingey, J. C., *Records of the City of Norwich*, Vol. II., p. 337.

Ante., p. 36.

in this, as in other trades, they shared to some extent in their husband's enterprises, is shown by the present-ment of " John Frank of New Malton, and Alice his wife, for forestalling the markett of divers paniers of fishe, buying the same of the fishermen of Runs-wick or Whitbye. . . . before it came into the markett."[1]

The position of the sisters of the Fishmongers' Com-pany, London, was recognised to the extent of provid-ing them with a livery, an ordinance of 1426 ordaining that every year, on the festival of St. Peter, " alle the brethren and sustern of the same frat'nite " should go in their new livery to St. Peters' Church, Cornhill.[2] An ordinance dated 1499 however, requires that no fishmonger of the craft shall suffer his wife, or servant, to stand in the market to sell fish, unless in his absence.[3] An entry in the Middlesex Quarter Sessions Records notes the " discharge of Sarah, daughter of Frances Hall. Apprenticed to Rebecca Osmond of the Parish of St. Giles' Without, Cripplegate, ' fishwoman ' "[4] A member of the important Fishmongers' Company would hardly be designated in this way, and Rebecca Osmond must be classed among the " Fishwives " who are so often alluded to in accounts of London. Their business was often too precarious to admit of taking apprentices, and their credit so low that a writer in the reign of Charles I., who advocated the establishment of " Mounts of Piety " speaks of the high rate of interest taken by brokers and pawnbrokers " above 400 in the hundred " from " fishwives, oysterwomen and others that do crye thinges up and downe the streets."[5]   It was in this humble class of

---

[1] Atkinson, J. C. *Yorks. N. R. Q. S. Records*, Vol. I., p. 121, 1608.

[2] Herbert, *Livery Companies of London*, Vol. II., p. 44.

[3] *Ibid*, Vol. II., p. 35.

[4] *Middlesex County Records*, p. 160, 1696.

[5] *A Project for Mounts of Piety. Lansdowne MSS.*, 351 fo., 18b.

trade rather than in the larger transactions of fishmongers, that women were chiefly engaged. In
London no impediments seem to have been placed
in the way of their business, but in the provinces
they, like the women who hawked meat, were per-
secuted under the bye-laws against regrating. At
Manchester, the wife of John Wilshawe was amerced
" for buyinge Sparlings [smelts] and sellinge them
the same day in 6d."[1] while at the same court others
were fined for selling unmarketable fish.

Brewers :—It has been shown that the position which
women occupied among butchers and bakers did not
differ materially from their position in other trades;
that is to say, the wife generally helped her husband
in his business, and carried it on after his death;
but the history of brewing possesses a peculiar interest,
for apparently the art of brewing was at one time
chiefly, if not entirely, in the hands of women. This
is indicated by the use of the feminine term brewster.
Possibly the use of the masculine or feminine forms
may never have strictly denoted the sex of the person
indicated in words such as brewer, brewster, spinner,
spinster, sempster, sempstress, webber, webster, and
the gradual disuse of the feminine forms may have
been due to the grammatical tendencies in the English
language rather than to the changes which were
driving women from their place in productive industry; but the feminine forms would never have
arisen in the first place unless women had been engaged
to some extent in the trades to which they refer,
and it often happens that the use of the feminine
pronoun in relation to the term " brewster " and even
" brewer " shows decisively that female persons are
indicated. At Beverley a bye-law was made in
1364 ordaining that " if any of the community abuse
the affeerers of Brewster-gild for their affeering,

[1] *Manchester Court Leet Records*, Vol. IV., p. 112, 1654.

in words or otherwise, he shall pay . . . . to the commuunity 6s. 8d."[1] In this case Brewster might no more imply a woman's trade than it does in the modern term " Brewster-Sessions," but in 1371 a gallon of beer was ordered to " be sold for 1½d. . . . . and if any one offer 1½d. for a gallon of beer anywhere in Beverley and the ale-wife will not take it, that the purchaser come to the Gild Hall and complain of the brewster, and a remedy shall be found,"[2] while a rule made in 1405 orders that " no brewster or female seller called tipeler " shall " permit strangers to remain after 9 p.m."[3] Similar references occur in the Records of other Boroughs. At Bury the Customs provided in 1327 that " if a woman Brewer (Braceresse) can acquit herself with her sole hand that she has not sold contrary to the assize [of ale] she shall be quit "[4] ; at Torksey " when women are asked whether they brew and sell beer outside their houses contrary to the assize or no, if they say no, they shall have a day at the next court to make their law with the third hand, with women who live next door on either side or with others."[5]

It was ordered at Leicester in 1335 that " no brew-eress, sworn inn-keeper or other shall be so bold as to brew except (at the rate of) a gallon of the best for 1d,"[6] and though the feminine form of the noun has been dropped, the feminine pronoun is still used in 1532 when " hytt is enacteyd y^{at} no brwar y^{at} brwys to sell, sell aboffe iid the gallan & sche schall typill

---

[1] *Beverley Town Documents*, p. 41.

[2] *Ibid*, p. 41.

[3] *Ibid*, p. lv.

[4] Bateson, (M.), *Borough Customs*, Vol. I., p. 185

[5] *Ibid*, Vol. I., p. 185, 1345.

[6] Bateson, (M.), *Records of Leicester*, Vol. II., p. 21

be no mesure butt to sell be ye dossyn & ye halfe
dossyn."[1]

The exclusive use of the feminine in these bye-
laws differs from the expressions used in regard to
other trades when both the masculine and feminine
pronouns are habitually employed, suggesting that
the trade of brewing was on a different basis.

It must be remembered that before the introduction of cheap sugar, beer was considered almost
equally essential for human existence as bread. Beer
was drunk at every meal, and formed part of the
ordinary diet of even small children. Large households brewed for their own use, but as many families
could not afford the necessary apparatus, brewing was
not only practised as a domestic art, but became
the trade of certain women who brewed for their
neighbours. It is interesting to note the steps which
led to their ultimate exclusion from the trade, though
many links in the chain of evidence are unfortunately missing. In 1532 brewers in Leicester are
referred to as " sche," but an Act published in
1574 shows that the trade had already emerged from
petticoat government. It declares that " No in-
habitantes what soeuer that nowe doe or hereafter
shall in theire howsses vse tiplinge and sellinge of
ale or beare, shall not brewe the same of theare owne,
but shall tunne in the same of the common brewars
therfore appoynted ; and none to be common brewars
but such as nowe doe vse the same, ... and
non of the said common brewars to sell, or . . . .
to tipple ale or beare by retayle . . . . the
Brewars shall togeyther become a felloweship. etc."[2]
This separation of brewing from the sale of beer was
a policy pursued by the government with the object
of simplifying the collection of excise, but it was

---

[1] Bateson, (M.), *Records of Leicester*, Vol. III., p. 33.

[2] *Ibid*, Vol. III., p. 153.

also defended as a means for maintaining the quality
of the beer brewed. It was ordayned in the Assize for
Brewers, Anno 23, H. 8, that " Forasmuch as the misterie of brewing as a thing very needfull and necessarie
for the common wealth, hath been alwaies by auncient
custom & good orders practised & maintained within
Citties, Corporate Boroughs and market Townes
of this Realm, by such expert and skilfull persons,
as eyther were traded and brought up therein, by the
space of seuen yeares, and as prentizes therin accepted :
accordingly as in all other Trades and occupations,
or else well knowne to be such men of skill and honestie,
in that misterie, as could and would alwaie yeeld unto
her Maiesties subiects in the commonwealth, such
good and holsome Ale and Beere, as both in the
qualitie & for the quantitie thereof, did euer agree
with the good lawes of the Realme. And especiallie
to the comfort of the poorer sort of subiectes, who
most need it, untill of late yeares, sondrie persons
. . . . rather seeking their owne private gaine,
then the publike profite of their countrie, haue not
onelie erected and set uppe small brewhouses at their
pleasures : but also brew and utter such Ales and Beere,
for want of skill in that misterie as both in the prices
& holesomnes thereof, doth utterlie disagree with
the good lawes and orders of this Realm ; thereby
also ouerthrowing the greater and more auncient
brewhouses." It is therefore recommended that
these modern brewhouses should be suppressed in
the interest of the old and better ones.[1]

The argument reads curiously when one reflects
how universal had been the small brewhouses in former
days. The advantages from the excise point of
view which would be gained by the concentration
of the trade in a few hands is discussed in a pamphlet
which remarks that " there is much Mault made in

Powell, John. *The Assize of Bread*,

private Families, in some Counties half, if not two thirds of the Maults spent, are privately made, and undoubtedly as soon as an Imposition is laid upon it, much more will, for the advantage they shall gain by saving the Excise . . . . if Mault could be forbidden upon a great penalty to be made by any persons, but by certain publick Maulsters, this might be of availe to increase the Excise."[1] The actual conditions prevailing in the brewing industry at this time are described as follows in another pamphlet. Brewers are divided into two classes, " The Brewer who brews to sell by great measures, and wholly serves other Families by the same ; which sort of Brewers are only in some few great Cities and Towns, not above twenty through the land . . . . The Brewers who brews to sell by retail . . . . this sort of Brewers charges almost only such as drink the same in those houses where the same is brewed and sold . . . . and therefore supplies but a small proportion of the rest of the land, being that in almost all Market Towns, Villages, Hamlets, and private houses in the Countrey throughout the land, all the Inhabitants brew for themselves, at least by much the greatest proportion of what they use."[2]

In order to extend and strengthen their monopoly the " Common Brewers " brought forward a scheme in 1620, asking for a certain number of common brewers to be licensed throughout the kingdom, to brew according to assize. All other inn-keepers, alehouse keepers and victuallers to be forbidden to brew, " these brew irregularly without control," and " offering to pay the King 4d. on every quart of malt brewed." The scheme was referred to the Council who recommended " that a proclamation be issued forbidding ' taverners, innkeepers, etc. to sell any beer

---

[1] *Considerations Touching the Excise*, p. 7.

[2] Rockley, Francis.

but such as they buy from the brewers.'" To the objections " that brewers who were free by service or otherwise to use the trade of brewing would refuse to take a licence, and when apprentices had served their time there would be many who might do so," it was replied that it was " not usual for Brewers to take any apprentices but hired servants and the stock necessary for the trade is such as few apprentices can furnish."[1] Thus the rise of the " common brewer" signalises the complete victory of capitalistic organisation in the brewing trade. In 1636 Commissioners were appointed to " compound with persons who wished to follow the trade of common Brewers throughout the Kingdom."[2] The next year returns were received by the Council, giving the names and other particulars of those concerned in various districts. The list for the " Fellowshipp of Brewers now living in Newcastle-upon-Tyne with the breath and depth of their severall mash tunns " gives the names of fifty-three men and three women, widows.[3] A list of such brewers in the County of Essex " as have paid their fines and are bound to pay their rent accordingly"[4] (i.e. were licensed by the King's Commissioners for brewing) includes sixty-three men and four women, while the names of one hundred and twenty-four men and eight women are given in other tables containing the amounts due from brewers and maultsters in certain other counties,[5] showing that the predominance of women in the brewing trade had then disappeared, the few names appearing in the lists being no doubt those of brewers' widows.

---

[1] *S. P. D.*, cxii., 75. February 9, 1620.

[2] *C. R.* November 9, 1636.

[3] *S. P. D.* ccclxxvii., 62, 1637.

[4] *S. P. D.* ccclxxvii., 64, 1637.

[5] *S. P. D.* ccclxxxvii., 66.

The creation of the common brewers' monopoly was very unpopular. At Bury St. Edmunds a petition was presented by " a great no. of poor people " to the Justices of Assize, saying that for many years they had been relieved " by those inn-keepers which had the liberty to brew their beer in their own houses, not only with money and food, but also at the several times of their brewing (being moved with pity and compassion, knowing our great extremities and necessities) with such quantities of their small beer as has been a continual help and comfort to us with our poor wives and children : yet of late the common brewers, whose number is small and their benefits to us the poor as little notwithstanding in their estate they are wealthy and occupy great offices of malting, under pretence of doing good to the commonwealth, have for their own lucre and gain privately combined themselves, and procured orders from the Privy Council that none shall brew in this town but they and their adherents."[1] At Tiverton the Council was obliged to make a concession to popular feeling and agreed that " every person being a freeman of the town and not prohibited by law might use the trade of Common Brewer as well as the four persons formerly licensed by the Commissioners, " but the petition that the ale-house keepers and inn-keepers might brew as formerly they used was refused, " they might brew for their own and families use ; otherwise to buy from the Common Brewers."[2]

The monopoly involved the closing of many small businesses. Sarah Kemp a widow, petitioned the Council because she had " been forced to give up brewing in Whitefriars, and had been at g^t loss both in removing her implements and in her rents," asking " that in consideration of her loss she might

---

[1] *Hist. MSS. Com.*, 14 Rep. App., VIII., p. 142.

[2] *C. R.* June 12, 1640. Order concerning the Brewers of Tiverton.

have license to erect brick houses on her messuage
in Whitefriars." This was granted on conditions.[1]
A married woman, Mary Arnold, was committed to
the Fleet on March 31st, 1639, " for continuing to
brew in a house on the Millbank in Westminster,
contrary to an order against the brewers in Westminster
and especially against Michael Arnold." The Council
ordered her to be discharged, on her humble admission
to brew no more in the said house, but to remove
within ten days ; and on bond from her husband
that neither he nor she nor any other shall brew in
the said house, and that he will remove his brewing
vessels within ten days.[2]

The closing of the trade of brewing to women
must have seriously reduced their opportunities
for earning an independance; that they had
hitherto been extensively engaged in it is shown
by frequent references to women who were
brewsters ; for example, Mrs. Putland was rated 5s.
on her brew-house ;[3] Jennet Firbank, wife of
Steph. Firbank, of Awdbroughe, a recusant, was presented at Richmond for brewing, a side note adding
" she to be put down from brueing."[4] Margaret,
the wife of Ambrose Carleton and Marye Barton were
presented at Carlisle for " brewing (being foryners)
and therefore we doe emercye either of them vi[s] 8d."[5]
At Thirske, Widow Harrington, of Hewton, Chr.
Whitecake, of Bransbie, Rob. Goodricke, of the same
(for his wife's offence) were presented, all for brewing.[6]
And at Malton, a few years later, " Rob. Driffeld,

---

[1] *C. R.*   22nd March, 1638–9.

[2] *C. R.*   May 8, 1639.

[3] *Strood Churchwardens' Accounts*, Add. MSS., 36937, p. 263., 1683.

[4] Atkinson, (J. C.), *Yorks. N. R. Q. S. Records*, Vol. I., p. 95., 1607.

[5] Ferguson, *Carlisle*, p. 280, *Court Leet Roll's*.   October 21, 1625.

Atkinson, (J. C.), *Yorks. N. R. Q. S. Records*, Vol. I., p. 159, 1609.

a brewster of Easingwold, was presented for suffering
unlawful games att cardes to be used at unlawful times
in the night in his house. . . . . and the wife
of the said Driffeld for that she will not sell anie of
her ale forth of doores except it be to those whom
she likes on and makes her ale of 2 or thre sortes,
nor will let anie of her poore neighbours have anie
of her drincke called small ale, but she saith she will
rather give it to her Swyne then play it for them "[1]
Isabell Bagley and Janyt Lynsley " both of Cowburne
bruesters " were fined 10s. each " for suffering play
at cardes in their houses, &c,"[2] and at Norwich,
Judith Bowde, brewer, was fined 2s. 9d.[3]

Although women had lost their position in the
brewing trade by the end of the seventeenth century,
they were still often employed in brewing for domestic
purposes. Sometimes one of the women—servants
on a large farm, brewed for the whole family, including all the farm servants.[4] In other cases a
woman made her living by brewing for different
families in their own houses. Thus in the account
of a fire on the premises of a certain Mr. Reading
it is described how his " Family were Brewing within
this Place . . . . The Servants who were in
the House perceiving a great smoak rose out of Bed,
and the Maid running out cried Fire and said *Wo
worth this Bookers wife* (who was the Person whom
Mr. *Reading* imployed to be his Brewer) *she hath
undone us.*"[5] Lady Grizell Baillie enters in her
Household Account Book, " For Brewing 7 bolls
Malt by Mrs. Ainsly 10s. For a ston hopes to
the said Malt out of which I had a puntion very

---

[1] Atkinson, (J. C.), *Yorks N. R. Q. S. Records*, Vol. II., pp. 53-54, 1614.

[2] *Ibid*, Vol. I., p. 93, 1607.

[3] Tingey, (J. C.), *Records of City of Norwich*, Vol. I., p. 388, 1676.

[4] Ante., p. 50.

[5] *True Account how Mr. Reading's House.*

strong Ale 10 gallons good 2nd ale and four puntions of Beer. 14s."[1]

Naturally the women who brewed for domestic purposes sometimes wished to turn an honest penny by selling beer to thirsty neighbours at Fairs and on Holidays, but attempts to do so were severely punished. Annes Nashe of Welling, was presented "for selling beer by small jugs at Woolmer Grene and for laying her donng in the highway leading from Stevenage to London."[2] A letter to a Somerset Magistrate pleads for another offender :—" Good Mr. Browne, all happiness attend you. This poor woman is arrested with Peace proces for selling ale without lycense and will assure you shee hath reformed it and that upon the first warning of our officers ever since Easter last, which is our fayre tyme, when most commonly our poore people doe offend in that kinde ; I pray you doe her what lawful kindness you may, and hope she will recompense you for your paynes, and I shall be ready to requite it in what I may, for if she be committed she is absolutely undone. Thus hoping of your favour I leave you to God and to this charitable work towards this poor woman. Your unfeined friend, Hum. Newman."[3]

Though with the growth of capitalism and the establishment of a monopoly for " Common Brewers " women were virtually excluded from their old trade of brewing, they still maintained their position in the retail trade, their hold upon which was favoured by the same circumstances which turned their energies to the retail side of other businesses.

A tendency was shown by public opinion to regard licences as suitable provision for invalids and widows who might otherwise require assistance from the rates.

---

[1] Baillie, Lady Grizell, *Household Book.* p. 91. 1714.

[2] *Hertford County Records*, Vol. I., p. 68. 1641.

[3] *Somerset Q. S. Records*, Vol. II., pp. 40-1, 1627.

Thus an attempt made at Lincoln in 1628 to reduce the numbers of licences was modified, " for that it appeareth that divers poor men and widows, not freemen, have no other means of livelihood but by keeping of alehouses, it is agreed that such as shall be approved by the justices may be re-admitted, but that none hereafter be newly admitted untill they be first sworn freemen."[1]   According to a pamphlet published early in the next century, " Ale-houses were originally Accounted Neusances in the *Parish's* where they were, as tending to Debauch the Subject, and make the People idle, and therefore Licences to sell Beer and Ale, where allow'd to none, but Ancient People past their Labours, and Invalides to keep them from Starving, there being then no *Act* of *Parliament* that *Parishes* should Maintain their own Poor.   But the Primitive Intention in granting Licences being now perverted, and all sorts of People Admitted to this priviledge, it is but reason the Publick should have some Advantage by the Priviledges it grants. . ."[2] Many examples of this attitude of mind can be observed in the Quarter Sessions Records.   For instance, Mary Briggs when a widow was licensed by the Hertfordshire Quarter Sessions to sell drink, and by the good order she kept in her house and the goodness of the drink she uttered and sold she got a good livelihood, and brought up three children she had by a former husband.   She married John Briggs, woodard and servant to Lord Ashton, she continuing her business and he his.   Her husband was returned as a papist recusant, and on his refusing to take oaths the court suppressed their alehouse.   Mrs. Briggs appealed on the ground that her business was carried on separately and by it she maintained her children by her former husband.   Her claim was supported by a petition

---

[1] *Hist. MSS. Com.*, 14 Rep., app. viii., p. 99, 1629.

[2] Phipps, (Thomas), *Proposal for raising £1,000,000 Sterling yearly.*

from her fellow parishioners, declaring that John Briggs was employed by Lord Ashton and " meddles not with his wife's trade of victualling and selling drink."[1] Other examples may be found in an order for the suppression of Wm. Brightfoot's licence who had " by surprize " obtained one for selling beer . . showing that he was a young man, and capable to maintain his family without keeping an alehouse,[2] and the petition of John Phips, of Stondon, labourer, lately fallen into great need for want of work. He can get very little to do among his neighbours, " because they have little for him to do, having so many poore laborious men besides within the said parish." He asks for a licence to sell beer " for his better livelihood and living hereafter, towards the mayntenance of himself, his poor wife and children."[3] Licences were refused at Bristol to " John Keemis, Cooper, not fit to sell ale, having no child ; he keeps a tapster which is no treeman that have a wife and child," and also to " Richard Rooke, shipwright, not fit to sell ale, having no child, and brews themselves." A Barber Surgeon was disqualified, having no child, " and also for entertaining a strange maid which is sick."[4]

Very rarely were doubts suggested as to the propriety of the trade for women, though a bye-law was passed at Chester ordaining that " no woman between the age of xiii & xl yeares shall kepe any taverne or ale-howse."[5] At times complaints were made of the conduct of alewives, as in a request to the Justices of Nottingham " that your Worshipps wyll take some order wythe all the alewyfes in this towne, for we thinke that never an alewyfe dothe as hir husband is bownd

---

[1] *Hertford County Records*, Vol. I., p. 289, 1678.

[2] *Middlesex Sessions Book*, p. 23, 1690.

[3] *Hertford County Records*, Vol. I., p. 174, 1665.

[4] Latimer, *Bristol*, p. 359. 1670. *Court Leet for St. Stephen's Parish*.

[5] *Harl. MSS.*, 2054 (4), fo., 6.

to,"[1] but there is no evidence of any marked difference
in the character of the alehouses kept by men and
those kept by women. The trade included women
of the most diverse characters. One, who received
stolen goods at the sign of the " Leabord's Head " in
Ware, had there a " priviye place " for hiding stolen
goods and suspicious persons " at the press for
soldiers she hid five men from the constables, and
can convey any man from chamber to chamber into
the backside. There is not such a house for the
purpose within a hundred miles."[2] In contrast to
her may be quoted the landlady of the Inn at Truro,
of whom Celia Fiennes wrote, " My Greatest pleasure
was the good Landlady I had, she was but an ordinary
plaine woman but she was understanding in the best
things as most—ye Experience of reall religion and her
quiet submission and self-Resignation to ye will of
God in all things, and especially in ye placeing her in
a remoteness to ye best advantages of hearing, and being
in such a publick Employment wch she desired and
aimed at ye discharging so as to adorn ye Gospel of
her Lord and Saviour, and the Care of her children."[3]

Vintners :—The trade of the Vintner had no connection with that of the Brewer. Wine was sold in
Taverns. In London the Vintners' Company, like
the other London Companies, possessed privileges
which were continued to the wife upon her husband's
death, but women were probably not concerned in
the trade on their own account. A survey of all the
Taverns in London made in 1633 gives a total of
211, whereof six are licensed by His Majesty, 203
by the Vintners' Company and two are licensed
by neither, one is unlicensed, " inhabited by An
Tither, whoe lately made a tavern of the Starr on

---

[1] *Nottingham Records*, Vol. IV., p. 325, 1614.

[2] *Hertford County Records*, Vol. I., p. 59, 1626.

[3] Fiennes, (Celia), p. 226   *Through England on a Side-Saddle*.

Tower Hill where shee also keepes a victualling house
unlicensed." One licensed by the Earl of Middlesex.
Amongst those duly licensed are the names of a few
widows. In Cordwainer Street Ward, there was
only one Tavern, " kept by a widdowe whose deceased
husband was bound prentice to a Vintener and so
kept his taverne by vertue of his freedome of that
companye after his termes of apprentizhood expired."[1]

Conclusion.

The foregoing examination of the relation of women
to the different crafts and trades has shown them
occupying an assured position wherever the system
of family industry prevailed. While this lasted the
detachment of married women from business is
nowhere assumed, but they are expected to assist
their husband, and during his absence or after his
death to take his place as head of the family and manager
of the business.

The economic position held by women depended
upon whether the business was carried on at home or
elsewhere, and upon the possession of a small amount
of capital. The wives of men who worked as journeymen on their masters' premises could not share their
husbands' trade, and their choice of independent
occupations was very limited. The skilled women's
trades, such as millinery and mantua-making, were
open, and in these, though apprenticeship was usual,
there is no reason to suppose that women who worked
in them without having served an apprenticeship,
were prosecuted; but as has been shown the
apprenticeship laws were strictly enforced in other
directions, and in some cases prevented women from
using their domestic skill to earn their living.
While women could share their husbands'
trades they suffered little from these restrictions,

---

[1] S.P.D. ccl., 22, November 6, 1633. Lord Mayor and others to the Council.

but with the development of capitalistic organisation the numbers of women who could find no outlet for their productive activity in partnership with their husbands were increasing and their opportunities for establishing an independent industry did not keep pace ; on the contrary, such industry became ever more difficult. The immediate result is obscure, but it seems probable that the wife of the prosperous capitalist tended to become idle, the wife of the skilled journeyman lost her economic independence and became his unpaid domestic servant, while the wives of other wage earners were driven into the sweated industries of that period. What were the respective numbers in each class cannot be determined, but it is probable that throughout the seventeenth century they were still outnumbered by the women who could find scope for productive activity in their husbands' business.

CHAPTER VI

PROFESSIONS

Introductory—Tendencies similar to those in Industry.—Army—Church—Law closed to women. Teaching—Nursing—Medicine chiefly practised by women as domestic arts. Midwifery.

(A). *Nursing*. The sick poor nursed in lay institutions—London Hospitals—Dublin—Supplied by low class women—Women searchers for the plague—Nurses for small-pox or plague—Hired nurses in private families.

(B) *Medicine*. Women's skill in Middle ages—Medicine practised extensively by women in seventeenth century in their families, among their friends and for the poor—Also by the village wise woman for pay—Exclusiveness of associations of physicians, surgeons and apothecaries.

(C) *Midwifery*. A woman's profession—Earlier history unknown—Raynold's translation of "the byrthe of mankynd."—Relative dangers of child-birth in seventeenth and twentieth centuries—Importance of midwives—Character of their training—Jane Sharp—Nicholas Culpepper—Peter Chamberlain—Mrs. Cellier's scheme for training—Superiority of French training—Licences of Midwives—Attitude of the Church to them—Fees—Growing tendency to displace midwives by Doctors.

Conclusion. Women's position in the arts of teaching and healing lost as these arts became professional.

Introductory.

SIMILAR tendencies to those which affected the industrial position of women can be traced in the professions also, showing that, important as was the influence of capitalistic organisation in the history of women's evolution, other powerful factors were working in the same direction.

Three professions were closed to women in the seventeenth century, Arms, the Church and the Law.

The Law.—It must be remembered that the mass of the "common people" were little affected by "the law" before the seventeenth century. "Common law" was the law of the nobles,[1] while farming people and

---

[1] *Holdsworth*, Vol. III., p. 408.

artizans alike were chiefly regulated in their dealings with each other by customs depending for interpretation and sanction upon a public opinion which represented women as well as men. Therefore the changes which during the seventeenth century were abrogating customs in favour of common law, did in effect eliminate women from what was equivalent to a share in the custody and interpretation of law, which henceforward remained exclusively in the hands of men. The result of the elimination of the feminine influence is plainly shown in a succession of laws, which, in order to secure complete liberty to individual men, destroyed the collective idea of the family, and deprived married women and children of the property rights which customs had hitherto secured to them. From this time also the administration of the law becomes increasingly perfunctory in enforcing the fulfilment of men's responsibilities to their wives and children.

Church.—According to modern ideas, religion pertains more to women than to men, but this conception is new, dating from the scientific era.

Science has solved so many of the problems which in former days threatened the existence of mankind, that the " man in the street " instinctively relegates religion to the region in which visible beauty, poetry and music are still permitted to linger ; to the ornamental sphere in short, whither the Victorian gentleman also banished his wife and daughters. This attitude forms a singular contrast to the ideas which prevailed in the Middle Ages, when men believed that supernatural assistance was their sole protection against the " pestilence that walketh in darkness " or from " the arrow that flieth by day." Religion was then held to be such an awful power that there were men who even questioned whether women could, properly speaking, be considered religious at all. Even in the seventeenth century the practice of

religion and the holding of correct ideas concerning
it were deemed to be essential for the maintenance
of human existence, and no suggestion was then
made that religious observances could be adequately
performed by women alone.

Ideas as to the respective appropriateness of
religious power to men and women have differed
widely ; some races have reserved the priesthood for
men, while others have recognised a special power
enduing women ; in the history of others again no
uniform tendency is shown, but the two influences can
be traced acting and reacting upon each other.

This has been the case with the Christian religion,
which has combined the wide-spread worship of the
Mother and Child with a passionate splitting of hairs
by celibate priests in dogmatic controversies concerning intellectual abstractions. The worship of
the Mother and Child had been extirpated in England
before the beginning of the seventeenth century ;
pictures of this subject were denounced because they
showed the Divine Son under the domination of a
woman. One writer accuses the Jesuits of representing Christ always " as a sucking child in his
mothers armes "—" nay, that is nothing they make
him an underling to a woman," alleging that " the
Jesuits assert (1) no man, but a woman did helpe
God in the work of our Redemption, (2) that God
made Mary partaker and fellow with him of his
divine Majesty and power, (3) that God hath divided
his Kingdom with Mary, keeping Justice to himselfe,
and yielding mercy to her." He complains that
" She is always set forth as a woman and a mother,
and he as a child and infant, either in her armes,
or in her hand, that so the common people might
have occasion to imagine that looke, what power of
overruling and commanding the mother hath over
her little child, the same hath she over her son Jesus
. . . . the mother is compared to the son, not

as being a child or a man, but as the saviour and mediator, and the paps of a woman equalled with the wounds of our Lord, and her milke with his blood . . . . But for her the holy scriptures speake no more of her, but as of a creature, a woman . . . . saved by Faith in her Saviour Jesus Christ . . . . and yet now after 1600 yeares she must still be a commanding mother and must show her authority over him . . . . she must be saluted as a lady, a Queen, a goddesse and he as a child."[1]

The ridicule with which Peter Heylin treated the worship of the Virgin Mary in France seems to have been pointed more at the notion of honouring motherhood, rather than at the distinction given to her as a woman, for he wrote " if they will worship her as a Nurse with her Child in her arms, or at her breast, let them array her in such apparel as might beseem a Carpenter's Wife, such as she might be supposed to have worn before the world had taken notice that she was the Mother of her Saviour. If they must needs have her in her state of glory as at Amiens; or of honour (being now publikely acknowledged to be the blessedness among Women) as at Paris : let them disburden her of her Child. To clap them thus both together, is a folly equally worthy of scorn & laughter."[2]

The reform which had swept away the worship of divine motherhood had also abolished the enforced celibacy of the priesthood ; but the priest's wife was given no position in the Church, and a tendency may be noted towards the secularisation of all women's functions. Convents and nunneries were abolished, and no institutions which might specially assist women in the performance of their spiritual, educational or charitable duties were established in

---

[1] *C. W.* 1641. *The Bespotted Jesuite.*

[2] Heylin (Peter), *The Voyage of France,* p. 29, 1673.

their place. There was, in fact, a deep jealousy of any influence which might disturb the authority and control which the individual husband exercised over his wife, and probably the seventeenth century Englishman was beginning to realise that nothing would be so subversive to this authority as the association of women together for religious purposes. If a recognised position was given to women in the Church, their lives must inevitably receive an orientation which would not necessarily be identical with their husband's, thus creating a danger of conflicting loyalties. Naturally, therefore, women were excluded from any office, but it would be a mistake to suppose that their subordination to their husbands in religious matters was rigidly enforced throughout this period. Certainly in the first half of the century their freedom of thought in religion was usually taken for granted, and possibly amongst the Baptists, certainly amongst the Quakers, full spiritual equality was accorded to them. Women were universally admitted to the sacraments, and therefore recognised as being, in some sort, members of the Church, but this was consistent with the view of their position to which Milton's well known lines in " Paradise Lost " give perfect expression, the ideal which, in all subsequent social and political changes, was destined to determine women's position in Church and State :—

> " Whence true authoritie in men, though both
>   Not equal, as their sex not equal seem'd,
>   For contemplation hee and valour form'd
>   For softness shee, and sweet attractive Grace,
>   Hee for God only, shee for God in him :
>
>   .   .   .   .   .
>
>   To whom thus Eve with perfect beauty adornd
>   My Author and Disposer, what thou bidst
>   Unargu'd I obey ; so God ordains,
>   God is thy Law, thou mine ; to know no more
>   woman's happiest knowledge and her praise."

Nevertheless, though excluded from any position in the hierarchy of recognised servants of the Church, it must not be supposed that the Church was independent of women's service. To their hands necessity rather than the will of man had entrusted a duty, which when unfulfilled makes all the complicated organisation of the Church impotent ; namely, the bending of the infant mind and soul towards religious ideals and emotions. The lives of the reformers of the seventeenth century bear witness to the faithfulness with which women accomplished this task. In many cases their religious labours were extended beyond the care of their children, embracing the whole household for their field of service. The life of Lettice, Viscountess Falkland, gives an example of the sense of responsibility under which many religious women lived. Lady Falkland passed about an hour with her maids, early every morning " in praying, and catechizing and instructing them ; to these secret and private prayers, the publick morning and evening prayers of the Church, before dinner and supper ; and another form (together with reading Scriptures and singing Psalms) before bedtime, were daily and constantly added . . . . neither were these holy offices appropriate to her menial servants, others came freely to joyn with them, and her Oratory was as open to her neighbours as her Hall was . . . . her Servants were all moved to accompany her to the Sacrament, and they who were prevailed with gave up their names to her, two or three dayes before, and from thence, she applied herself to the instructing of them   . . . and after the Holy Sacrament she called them together again and gave them such exhortations as were proper for them."[1]

The quarrel between Church and State over the teaching profession is an old story which does not

---

[1] *Falkland, Lady Letice, Vi-countess, Life and Death of.*

concern this investigation. It is sufficient to note that in England neither Church nor State considered that the work of women in training the young entitled them to a recognised position in the general social organisation, or required any provision apart from the casual arrangements of family life.

Teaching. —The question of the standard and character of the education given to girls is too large a subject to be entered into here ; it can only be remarked that the number of professional paid women teachers was small. The natural aptitude of the average woman for training the young, however, enabled mothers to provide their children, both boys and girls, with a very useful foundation of elementary education.

The professions of medicine, midwifery and nursing are very closely allied to each other ; for neither was there any system of instruction on a scientific basis available for women, whose practice was thus empirical ; but as yet science had done little to improve the skill even of the male practitioner.

Nursing.—Nursing was almost wholly a domestic art.

Medicine. —Though we find many references to women who practised medicine and surgery as professions, in the majority of cases their skill was used only for the assistance of their family and neighbours.

Midwifery.—Midwifery was upon a different footing, standing out as the most important public function exercised by women, and being regarded as their inviolable mystery till near the beginning of the seventeenth century. The steady process through which in this profession women were then supplanted by men, furnishes an example of the way in which women have lost their hold upon all branches of skilled responsible work, through being deprived of opportunities for specialised training.

The relative deterioration of woman's capacity in comparison with the standard of men's efficiency

cannot be more clearly shown than in the history of
midwifery. Even though the actual skill of midwives
may not have declined during the seventeenth
century men were rapidly surpassing them in scientific knowledge, for the general standard of women's
education was declining, and they were debarred
from access to the higher branches of learning.
As the absence of technical training kept women out
of the skilled trades, so did the lack of scientific education drive them from the more profitable practice
of midwifery, which in former times tradition and
prejudice had reserved as their monopoly.

A—*Nursing.*

Whatever arrangements had been made by the
religious orders in England for the care of the sick
poor were swept away by the Reformation. The
provision which existed in the seventeenth century
for this purpose rested on a lay basis, quite unconnected
with the Church. Amongst the most famous charitable institutions were the four London Hospitals ;
Christ's Hospital for children under the age of sixteen,
St. Bartholomew's and St. Thomas's for the sick and
impotent poor, and Bethlehem for the insane.
There is no evidence that the women of the upper
classes took any part in the management of these
hospitals. The squalor and the ugly and disgusting
details which are associated with nursing the diseased
and often degraded poor, was unredeemed by the
radiance with which a mystic realisation of the Divine
Presence had upheld the Catholic Saints, or by the
passionate desire for the service of humanity which
inspired Florence Nightingale. Thus it was only
the necessity for earning their daily bread which
induced any women to enter the profession of nursing
during this period, and as the salaries offered were
considerably lower than the wages earned by a competent servant in London, it may be supposed that

the class attracted did not represent the most efficient type of women.

The rules appointed for the governance of nurses show that the renunciations of a nun's life were required of them, but social opinion in Protestant England set no seal of excellence upon their work, however faithfully performed, and the sacrifices demanded from the nurses were unrewarded by the crown of victory.

During the reign of Edward VI. there were a matron and twelve sisters at St. Bartholomew's who received in wages £26 6s. 8d. In addition the matron received 1s. 6d. per week for board wages and the sisters 1s. 4d. per week, and between them £6 per year for livery, while the matron received 13s. 4d. for this purpose.[1] The rules for the governance of the sisters were as follows :—" Your charge is, in all Things to declare and shew yourselves gentle, diligent, and obedient to the Matron of this House, who is appointed and authorised to be your chief Governess and Ruler. Ye shall also faithfully and charitably serve and help the Poor in all their Griefs and Diseases, as well by keeping them sweet and clean, as in giving them their Meats and Drinks, after the most honest and comfortable Manner. Also ye shall use unto them good and honest Talk, such as may comfort and amend them ; and utterly to avoid all light, wanton, and foolish Words, Gestures, and Manners, using yourselves unto them with all Sobriety and Discretion, and above all Things, see that ye avoid, abhor, and detest Scolding and Drunkenness as most pestilent and filthy Vices. Ye shall not haunt or resort to any manner of Person out of this House, except ye be licensed by the Matron ; neither shall ye suffer any light Person to haunt or use unto you, neither any dishonest Person, Man or Woman ; and so much as in you shall lie, ye shall avoid and shun the Conversation and Company of all Men.

---

[1] Stow, *London*, I., pp., 185-186.

Ye shall not be out of the Woman's Ward after the Hour of seven of the Clock in the Night, in the Winter, Time, nor after Nine of the Clock in the Night in the Summer : except ye shall be appointed and commanded by the Matron so to be, for some great and special cause that shall concern the Poor, (as the present Danger of Death or extreme Sickness), and yet so being commanded, ye shall remain no longer with such diseased Person than just Cause shall require. Also, if any just Cause of Grief shall fortune unto any of you, or that ye shall see Lewdness in any Officer, of other Person of this House, which may sound or grow to the Hurt or Slander thereof, ye shall declare the same to the Matron, or unto one or two of the Govenours of this House, that speedy Remedy therein may be had; and to no other Person neither shall ye talk or meddle therein any farther. This is your Charge, and with any other Thing you are not charged."[1]

The Matron was instructed to " receive of the Hospitaler of this House all such sick and diseased Persons as he . . . . shall present unto you," and to " have also Charge, Governance & Order of all the Sisters of this House. . . .that every of them. . . . do their Duty unto the Poor, as well in making of their Beds, and keeping their Wards, as also in washing and purging their unclean Cloaths, and other Things. And that the same Sisters every night after the Hour of seven of the Clock in the Winter, and nine of the Clock in the Summer, come not out of the Woman's Ward, except some great and special Cause (as the present Danger of Death, or needful Succour of some poor Person). And yet at such a special time it shall not be lawful for every Sister to go forth to any Person or Persons (no tho' it be in her Ward) but only for such as you shall think virtuous, godly, and discreet. And the

---

[1] Stow, *London*, app., p. 58.

same Sister to remain no longer with the same sick Person then needful Cause shall require. Also at such times as the Sisters shall not be occupied about the Poor, ye shall set them to spinning or doing some other Manner of Work, that may avoid Idleness, and be profitable to the Poor of this House. Also ye shall receive the Flax . . . . the same being spun by the Sisters, ye shall commit to the said Governors . . . . You shall also . . . . have special Regard to the good ordering & keeping of all the Sheets, Coverlets, Blankets, Beds, and other Implements committed to your Charge, ... Also ye shall suffer no poor Person of this House to sit and drink within your House at no Time, neither shall ye so send them drink into their Wards, that thereby Drunkenness might be used and continued among them."[1]

In Christ's Hospital there were two Matrons with salaries of £2 13s. 4d. per annum and forty-two women keepers with salaries of 40s. per annum. Board wages were allowed at the rate of 1s. 4d. per week for the "keepers" and 1s. 6d. for the Matrons. There was one keeper for fifteen persons.[2] The Matron was advised "Your office is an office of great charge and credite. For to yow is committed the Governance and oversight of all the women and children within this Hospital. And also to yow is given Authoritie to commaunde, reprove, and rebuke them or any of them . . . . Your charge is also to search and enquire whether the women do their Dutie, in washing of the children's sheets and shirts, and in kepeing clean and sweet those that are committed to their Charge ; and also in the Beddes, Sheets, Coverlets, and Apparails (with kepeing clean Wards and Chambers) mending of such as shall be

---

[1] Stow, *London*, App. pp. 57–58.

[2] *Ibid*, I. pp. 175. 6.

broken from Time to Time. And specially yow shall give diligent Hede, that the said Washers and Nurses of this Howse be alwaies well occupied and not idle ; . . . . you shal also once every Quarter of the Year examine the Inventorie."[1]

The nurses were instructed that they must " carefully and diligently oversee, kepe, and governe all those tender Babes & yonglings that shal be committed to your Charge, and the same holesomely, cleanely and swetely nourishe and bring up . . . . kepe your Wardes and every Part thereof swete and cleane . . . . avoid all Idleness when your Charge and Care of keping the Children is past, occupie yourselves in Spinning, Sewing, mending of Sheets and Shirts, or some other vertuous Exercise, such as you shal be appointed unto. Ye shal not resort or suffer any Man to resort to you, before ye have declared the same to the almoners or Matron of this Howse and obtained their Lycense and Favour, so to do . . . . see that all your children, before they be brought to Bed, be washed and cleane, and immediately after, every one of yow quietly shal go to your Bed, and not to sit up any longer ; and once every night arise, and see that the Children be covered, for taking of Colde."[2]

Some idea of the class of women who actually undertook the important duties of Matron for the London Hospitals may be gathered from a petition presented by Joane Darvole, Matron of St. Thomas's Hospital, Southwark, to Laud. She alleged " that she was dragged out of the Chapel of the Hospital at service and dragged along the streets to prison for debt, to the hazard of her life, " she being a " very weak sickly and aged woman," clothes torn from her back and cast into a swoon. She petitions against the

---

[1] Stow, *London*, app., p. 42.

[2] Stow *London*, app., p. 43.

profanation of God's house and the scandal to the congregation.[1]

Sick and wounded soldiers were tended at the Savoy, where there were thirteen Sisters, whose joint salaries amounted to £52 16s. 8d. per annum.[2] Among the orders for the patients, nurses and widows in the Savoy and other hospitals in and about London occur the following regulations :—4[thly] " That every soldier or nurse . . . . that shall profanely sweare " to pay 12d. for the first offence, 12d. for the second, and be expelled for the third. 8[thly] " That if any souldier shall marye any of the nurses of the said houses whilst hee is there for care or (recov)ery they both shall be turned forth of the House. 11[thly] No soldier under cure to have their (wiv)es lodge with them there except by the approbation of the Phisicion. 12[thly] No nurse to be dismissed without the approval of 2 of the Treasurers for the relief of maimed soldiers at least. Nurses to be chosen from among the widows of soldiers if there are among them those that be fit, and those to have 5s. per weeke as others usually have had for the service. 14[thly] soldiers, wounded and sick, outside the hospitals not to have more than 4s. per week. Those in St. Thomas's and Bartholomew's hospital 2s. a week, those in their parents', masters' or friends' houses, according to their necessities, but not more than 4s. per week. 15[thly] Soldiers' widows to receive according to their necessities, but not more than 4s. a week. 19[thly] If any of the nurses . . . . . shalbee negligent in their duties or in giving due attendance to the . . . . sicke souldiers by daye or night or shall by scoulding, brawlinge or chidinge make any disturbance in the said hospitall, she shall forfeite 12d. for 1st offence, week's pay for second,

---

[1] *S.P.D.*, cccclv., 87. May 30th, 1640.

[2] Stow, *London* I., p. 211.

be dismissed for the third. 20[thly] If any widow after marriage shall come and receive weekly pensions as a soldier's widow contrary to the ordinance of parl[t] he which hath married her to repay it, & if he is unable she shall be complained of to the nearest J.P. and be punished as a de(ceiver)."[1]

There was one nurse for every ten patients in the Dublin hospitals, and the salary was £10 per annum, out of which she had to find her board.[2]

The opportunity which the hospitals afforded for training in the art of nursing was entirely wasted. The idea that the personal tending of the sick and forlorn poor would be a religious service of special value in the sight of God had vanished, and their care, no longer transformed by the devotion of religious enthusiasm, appeared a sordid duty, only fit for the lowest class in the community. Well-to-do men relieved their consciences by bequeathing money for the endowment of hospitals, but the sense of social responsibility was not fostered in girls, and the expression of charitable instincts was almost confined in the case of women to their personal relations.

Outside the hospitals employment was given to a considerable number of women in the tending of persons stricken with small-pox or the plague, and in searching corpses for signs of the plague. London constables and churchwardens were ordered in 1570 " to provide to have in readiness Women to be Provyders & Deliverers of necessaries to infected Howses, and to attend the infected Persons, and they to bear reed Wandes, so that the sick maie be kept from the whole, as nere as maie be, needful attendance weyed."[3]

In the town records of Reading it is noted " at this daye Marye Jerome Wydowe was sworn to be

---

S. P. D., dxxxix, 231. November 15, 1644.

[2] S. P. D., Interreg : I. 62, p. 633. 17 Aug., 1649.

Stow, London, V., p. 433.

a viewer and searcher of all the bodyes that shall dye within this boroughe, and truly to report and certifye to her knowledge of what disease they dyed, etc. ; and Anne Lovejoy widowe, jurata, 4^s a weeke a peice, allowing iiijs. a moneth after."[1] " Mary Holte was sworne to be a searcher of the dead bodyes hencefovrth dyeinge within the boroughe (being thereunto required) having iiijs. a weeke for her wages, and iiid a corps carryeing to buryall, and iiijs a weeke a moneth after the ceassinge of the plague."[2]

In 1637 it was " agreed . . . . with old Frewyn and his wief, that she shall presentlye goe into the house of Henry Merrifeild and be aidinge & helpinge to the said Merrifeild and his wief, during the time of their visitacion [plague] . . . . She shall have dyett with them, and six weekes after their visitacion ended. And old Frewin to have 2s. a week duringe all that tyme paid him, and 2s. in hand. And she shall have 2^s a weeke kept for her & paid her in th'end of the sixe weekes after."[3] Later " it was thought fitt the Woman keeper and Merifielde's wenche in the Pest-house, it beinge above vj weekes past since any one dyed there, should be at libertie and goe hence to her husbande's house, she havinge done her best endevour to ayre and cleanse all the beddes & beddinge & other things in both the houses. . . . for her mayntenance vj weekes after the ceassinge of the sicknes, she keepinge the wenche with her, they shalbe paid 3s. a weeke for and towardes their mayntenance duringe the vj weekes."[4] In 1639 the Council "Agree to geve the Widowe Lovejoye in full satisfaccion for all her paynes taken in and about the visited people in this Towne in this last

---

[1] Guilding, *Reading Records*, Vol. II., p. 241, 1625.

[2] *Ibid*, Vol. II., p. 244, 1625.

[3] *Ibid*, Vol. III., p. 371.

[4] *Ibid*, Vol. III., p. 384, 1637.

visitacion xls. in money, and cloth to make her a kirtle and a wascote, and their favour towards her two sonnes-in-lawe (beinge forreynours) about their fredome."[1] On a petition in 1641 from Widow Lovejoy " for better allowance & satisfaction for her paines aboute the visited people ; . . . . it was agreed that she shall have xxxs. soe soone as the taxe for the visited people is made uppe."[2]

In rural districts where hospitals were seldom within reach, entries are not infrequently found in the parish account books of payments made to women for nursing the poor. " Item. To Mother Middleton for twoe nights watchinge with Widow Coxe's child being sick."[3] " To Goody Halliday, for nursing him & his family 5 weeks £1 5 ; to Goody Nye, for assisting in nursing, 2s. 6d.[4] . . . . to Goody Peckham for nursing a beggar, 5s. For nursing Wickham's boy with the small pocks 12s."[5] A Hertfordshire parish paid a woman 15s. for her attendance during three weeks on a woman and her illegitimate child.[6] A Morton man was ordered to pay out of his next half-year's rent for the grounds he farmed of Isabelle Squire " 20s to Margt. Squire, who attended and looked to her half a year during the time of her distraction."[7]

Sometimes nurses were provided for the poor by religious and charitable ladies, who, like Lettice, Viscountess Falkland, " hired nurses to serve them."[8] Sick nurses were also engaged by well-to-do people to attend upon themselves or their servants. Thus the Rev.

---

[1] Guilding, *Reading Records*, Vol. III., p. 459.

[2] *Ibid*, Vol. IV., p. 8.

[3] *Sussex Arch. Coll.*, Vol. XXIII., p. 90. Hastings Documents. 1601.

[4] *Sussex Arch. Coll.*, Vol. XX., p. 117. *Acc. Book of Cowden.* 1704.

[5] *Ibid*, p. 118.

[6] *Hertford County Records*, Vol. I., p. 435, 1698.

[7] Atkinson, J. C., *Yorks. N. R Q. S. Records*, Vol. VII., p. 91. 1682.

[8] *Falkland, Lady Letice, Vi-countess, Life and Death of.*

Giles Moore enters in his journal " My mayde being sicke I payd for opening her veine 4d. to the Widdow Rugglesford, for looking to her, I gave 1s. and to old Bess for tending her 3 days and 2 nights I gave 1ˢ; in all 2ˢ 4ᵈ."[1] A little later, when the writer himself was " in an ague. Paid Goodwyfe Ward for being necessary to me 1s."[2] Though his daughter was with him, a nurse watched in the chamber when Colonel Hutchinson died in the prison at Dover.[3]

A few extracts from account books will supply further details as to the usual scale of remuneration for nurses ; no doubt in each case the money given was in addition to meat and drink. Sarah Fell enters " by mᵒ given Ann Daniell for her paines about Rachell Yeamans when she died 05.00."[4] Timothy Burrell " pd. Gosmark for tending Mary 3 weeks 6s."[5] Lady Grisell Baillie engaged a special nurse for her daughter Rachy at a fee of 5s.[6] At Herstmonceux Castle they " pd Hawkin's wife for tending the sick maiden 10 days 3s. Pd. Widdow Weeks for tending sick seruants a fortnight 4s."[7] Sir John Foulis in Scotland paid " to Ketherin in pᵗ paymᵗ & till account for her attendance on me the time of my sickness 12. 0. 0 " [scots].[8] " To Katherine tueddie in compleat paymᵗ for her attendance on me wⁿ I was sick 20. 0. 0." [scots].[9] " To my good douchter jennie to give tibbie tomsone for her attendance on my wife the time of her sickness 5. 16. 0. [scots]."[10]

---

[1] *Sussex Arch. Coll.*, Vol. I., p. 72. *Rev. Giles Moore's Journal.*

[2] *Ibid*, Vol. l., p. 100. 1667.

[3] *Memoirs of Col. Hutchinson*, p. 377.

[4] Fell (Sarah), *Household Accounts*, p. 285. June 20, 1676.

[5] *Sussex Arch. Coll.*, Vol. III., p. 123. *Journal of Timothy Burrell.* 1688.

[6] *Baillie, Lady Grisell, Household Book.* Intro. lxvii.

[7] *Sussex Arch. Coll.*, Vol. XLVIII., p. 121. 1643-1649.

[8] Foulis, Sir John, *Account Book*, p. 346. May 23, 1704.

[9] *Ibid*, p. 396. August 22, 1705.

[10] *Ibid*, p. 314. January 28, 1703.

All the above instances refer to professional nursing ; that is to say to the tending of the sick for wages, but nursing was more often of an unprofessional character. Sickness was rife in all classes, and for the most part the sick were tended by the women of their household or family. The claim for such assistance was felt beyond the limits of kinship, and in the village community each woman would render it to her neighbour without thought of reward. The solidarity of the community was a vital tradition to the village matron of the early seventeenth century, and it was only in cases of exceptional isolation or difficulty, or where the sick person was a stranger or an outcast that the services of a paid nurse were called in. Probably the standard of efficiency was higher in domestic than in professional nursing, because professional nurses received no systematic training. Their rate of remuneration was low, the essential painfulness of their calling was not concealed by the glamour of a religious vocation, still less was it rewarded by any social distinction. Therefore the women who took up nursing for their livelihood did so from necessity, and were drawn from the lower classes.

Illness was so frequent in the seventeenth century that few girls can have reached maturity without the opportunity of practising the art of nursing at home ; but amongst the " common people," that is to say all the class of independent farmers and tradesmen, the housewife can hardly have found time to perfect her skill in nursing to a fine art. Probably the highest level was reached in the households of the gentry, where idleness was not yet the accepted hall-mark of a lady, and the mistress felt herself to be responsible for the training of her children and servants in every branch of the domestic arts, amongst which were reckoned both medicine and nursing.

(B). *Surgery and Medicine.*

The position held by mediæval women in the arts

of healing is shown in such books as Mallory's " Morte
d'Arthur." When wounds proved intractable to
the treatment of the rough and ready surgeons who
attended in the vicinity of tourneys, knights sought
help from some high-born lady renowned for her
skill in medicine. It is true that popular belief
assigned her success to witchcraft rather than to the
knowledge and understanding acquired by diligent
study and experience, but a tendency to faith in the
occult was universal, and the reputation of the ladies
probably bore some relation to their success in the
cures attempted, for, according to the author of
" The Golden Bough," science is the lineal descendant
of witchcraft. The position of pre-eminence as con-
sultants was no longer retained by women in the seventeenth century. Schools and Universities had been
founded, where men could study medicine and
anatomy, and thus secure for themselves a higher
standard of knowledge and efficiency ; but, though
women were excluded from these privileges they were
not yet completely ousted from the medical profession,
and as a domestic art medicine was still extensively
practised by them.

Every housewife was expected to understand the
treatment of the minor ailments at least of her household, and to prepare her own drugs. Commonplace
books of this period contain recipes for making mulberry
syrup, preserving fruit and preparing meats, mingled
with, for example, prescriptions for plague water,
which is " very good against the plague, the
smallpox, the measles, surfeitts . . . . and is
of a sovereign nature to be given in any sickness "
" An oyle good for any ach—and ointments for
sore eyes or breasts, or stone in the kidney or bladder."
And in addition, " my brother Jones his way of making
inks."[1] " The Ladies Dispensatory " contains " the
Natures, Vertues and Qualities of all Herbs, and Simples

---

[1] *Add. MSS.* 36308.

usefull in Physick. Reduced into a Methodical Order,"
the diseases to be treated including those of men,
as well as women and children.[1]

As was the case in other domestic arts, girls depended for
their training in medicine chiefly on the tradition they
received from their mothers, but this was reinforced
from other sources as occasion offered. "The Ladies
Dispensatory" was not the only handbook published
for their use ; sometimes, though schools were closed
to women, an opportunity occurred for private coach-
ing. Thus Sarah Fell entered in her account book,
"July ^{ye} 5° 1674 by m° to Bro : Lowe^r y^t hee gave
Thomas Lawson fo^r comeinge over hithe^r to Instruct
him & sist^{rs}, in the knowledge of herbs. 10.00,"[2]
and when Mrs. Hutchinson's husband was Governor
of the Tower she allowed Sir Walter Raleigh and Mr.
Ruthin during their imprisonment to make experiments
in chemistry " at her cost, partly to comfort and divert
the poor prisoners, and partly to gain the knowledge
of their experiments, and the medicines to help such
poor people as were not able to seek physicians.
By these means she acquired a great deal of skill,
which was very profitable to many all her life."[3]

Neither did ladies confine their services to their
own household, but extended their benefits to all
their suffering neighbours. The care of the sick poor
was considered to be one of the duties of a " Person of
Quality," whose housekeepers were expected " to have
a competent knowledge in Physick and Chyrurgery,
that they may be able to help their maimed, sick and
indigent Neighbours ; for Commonly, all good and
charitable Ladies make this a part of their House-
keepers business."[4] The " Good Woman " is des-

[1] Sowerby (Leonard) *The Ladies' Dispensatory.* 1651.

[2] Fell, (Sarah). *Household Accounts,* p. 95. July 5, 1674.

[3] *Memoirs of Col. Hutchinson,* p. 12.

[4] *Compleat Servant-maid,* p. 40.

cribed as one who " distributes among the Indigent, Money and Books, and Cloaths, and Physick, as their severall Circumstances may require," to relieve " her poorer Neighbours in sudden Distress, when a Doctor is not at Hand, or when they have no Money to buy what may be necessary for them; and the charitableness of her Physick is often attended by some cure or other that is remarkable. God gives a *peculiar Blessing* to the Practice of those Women who have no other design in this Matter, but the doing Good : that neither prescribe where they may have the Advice of the Learned, nor at any time give or recommend any thing to try Experiments, but what they are assured from former Tryals is safe and innocent ; and if it do not help cannot hurt."[1]

The provision made by Lady Falkland of " antidotes against infection and of Cordials, and other several sorts of Physick for such of her Neighbours as should need them, amounted yearly to very considerable summes . . . her skil indeed was more than ordinary, and her wariness too . . . . Bookes of spiritual exhortations, she carried in her hand to these sick persons."[2] Mrs. Elizabeth Bedell " was very famous and expert in Chirurgery, which she continually practised upon multitudes that flock'd to her, and still *gratis*, without respect of persons, poor or rich. It hapned occasionally that some would return like the heald Samaritan, with some token of thankfulness ; though this was seldom. But God did not fail to reward them with (that which in Scripture is most properly call'd his reward) children, and the fruit of the womb. 3 sons and 4 daughters."[3]

Expressions of gratitude to women for these medical services occur in letters and diaries of the time. The

[1] Rogers, Timothy. *Character of a Good Woman*, p. 42-43.

[2] *Falkland, Lady Lettice, Vi-countess, The Life and Death of.*

[3] *Bedell, (Wm.), Life and Death of*, p. 2.

Rev. R. Josselin enters January 27th, 1672, " My
L. Honeywood sent her coach for me : y^r I stayd
to March 10, in wch time my Lady was my nurse &
Phisitian & I hope for much good : . . . . they
considered ye scurvy.   I tooke purge & other things
for it ; "[1]   Marmaduke Rawdon met with a carriage
accident, in which he strained his " arme, but comminge
to Hodsden his good cossen Mrs. Williams, with hir
arte and care, quickly cured itt, and in ten dayes
was well againe."[2]

Nor was the practice of medicine confined to Gentlewomen ; many a humble woman in the country,
the wife of farmer or husbandman, used her skill for
the benefit of her neighbours.   In their case, though
many were prompted purely by motives of kindness
and goodwill, others received payment for their
services.   How much the dependence of the common
people on the skill of these " wise women " was taken
for granted is suggested by some lines in " The
Alchemist," where Mammon assures Dol Common

> " This nook, here, of the Friers is no Climate
> For her to live obscurely in, to learne
> Physick, and Surgery, for the Constable's wife
> Of some odde Hundred in Essex."[3]

Though their work was entirely unscientific, experience and common sense, or perhaps mere luck,
often gave to their treatment an appearance of success
which was denied to their more learned rivals.   Thus
Adam Martindale describing his illness says that
it was " a vehement fermentation in my body
. . . ugly dry scurfe, eating deep and spread-
ing broad.   Some skilfull men, or so esteemed, being
consulted and differing much in their opinions, we were
left to these three bad choices . . . . in this greate

---

[1] Josselin, (R.), *Diary*, pp. 163-4.

[2] *Rawdon, (Marmaduke), Life of*, p. 85.

[3] Jonson, (Ben.) *The Alchemist,* Act IV., Sc. I.

straite God sent us in much mercie a poore woman, who by a salve made of nothing but Celandine and a little of the Mosse of an ashe root, shred and boyled in May-butter, tooke it cleare away in a short time, and though after a space there was some new breakings out, yet these being annointed with the same salve . . . . . were absolutely cleared away."[1]

The general standard of efficiency among the men who professed medicine and surgery was very low, the chief work of the ordinary country practitioner being the letting of blood, and the wise woman of the village may easily have been his superior in other forms of treatment. Sir Ralph Verney, writing to his wife advises her to " give the child no phisick but such as midwives and old women, with the doctors approbation, doe prescribe; for assure yourselfe they by experience know better than any phisition how to treat such infants."[2] Of Hobbes it was said that he took little physick and preferred " an experienced old woman " to the " most learned and inexperienced physician."[3]

Dr. Turbeville, a noted oculist in the West Country, was sent for to cure the Princess of Denmark, who had a dangerous inflammation of the eyes. On his return he is reported to have said that " he expected to learn something of these Court doctors, but, to his amazement he found them only spies upon his practice, and wholly ignorant as to the lady's case ; nay, farther, he knew several midwives and old women, whose advice he would rather follow than theirs."[4] He died at Sarum in 1696, and his sister, Mrs. Mary Turbeville, practised afterwards in London " with good

---

[1] *Martindale (Adam), Life of,* p. 21. 1632.

[2] *Verney Family,* Vol. 2, p. 27c. 1647.

[3] *Dictionary of National Biography.*

[4] Hoare, Sir R. C., *History of Modern Wilts.* Vol. VI. p. 465

reputation and success. She has all her brother's receipts, and having seen his practice, during many years, knows how to use them. For my part, I have so good an opinion of her skill that should I again be afflicted with sore eyes, which God forbid! I would rely upon her advice rather than upon any pretenders or professors in London or elsewhere."[1]

Events, however, were taking place which would soon curtail the practice of women whose training was confined to personal experience, tradition and casual study. The established associations of physicians, surgeons and apothecaries, although of recent growth, demanded and obtained, like other companies, exclusive privileges. Their policy fell in with the Government's desire to control the practice of medicine, in order to check witchcraft. Statute 3, Henry VIII., enacted that " none should exercise the Faculty of Physick or Surgery within the City of *London* or within Seven Miles of the same, unless first he were examined, approved and admitted by the Bishop of *London*, or the Dean of *St. Paul's*, calling to him or them Four Doctors of Physick, and for Surgery other expert Persons in that Faculty, upon pain of Forfeiture of £5 for every Month they should occupy Physick or Surgery, not thus admitted " because " that common Artificers, as Smiths, Weavers, and Women, boldly and accustomably took upon them great Cures, and Things of great Difficulty, in the which they partly used Sorceries and Witchcraft, and partly applied such Medicines unto the Diseased, as were very noyous, and nothing meet therefore."[2]

The restrictions were extended to the provinces. A Charter given to the Company of Barber-Surgeons at Salisbury in 1614 declared that " No surgeon or barber is to practise any surgery or barbery, unless

---

[1] Hoare, Sir R. C., *History of Modern Wilts*, Vol. VI., p. 467.

[2] Stow, *London* I., p. 132.

first made a free citizen, and then a free brother of the company. Whereas, also, there are divers women and others within this city, altogether unskilled in the art of chirurgery, who do oftentimes take cures on them, to the great danger of the patient, it is therefore ordered, that no such woman, or any other, shall take or meddle with any cure of chirurgery, wherefore they, or any of them shall have or take any money, benefit or other reward for the same, upon pain that every delinquent shall for every cure to be taken in hand, or meddled with, contrary to this order, unless she or they shall be first allowed by this Company, forfeit and lose to the use of this Company the sum of ten shillings."[1]

The Apothecaries were separated from the Grocers in 1617, the charter of their company providing that " No person or persons whatsoever may have, hold, or keep an Apothecaries Shop or Warehouse, or that may exercise or use the Art or Mystery of Apothecaries, or make, mingle, work, compound, prepare, give, apply, or administer, any Medicines, or that may sell, set on sale, utter, set forth, or lend any Compound or Composition to any person or persons whatsoever within the City of London, and the Liberties thereof, or within Seven Miles of the said city, unless such person or persons as have been brought up, instructed, and taught by the space of Seven Years at the least, as Apprentice or Apprentices, with some Apothecary or Apothecaries exercising the same Art, and being a Freeman of the said Mystery." Any persons wishing to become an Apothecary must be examined and approved after his apprenticeship.[2]

It will be observed that there is little in their charters to distinguish the medical from other city Companies, and while the examination required

---

[1] Hoare, Sir R. C., *History of Modern Wilts*, Vol. VI., p. 341.

[2] Barrett, *History of Apothecaries*, Intro., p. xxvii.

by the Faculties of Medicine and Surgery in the City of London excluded women altogether, the Apothecaries still admitted them by marriage or apprenticeship. " M[ris] Lammeere Godfrey Villebranke her son both Dutch Pothecarys " are included in a certificate made by the Justices of the Peace to the Privy Council, of the foreigners residing in the Liberty of Westminster.[1] A journeyman who applied for the freedom of the company, stated that he was serving the widow of an apothecary. His application was refused time after time through difficulties owing to a clause in the Charter. Counsel's opinion was taken, and finally he was admitted provided he kept a journeyman and entered into a bond of £100 to perform the same, that he gave £10 and a spoon to the Company, took the oaths and paid Counsel's fees.[2] He subsequently married the widow. Similar rules obtained in the provinces, as is shown by the admittance of Thomas Serne in 1698–9 to the freedom of the City of Dorchester on payment of 40s. because he had " married a wife who had lived as apprentice for 20 years to an apothecary."[3]

The jurisdiction of companies was local, and where no company existed boys were apprenticed to surgery for the sake of training, though such an apprenticeship conferred no monopoly privilege. Surgery was sometimes combined with another trade. John Croker describes in his memoir how he was bound apprentice in 1686 to one John Shilson " by trade a serge-maker, but who also professed surgery ; with whom I went to be instructed in the art of surgery."[4] The operation of these various Statutes and Charters being local and their enforcement depending upon

---

[1] *S. P. D.*, ccc., 75.   October 1635.

[2] Barrett, *History of Apothecaries*, pp., 28–9.

Mayo, C. H., *Municipal Records of Dorchester*, p. 428.

Croker, (John), *Brief Memoirs*, p. 5.

the energy of the parties interested, it is difficult to determine what was their actual and immediate effect on the medical practice of women. Statute 3, Henry VIII., must have been enforced with some severity, for a later one declares " Sithence the making of which said Act the companie & felowship of surgeons of London, minding oonly their own lucres, and nothing the profit or ease of the diseased or patient, have sued, troubled and vexed divers honest persons as well men as women, whom God hath endued with the knowledge of the nature, kind, and operation of certain herbes, roots and waters, and the using & ministering of them to such as been pained with customable diseases, as women's breasts being sore, a pin and the web in the eye, &c., &c., and yet the said persons have not taken any thing for their pains or cunning."[1]

Not only the Surgeons but the Apothecaries also, enforced observance of the privileges which the King had granted to them, and in consequence a Petition of many thousands of citizens and inhabitants in and about London was presented on behalf of Mr. William Trigg, Practitioner of Physick, saying that he " did abundance of good to all sorts of people in and about this City: when most of the Colledge Doctors deserted us, since which time your Petitioners have for above twenty yeares, in their severall times of Sicknesses, and infirmities taken Physick from him . . . . in which time, we doe verily believe in our consciences, that he hath done good to above thirty thousand Persons; and that he maketh all his Compositions himselfe, not taking anything for his Physick from poor people ; but rather releiving their necessities, nor any money from any of us for his advice ; and but moderately for his Physick : his custome being to take from the middle sort of Patients 12d., 18d., 2s., 2s. 6d. as they please to give, very seldom five shillngs unlesse from such as take

---

Statutes at Large. 34 Henry VIII. C.8.

much Physick with them together into the Countrey.
. . . . there is a good and wholesome law made
in the 34th year of King Henry 8 C. 8. Permitting
every man that hath knowledge and experience in
the nature of Herbs, Roots and waters, to improve
his Talent for the common good and health of the
people," and concluding that unless Dr. Trigg is
allowed to continue his practice " many poore
people must of necessity perish to death . . . . .
for they are not able to pay great fees to Doctors
and Apothecaries bills which cost more then his
advice and Physick; nor can we have accesse unto
them when we desire, which we familiarly have to
Dr. *Trigg* to our great ease and comfort."[1]

Prudence Ludford, wife of William Ludford of
Little Barkhampton, was presented in 1683 " for
practising the profession of a chyrurgeon contrary
to law,"[2] but many women at this time continued
their practice as doctors undisturbed ; for example,
Mrs. Lucy Hutchinson casually mentions that one
of her maids went to Colson, to have a sore eye cured
by a woman of the town.[3] While Mrs. D'ewes was
travelling from Axminster to London by coach, her
baby boy cried so violently all the way, on account
of the roughness of the road that he ruptured himself, and was left behind at Dorchester under the care
of Mrs. Margaret Waltham, " a female practitioner."[4]

The account books of Boroughs and Parishes show
that the poor received medical treatment from men
and women indiscriminately. A whole series of such
payments occur in the minute book of the Dorchester
Corporation. " It is ordered that the V^{li} to
be paid to Peter Salanova for cutting of Giles

---

[1] *Humble Petition of many thousands of Citizens, and Inhabitants in and about London*

[2] *Hertford Co. Records*, Vol. I. p. 328.

[3] *Memoirs of Col. Hutchinson*, p. 427.

[4] Yonge, Walter, *Diary*, Intro., xxii.

Garrett's leg shall be paid out of the X^{li} yearly paiable out of the Hospitall for pious vses . . . . to have the one halfe having cutt of his leg already, and the other halfe when he is thoroughly cured.[1] . . . . Unto the Widdow Foote xs. for the curing of the Widow Huchins' lame leg at present; and xs. more when the cure is finished[2]. . . . Mr. Losse should be payed by the Steward of the Hospital the somme of viij li for his paynes and fee as Phisitian in taking care of the poore of the Towne for the last yeare . . . . as it hath bin formerly accustomed . . . . Vnto Mr. Mullens the somme of thirty shillings for curing Hugh Rogers of a dangerous fistula."[3] Three pounds more (three having already been paid) was ordered to be given to "Cassander Haggard for finishing the great cure on John Drayton otherwise Keuse."[4] In another case the Council tendered to Mr. Mullens, "the chirurgeon, the some of xxx^s for curing of Thomas Hobbs, but he answered hee would consider of it next weeke [He declined]."[5]

At Cowden the overseers paid to Dr. Willett for "reducing the arm of Elizth Skinner, and for ointment, cerecloths and journeys, £2; three years later a further sum of 10s. was given "to Goodwife Wells for curing Eliz Skinner's hand."[6] "Mary Olyve was paid 6s. 8d. "for curing a boye that was lame" at Mayfield,[7] and 15s. was given to "Widow Thurston for healing of Stannard's son," by the churchwardens at Cratfield.[8] In Somerset £5 was

---

[1] Mayo, C. H., *Municipal Records of Dorchester*, p. 516, 1640.

[2] *Ibid*, p. 518. 1651

[3] *Ibid*, p. 518, 1649-50.

[4] *Ibid*, pp. 518-9. 1652-1654.

[5] *Ibid*, p. 519.

[6] *Sussex Arch. Coll.*, Vol. XX., p. 114. *Account Book of Cowden*, 1690.

[7] *Ibid*, Vol. XVIII., p. 196. *Accounts of Parish of Mayfield*.

[8] *Cratfield Parish Papers*, p. 179. 1640.

paid to " Johane Shorley towards the cure of Thomas Dudderidge. Further satisfaction when cure is don."[1]

Such entries show that though women may have practised surgery and medicine chiefly as domestic arts, nevertheless their skill was also used professionally, their natural aptitude in this direction enabling them to maintain their position throughout the seventeenth century even when deprived of all opportunities for systematic study and scientific experiments, and in spite of the determined attacks by the Corporations of physicians and surgeons ; but their success was owing to the fact that Science had as yet achieved small results in the standard of medical efficiency.

(C). *Midwifery.*

It has been shown that the employment of women in the arts of medicine, nursing and teaching was chiefly, though not entirely, confined to the domestic sphere ; midwifery, on the other hand, though occasionally practised by amateurs, was, in the majority of cases, carried on by women who, whether skilled or unskilled, regarded it as the chief business of their lives, and depended upon it for their maintenance. Not only did midwifery exist on a professional basis from immemorial days, but it was formerly regarded as a mystery inviolably reserved for women ; and though by the seventeenth century the barrier which excluded men had broken down, the extent to which the profession had in the past been a woman's monopoly is shown by the fact that the men who now began to practise the art were known as men-midwives.

The midwife held a recognised position in Society and was sometimes well-educated and well-paid. Nothing is known as to the mediæval history of midwifery in England ; and possibly nothing ever will be known concerning it, for the Englishwoman of that period had no impulse to commit her experience and ideas to writing. All the wisdom which touched her special sphere in life was transmitted orally from mother to daughter, and thus at any change, like the Industrial Revolution, which silently undermined the foundations of society, the traditional womanly wisdom could vanish, leaving no trace behind it. Even in the Elizabethan period and during the seventeenth century, when most women could read and many could write, they show little tendency to record information concerning their own affairs. But the profession of midwifery was then no longer reserved exclusively for women. The first treatise on the subject published in England was a translation by Raynold of " The Byrth of Mankynd." He says in his preface that the book had already been translated into " Dutche Frenche, Spanyshe and dyvers other languages. In the which Countries there be fewe women that can reade, but they wyll haue one of these bookes alwayes in readinesse . . . . it beinge lykewyse sette foorth in our Englyshe speeche . . . . it may supply the roome and place of a good Mydwyfe, ... and truly . . . . there be syth the fyrst settynge forth of this booke, right many honourable Ladyes, & other Worshypfull Gentlewomen, which have not disdayned the oftener by the occasion of this booke to frequent and haunt women in theyr labours, caryinge with them this booke in theyr handes, and causyng such part of it as doth chiefely concerne the same pourpose, to be read before the mydwyfe, and the rest of the women then beyng present ; whereby ofttymes, then all haue been put in remembraunce of that, wherewith the laboryng woman hath bene greatly comforted, and alleuiated of her thronges and travayle . . . . But here now let not the good Mydwyves be offended with that, that is spoken of the badde. For verily there is no

science, but that it hath his Apes, Owles, Beares and
Asses . . . . at the fyrst commyng abroade
of this present booke, many of this sorte of mydwyves,
meuyd eyther of envie, or els of mallice, or both,
diligented . . . . to fynde the meanes to sup-
presse . . . . the same; makyng all wemen of
theyr acquayntaunce . . . . to beleeue, that
it was nothyng woorth: and that it shoulde be a
slaunder to women, forso muche as therein was descried
and set foorth the secretes and priuities of women,
and that euery boy and knaue hadd of these bookes,
readyng them as openly as the tales of Robinhood &c."[1]

It is sometimes supposed that childbirth was an
easier process in former generations than it has become
since the developments of modern civilisation. The
question has a direct bearing on the profession of
midwifery, but it cannot be answered here, nor
could it receive a simple answer of yes or no, for it
embraces two problems for the midwife, the ease and
safety of a normal delivery and her resources in face
of the abnormal.

No one can read the domestic records of the seventeenth century without realising that the dangers of
childbed were much greater then than now; nevertheless the travail of the average woman at that time may
have been easier. There was clearly a great difference
in this respect between the country woman, inured
to hard muscular labour, and the high born lady or
city dame. The difference is pointed out by contemporary writers. McMath dedicated " the *Expert
Midwife*" to the Lady Marquies of Douglas because
" as it concerns all Bearing Women . . . . so
chiefly the more Noble and Honourable, as being more
Excellent, more Tender, and Delicate, and readily
more opprest with the symptoms." Jane Sharp confirms this, saying that " the poor Country people,

---

[1] Raynold, *The Byrth of Mankynd*, Prologue.

where there are none but women to assist (unless it
be those that are exceeding poor and in a starving
condition, and then they have more need of meat
than Midwives) . . . . are as fruitful and as
safe and well delivered, if not much more fruitful,
and better commonly in Childbed than the greatest
Ladies of the Land."[1]

Rich and poor alike depended upon the midwife to
bring them safely through the perils of childbirth,
and it is certain that women of a high level of intelligence and possessing considerable skill belonged to the
profession. The fees charged by successful midwives
were very high, and during the first half of the century
they were considered in no way inferior to doctors
in skill. It was natural that Queen Henrietta Maria
should send for one of her own country women to
attend her, French midwives enjoying an extraordinarily high reputation for their skill at this time.
The payment in 1630 of £100 to Frances Monnhadice,
Nurse to the Queen, " for the diet & entertainment
of Madame Peron, midwife to the Queen," and further
of a "Warrant to pay Madame Peron £300 of the
King's gift "[2] shows the high value attached to her
services.

That English midwives were often possessed of
ample means is shown by a deposition made by
" Abraham Perrot, of Barking parish, Gentleman,"
who " maketh oath that a month before the fire
. . . . he . . . . paid unto Hester Shaw
Widow, ... the summe of £953. 6. 8."[3] the said
Mrs. Shaw being described as a midwife ; but
relations who were members of this profession
are never alluded to in letters, diaries or memoirs.
From this absence of any social reference it is difficult

---

[1] Sharp (Jane), *The Midwives Book*, p. 3.

[2] S. P. D. 1630. Sign Manual Car. I., Vol. VII. No. 11.

[3] *Mrs. Shaw's Innocency Restored.* 1653.

to determine from what class of the community
they were drawn, or what were the circumstances
which led women to take up this responsible and
arduous profession. No doubt necessity led many
ignorant women to drift into the work when they were
too old to receive new ideas and too wanting in ambition to make any serious effort to improve their
skill, but the writings of Mrs. Cellier and Mrs. Jane
Sharp prove that there were others who regarded
their profession with enthusiasm, and who possessed
an intelligence acute enough to profit by all the
experience and instruction which was within their
reach.

The only training available for women who wished
to acquire a sound knowledge of midwifery was by
apprenticeship ; this, if the mistress was skilled in
her art, was valuable up to a certain point, but as no
organisation existed among midwives it was not possible to insist upon any general standard of efficiency,
and many midwives were ignorant of the most elementary circumstances connected with their profession.
In any case such an apprenticeship could not supply
the place of the more speculative side of training,
which can only be given in connection with schools
of anatomy where research work is possible, and from
these all women were excluded.

As has been said, many women who entered the
profession did not even go through a form of apprenticeship, but acquired their experience solely, to
use Raynold's words, " by haunting women in their
labours." In rural England it was customary when
travail began, to send for all the neighbours who were
responsible women, partly with the object of securing
enough witnesses to the child's birth, partly because
it was important to spread the understanding of
midwifery as widely as possible, because any woman
might be called upon to render assistance in an
emergency.

Several handbooks on Midwifery were written in response to the demand for opportunities for scientific training by the more intelligent members of the profession. One of the most popular of these books, which passed through many editions, was published in 1671 by Jane Sharp "Practitioner in the art of Midwifery above 30 years." The preface to the fourth edition says that "the constant and unwearied Industry of this ingenious and well-skill'd midwife, Mrs. Jane Sharp, together with her great Experience of Anatomy & Physick, by the many years of her Practice in the art of Midwifery hath . . . . . made them . . . . much desired by all that either knew her Person . . . . or ever read this book, which of late, by its Scarceness hath been so much enquired after . . . . as to have many after impressions." The author says that she has "often sate down sad in the Consideration of the many Miseries Women endure in the Hands of unskilful Midwives ; many professing the Art (without any skill in anatomy, which is the Principal part effectually necessary for a Midwife) meerly for Lucres sake. I have been at Great Cost in Translations for all Books, either French, Dutch or Italian of this kind. All which I offer with my own Experience."[1]

Jane Sharp points out that midwives must be both speculative and practical, for "she that wants the knowledge of Speculation, is like one that is blind or wants her sight : she that wants the Practice, is like one that is lame & wants her legs, ... Some perhaps may think, that then it is not proper for women to be of this profession, because they cannot attain so rarely to the knowledge of things as men may, who are bred up in Universities, Schools of Learning, or serve their Apprenticeship for that end and purpose, where anatomy Lectures being frequently read the

---

[1] Sharp, Mrs. Jane, *The Midwives Book, or the whole Art of Midwifery discovered.*

situation of the parts both of men and women . . . are often made plain to them. But that objection is easily answered, by the former example of the Midwives amongst the Israelites, for, though we women cannot deny that men in some things may come to a greater perfection of knowledge than women ordinarily can, by reason of the former helps that women want; yet the Holy Scriptures hath recorded Midwives to the perpetual honour of the female Sex. There not being so much as one word concerning men midwives mentioned there . . . . it being the natural propriety of women to be much seeing into that art; and though nature be not alone sufficient to the perfection of it, yet further knowledge may be gain'd by a long and diligent practice, and be communicated to others of our own sex. I cannot deny the honour due to able Physicians and Chyrurgions, when occasion is, Yet . . . . where there is no Men of Learning, the women are sufficient to perform this duty . . . . It is not hard words that perform the work, as if none understood the Art that cannot understand Greek. Words are but the shell, that we oftimes break our Teeth with them to come at the kernel, I mean our brains to know what is the meaning of them; but to have the same in our mother tongue would save us a great deal of needless labour. It is commendable for men to employ their spare time in some things of deeper Speculation than is required of the female sex; but the art of Midwifery chiefly concerns us."[1]

Though the schools of Medicine and Anatomy were closed to women, individual doctors were willing to teach the more progressive midwives some of the science necessary for their art; thus Culpeper dedicated his " Directory " to the midwives of England in the following words:—" Worthy Matrons, You are of

---

[1] Sharp, Mrs. Jane The Midwives Book, pp. 2–4.

the number of those whom my soul loveth, and of whom I make daily mention in my Prayers : . . . . If you please to make experience of my Rules, they are very plain, and easie enough ; . . . . If you make use of them, you wil find your work easie, you need not call for the help of a Man-Midwife, which is a disparagement, not only to yourselves, but also to your Profession : . . . . All the Perfections that can be in a Woman, ought to be in a Midwife ; the first step to which is, To know your ignorance in that part of Physick which is the Basis of your Act . . . . If *any want Wisdom, let him ask it of God* (not of the *Colledg of Physitians*, for if they do, they may hap to go without their Errand, unless they bring Money with them)."[1]

Efforts made by Peter Chamberlain to secure some systematic training for midwives drew upon himself the abuse, if not persecution, of his jealous contemporaries. In justifying the course he had taken he pleads " Because I am pretended to be Ignorant or Covetous, or both, therefore some ignorant Women, whom either extream Povertie hath necessitated, or Hard-heartedness presumed, or the Game of Venus intruded into the calling of Midwifry (to have the issues of Life & Death of two or three at one time in their hands, beside the consequence of Health and Strength of the Whole Nation) should neither be sufficiently instructed in doing Good, nor restrained from doing Evil ? . . . . . The objection infers thus much. Because there was never any Order for instructing and governing of Midwives, therefore there never must be . . . . It may be when Bishops are restored again, their Ordinaries will come in to plead their care. Of what ? Truly that none shall do good without their leave. That none shall have leave, but such as will take their Oath and pay Money. That

---

[1] Culpeper, Nich., Gent., Student in Physick and Astrologie, *Directory for Midwives.*

taking this Oath and paying their Money with the testimonie of two or three Gossips, any may have leave to be as ignorant, if not as cruel as themselves, ... but of Instruction or Order amongst the Midwives, not one word."[1]

The danger which threatened midwives by the exclusion of women from the scientific training available for men, did not pass unnoticed by the leading members of the Profession. They realised that the question at stake did not concern only the honour of their Profession, but involved the suffering, and in many cases even the death, of vast numbers of women and babies who must always depend on the skill of midwives and urged that steps should be taken to raise the standard of their efficiency. Mrs. Cellier[2] pointed out

---

[1] Chamberlain (Peter), *A Voice in Rhama, or the Crie of Women and Children*. 1646.

[2] Cellier (Mrs.). *A scheme for the foundation of a Royal Hospital, Harleian Miscellany, Vol. IV. pp.* 142-147.

The scheme was well thought out, and some details from it may be given here as showing the aspirations of an able woman for the development of her profession. Mrs. Cellier proposed that the number of midwives admitted to the first rank should be limited to 1000, and that these should pay a fee of £5 on admittance and the like sum annually. All the midwives entering this first rank should be eligible for the position of Matron, or assistant to the Government.

Other midwives may be admitted to the second thousand on payment of half the above fees.

The money raised by these fees is to be used for the purpose of erecting "one good, large and convenient House, or Hospital," . . . . for the Receiving and Taking in of exposed Children, to be subject to the Care, Conduct and Management of one Governess, one female Secretary, and twelve Matron Assistants, subject to the visitation of such Persons, as to your Majesty's Wisdom shall be thought necessary . . . . the children to be afterwards educated in proper Learning, Arts and Mysteries according to their several capacities. As a further endowment for this institution, Mrs. Cellier asks for one fifth part of the voluntary charity collected in the Parishes comprised within the Limits of the weekly Bills of Mortality, and that in addition collecting Boxes may be placed in every Church, Chapel, or publick Place of Divine Service of any Religion whatsoever within their limits. The scheme further provides "that such Hospital may be allowed to establish twelve lesser convenient houses, in twelve of the greatest parishes, each to be governed by one of the twelve Matrons, Assistants to the Corporation of the Midwives, which Houses may be for the taking in, delivery and month's Maintenance, at a price certain of any woman, that any of the parishes within the limits aforesaid, shall by the overseers of the poor place in them; such women being to be subject, with the Children born of them, to the future care of that parish, whose overseers place them there to be delivered, notwithstanding such House shall not happen to stand in the proper Parish." . . . .

" That, within the Space of twenty years last past, above six thousand women have died in child-bed, more than thirteen thousand children have been born abortive, and above five thousand chrysome infants have been buried, within the weekly bills of mortality ; above two-thirds of which, amounting to sixteen thousand souls, have in all probability perished, for want of due skill and care, in those women who practise the art of midwifery . . . . To remedy which, it is humbly proposed, that your Majesty will be graciously pleased to unite the whole number of skilful midwives, now practising within the limits of the weekly bills of mortality, into a corporation, under the government of a certain number of the most able and matron-like women among them, subject to the visitation of such person or persons, as your Majesty shall appoint ; and such Rules for their good government, instruction, direction, and administration as are hereunto annexed."

Then follow proposals for the care of the children, requiring that they may be privileged to take to themselves Sirnames and to be made capable, by such names, of any honour or employment, without being liable to reproach, for their innocent misfortune, and that the children so educated may be free members of every city and corporation.

After the first settlement, no married woman shall " be admitted to be either governess, secretary, or any of the twelve principal assistants to the Government and that no married person of either sex shall be suffered to inhabit within the said Hospital, to avoid such inconveniences as may arise, as the children grow to maturity ; . . . . if any of these Persons do marry afterwards, then to clear their accounts and depart the house, by being expelled the society."

Among many interesting rules for governing the Hospital, Mrs. Cellier appoints " That a woman, sufficiently skilled in writing and accounts, be appointed secretary to the governess and company of midwives, to be present at all controversies about the art of midwifery, to register all the extraordinary accidents happening in the practise, which all licensed midwives are, from time to time, to report to the society ; that the female secretary be reckoned an assistant to the government, next to the governess and capable of succeeding in her stead."

" That the principal physician or man-midwife, examine all extraordinary accidents and, once a month at least, read a publick Lecture to the whole society of licensed midwives, who are all to be obliged to be present at it, if not employed in their practise." The lectures to be kept for future reference by the midwives.

" That no men shall be present at such public lectures, on any pretence whatsoever, except such able doctors and surgeons, as shall enter themselves students in the said art, and pay, for such their admittance, ten pounds, and ten pounds a year." The physicians and surgeons so admitted were to be " of Council with the principle man-midwife and be capable of succeeding him, by election of the governess, her secretary, twelve assistants, and the twenty-four lower assistants,"

Mrs. Cellier succeeded with her proposal, in so far
that His Majesty agreed to unite the midwives into
a Corporation by Royal Charter, but there the matter
rested."[1]

In France women were more fortunate, for a noted
school of midwifery had already been established
at the Hotel Dieu in Paris, at which every six weeks
dissections and anatomies were especially made for the
apprentices of the institution, both past and present.[2]
Before entering on their profession the French midwives were required to pass an examination before the
chirurgeons. Their professional reputation stood so
high that Pechey alludes to one of them as " that
most Famous Woman of the World, *Madam Louise
Burgeois*, late Midwife to the Queen of *France*. The
praises that we read of all those that ever heard of her
are not so much a flourish as truth ; for her reasons are
solid experiences, and her witnesses have been all
of the most eminent Persons of *France :* and not only
of her, but as we have already exprest, of the most
excellent known Men and Women of this Art of
other Countries."[3]

According to Mrs. Cellier, English midwives were
for a time examined by the College of Surgeons, but
as their records for the years in question are missing
there is no means of ascertaining the numbers of those
who presented themselves for examination. She
says that Bishops did not " pretend to License Midwives till Bp. *Bonner's* time, who drew up the
Form of the first License, which continued in full
force till 1642, and then the Physicians and Chirurgeons contending about it, it was adjudged a Chy-
rurgical operation, and the Midwives were Licensed
at *Chirurgions-Hall, but not till they had passed three*

---

[1] Cellier, (Eliz.). *To Dr. ———, an answer to his Queries concerning the Colledg of Midwives*, p. 7.

[2] Carrier (Henriette.) *Origine de la Maternité de Paris.*

[3] Pechey, *Compleat Midwife*, Preface.

*examinations, before six skilful Midwives, and as
many Chirurgions expert in the Art of Midwifery.*
Thus it continued until the Act of Uniformity passed,
which sent the Midwives back to *Doctors Commons,*
where they pay their money (*take an oath which it
is impossible for them to keep*) and return home as skilful as they went thither. I make no reflections on those
learned Gentlemen, the Licensers, but refer the
curious for their further satisfaction to the Yearly
Bills of Mortality, from 42 to 62 ; Collections of which
they may find at *Clerkshall.* Which if they please
to compare with these of late Years, they will find there
did not then happen the eight part of the Casualities
either to Women or Children, as do now."[1]

In granting licences to midwives the Bishops were
supposed to make some enquiry as to their professional
attainments. Among the " articles to be enquired
of " during Diocesan visits was one " whether any man
or woman within your Parish, hath professed or practised Physick or Chyrurgery ; by what name or names
are they called, and whether are they licensed by the
Bishop of the Diocesse, or his Vicar Generall, and upon
whom have they practised, and what good or harm
have they done ? "[2]   And again, " whether any in
your Parish do practise Physicke or chirurgery, or that
there be any mid-wife there, or by what authority
any of them do practise, or exercise that profession."[3]
But the interest of the Bishops was concerned more
with the orthodoxy of the midwife than with her
professional skill.

A midwife's licence was drawn up as follows :
beginning :—" Thomas Exton, knight, doctor of
laws, commisary general, lawfully constituted of
the right worshipful the dean & chapter of St.

[1] Cellier (Eliz.). *to Dr. —— an answer to his Queries concerning the Colledg
of Midwives,* p. 6.

[2] *Exeter, Articles to be enquired of by the Churchwardens.* 1646.

[3] *Canterbury, Articles to be enquired.* 1636.

Paul's in London ; to our beloved in Christ, Anne
Voule, the wife of Jacob Voule, of the parish of St
Gile's Cripplegat, sendeth greeting in our Lord God
everlasting : Whereas, by due examination of diverse,
honest, and discreet women, we have found you apt
and able, cunning and experte, to occupy & exercise
the office, business & occupation of midwife," and
continuing after many wise and humane rules for her
guidance with an exhortation " to be diligent, faithful
and ready to help every woman travelling of child,
as well the poor as the rich, and you shall not forsake
the poor woman and leave her to go to the rich ;
you shall in no wise exercise any manner of witchcraft,
charms, sorcery, invocation, or other prayers, than
such as may stand with God's laws, and the king's,"
concluding thus :—" Item, you shall not be privy
to or consent that any priest or other party shall in
your absence, or your company, or of your knowledge
or sufferance, baptize any child by any mass, Latin
service, or prayers than such as are appointed by the
laws of the Church of England ; neither shall you
consent that any child borne by any woman, who shall
be delivered by you, shall be carried away without
being baptized in the parish by the ordinary minister
where the said child is born."[1]

The Bishops' interest in midwives may have been
caused partly by a praiseworthy desire to secure an
adequate supply for the assistance of women in each
parish. But from the Church's point of view, the
midwife's chief importance was not due to the fact
that the life of mother and child might depend on
her skill, but to her capacity for performing the rites
of baptism. The reasons for granting her this authority are explained as follows :—" in hard Labours
the Head of the Infant was sometimes baptized
before the whole delivery. This Office of Baptizing

---

[1] *Sussex Arch. Coll.*, Vol. IV., pp., 249-50. Extracts from Parish Registers.

in such Cases of Necessity was commonly performed
by the Midwife; and 'tis very probable, this gave
first Occasion to Midwives being licensed by the
Bishop, because they were to be first examined by the
Bishop or his delegated Officer, whether they could
repeat the Form of Baptism, which they were in
Haste to administer in such extraordinary Occasion.
But we thank God our times are reformed in Sense,
and in Religion."[1]   Though the midwife was only
expected to baptize in urgent cases she might strain
her privilege, and baptize even a healthy infant
into the Roman Church.   Her power in this respect
was regarded with suspicion and jealousy by English
Protestants, not only because she might inadvertently
admit the infant to the wrong fold, but because it
resembled the conferring of office in the Church upon
women; however, as no man was usually present at
the birth of a child, and it was fully believed that delay
might involve che perpetual damnation of the dying
infant's soul, no alternative remained.   Peter Heylyn,
in writing of Baptism, comments on the difficulty,
saying that " the first Reformers did not only allow
the administration of this Sacrament [Baptism] in
private houses, but permitted it to private persons,
even to women also."   He continues that when King
James, in the Conference at Hampton Court, seemed
offended because of this liberty to women and
laicks, Dr. Whitgift, Archbishop of Canterbury, denied
that the words gave this liberty, and Dr. Babington
alledged " that the words were purposely made
ambiguous as otherwise the Book might not have
passed Parliament.   To whom it was replied by the
Bishop of London that there was no intent to deceive
any, but the words did indeed " intend a permission
of private persons to Baptize in case of *necessity*."[2]
    The fear of secret baptisms into the Catholic

    [1] Watson, *Clergyman's Law*, p. 318.
    [2] *Heylyn (Peter), Cyprianus Anglicus, p. 27.*

Church is shown in a letter which states that " the wief of Frances Lovell esq^r of West Derh^m is noted for a recusant. And the said Frances had a childe about three yeares past christianed by a midwief sent thither by the La. Lovell, and the midwief's name cannot be learned."[1]

It was this danger which led to the prosecution of women who practised without licences. The Church-wardens at Lee presented " the Widow Goney and the wife of Thomas Gronge being midwives & not sworne." In Hadingham they report " We have two poore women exercising the office of midwives, one Avice Rax and the wife of one John Sallerie,"[2] and elsewhere " Dorothye Holding wief of Jo. Holding & Dorothye Parkins wief of Wm Parkins " were presented " for exercising the office of midwives without License."[3]

The fees charged by midwives varied from £300 in the case of the French Midwife who attended the Queen, to the sum of 1s. 6d. paid by the Parish of Aspenden to the midwife who delivered a woman " received by virtue of a warrant from the justices."[4] In most cases the amount paid by the parents was supplemented by gifts from the friends and relations who attended the christening.[5] Thus the baby's

[1] Bacon, (Sir Nat.). *Official Papers*, p. 176. 1591.

[2] *S. P. D.*, ccxcvi., 17. August 21, 1635. *Visitation presentments by the Churchwardens.*

[3] *S. P. D.*, ccxcv., 6. August 19, 1636.

[4] *Hertford County Records*, Vol. I., p. 435. 1698.

[5] The Rev. Giles Moore " gave Mat [his adopted daughter] then answering for Edwd. Cripps young daughter 5s. whereof shee gave to the mydwyfe 2s & 1s. to the Nurse. Myself gave to the mydwyfe in the drinking bowle 1s. (*Sussex Arch. Coll.*, Vol. I., p. 113. *Rev. Giles Moore, Journal.*)

Later is entered in the Journal, he being god-father " 1674. Mat was brought to bed of a daughter. Gave the mydwyfe, goodwyfe & Nurse 5s. each." (*Ibid*, p. 119.)

After Lady Darce's confinement at Herstmonceux Castle, is entered in the accounts " paid my Lord's benevolence to Widdow Craddock the midwife of Battle £5. 0. 0. (*Sussex Arch. Coll.*, Vol. xlviii. 1643-1649.)

Entries in a similar book of the Howard family give " To my young ladye's mid-wyfe xx^s (p. 227-8) To Mrs. Fairfax her Midwife by my Lord xx^s . . . . by my Ladie xx^s. More to Mrs. Fairefax her midwife by my Ladie's commaund iij^{li} " (*Howard Household Book*, p. 263. 1629.)

death meant a considerable pecuniary loss to the
midwife. An example of her payment in such a case
is given in Nicholas Assheton's diary; he enters on
Feb. 16, 1617. " My wife in labour of childbirth.
Her delivery was with such violence as the child
dyed within half an hour, and, but for God's wonderful
mercie, more than human reason could expect, shee
had dyed, ... divers mett and went with
us to Downham; and ther the child was buried . . .
my mother wth me laid the child in the grave . . .
Feb. 24, the midwyfe went from my wyffe to Cooz
Braddyll's wyffe. She had given by my wyffe xxs
and by me vs."[1]

The Churchwardens at Cowden entered in their
account book 1627 " Item, paide for a poore woman's
lying in 3. o." 1638. " to John Weller's wife for her
attendance on the widow Smithe when she lay in 2. o."[2]

The account book of Sir John Foulis of Ravelstone
gives many details of the expenses incurred at confine-
ments in Scotland. His wife appears to have been
attended by a doctor, as well as a midwife, and the
latter's fee was the higher of the two. The payments
are in Scots money.[3] " Mar. 26 1680, to the doctor
Steinsone for waiting on my wife in her labour 2
guines at 33 P. sterl. p.piece, 27. 16. o, to Elspie
dicksone, midwife, 40. 12. o, to her woman 2. 18. o."
On November 26, 1692 there is another payment

Sarah Fell records the presents given to her sister's midwife —Jan ye 1st 1675
by m^o Lent Bro. Lowe^r to give Jane Chorley his wifes midwife   1. oo.oo
by m^o Mothe^r gave to s^d midwife   5. oo
by m^o Sist^r Sus : sist^r Rach : & I gave he^r   5. oo
(Dec. 6. 1676. By M^o Given ffran. Laite Sister Lowers middwife by ffathe^r &
Mothe^r 5s. by sist^r Sus : 2s. by sist^r Rach : 2s. myselfe 4s.   Dec. 10, 1677
by m^o Mothe^r gave ffrances Layte when she was middwife to Sist^r Lower of litle
Love-day Lowe^r 02.06, by m^o sist^r Susannah gave he^r then 01.oo by m^o sister Rachell
gave her then 01.oo (Fell, Sarah, *Household Accounts*).

[1] Assheton (Nicholas), *Journal*, p. 81.

[2] *Sussex Arch. Coll.*, Vol. XX., p. 101 and p. 104. *Account Book of Cowden*.

[3] One pound Scots—2od. sterling.

" to my wife to give doctor Sibbald for his attendance on her in childbed and since to this day 5 guineas 66. o. o." Jan. 31, 1704 " to my son W^m to give the midwife when his wife was brought to bed of her sone Jo^n 3 guineas 42. 12. o. to my douchter Crichtoune to give the midwife for me halfe a guinie.7. 2. o.

The size of the gratuities given to the midwife by the friends and acquaintances who gathered at a society christening in London may be judged from Pepys, who enters in his diary when he was Godfather with Sir W. Pen to Mrs. Browne's child " I did give the midwife 10s."[1] His gratuities to people of lower rank were smaller, and of course the gifts made by the " common people " and those of the gentry in the provinces were much more modest.

In the latter part of the century there are indications of a growing tendency among the upper classes to replace the midwife by the doctor. The doctors encouraged the tendency. Their treatises on midwifery, of which several were published during this time, deprecate any attempt on the midwife's part to cope with difficult cases. Dr. Hugh Chamberlain points out " nor can it be so great a discredit to a Midwife . . . . to have a Woman or Child saved by a Man's assistance, as to suffer either to die under her own hand."[2] In making this translation of Maurice's work on Midwifery, Chamberlain omitted the anatomical drawings, " there being already severall in English ; as also here and there a passage that might offend a chast English eye ; and being not absolutely necessary to the purpose ; the rest I have, as carefully as I could, rendered into English for the benefit of our midwives."[3] This line of thought is

---

[1] Pepy's *Diary*, Vol. I., p. 3o8. 1661.

[2] Chamberlain (Dr. Hugh). *Accomplisht Midwife* : *Epistle to the Reader.*

[3] *Ibid.*

carried yet further by McMath, who says in the preface to " The Expert Midwife " that he has " of purpose omitted a Description of the parts in a woman destined to Generation, not being absolutely necessary to this purpose, and lest it might seem execrable to the more chast and shamfaced through Baudiness and Impurity of words ; and have also endeavoured to keep all Modesty, and a due Reverence to Nature : nor am I of the mind with some, as to think there is no Debauchery in the thing, except it may be in the abuse."[1]

The notion that it was indecent for a woman to understand the structure and functions of her own body fitted in with the doctors' policy of circumscribing the midwife's sphere ; McMath continues " Natural Labour, where all goes right and naturally, is the proper work of the Midwife, and which she alone most easily performs aright, being only to sit and attend Nature's pace and progress . . . . and perform some other things of smaller moment, which Physicians gave Midwifes to do, as unnecessary & indicent for them, and for the Matronal chastity (tho some of Old absurdly assigned them more, and made it also their office to help the Delivery, and not by Medicaments only and others, but Inchantments also.)."[2]

Clearly in a profession which often holds in its hands the balance between life and death, those members who are debarred from systematic study and training must inevitably give way sooner or later to those who have access to all the sources of learning, but the influences which were prejudicing women's position in midwifery during the seventeenth century were not wholly founded on such reasonable grounds ; they were also affected by much more

---

[1] McMath (Mr. James, M.D.). *The Expert Mid-wife.*

[2] *Ibid.*

general, undefined and subtle causes. It may even be doubted whether the superior knowledge of the seventeenth century doctor actually secured a larger measure of safety to the mother who entrusted herself to his management than was attained by those who confided in the skill of an experienced and intelligent midwife. Chamberlain admits that the practice of doctors " not onely in England but thoughout Europe ; . . . . hath very much caused the report, that where a man comes, one or both [mother or child] must necessarily dye ; and makes many for that reason forbear sending, untill either be dead or dying."* He continues " my Father, Brothers and myself (though none else in Europe that I know) have by God's blessing, and our industry, attained to, and long practised a way to deliver a woman in this case without any prejudice to her or her Infant."

The discovery to which Chamberlain refers was the use of forceps, which he and his family retained as a profound secret. Therefore this invention did not rank among the advantages which other doctors possessed over midwives at this period. Even when, a century later, the use of forceps became generally understood, the death rate in childbed was not materially reduced, for it was only with the discovery of the value of asepsis that this heavy sacrifice was diminished. We must therefore look for the explanation of the growing ascendancy of male practitioners to other causes beside the hypothetical standard of their greater efficiency. Their prestige rested partly on an ability to use long words which convinced patients of their superior wisdom ; it was defended by what was fast becoming a powerful corporation ; and more potent in its effect was the general deterioration in the position of women which took place during the century. A lessening

---

¹ Chamberlain (Hugh). *Accomplisht Midwife : Epistle to Reader.*

of confidence in womanly resourcefulness and capacity in other walks of life, could not fail to affect popular estimation of their value here too ; and added to this were the morbid tendencies of the increasing numbers of oversexed society women who were devoted to a life of pleasure. The fact that similar tendencies were visible in France, where an excellent scientific training was open to women, shows that the capture of the profession by men was not only due to superior skill.

The famous French Midwife, Madame Bourgeois, told her daughter " There is a great deal of artifice to be used in the pleasing of our Women, especially the young ones, who many times do make election of Men to bring them to bed. I blush to speak of them, for I take it to be a great peice of impudence to have any recourse unto them, unless it be a case of very great danger. I do approve, I have approved of it, and know that it ought to be done, so that it be concealed from the Woman all her life long ; nor that she see the surgeon any more."[1]

Whatever may have been the explanation, midwifery had ceased to be a monopoly for women when the " man-midwife " made his appearance in the sixteenth century, but it is only in the latter half of the seventeenth century that the profession passes definitely under the control of men. The doctors who then secured all the more profitable class of work, were united in a corporation which was often directed by men possessed of a disinterested enthusiasm for truth, and considerable proficiency in their art, even though many in their ranks might regard their profession merely as a means for acquiring personal fame or wealth. But the interest of the corporations of physicians and surgeons was centred more upon their profession than upon the general well-being of the community,

---

[1] Pechey, *Compleat Midwife*, p. 349.   Secrets of Madame Louyse Bourgeois, midwife to the Queen of France, which she left to her Daughter as a guide for her.

and they did not regard it as part of their duty to secure competent assistance in childbirth for every woman in the community. They took a keen professional interest in the problems of midwifery, but the benefits of their research were only available for the wives or mistresses of rich men who could afford to pay high fees. Far from making any effort to provide the same assistance for the poor, the policy of the doctors, with some exceptions, was to withold instruction from the midwives on whom the poor depended, lest their skill should enable them to compete with themselves in practice among the wealthy.

Conclusion.

The foregoing examination of the character and extent of women's professional services has brought several interesting points to light. It has been shown that when social organisation rested upon the basis of the family, as it chiefly did up to the close of the Middle Ages, many of the services which are now ranked as professional were thought to be specially suited to the genius of women, and were accordingly allotted to them in the natural division of labour within the family. The suggestions as to the character and conditions of these services during the Middle Ages, rest upon conjectures drawn from the comparison of a few generally accepted statements concerning the past, with what appears at the opening of the seventeenth century to be a traditional attitude to women, an attitude which was then undergoing rapid modifications. A more thorough and detailed examination of their position in the preceding centuries may show that it was far less stable than is generally supposed, but such a discovery need not disturb the explanation which is here given of the tendencies deciding the scope of women's professional activity within in the seventeenth century.

First among these was the gradual emergence of the arts of teaching and healing, from the domestic or family sphere to a professional organisation. Within the domestic sphere, as women and men are equally members of the family, no artificial impediment could hinder women from rendering the services which nature had fitted them to perform ; moreover, the experience and training which family life provided for boys, were to a large extent available for girls also. Coincident with a gradual curtailment of domestic activities may be observed a marked tendency towards the exclusion of women from all interests external to the family. The political theories of the seventeenth century regarded the State as an organisation of individual men only or groups of men, not as a commonwealth of families ; in harmony with this idea we find that none of the associations which were formed during this period for public purposes, either educational, economic, scientific or political, include women in their membership. The orient- ation of ideas in the seventeenth century was drawing a rigid line between the State, in which the individual man had his being, and family matters. The third tendency was towards the deterioration of women's intellectual and moral capacity, owing to the narrowing of family life and the consequent impoverishment of women's education. The fourth tendency was towards an increasing belief in the essential inferiority of women to men.

It will be seen that these tendencies were interdepen- dent. Their united effect was revolutionary, gradually excluding women from work for which in former days, nature, it was supposed, had specially designed them. Thus the teaching of young children, both girls and boys, had been generally entrusted to women, many men acknowledging in later life the excellence of the training which they had received from their mothers, and it cannot be doubted that women were upon the whole successful in transmitting to their children the benefit of the education and experience which they had themselves received. But no amount of didactic skill can enable persons to teach what they do not themselves possess, and so the scope of the training given by women depended upon the development of their own personalities. When family traditions and family organisation were disturbed, as perhaps they would have been in any case sooner or later, but as they were to a more marked extent during the Civil War, the sources from which women derived their mental and spiritual nourishment were dried up, and without access to external supplies their personality gradually became stunted.

Women were virtually refused access to sources of knowledge which were external to th family, and hence, with a few exceptions they were confined in the teaching profession to the most elementary subjects. Women were employed in the " dames schools " attended by the common people, or, when they could read and write themselves, mothers often instructed their children in these arts ; but the governesses employed by gentlefolks, or the schoolmistresses to whom they sent their daughters for the acquisition of the accomplishments appropriate to young ladies, were seldom competent to undertake the actual teaching themselves ; for this masters were generally engaged, because few women had gone through the training necessary to give them a sound understanding of the arts in question. Women were not incapable of teaching, but as knowledge became more specialized and technical, the opportunities which home life provided for acquiring such knowledge proved inadequate ; and consequently women were soon excluded from the higher ranks of the teaching profession.

The history of their relation to the arts of Healing is very similar. Other things being equal, as to some extent they were when the greater part of human life was included within the family circle, the psychic and emotional female development appears to make women more fitted than men to deal with preventive and remedial medicine. The explanation of this fact offers a fascinating field for speculation, but involves too wide a digression for discussion here, and in its support we will only point out the fact that in the old days, when no professional services were available, it was to the women of the family, rather than to the men, that the sick and wounded turned for medicine and healing. Yet in spite of this natural affinity for the care of suffering humanity, women were excluded from the sources of learning which were being slowly organised outside the family circle, and were thus unable to remain in professions for which they were so eminently suited.

The suspicion that the inferior position which women occupied in the teaching profession and their exclusion from the medical profession, was caused rather by the absence of educational opportunities than by a physiological incapacity for the practice of these arts, is strengthened by the remarkable history of Midwifery; which from being reserved exclusively for women and practised by them on a professional basis from time immemorial, passed in its more lucrative branches into the hands of men, when sources of instruction were opened to them which were closed to women. Just as the amateur woman teacher was less competent than the man who had made art or the learned languages his profession, so did the woman who treated her family and neighbours by rule of thumb, appear less skilful than the professional doctor, and the uneducated midwives brought their profession into disrepute. The exclusion of women from all the sources of specialised training was bound to re-act unfavourably upon their characters, because as family life depended more and more upon professional services for education and medical assistance, fewer opportunities were offered to women for exerting their faculties within the domestic sphere and the general incompetence of upper class women did in fact become more pronounced.

CHAPTER VII

CONCLUSION

Great productive capacity of women under conditions of Family and Domestic Industry—no difference between efficiency of labour when applied for domestic purposes or for trade.

Rate of wages no guide to real value of goods produced—married women unlikely to work for wages when possessing capital for domestic industry—Women's productiveness in textile industries—Agriculture—Other industries—Professional services.

Capitalism effected economic revolution in women's position—By (a) substitution of individual for family wages—(b) employment of wage-earners on master's premises—(c) rapid increase of master's wealth.

Exclusion of women from skilled trades not originally due to sex jealousy—Women's lack of specialised training due, (a) to its being unnecessary ; (b) the desire to keep wife in subjection to husband—Reduction in the value to her family of woman's productive capacity by substitution of wage-earning for domestic industry—Effect of her productive energy on her maternal functions and her social influence.

THE preceding chapters have demonstrated the great productive capacity which women possessed when society was organised on the basis of Family and Domestic Industry. There was then no hard and fast line dividing domestic occupations from other branches of industry, and thus it has not been possible to discover how much of women's labour was given to purposes of trade and how much was confined to the service of their families ; but as labour was at this time equally productive, whether it was employed for domestic purposes or in Trade, it is not necessary to discriminate between these two classes of production in estimating the extent to which the community depended upon women's services. The goods produced and the services rendered to their families by wives and daughters, must if they had been idle have employed labour otherwise available for Trade ; or to put the position in another way, if the labour of women had been withdrawn from the domestic industries and applied to Trade, more goods would have been produced for the market, which goods the said women's families would then have obtained by purchase; but while by this means the trade of the country would be greatly increased, unless the efficiency of women's labour had been raised by its transference from domestic to other forms of industry, the wealth of the community would remain precisely the same.

Nevertheless, in estimating a country's prosperity domestic production is generally overlooked, because, as the labour devoted to it receives no wages and its results do not enter the market, there is no mechanical standard for estimating its value. For similar reasons Home Trade is commonly considered to be of less importance than Foreign Trade, because, as the latter passes through the Customs, its money value can be much more readily computed, and because the man in the street, like King Midas, has imagined that gold is wealth. But we are here considering the production of goods and services, not of gold, and from this point of view, the woman who spins thread to clothe her family, and she who furnishes by her industry milk and cheese, eggs and pork, fruit and vegetables for the consumption of her family, has produced exactly the same goods, no more and no less, than if she had produced them for the market, and whether these goods are consumed by her own family or by strangers makes absolutely no difference to their real value.

Neither can the value of a woman's productive activity be judged by the wages she receives, because the value of a pair of sheets is the same, whether the flax has been spun by a well-to-do farmers' wife who meanwhile lives in affluence, or by a poor woman earning wages which are insufficient to keep body and soul together. The labour required for spinning the flax was the same in either case, for there was no difference in the type of spinning wheel she used, or in her other facilities for work ; it was only later, when organisations for trading purposes had enormously increased productive capacity by the introduction of power and the sub-division of labour, that the same productive capacity, devoted to domestic purposes, became relatively inferior in results. This change between the relative efficiency of domestic and industrial labour could not fail, when it took place, to exert a marked influence on the economic position of married women, because while their husbands earned sufficient money to pay rent and a few outgoing expenses, they had no inducement to work for wages, their labour being more productive at home. Women who fed and clothed themselves and their children by means of domestic industry gratified in this way their sense of independence as effectively as if they had earned the equivalent money by trade or wages. Considering the low rates paid to women, it may be supposed that few worked for wages when possessed of sufficient stock to employ themselves fully in domestic industries ; on the other hand there were a considerable number who were in a position to hire servants, and who, having learnt a skilled trade, devoted themselves to business, either on their own account or jointly with their husbands.

If the general position of women in the whole field of industry is reviewed, it will be seen that, beyond question, all the textile fabrics used at this time, with the exception of a few luxuries, were made from the thread which was spun by women and children, the export trade in cloth also depending entirely on their labour for spinning and to some extent for the other processes. In agriculture the entire management of the milch cows, the dairy, poultry, pigs, orchard and garden, was undertaken by the women, and though the mistress employed in her department men as well as women servants, the balance was redressed by the fact that women and girls were largely employed in field work. The woman's contribution to farming is also shown by the fact that twice as much land was allowed to the colonists who were married as to those who were single. The expectation that the women and children in the husbandman class would produce the greater part of their own food is proved by the very low rate of wages which Quarter Sessions fixed for agricultural labour, and by the fact that when no land was available it was recognised that the wage earner's family must be dependent on the poor rate.

Though the part which women played in agriculture and the textile industries is fairly clear, a great obscurity still shrouds their position in other directions. One fact however emerges with some distinctness ; women of the tradesman class were sufficiently capable in business, and were as a rule so well acquainted with the details of their husband's concerns, that a man generally appointed his wife as his executrix, while custom universally secured to her the possession of his stock, apprentices and goodwill in the event of his death. That she was often able to carry on his business with success, is shown by incidental references, and also by the frequency with which widow's names occur in the lists of persons occupying various trades.

How much time the wives of these tradesmen actually spent over their husband's business is a point on which practically no evidence is forthcoming, but it seems probable that in the skilled trades they were seldom employed in manual processes for which they had received no training, but were occupied in general supervision, buying and selling. It is not therefore surprising to find women specially active in all branches of the Retail Trade, and girls were apprenticed as often to shop-keepers as to the recognised women's trades such as millinery and mantua-making.

The assistance of the wife was often so important in her husband's business, that she engaged servants to free her from household drudgery, her own productive capacity being greater than the cost of a servant's wages. Apart from exceptional cases of illness or incompetence, the share which the wife took in her husband's business, was determined rather by the question whether he carried it on at home or abroad than by any special appropriateness of the said business to the feminine disposition. Thus, though women were seldom carpenters or masons, they figure as pewterers and smiths. In every business there are certain operations which can conveniently be performed by women, and when carried on at home within the compass of the family life, the work of a trade was as naturally sorted out between husband and wife, as the work on a farm. No question arose as to the relative value of their work, because the proceeds became the joint property of the family, instead of being divided between individuals.

With regard to the services which are now classed as professional, those of healing and teaching were included among the domestic duties of women. Illness was rife in the seventeenth century, for the country was devastated by recurrent epidemics of small-pox and the plague, besides a constant liability to ague and the other ordinary ailments of mankind; thus the need for nursing must have been very great. The sick depended for their tending chiefly upon the women of their own households, and probably the majority of English people at this time, received medical advice and drugs from the same source. Women's skill in such matters was acquired by experience and tradition, seldom resting upon a scientific basis, for they were excluded from schools and universities. Acquired primarily with a view to domestic use, such skill was extended beyond the family circle, and women who were wise in these matters sometimes received payment for their services. Midwifery alone was really conducted on professional lines, and though practised in former days exclusively by women, it was now passing from their hands owing to their exclusion from the sources of advanced instruction.

It is difficult to estimate the respective shares taken by men and women in the art of teaching, for while the young were dependent on home training, they received attention from both father and mother, and when the age for apprenticeship arrived the task was transferred to the joint care of master and mistress. With regard to learning of a scholastic character, reading was usually taught by women to both boys and girls, who learnt it at home from their mothers, or at a dame's school; but the teaching of more advanced subjects was almost exclusively in the hands of men, although a few highly educated women were engaged as governesses in certain noble families where the Tudor tradition still lingered. Generally speaking, however, when a girl's curriculum included such subjects as Latin and Arithmetic her instruction, like her brothers, was received from masters, and this was equally true in the case of accomplishments which were considered more appropriate to the understanding of young ladies. Women rarely, if ever, undertook the teaching of music, painting or dancing. From these branches of the teaching profession they were debarred by lack of specialised training.

Thus it will be seen that the history of women's position in the professions, follows a very similar course to that of the developments in the world of Industry; work, for which they appeared peculiarly fitted by disposition or natural gifts, while it was included within the domestic sphere, gradually passed out of their hands when the scene of their labour was transferred to the wider domains of human life. Capitalism was the means by which the revolution in women's economic position was effected in the industrial world. The three developments which were most instrumental to this end being :—

(a) the substitution of an individual for a family wage, enabling men to organise themselves in the competition which ruled the labour market, without sharing with the women of their families all the benefits derived through their combination.

(b) the withdrawal of wage-earners from home-life to work upon the premises of the masters, which prevented the employment of the wage-earner's wife in her husband's occupation.

(c) the rapid increase of wealth, which permitted the women of the upper classes to withdraw from all connection with business.

Once the strong hand of necessity is relaxed there has been a marked tendency in English life for the withdrawal of married women from all productive activity, and their consequent devotion to the cultivation of idle graces ; the parasitic life of its women has been in fact one of the chief characteristics of the parvenu class. The limitations which surrounded the lives of the women belonging to this class are most vividly described in Pepys' Journal, where they form a curious contrast to the vigour and independence of the women who were actively engaged in industry. The whole Diary should be read to gain a complete idea of the relations of married life under these new circumstances, but a few extracts will illustrate the poverty of Mrs. Pepys' interests and her abject dependence on her husband. Most curious of all is Pepys' naïve admission that he was trying to " make " work for his wife, which furnishes an illustration of the saying " coming events cast their shadows before them."

" Nov. 12, 1662. much talke and difference between us about my wife's having a woman, which I seemed much angry at that she should go so far in it without . . . . my being consulted. 13th. Our discontent again and sorely angered my wife, who indeed do live very lonely, but I do perceive that it is want of worke that do make her and all other people think of ways of spending their time worse. June 8. 1664. Her spirit is lately come to be other than it used to be, and now depends upon her having Ashwell by her, before whom she thinks I shall not say nor do anything of force to her, which vexes me, and makes me wish that I had better considered all that I have done concerning my bringing my wife to this condition of heat. Aug. 20. I see that she is confirmed in it that all I do is by design, and that my very keeping of the house in dirt, and the doing this and anything else in the house, is but to find her employment to keep her within, and from minding of her pleasure, which though I am sorry to see she minds it, is true enough in a great degree. Jan. 14. 1667-8. I do find she do keep very bad remembrance of my former unkindness to her and do mightily complain of her want of money and liberty, which will rather hear and bear the complaint of than grant the contrary . . . . . Feb. 18. a ring which I am to give her as a valentine. It will cost me near £5 she costing me but little in comparison with other wives, and I have not many occasions to spend money on her. Feb. 23. with this and what she had she reckons that she hath above £150 worth of jewels of one kind or another ; and I am glad of it, for it is fit the wretch should have something to content herself with."

While the capitalistic organisation of industry increased the wealth of the masters, it condemned a large proportion of the craftsmen to remain permanently in the position of journeymen or wage-earners with the incidental result that women were excluded from their ranks in the more highly skilled trades. Under the old system of Family Industry, labour and capital had been united in one person or family group of persons, but capitalism brought them into conflict ;

and the competition which had previously only existed
between rival families was introduced into the
labour market, where men and women struggled
with each other to secure work and wages from the
capitalist. The keystone of the journeymen's position
in their conflict with capital, lay in their ability
to restrict their own numbers by the enforcement
of a long apprenticeship and the limitation of the
number of apprentices. On gaining this point the
journeymen in any trade secured a monopoly which
enabled them to bargain advantageously with the
masters. Their success raised them into the position
of a privileged class in the world of labour, but did
nothing to improve the position of the other wage-
earners in unskilled or unorganised trades.

When their organisation was strong enough the
journeymen allowed no unapprenticed person to be
employed upon any process of their trade, however
simple or mechanical; a policy which resulted in the
complete exclusion of women, owing to the fact that
girls were seldom, if ever, apprenticed to these trades.
It has been shown that under the old system, craftsmen had been free to employ their wives and
daughters in any way that was convenient, the widow
retaining her membership in her husband's gild or
company with full trading privileges, and the daughters
able, if they wished, to obtain their freedom by
patrimony. Journeymen however now worked on
their masters' premises, their traditions dating from
a time when they were all unmarried men; and
though the majority of them had renounced the expectation of rising above this position of dependence,
the idea that they should extend their hardly won
privileges to wife or daughter never occurred to
them.

Thus came about the exclusion of women from the
skilled trades, for the wives of the men who became
capitalists withdrew from productive activity, and the

wives of journeymen confined themselves to domestic work, or entered the labour market as individuals, being henceforward entirely unprotected in the conflict by their male relations. Capitalistic organisation tended therefore to deprive women of opportunities for sharing in the more profitable forms of production, confining them as wage-earners to the unprotected trades. It would be an anachronism to ascribe this tendency to sex-jealousy in the economic world. The idea of individual property in wages had hardly arisen, for prevailing habits of thought still regarded the earnings of father, mother and children as the joint property of the family, though controlled by the father ; and thus the notion that it could be to men's advantage to debar women from well-paid work would have seemed ridiculous in the seventeenth century. Though the payment of individual wages was actually in force, their implication was hardly understood,and motives of sex-jealousy do not dominate the economic world till a later period. While the family formed the social unit the interests of husband and wife were bound so closely together, that neither could gain or suffer without the other immediately sharing the loss or advantage.

The momentous influence which some phases of Capitalism were destined to exert upon the economic position of women, were unforeseen by the men who played a leading part in its development, and passed unnoticed by the speculative thinkers who wrote long treatises on Theories of State Organisation. The revolution did not involve a conscious demarcation of the respective spheres of men and women in industry ; its results were accidental, due to the fact that women were forgotten, and so no attempt was made to adjust their training and social status to the necessities of the new economic organisation. The oversight is not surprising, for women's relation to the " Home " was regarded as an immutable law of Nature, inviolable by any upheaval in external social arrangements.

Thus the idea that the revolution in women's economic position was due to deliberate policy may be dismisssed. Capitalism is a term denoting a force rather than a system ; a force that is no more interested in human relations than is the force of gravitation; nevertheless its sphere of action lies in the social relations of men and women, and its effects are modified and directed by human passions, prejudices and ideals. The continuance of human existence and its emancipation from the trammels that hamper its progress, must depend upon the successful mastery of this as of the other forces of Nature.

If we would understand the effect of the introduction of Capitalism on the social organism, we must remember that the subjection of women to their husbands was the foundation stone of the structure of the community in which Capitalism first made its appearance. Regarded as being equally the law of Nature and the Law of God, no one questioned the necessity of the wife's obedience, lip service being rendered to the doctrine of subjection, even in those households where it was least enforced. Traditional ideas regarded the common wealth, or social organisation, as an association of families, each family being a community which was largely autonomous, and was self-contained for most of life's purposes; hence the order and health of the commonwealth depended upon the order and efficiency of the families comprised within it. Before the seventeenth century the English mind could not imagine order existing without an acknowledged head. No one therefore questioned the father's right to his position as head of the family, but in his temporary absence, or when he was removed by death, the public interest required his family's preservation, and the mother quite naturally stepped into his place, with all its attendant responsibilities and privileges. In this family organisation all that the father gained was shared by the mother and children, because his whole life, or almost his whole life, was shared by them. This is specially marked in the economic side of existence, where the father did not merely earn money and hand it to the mother to spend, but secured for her also, access to the means of production; the specialised training acquired by the man through apprenticeship did not merely enable him to earn higher wages, but conferred upon his wife the right to work, as far as she was able, in that trade.

Capitalism, however, broke away from the family system, and dealt direct with individuals, the first fruit of individualism being shown by the exclusion of women from the journeymen's associations; and yet their exclusion was caused in the first place by want of specialised training, and was not the necessary result of Capitalism, for the history of the Cotton Trade shows, in later years, that where the labour of women was essential to an industry, an effective combination of wage-earners could be formed which would include both sexes.

Two explanations may be given for women's lack of specialised training. The first, and, given the prevailing conditions of Family Industry, probably the most potent reason lay in the belief that it was unnecessary. A specialised training, whether in Science, Art or Industry, is inevitably costly in time and money; and as in every trade there is much work of a character which needs no prolonged specialised training, and as in the ordinary course of a woman's life a certain proportion of her time and energy must be devoted to bearing and rearing children, it seemed a wise economy to spend the cost of specialised training on boys, employing women over those processes which chiefly required general intelligence and common-sense.

It has been shown that this policy answered well
enough in the days of Domestic and Family Industry
when the husband and wife worked together, and
the wife therefore reaped the advantages of the
trading privileges and social position won by her
husband. It was only when Capitalism re-
organised industry on an individual basis, that the
wife was driven to fight her economic battles
single handed, and women, hampered by the want
of specialised training, were beaten down into
sweated trades.

The second explanation for women's lack of specialised training is the doctrine of the subjection of women
to their husbands. While the first reason was more
influential during the days of Family and Domestic
Industry, the second gains in force with the development of Capitalism. If women's want of specialised
training had been prejudicial to their capacity for
work in former times, such training would not have
been withheld from them merely through fear of
its weakening the husband's power, because the husband
was so dependent upon his wife's assistance. There
was little talk then of men " keeping " their wives ;
neither husband nor wife could prosper without
the other's help. But the introduction of Capitalism,
organising industry on an individual basis, freed men
to some extent from this economic dependence on
their wives, and from henceforward the ideal of the
subjection of women to their husbands could be
pursued, unhampered by fear of the dangers resulting
to the said husbands by a lessening of the wife's
economic efficiency.

A sense of inferiority is one of the prime requisites
for a continued state of subjection, and nothing
contributes to this sense so much, as a marked
inferiority of education and training in a society
accustomed to rate everything according to its
money value. The difference in earning capacity

which the want of education produces, is in itself sufficient to stamp a class as inferior.

There is yet another influence which contributed to the decline in the standard of women's education and in their social and economic position, which is so noticeable in the seventeenth century. This period marks the emergence of the political idea of the "mechanical state" and its substitution for the traditional view of the nation as a commonwealth of families. Within the family, women had their position, but neither Locke, nor Hobbes, nor the obscure writers on political theory and philosophy who crowd the last half of the seventeenth century, contemplate the inclusion of women in the State of their imagination. For them the line is sharply drawn between the spheres of men and women; women are confined within the circle of their domestic responsibilities, while men should explore the ever widening regions of the State. The really significant aspect of this changed orientation of social ideas, is the separation which it introduces between the lives of women and those of men, because hitherto men as well as women lived in the Home.

The mechanical State *quâ* State did not yet exist in fact, for the functions of the Government did not extend much beyond the enforcement of Justice and the maintenance of Defence. Englishmen were struggling to a realisation of the other aspects of national life by means of voluntary associations for the pursuit of Science, of Trade, of Education, or other objects, and it is in these associations that the trend of their ideas is manifested, for one and all exclude women from their membership; to foster the charming dependence of women upon their husbands, all independent sources of information were, as far as possible, closed to them. Any association or combination of women outside the limits of their own families was discouraged, and the benefits which had been extended to them in this respect by the Catholic Religion were specially deprecated. Milton's statement sums up very fairly the ideas of this school of thought regarding the relations that should exist between husband and wife in the general scheme of things. They were to exist " He for God only, she for God in him." The general standard of education resulting from such theories was inevitably inferior ; and the exclusion of women from skilled industry and the professions, was equally certain to be the consequence sooner or later, of the absence of specialised training.

The general effect upon women of this exclusion, which ultimately limited their productive capacity to the field of household drudgery, or to the lowest paid ranks of unskilled labour, belongs to a much later period. But one point can already be discerned and must not be overlooked. This point is the alteration which took place in the value to her family of a woman's productive capacity when her labour was transferred from domestic industry to wage-earning, under the conditions prevailing in the seventeenth century. When employed in domestic industry the whole value of what she produced was retained by her family ; but when she worked for wages her family only received such a proportion of it as she was able to secure to them by her weak bargaining power in the labour market. What this difference amounted to will be seen when it is remembered that the wife of a husbandman could care for her children and feed and clothe herself and them by domestic industry, but when working for wages she could not earn enough for her own maintenance.

This depreciation of the woman's productive value to her family did not greatly influence her position in the seventeenth century, because it was then only visible in the class of wage-earners, and into this position women were forced by poverty alone. The productive efficiency of women's services in domestic industry remained as high as ever, and every family which was possessed of sufficient capital for domestic industry, could provide sufficient profitable occupation for its women without their entry into the labour market. Independent hard-working families living under the conditions provided by Family and Domestic Industry, still formed the majority of the English people. The upper classes, as far as the women were concerned, were becoming more idle, and the number of families depending wholly on wages was increasing, but farmers, husbandmen and tradesmen, still formed a class sufficiently numerous to maintain the hardy stock of the English race unimpaired. Thus, while the productive capacity of women was reduced in the seventeenth century by the idleness of the *nouveau riche* and by the inefficiency of women wage-earners which resulted from their lack of nourishment, it was maintained at the former high level among the intermediate and much larger class, known as " the common people."

Though from the economic point of view intense productive energy on the part of women is no longer necessary to the existence of the race, and has been generally abandoned, an understanding of its effect upon the maternal functions is extremely important to the sociologist. No complete vital statistics were collected in the seventeenth century, but an examination of the different evidence which is still available, leaves no doubt that the birth rate was extremely high in all classes, except perhaps that of wage-earners. It was usual for active busy women amongst the nobility and gentry, to bear from twelve to twenty children, and though the death rate was also high, the children that survived appear to have possessed abundant vitality and energy. Neither does the toil which fell to the lot of the women among the common people appear to have injured their capacity for motherhood; in fact the wives of husbandmen were the type selected by the wealthy to act as wet nurses for their children. It is only among the class of wage-earners that the capacity for reproduction appears to have been checked, and in this class it was the under-feeding, rather than the over-working of the mothers, which rendered them incapable of rearing their infants.

The effect of the economic position of women, must be considered also in relation to another special function which women exercise in society, namely the part which they play in the psychic and moral reactions between the sexes. This subject has seldom been investigated in a detached and truly scientific spirit, and therefore any generalisations that may be submitted have little value. It will only be observed here that the exercise by women of productive energy in the Elizabethan period, was not then inconsistent with the attainment by the English race of its high-water mark in vitality and creative force, and that a comparison of the social standards described by Restoration and Elizabethan Dramatists, reveals a decadence, which, if not consequent upon, was at least coincident with, the general withdrawal of upper-class women from their previous occupation with public and private affairs.

Undoubtedly the removal of business and public interests from the home, resulted in a loss of educational opportunities for girls ; a loss which was not made good to them in other ways, and which therefore produced generations of women endowed with a lower mental and moral calibre. The influence of women upon their husbands narrowed as men's lives drifted away from the home circle and centred more round clubs and external business relations. Hence it came about that in the actual social organisation prevailing in England during the last half of the seventeenth century, the influence or psychic reaction of women upon men was very different in character and much more limited in scope, than that exercised by them in the Elizabethan period. When considered in regard to the historical facts of this epoch, it will be noticed that the process by which the vital forces and energy of the people were lowered and which in common parlance is termed emasculation, accompanied an evolution which was in fact depressing the female forces of the nation, leaving to the male forces an ever greater predominance in the directing of the people's destiny. The evidence given in the preceding chapters is insufficient to determine what is cause and what is effect in such complicated issues of life, and only shows that a great expenditure of productive energy on the part of women is not, under certain circumstances, inconsistent with the successful exercise of their maternal functions, nor does it necessarily exhaust the creative vital forces of the race.

The enquiry into the effect which the appearance of Capitalism has produced upon the economic position of women has drawn attention to another isssue, which concerns a fundamental relation of human society, namely to what extent does the Community or State include women among its integral members, and provide them with security for the exercise of their functions, whether these may be of the same character or different from those of men.

It has been suggested that the earlier English Commonwealth did actually embrace both men and women in its idea of the "Whole," because it was composed of self-contained families consisting of men, women and children, all three of which are essential for the continuance of human society; but the mechanical State which replaced it, and whose development has accompanied the extension of Capitalism, has regarded the individual, not the family, as its unit, and in England this State began with the conception that it was concerned only with male individuals. Thus it came to pass that every womanly function was considered as the private interest of husbands and fathers, bearing no relation to the life of the State, and therefore demanding from the community as a whole no special care or provision.

The implications of such an idea, together with the effect which it produced upon a society in which formerly women had been recognised as members, though perhaps not equal members, cannot be fully discussed in this essay; the investigation would require a much wider field of evidence than can be provided from the survey of one century. But from the mere recognition that such a change took place, follow ideas of the most far-reaching significance concerning the structure of human society; we may even ask ourselves whether the instability, superficiality and spiritual poverty of modern life, do not spring from the organisation of a State which regards the purposes of life solely from the male standpoint, and we may permit ourselves to hope that when this mechanism has been effectively replaced by the organisation of the whole, which is both male and female, humanity will receive a renewal of strength that will enable them to grapple effectively with the blind force Capitalism;—that force which, while producing wealth beyond the dreams of avarice, has hitherto robbed us of so large a part of the joy of creation.

AUTHORITIES.

(The numbers in leaded type are the press marks in the British Museum.)

Account of Several Workhouses for Employing and Maintaining the Poor, etc. *London* 1725. **1027 i. 18 (9).**

Act of Common Council for the reformation of sundry abuses practised by divers persons upon the common markets and streets of the City of London. 1631. **21 l. 5 (4).**

Act for the settlement and well ordering of the severall Publick Markets within the City of London.
1674. **21 l. 5 (58).**

Acts and Ordinances of the Interregnum II. 1651.

Add. MSS. 36308.

Answer to a Paper of Reflections on the Project for laying a Duty on English Wrought Silks. **8223 e. 9 (75).**

Arber, Edward. Transcript of the Registers of the Company of Stationers of London. 1554-1640. *London,* 1876.

Assheton, Nicholas, Esq. Journal of; ed. by Rev. F. R. Raines. *Chetham Soc.,* 1848

Astell, Mary. A serious proposal to the Ladies for the advancement of their true and greatest Interest, by a Lover of her sex. 1694. **12314 a. 22.**

Atkinson, J. C. Quarter Sessions Records for the North Riding of Yorkshire. *London,* 1884. **R. ac. 8190.**

Bacon, Francis. Works of; ed. by Spedding. *London,* 1858.

Bacon, Sir Nathaniel, of Stiffkey, Norfolk. Official Papers of, 1580-1620. *Royal Hist. Soc. Camden, 3rd Series.* 1915

Baillie, Lady Grisell. Household Book of, ed. by R. Scott-Moncrieff. *Edinburgh,* 1911. **R. ac. 8256.**

Banks, John. A Journal of the Life of. *London,* 1712.

Barrett, C. R. B. History of the Society of Apothecaries of London. *London,* 1905. **7680 f. 14.**

Bateson, Mary. Borough Customs.
Selden Society, Vol. XVIII., 1904. **R. ac. 2176.**

———— Records of the Borough of Leicester.
Cambridge, 1905. **2367 b. 5.**

Batt, Mary. Testimony to the Life and Death of. 1683.

Bedell, Wm. True relation of the life and death of the Right Reverend Father in God, Lord Bishop of Kilmore In Ireland. *Camden Society,* 1872. **R. ac. 8113/98.**

Best, Henry. Rural Economy in Yorkshire in 1641.
Surtees Society, 33. *Durham,* 1857.

Black, W. H. History and Antiquities of the Worshipful Company of Leathersellers of the City of London.
London 1871. **1890 c. 5.**

Bownas, Samuel. Life and Travels of. *London* 1756.

Brathwaite, Richard. Anniversaries upon his Panarete continued—with her contemplations penned in the languishing time of her sicknesse. *London* 1635. **Huth 68.**

———— The English gentleman and English gentlewoman in one volume concluded : the 3rd edition with a Ladies Love Lecture and a supplement. *London* 1641. **30 e. 6.**

Brewster, John. Parochial History and Antiquities of Stockton upon Tees. *Stockton* 1796. **2368 d. 3**

Brief State of the Inland or Home Trade of England, and of the oppressions it suffers, and the Dangers which threaten it from the Invasion of Hawkers, Pedlars and Clandestine Traders of all sorts. *London* 1730. **104 h. 20.**

British Friend.

Bund, J. W. Willis. Worcestershire County Records.
Worcester 1900. **010360 i.**

Burton, John Richard. History of Kidderminster.
1890. **10368 h. 27.**

C. W. The Bespotted Jesuite. *London* 1641. **E. 166 (3).**

Calendar State Papers. Domestic Series (C. S. P. D.).

Canterbury. Articles to be enquired of by the Churchwardens, etc. **698 n. 20 (18).**

Carpenters, Records of the Worshipful Company of.
1913. **W.P. 2524.**

Cary, John. Account of the Proceedings of the Corporation of Bristol in execution of the Act of Parliament for the better Employing and Maintaining the Poor of that City. *London* 1700. **1027 i. 18 (3).**

Carrier, Henriette. Origines de la Maternité de Paris.
1888. **7687 eee. 31.**

Case of the Linen Drapers and other Dealers in Printed Callicoes and Linens. **816 m. 13 (49).**

Case of British and Irish Manufacture of Linnen, Threads, and Tapes, etc. **1887 b. 60 (6).**

Case of the Manufacturers of Gilt and Silver Wire. **1887 b. 60 (9).**

Case of the Parish of St. Giles. 8223 e. 9 (23).

Case of the Woollen Manufacturers of Great Britain, and of the Poor they imploy. 1887 b. 60 (32).

Case or Petition of the Corporation of Pin-makers. 816 m. 13.

Cellier, Elizabeth, Mrs. Scheme for the foundation of a Royal Hospital. *London* 1687. *Harl. Misc. Vol. iv.*

———— To Dr.——an answer to his Queeries concerning the Colledg of Midwives. 1687-8. 1178 h. 2 (2).

———— Malice Defeated. 1680. 515 l. 1 (10).

Chalkley, Thomas. Collection of the Works of. *London* 1751.

Chamberlain, Hugh, Dr. Trans. Treatise on Midwifery by F. Maurice. 1672.

Chamberlain, Peter. Dr. in Physick, Fellow of the Colledge of London, and one of His Majestie's Physicians Extraordinary. A voice in Rhama or the Crie of Women and Children. *London* 1646. **B.M. E. 1181.**

Charter of the Joiners' Co. Chester. *Harl. MSS.* 2054, *fo.* 5.

Charter and By-laws of the Company of Armourers and Brasiers, in the City of London. 1554-1640.
1873. **08227 b. 13.**

Child, Sir Josiah. A New Discourse of Trade, etc.
2nd ed. London 1694. **712 c. 5.**

———— Short Addition. 1668. **1029 b. 1.**

Churchwardens' Accounts. Steeple Ashton. *Wilts Notes and Queries.* *London* 1911. **R. pp. 6049 m.**

———— St. Michael's in Bedwardine, Worcester.
Oxford 1896. **R. Ac. 8166/8.**

Clode, Charles M. Memorials of the Guild of Merchant Taylors, City of London. *London* 1875. **2366 d. 2.**

———— Early History of the Guild of Merchant Taylors of the Fraternity of St. John the Baptist, London.
London 1888. **8248 f. 18.**

Clothiers' Complaint, or Reasons for Passing the Bill.
London 1692. **711 f. 28.**

Compleat Servant-maid, or the Young Maiden's Tutor.
London 1700. **1037 a. 42.**

Congreve, Wm. Works of. *London* 1710. **641 d. 3.**

Considerations touching the Excise of Native and Forreign Commodities (as formerly established) as also how the present Excise settled on His Majesty may (with some additions) be improved to the sum resolved on by the Commons in Parliament. **712 m. 1 (3).**

Costello, Louisa S. Memoirs of Eminent Englishwomen.
                          London 1844. 1023 i. 8.
Council Register.

Cox, Rev. J. C. Churchwardens' Accounts.   1913.   2260 b. 3.
———— Three Centuries of Derbyshire Annals as illus-
    trated by the Records of the Quarter Sessions of the
    County of Derby.   *London* 1890.   01035 8 l. 28.

Cratfield. Accounts of the Parish of.   Ed. by Wm. Holland
    and J. J. Raven.   1895.   01035 8 l. 42.

Croker, John. Brief Memoirs of.   *London* 1839.

Cromwell Family. Bills and Receipts. Vol. II. 1546-1672.
                                    Add. Mss. 33,461.

Crosfield, Helen G. Margaret Fox of Swarthmoor Hall.
                                        London 1913

Culpeper, Nicholas, Gent., Student in Physick and Astrologie.
    Directory for Midwives.   1651.   E. 1340.

Davenant (Inspector-General of Exports and Imports).   An
    Account of the trade between Greate Britain, France,
    Holland, etc.,   .   .   .   delivered in his reports made to
    the Commissioners for Publick Accounts.   1715.

Davies, J. S. History of Southampton. *London* 1883.   2368 cc. 5.

Decker, Thomas. Best Plays. *Ed. by E. Rhys.*
                                London 1887. 11773 bb. 14.

Declaration of the Estate of Clothing now used within this
    Realme of England.   712 G. 16 (1).

Defoe, Daniel. The Behaviour of Servants in England.
                                London 1724.   1137 h. 6.
———— Every-Body's Business is No-Body's Business.
                                London 1725.   1137 h. 6 (2).

Dunning, Richard, Gent.   A plain and easie Method shewing
    how the office of overseer of the Poor may be managed,
    whereby it may be £9,000 per annum Advantage to the
    County of Devon, without abating the weekly Relief of
    any Poor, or doing a Penny damage to any Person.
                                London 1686.   1027 i. 17.

Dunsford, M.   Historical Memoirs of the Town and Parish of
    Tiverton.   *Exeter* 1790.   2368 d. 3.

Englands Way to win wealth and to employ Ships and
    Mariners, etc., by Tobias, Gentleman, Fisherman and
    Mariner.   1614. *Harleian Misc., Vol. III.*

Evelyn, John. Diary of. *Ed. by Wm. Bray.* 1906. 10854 f. 11.

Exeter. Articles to be enquired of by the Churchwardens.
                                1636. 698 n. 20 (19).

Eyre, Captain Adam. A Dyurnall. 1646. *Surtees Society,*
    Vol. LXV.   *Durham* 1877. **R. ac. 8045/53.**

Falkland, Lady Letice Vi-countess. The Virtuous, Holy,
    Christian Life and Death of the late, by John Duncon.
                              London 1653. **701 b. 12.**

Fanshawe, Lady. Memoirs of. Wife of Sir Richard
    Fanshawe, Bart.   *London* 1905. **012207 i.**

Fell, Sarah. Swarthmoor Household Accounts.

Ferguson, R. S. Municipal Records of the City of Carlisle.
                     Carlisle 1887. **R. ac. 5630/5.**

Fiennes, Celia. Through England on a Side Saddle in the
    time of William and Mary. Being the Diary of C. F.
                     London 1888. **10854 g. 23.**

Firmin, Thomas. The Life of.   *London* 1698. **857 h. 26.**

———— Some Proposals for the imploying of the Poor,
    especially in and about the City of London.
                     London 1678. **1027 i. 32.**

Fitzherbert, Sir Anthony. Book of Husbandrye. 1555. **969 a. 32 (1).**

Foulis, Sir John, of Ravelston. Account Book of. 1671-1707.
                     Edinburgh 1894. **R. ac. 8256.**

Fox, F. F. Some Account of the Merchant Taylors, Bristol.
                     Bristol 1880. **10352 l. 17.**

Further Considerations for encouraging the woollen Manu-
    facturers of this Kingdom.   **1852 d. 1 (41).**

Gentlemen's Magazine. May, 1834. Vol. I., Letter to
    Lord Althorp on the Poor Laws by Equitas.

Gibbs, A. E. Corporation Records—St. Albans.
                 St. Albans 1890. **10351 cc. 56.**

Grasier's Complaint.   *London* 1726. **712 G. 16.**

Guilding, J. M. Reading Records.   1892. **2366 d. 4·**

Hale, Sir Matthew. Method Concerning Relief and
    Employment of the Poor.   *London* 1699. **1027 i. 18 (1).**

———— Discourse touching Provision for the Poor.

Hamilton, A. H. A. Quarter Sessions Records, Queen
    Elizabeth to Queen Anne.   1878. **6006 a. 14.**

Hardy, W. J. Hertford County Records, 1581-1698.
                   Hertford 1905. **010360 K. 7.**

———— Middlesex County Records.   1905. **5805 d. f. 2.**

Harl, MSS. 2054, 2105, relating to City of Chester.

Harley, Letters of the Lady Brilliana. *Intro. and notes by*
    Thos. Taylor Lewis.   *London* 1853. **R. ac. 8113/56**

Haynes, John. Great Britain's Glory, or an account of the Great Numbers of Poor employed in the woollen and silk manufactures.   *London* 1715. **1029 a. 6 (3).**

———— View of the Present State of the Clothing Trade in England.   *London* 1706. **1029 a. 6 (2).**

Heath, J. B. Some account of the Worshipful Company of Grocers of the City of London.   *London* 1854. **1302 m. 2.**

Herbert, Wm. History of the Twelve Great Livery Companies of London.   1836.

Heylyn, Peter, D.D. The Historical and Miscellaneous Tracts of ; and an account of the life of the Author.
        London 1681. **479 d. 11.**

———— Cyprianus Anglicus.   1668. **C82 f. 2.**

———— Voyage of France.   1673. **10170 aaa. 8.**

Heywood, Rev. Oliver, 1630-1702. His autobiography, diaries, anecdote and event books, *ed. by J. Horsfall Turner.*   1882. **4907 e. 4.**

Historical MSS. Commission 14 Rep. App. VIII.

———— Various Collections. Vol. I.

———— ———— Vol. IV.

Hoare, Sir R. C. History of Modern Wiltshire. Old and New Sarum or Salisbury.   *London* 1843.

Holdsworth, W. S. A History of Eng. Law.   1903.

Holroyd, Joseph, cloth factor, and Sam. Hill, Clothier, Letter Books of.   *Halifax* 1900. **7958 h.**

Howard, Lord William of Naworth Castle. Selections from the Household Books of.
        Surtees Society, Vol. LXVIII. Durham 1878. **R. ac. 8045/55.**

Howell, James. Familiar Letters.   *London* 1754. **G. 2118.**

Humble Petition and Case of the Tobacco Pipe Makers of the City of London and Westminster.   1695. **816 m. 12.**

Humble Petition of many thousands of Courtiers', Citizens', Gentlemen's and Tradesmen's wives, etc.
        Feb. 10, 1641. **669 f. 4 (59).**

Humble Petition of the Master, Wardens and Assistants of the Company of Silk Throwers, London.   **816 m. 13 (115).**

Hunter, Joseph. History and Topography of Ketteringham.   *Norwich* 1851. **10351 h. 10.**

Hutchinson, Memoirs of the Life of Colonel, written by his widow, Lucy. *Ed. by C. H. Firth.*   1906. **12207 p.p.**

Irish Friend. Vol. IV. Account of remvarkable visions and passages of John Adams, of Yorkshire.

James, John. History of the Worsted Manufacture in England. *London* 1857. **2270 bb. 16.**

Johnson, Rev. A. H. History of the Worshipful Company of Drapers of London. 1914. **W.P. 3016.**

Jonson, Ben. Plays. 1756. **673 f. 13-19.**

Josselin, Rev. Ralph. The Diary of. 1616-1683, *ed. for the Royal Historical Society by E. Hockcliffe.* 1908. **R. ac. 8118/17.**

Jupp, Ed. B. Historical Account of the Worshipful Company of Carpenters of the City of London. *London* 1887. **10350 dd. 17.**

King, Gregory (Rouge Dragon). Natural and Political Observations and Conclusions upon the state and condition of England, 1696. *Ed. by G. Chalmers.* *London* 1910. **1137 k. 27.**

Lambert, Rev. J. Malet. 2,000 years of Gild Life, Kingston-upon-Hull. **2240 f. 9.**

Lamond, Eliz. Discourse of the Common Weal of this Realm of England. First printed in 1581. *Cambridge* 1893. **8009 aaa. 33.**

Lansdowne MSS. 161 fo. 127. Letter from Mayor of Southampton to Sir J. Cæsar *re* suit of Rachell Tierry.

———— 351 fo. 18 b. A Project for Mounts of Piety.

Latimer, John. Annals of Bristol. *Bristol* 1900. **2367 bb. 1.**

Leach, Arthur F. Beverley Town Documents. *Selden Society, Vol. xiv.* *London* 1900. **R. ac. 2176.**

Leader, John Daniel. Extracts from the earliest book of Accounts belonging to the Town Trustees of Sheffield. 1566-1707. *Sheffield* 1879. **8228 aa. 11.**

———— Records of the Burgery of Sheffield, commonly called the Town Trust. *London* 1897. **010358 f. 63.**

Leader, Robert Eadon. History of the Company of Cutlers in Hallamshire. *Sheffield* 1905. **1889 e. 10.**

Leland, John. The Itinerary of, 1535-1543. *Ed. by L. Toulmin Smith.* *London* 1907. **2366 d. 6.**

Linnen and Woollen Manufactory discoursed, with the Nature of Companies and Trade in General. *London* 1691. **712 m. 1 (14).**

Lipson, E. An Introduction to the Economic History of England. I. the Middle Ages. *London* 1915. **W.P. 2753.**

Little Red Book of Bristol. *Ed. by F. B. Bickley.* **10370 h. 22.**

Lyon, John. History of Town and Port of Dover. *Dover* 1813. **191 b. 6.**

Manchester Court Leet Records. **1887.**

Martindale, Adam, The Life of, written by himself. *Ed. by Richard Parkinson. Cheetham Society, Vol. IV.* 1845. **R. ac. 8120.**

McMath, James, M.D. The Expert Midwife. 1694. **7581 de. 19.**

Mayo, C. H. Municipal Records of the Borough of Dorchester. Dorset. *Exeter* 1908. **010360 k. 11.**

Monthly Meeting Minute Books of the Society of Friends, Horselydown and Peele.

Mournfull Cryes of many thousand Poore Tradesmen, 1647. **669 f. 11 (116).**

Murray, Lady Mary, of Stanhope. Memoirs of Lives and Characters of the Rt. Hon. Geo. Baillie of Jerviswood, and of Lady Grisell Baillie. *Edinburgh* 1822. **614 g. 29.**

Nash, T. History and Antiquities of Worcester. 1781.

Nicholas Papers. Correspondence of Sir Edward Nicholas, Secretary of State. *Ed. by G. F. Warner.* *Camden Society* 1886. **R. ac. 8113/127.**

Nicholson, Dame Magdalen, widow of Sir Gilbert Elliot, first Baronet of Stobbs, by Alexander O. Curle. Some notes of the Account Book of. *In Proceedings of the Society of Antiquaries of Scotland.* 1904-1905. Vol. *XXXIX., pp.* 120-132. **R. ac. 5770. 2.**

Nottingham, Records of the Borough of. *London* 1889. **2366 d. 1.**

Osborne, Dorothy. Letters to Sir William Temple. *Ed. by E. A. Parry.* **10921 bbb. 34.**

Overall, W. H. Analytical Index to the Series of Records known as the Remembrancia, preserved among the Archives of the City of London. 1579-1664. *London* 1878.

————— Some account of the Company of Clockmakers of the City of London. *London* 1881. **10349 gg. 11.**

Pechey, John. Fellow of the Colledge of Physicians. The Compleat Midwife's practice enlarged. *London* 1698. **778 b. 44.**

Pepys, Samuel. Diary and Correspondence. *Ed. by* Rev. Mynors Bright. *London* 1875. **100854 ee. 1.**

Petty, Dorothy, the case of, in Relation to the Union Society, at the White Lyon by Temple Bar, whereof she is Director. 1710. **816 m. 10/82.**

Phipps, Thomas, Esq. His Proposal for Raising 1,000,000 of Pounds Sterling Yearly. 1712. **8223 e. 9 (60).**

Poor out-cast Children's Song and Cry. *London* 1653. **669 f. 16 (93).**

Powell, John. The Assize of Bread. *London* 1600. **C. 40 d. 54.**

The Proverb Crossed or a new Paradox maintained, etc.,
Being a Full Clear and Distinct answer to a Paper of an
English Gentleman, who endeavours to demonstrate
that it is for the Interest of England, that the Laws
against the Transportation of Wooll should be repealed.
London 1677. 712 g. 16 (16).

Pseudonismus, Considerations concerning Common-fields and
Inclosures. 1654. E. 719 (9).

Ramsey, Wm. History of Worshipful Company of Glass-
sellers of London. 1898. 8248 g. 19.

Rawdon, Marmaduke, of York, the Life of. *Ed. by Richard
Davies. Camden Society, Vol. LXXXV.* R. ac. 8113/80

Raynold, Thomas. The byrth of Mankynde, otherwyse
named the woman's booke, newly set furth, corrected
and augmented. London 1545. 1177 h. 1.

Reasons for a Limited Exportation of Wooll. 1677. 712 g. 16 (14).

Reasons humbly offered to the Honourable House of Commons by the Leather-dressers and Glovers. 816 m. 13 (39).

Remarks upon Mr. Webber's Scheme and the Draper's
Pamphlet. 1741. 1029 d. 4 (5).

Report of Commission on Decay of Clothing Trade. 1622.
Stowe 554 fo. 45-49.

Report of the Commissioners on the Condition of the Hand-
loom weavers, 1841. Mr. Chapman's Report.

Riley, H. T. Chronicles of the Mayors and Sheriffs of
London, 1188-1274. London 1863. 9510 h. 12.

———— Memorials of London and London Life. 1868.

Riley, W. H. Translation of the Liber Albus, of the City
of London. Compiled 1419, by John Carpenter, clerk,
and Richard Whittington, Mayor. London 1861. 9510 f. 22.

Rockley, Francis, Esq., Presenteth that the Revenue of Excise.
816 m. 6 (2).

Rogers, J. E. Thorold. History of Agriculture and Prices.
Oxford 1866-1902.

———— Oxford City Documents. 1891. R. ac. 8126/10.

Rogers, Timothy, M.A. The Character of a Good Woman,
both in a Single and Marry'd State, in a Funeral Discourse on Prov. 31, 10, occasion'd by the Decease of Mrs.
Elizabeth Dunton. London 1697. 1417 b. 29.

Rolls of Parliament.

Salford, The Portmote or Court Leet Records of the Borough
or Town and Royal Manor of, 1597-1669.
Cheetham Society 1902. Vol. xlvi. new series. R. ac. 8120,

Scheme to prevent the running of Irish Wools to France. By a Merchant of London. *London* 1743. **1029 d. 4** (3).

Second Humble Address from the Poor Weavers and Manufacturers to the Ladies. **816 m. 14** (84).

Sharp, Jane. The Midwives Book or the whole art of Midwifery discovered, by Mrs. Jane Sharp, Practioner in the art of Midwifery above thirty years. *London* 1671. **1177 b. 19.**

Shaw's, Mrs., Innocency restored and Mr. Clendon's Calumny retorted, notwithstanding his late Triumphing, by sundry Depositions, making out more than ever she by Discourse or writing did positively charge upon him. *London* 1653. **E. 730 596** (8).

Short Essay upon Trade in General, etc., by a Lover of his Country. *London* 1741. **1029 d. 4** (2).

Smith, L. Toulmin. English Gilds. 1870. **R. ac. 9925/33.**

Smith's Book of Accounts, Chester, 1574. **Harl. MSS. 2054 fo. 22.**

Smyth, Richard, The Obituary of. Secondary of the poultry Compter, London; being a catalogue of all such persons as he knew in their life. *Ed. by Sir Henry Ellis.* *Camden Society,* 1849. **R. ac. 8113/44.**

Smythe, W. Dumville. Historical Account of the Worshipful Company of Girdlers, London. *London* 1905. **8248 e. 44.**

Somerset Quarter Sessions Records. *Ed. by Rev. E. N. Bates Harbin.* 1913. **R. ac. 8133/17.**

Sowerby, Leo. Ladies Dispensatory, containing the nature, virtues and qualities of all Herbs and simples usefull in Physick reduced into a methodical order, for their more ready use in any sicknesse, or other accident of the Body. *London* 1651. **E. 1258.**

State Papers. Domestic Series (S.P.D.).

Statutes at Large.

Stone, Jolley. Court Precedents. 1673, **Harl. MSS. 1628.**

Stopes, Mrs. C. C. Shakespeare's Warwickshire Contemporaries. 1897. **11765 d. 17.**

Stow, John. Survey of the cities of London and Westminster. Written at first MDXCVIII., brought down from the year 1633 to the present time by John Strype. *London* 1720. **1791 d. 5.**

Strood, Churchwarden's Acc. Book. 1555-1763. **Add. MSS. 36937.**

Sussex Archeological Collections.
    Account Book of Cowden. Vol. XX.
    Burrell, Timothy, Journal of. Vol. III.
    Danny Papers. Vol. X.
    East Sussex Parochial Documents. Vol. IV.

AUTHORITIES 319

Everenden and Frewen Account Books. Vol. IV.
Hastings Documents. Vol. XXIII.
Herstmonceux Castle House Accounts. Vol. XLVIII.
Mayfield Overseer's Accounts. Vol. XVIII.
Moore, Rev. Giles, Journal of. Vol. I.
Stapley, Rich., Diary of. Vol. II.
Taylor, Randall. A Discourse of the Growth of England
in Populousness and Trade since the Reformation.
1689. 712 m. 1 (13).
Tawney, R. H. The assessment of Wages in England by the
Justices of the Peace—*in the vierteljahrschrift für
Sozial und Wirtschaftsgeschichte. XI. Band Drittes
Heft and Viertes Heft.* 1913.
Thornton, Mrs. Alice. of East Newton, Co. York. Auto-
biography. *Surtees Society, Vol. LXII.* 1873 R. ac. 8045/50
Tingey, J. C. Assessment of Wages for Norfolk. *English
Historical Review, Vol. XIII.*
———— Records of the City of Norwich.
Norwich 1906. 2368 cc. 4.
Trade of England. Revived and the abuses thereof Rectified.
London 1681. 712 g. 16 (20).
True Account how Mr. Reading's House at Santoft happened
to be Burnt. 816 m. 10/112.
True Case of the Scots Linen Manufacture. 816 m. 13 (55).
Verney, F. P. Memoirs of the Verney Family during the
Civil Wars. *London* 1892. 2407 f. 12.
Vives, office and duetie of an husband. Trans. by Thos.
Paynell. 1550. G. 10325.
Watson, Wm. The Clergyman's Law. 1747. 516 m. 10.
Weavers True Case, or the wearing of Printed Calicoes and
Linnen Destructive to the Woollen and Silk Manu-
facturers. 1719. T. 1814 (8).
Welch, Charles. History of the Worshipful Company of
Pewterers of the City of London. *London* 1902. 8248 f., 15.
Welford, Richard. History of Newcastle and Gateshead.
London 1885. 2367 bb. 7.
Wilkinson, Robert. The Merchant Royal, or woman a ship,
etc. in conjugal duty, set forth in a collection of ingenious
and delightful wedding sermons. Original ed., 1607.
London 1732. 4454 b. 9.
Wycherley, Wm. Plays. *London* 1735. 644 a. 19.
Yonge, Walter. Diary at Colyton and Axminster, Co.
Devon. 1604-1628. *Ed. by Geo. Roberts.*
Camden Society 1848. R. ac. 8113/41.

WAGES ASSESSMENTS.

County.		Reference.
Buckingham	..	Hamilton, A. H. A., Quarter Sessions Records from Queen Eliz. to Queen Anne.
Cardigan ..	..	Dyson, Humfrey., Proclamations of Queen Elizabeth. G6463 (331b.).
Chester ..	..	Harleian MSS., 2054 (3), f. 5 2b.
Derbyshire ..	..	Cox, J. C., Three Centuries of Derbyshire Annals.
Devonshire ..	..	Hamilton, A. H. A., Quarter Sessions Record.
Dorsetshire ..	..	Sussex Archeological Collections, Vol. I., p. 75.
Essex ..	..	Ruggles, Thomas, History of the Poor, pp. 123-5. 1027 i. 1.
Gloucestershire	..	Rogers, J. E. Thorold, History of Agriculture and Prices. Vol. VI., p. 694.
Hertfordshire	..	Hardy, W. J., Hertford County Records.
Kent ..	..	Rogers, J. E. T., History of Agriculture and Prices. Vol. VII., p. 623.
Kingtson-upon-Hull		Dyson, Humfrey, Proclamations. G6463 (77).
Lancashire ..	..	Rogers, J. E. T., History of Agriculture and Prices. Vol. VI., p. 689.
Lincolnshire	..	Hist. MSS. Com., Duke of Rutland, Vol. I., p. 460.
London ..	..	Lord Mayor's Proclamations. 21 h. 5 (61).
Middlesex ..	..	Hardy, W. J., Middlesex County Records.
Norfolk ..	..	English Historical Review, Vol. XIII., p. 522.
Rutland ..	..	Archeologia, Vol. XI., pp. 200-7.
St. Albans ..	..	Gibbs, Corporation Records.
Somerset ..	..	Somerset Quarter Sessions Records.
Suffolk ..	..	Cullum, Sir John., History of Hawstead.
Warwickshire	..	Archeologia, Vol. XI., p. 208.
Wiltshire ..	..	Hist. MSS. Com. Var. Coll., Vol. I., p. 163.
Worcestershire	..	Hist. MSS. Com. Var. Coll., Vol. I., p. 323.
Yorkshire :		
East Riding	..	Rogers, J. E. T., History of Agriculture and Prices, Vol. VI., p. 686.
North Riding	..	Atkinson, J. C., Yorkshire, North Riding Quarter Sessions Records, Vols. VI. and VII.

INDEX.

INDEX

Cost of living, 68-79 *passim*, 134; *diet of children*, 68, 71, 223; *servants*, 68; *difference between men, women and children*, 71-73 *passim*, 127; *Family of three Children*, 68, 73.

Cotton trade, 94, 124.

Cowden, parish of, 131, 264, 280.

Cows, 45, 47, 53, 55, 57, 209, 292; *see* Dairy, Milking.

Crafts, 10, 150-197; *see* Gilds, Trades.

Craftsman, 10, 197.

Cromwell family, 18, 69.

Culpeper, Nicholas, 271 *seq.*

Custom (habit), 155, 158-161.

Customs, 160; *see* Corporations; *excise*, 140.

Cutler, 187.

Cutworks, 32.

Dairy, *see* Butter, Cheese, Cows, Milking; *produce for domestic consumption*, 5, 43; *as pin-money*, 54; *supplementing family income*, 55; *women's sphere*, 5, 50, 53, 292.

Dant, Joan, 32 *seq.*, 206.

Daughters, 176 *seq.*, 197 *seq.*, 252, 284; *see* Burling, Education; *employed in parents' trade*, 184, *seq.*, 195, 200, 217, 298; *enters company by patrimony*, 191, 298; *hired out as weavers*, 103; *sustaining parents*, 115.

Decker, Thos., 158 *seq.*

Defoe, Daniel, 96, 115 *seq.*, 156 *seq.*

Distaff, 13, 48, 107, 111.

Doctor, *see* Apothecaries, Barber-surgeons, Physicians, Midwifery.

Domestic Industry, 4 *seq.*, 8, 40, 47-49, 151, 210, 254, 302; *see* Baking, Brewers, Capitalism, Dairy, Family Industry, Servants, Spinning, Textile Trades; *definition of*, 4-6 *passim*; *drudgery performed by servants*, 156 *seq.*, 294, 304; *effect on women's economic position*, 145, 290, 292; *girls' work*, 11 *seq.*; *men's work*, 5.

Dorchester, 132 *seq.*, 185, 200, 217, 261, 263 *seq.*

Drapers, 184, 200; *see* Gild.

Dunning, Richard, 132.

Dyer, 111, 155; *of leather*, 158; *in Ireland*, 18.

Education, 36, 242, 286 *seq.*, 295, 302-306 *passim*; *see* Apprentice, Children, Mother, Poor Relief, Teaching; *arithmetic unnecessary for girls*, 52; *industrial*, 71, 130-

135 *passim*; *influence of domestic and family industry*, 40; *institutions*, 239; *medical*, 255, 288; *nurses*, 249; *want of specialised training for girls*, 243, 288, 301, 304.

Embroiderer, 184.

Elizabethan Period, Women of, 2, 3, 9, 38, 41.

Estate Management, 14, 15, 17.

Evelyn, John, 115.

Everenden, 62.

Executrix, 39, 188, 293.

Exeter, 206.

Eyre, Adam, 54.

Farmer, 42-56 *passim*, 108, 155; *see* Agriculture, Capitalism; *definition of*, 43; *demand for labour*, 81, 83, 90, 91; *finds sureties for married labourers*, 83 *seq.*; *preference for unmarried labourers*, 12; *wife's occupation*, 46-50 *passim*, 111, 112; *women's characteristics*, 43 *seq.*

Farrier, 155.

Father, 39, 45, 56, 79, 86, 145, 237; *deserts starving family*, 118, 148; *head of family*, 6, 300; *interest in children*, 5, 54, 160, 295; *profits of family industry vested in father*, 6, 7, 182, 294, 299.

Falkland, The Lady, 18-20 *passim*.

Falkland, The Lady Letice, 241, 251, 256.

Family, 73, 80, 100, 106, 122, 144, 204, 219, 242, 286, 291, 294, 299, 304, 307; *see* Business, Capitalism, Father, Mother, Wages, Wage-earners, Widow, Wife; *basis of social organisation*, 285, 288, 290, 299 *seq.*; *chargeable to Parish*, 80-88 *passim*, 134, 142, 146, 204; *dependence on wages*, 43, 56, 178, *see* Husbandmen, Wage-earners; *size of*, 86 *seq.*; *traditions lost*, 118, 148, 237, 287;

Family Industry 6-11 *passim*, 92, 94, 96 *seq.*, 102, 142, 151, 156, 165, 192 *seq.*, 196, 216, 234, 290, 297, 301 *seq.*, 305, *see* Capitalism;

Fanshawe, Lady, 22.

Fell, Sarah, 17, 51, 255.

Felt-maker, 190.

Fiennes, Celia, 62, 73, 124, 233.

Firmin, Thomas, 135-137 *passim*.

Fishmonger, 219 *seq.*

Fishwives, 36, 209, 219-221; *oyster-wives*, 202, 220.

Fitzherbert, Sir Anthony, 46-50, 129.